William Huntington

Pastor Of Providence

William Huntington
Pastor Of Providence

George M. Ella

Go *publications*

Go Publications
3 South Parade, Seascale, Cumbria, CA20 1PZ, ENGLAND.

ISBN 978-1-908475-27-5

Publisher's Foreword

William Huntington (1745-1813) was from a very humble background with almost no formal education yet by God's grace became one of the foremost preachers and influential pastors the United Kingdom has ever produced. He ministered to a large church in London called Providence Chapel with a congregation of almost two thousand listeners. Midweek services in a larger building drew audiences of even more.

An early biographer, Thomas Wright, called Huntington 'by far the most impressive and most famous preacher of his age' and remarked that his literary 'masterpieces' *The Bank of Faith, The Kingdom of Heaven Taken by Prayer* and *Contemplations on the God of Israel* have been read and treasured by millions both in the United Kingdom and in America. Huntington's '*Contemplations*' together with his extensive pastoral correspondence was considered by another great admirer, J. C. Philpot, to be of the highest spiritual value.

Despite these high tributes many Christians today have never heard of William Huntington. This is largely because the doctrines Huntington preached have been spurned by more recent generations. Huntington believed in divine election, particular redemption and emphasised the need for a true spiritual work of grace in conversion.

He wrote against believers being brought under the law of Moses as their rule of life and taught, like Paul (Titus 2:11, 12), that the gospel teaches true holiness to a believer and is a sufficient rule of life (Galatians 6:16). Huntington would be aghast that so many today are called 'believers' not because they have experienced an internal act of transforming grace, but merely for following external moral codes of conduct.

This is a new edition of Dr George M. Ella's book of the same title first published in 1994 by Evangelical Press. At the time of its publication the book was poorly reviewed because of perceived criticism it contained concerning the theological position adopted by another evangelical publisher in the United Kingdom, The Banner Of Truth Trust, though as any fair-minded reader will realise Dr Ella was merely responding to that publisher's own unfounded criticism of Huntington's doctrinal ministry.

Notwithstanding the strengths and merits of Dr Ella's arguments, the book drew high-level disapproval from within a small group that one evangelical publisher should censure another. The criticism stung and as a consequence Dr Ella's *Huntington* was quietly shelved with little marketing effort expended and soon found itself relegated to a few discount bins at conferences.

This led to the following interesting story. At one such conference in Wales a gospel minister and his wife were browsing the book stall between sessions. The lady picked up *Huntington* but her husband was dismissive telling her the book had been poorly reviewed and should not be purchased. She persisted saying at the price being asked she could not lose, and she would make up her own mind if it was good. The book was bought, read and thoroughly enjoyed by the lady and then her husband. In the following years a long and fruitful acquaintance grew between the couple and the author.

We believe Dr Ella's warnings at the time, gentle as they were, of a new downgrading in British evangelicalism in the late-twentieth century were justified. Looking back there is little doubt many doctrinally sound congregations have traded the clear gospel preaching of earlier decades for a nominally reformed ministry invariably delivered with universal applications. This has been fuelled by the promotion of John Wesley and Andrew Fuller by publishing houses on both sides of the Atlantic.

In his own generation William Huntington stood against such downgrading of Biblical truth and preached the gospel of free grace which fed the minds and touched the hearts of his hearers. He brought them into a deep personal knowledge of God who forgives sin, imputes righteousness, and bestows gospel blessings on His chosen people according to His purpose in the everlasting covenant of grace and peace. William Huntington knew this by personal experience and preached it accordingly.

Huntington's ministry was successful because it met people at the point of their greatest need and his preaching, saturated as it was with scripture and scriptural references, brought light to darkened souls. In his own day the gospel of free grace which Huntington preached changed people's lives as they were converted under his guidance and comforted in their hearts. We believe with William Huntington it is still this gospel, and not another, which is the power of God unto salvation and we are delighted to recommend this volume for the encouragement and edification of the Lord's people.

Peter L. Meney

Table Of Contents

An Appreciation Of Huntington

His eminent gifts and grace, his great abilities as a preacher and writer, his separating, discriminating ministry, and the power of God so evidently resting upon him, not only gathered together a large congregation, but wherever there was a saint of God of any deep experience of the law in other congregations seeking rest and finding none under a letter ministry, he as it were instinctively crept in to hear the man who could and did describe the feelings of his heart. And when from the same lips the gospel was preached, with the Holy Ghost sent down from heaven, and pardon and peace reached his conscience, the wanderer settled under his ministry, as fraught with a divine blessing, and loved and revered him as the mouth of God to his soul. When he went into different parts of the country it was still the same. In Kent and Sussex, in the Isle of Ely, in Lincolnshire at Grantham, in Nottinghamshire at Newark and Nottingham, wherever he went, his Master went with him, and accompanied the word with signs following. His ministry was especially blessed to the gathering together of the outcasts of Israel, those peculiar characters whom Hart so well describes:

> The poor dependents on his grace,
> That men disturbers call;
> By sinners and by saints withstood,
> For these too bad, for these too good,
> Condemn'd or shunn'd by all.

Like Simon Peter, he was made a fisher of men. He could throw the hook into deep waters, where his brethren of the rod and line knew not where or how to angle. His own deep experience of the law, of divers temptations, of soul distress, of spiritual jealousy, of the hiding of God's face, enabled him to drop his line into the dark waters and gloomy sunken holes, where some spiritual fish hide and bury themselves out of sight and light; and his clear and blessed deliverance qualified him to angle also for those which leap and bask in the bright beams of the noonday sun.

By his writings, occasional visits, and constant correspondence, he kept up the tie which knit him to his country friends. His liberal hospitality opened his house to them when they came to London, where he fed body and soul, entertaining them with his lively, witty, cheerful, yet spiritual conversation, reading at a glance their foibles and failings, and entering into their varied experience of sorrow and joy, with all the freedom and familiarity of an intimate friend, and all the authority of a revered and beloved teacher.

J. C. Philpot

Introduction

Anyone taking the trouble to read through the pages of The Gospel Standard, The Gospel Magazine, The Gospel Advocate and Zion's Watchtower published last century will be well rewarded by the meaty articles presented there. He or she will also be struck by the fact that many of these articles are by, or refer to, the Rev. William Huntington (1745-1813). It will also soon become evident that a great number of the other excellent articles in these magazines were written by those who came to be called 'Huntingtonians' because of their love for the doctrines which Huntington so ably preached and defended. These were the doctrines of the Reformation, the Puritans and the Calvinistic leaders of revival, such as George Whitefield (1714-1770).

Whitefield was a great eighteenth-century evangelist whose doctrine was as sound as his heart. Year after year he travelled between two continents preaching the sinfulness of man and the righteousness of Christ. In church, chapel, barn, field and country lane, wherever an opportunity arose, he would use it to preach reconciliation and justification in Christ and in him alone. Whitefield was a sower and a reaper but, because he was always on the move, he could hardly be called a gatherer or a winnower of the wheat he had reaped. He never settled down in a pastorate and never had a regular ministry to a gathered church. This was no weakness on his part. He was called to be an itinerant evangelist and performed that task better than perhaps any man has ever done since biblical times. He was not called to be a pastor. This task was left to others. But just as there were few evangelists available in the eighteenth century who could match Whitefield in their fervour and outreach for the Lord, so there were few pastors who could answer the challenge to winnow and gather in the results of his labours and build a spiritual and permanent home for the converted.

This might seem a bold thing to say as the eighteenth century is well known amongst evangelicals as a time of great revivals. This is true, but most of these revivals occurred through God's raising up evangelists and itinerant preachers who were men of pure doctrine but who neither founded local churches, nor pastored them. When they died, or their influence waned, the churches who took care of the newly saved were, in many cases, incapable of teaching them sound doctrine. This was because during the latter half of the eighteenth century the Reformed Calvinistic doctrines of the total depravity of man, unconditional election, the imputed righteousness of Christ and the sanctifying work of the Holy Spirit were being dropped like hot potatoes in favour of Amyraldian[1], Neonomian[2], and Arminian[3] teaching. Many sound Dissenting churches had left the faith of their fathers completely and followed Dr Joseph Priestly (1733-1804), who exchanged Calvinism for a thorough rejection of the atonement and even the Trinity and taught the views of the French Revolution. The Bible's teaching on the roles of men and women in Christian society was largely ignored and one rich and powerful woman, the then Countess of Huntingdon, formed a large movement in which she appointed and defrocked ministers under her patronage at will. Nominal Calvinists and active Arminians alike were thrusting on their church members doctrines which were as anathema to Whitefield as they were to John Bunyan, John Owen and Paul of Tarsus. The fact that Christ had died for his sheep alone, thus saving every lamb, ewe and ram in his flock was seen as heresy and churches who were Calvinistic by name were

---

[1] After the French pastor Moses Amyrald (1596-1664), who taught that God sent Christ into the world to die for all men but, as no one would believe, God had second thoughts and thus elected some to salvation through his own sovereign will. The view was accepted by Richard Baxter and Andrew Fuller in England.

[2] The teaching that Christ atoned for all men in the sense that he made salvation possible for all by placing all in a salvable state. A new law was then introduced, the law of the gospel, which required faith and conversion. These are the marks of evangelical righteousness in the believer which, imperfect as they may be, are the ground of his justification. This theory was an outright denial of the imputed righteousness of Christ and was widespread in Huntington's day, often combined with Amyraldianism and Arminianism.

[3] After Jacobus Arminius (Jakob Hermandszoon, 1560-1609) who taught that the atonement was universal and God saves all who believe and persevere in the faith. God's saving grace is not irresistible and the believer can have his name rubbed out of the Lamb's Book of Life. The Council of Dort (1618-1619) declared Arminius' teaching to be heresy but it was adopted by John Wesley and since then has been the main doctrine of his followers.

excommunicating their members for believing so. What decent home for Whitefield's converts could be found in such a spiritual shambles?

Not only were evangelicals in such disarray theologically, they had become chaotic, even anarchic, in their politics. Many had a confused notion in their heads that a revolution such as the one in France would be good for England. This led them to leave the established church and adopt Paineite views and, with them, ideas of disestablishing the Church of England and granting full freedom for Dissenters – including Roman Catholics. Always ready to see both the Crown and the established church criticised, the Jacobites[4], who were still numerous in England, joined the throng. The Jacobites, of course, were, on the whole, pro-Roman Catholic and we are presented with the incredible picture of English evangelicals hobnobbing with Jacobins[5], who were professing atheists and Jacobites who wanted a Stuart on the British throne. William Wilberforce, a leading Evangelical, had French citizenship bestowed on him by the revolutionary French Convention. Soon it seemed that the only political powers in England who were not in favour of fraternizing with France and opening the doors to Roman Catholicism were King George III of England and the Anglican bishops in the House of Lords.

A man raised up by God

A strong pastoral hand was necessary to gather these scattered sheep. Just as God raised up Whitefield as the evangelist *par excellence*, he provided his church with a shepherd second to none in William Huntington. Both men were raised up when the need was greatest. God's timing is always perfect.

But 'Stop!', the reader might say. 'Who is William Huntington? I have hardly even heard of him'. This is not surprising. Whitefield himself was almost unknown to twentieth-century readers until a revival of interest in his work occurred by the grace of God some few

---

[4] Supporters of James II and his descendants after the Glorious Revolution of 1688 in which James was removed from the throne by Protestant powers.

[5] Radical French Republicans who met in an old Jacobin convent.

years ago. So great has been the influence of Wesleyanism that only a generation or two ago most evangelicals believed that Wesley had pioneered the Evangelical Awakening and had been the first to take to the streets with the gospel.[6] A movement which believes Wesley's doctrines that election is 'the devil's decree' and that imputed righteousness is 'imputed nonsense' and tops that with the notion that those who do not reach perfection in this life will find no perfection in the life to come can hardly be expected to hold the name of Whitefield in honour.[7] Now, however, since the Reformed banner is once again being used as a rallying point, Whitefield is coming back to his own. The evangelist has been reinstated, but not yet his successor, William Huntington. It is high time that this Boanerges of the pulpit, saint of the writing desk and comforter of the dying should be vindicated and re-established as the great winnower of the eighteenth-century revival, standing not a whit behind Whitefield, Bunyan or any saint one might care to mention. This is not just the whim and fancy of a modern writer. The Reformed newspapers and magazines after Huntington's death widely proclaimed him as being a great consolidator of the church.

The Gospel Magazine, not given to emotional effervescence, published in 1850 a long appraisal of Huntington, ranking him with the very greatest in the history of the church. The writer states that 'Mr Huntington's great work was to manifest to the Church the various phases of experience that the soul passes through while here below. *No one since the apostolic age*,[8] I think, has so plainly instructed, and so clearly set forth to the Church, the manner in which the Lord carries out his work in the souls of his people'. The author regards Huntington as emphasizing true Christian experience more than Whitefield, whom he followed in days when 'the doctrines of Regeneration and Eternal Election were called the whines of enthusiasts and fools'.

When Huntington began to preach in London around 1780, he and William Romaine were two of the very few who preached the whole

---

[6] This is also the stance of High Church historians such as Overton and Relton who in their *History of the English Church* argue that 'John Wesley must surely be regarded as the prime mover of the Evangelical Revival'. Whitefield is hardly dealt with in this connection.

[7] See Wesley's correspondence with the saintly James Hervey to find many a heretical – if not blasphemous – statement concerning the atonement and Christ's righteousness.

[8] My italics.

gospel and free love of God in the metropolis. After his death in 1813, there were hundreds of Anglican, Dissenting and Baptist pastors who looked upon him, rightly, as a great teacher sent from God and sought to follow his Christian example. Two of his most faithful early nineteenth-century apologists were J. C. Philpot[9], editor of The Gospel Standard, a university don and no mean preacher himself, and Dr D. A. Doudney, an Anglican minister who was the editor of The Gospel Magazine for many years. Anyone familiar with the lives of these two men will receive deep insight into the kind of piety and personal holiness Huntington's doctrines cultivated.[10] J. C. Philpot was one of the many who recognised Huntington's genius as a winnower. Writing of this aspect of Huntington's calling when reviewing his *Posthumous Letters*, Philpot says,

> Whitefield first, and then Toplady, Romaine, and many other good and gracious men had threshed out the corn, and it lay upon the floor, mingled with straw and chaff. Wesley, with his Arminian zeal and free-will doctrines, and Lady Huntingdon's preachers, with their mixture of truth and error, had added to the heap, and it is to be feared much more chaff than wheat. An able, experienced workman was needed to sift the heap. This workman was the immortal Coalheaver[11], who, by a deep personal experience of law and gospel, could well winnow the floor.[12]

Philpot was mainly taken with Huntington's fine doctrine; Dr Doudney with his shining life and holy Christian living. William Romaine had compared Huntington with Bunyan and said that God raised up such people but once in a hundred years. Doudney took up the comparison and wrote in an editorial:

---

[9] Philpot was a minister of a church but felt it wrong to be called 'Reverend'.

[10] See J. H. Philpot's *The Seceders*, Banner of Truth Trust, undated, for a fine biography of J. C. Philpot. The Gospel Magazine reprints Doudney's articles from time to time. See especially 'No Ordinary Man', March-April, 1993, for a short biography.

[11] A reference to Huntington's former occupation.

[12] Gospel Standard, August, 1856, p. 259.

> If it be desirable that the character of a real pilgrim should be portrayed, the Holy Ghost will neither employ an Oxford, a Cambridge, nor a Highbury man to write it, but in the exercise of His sovereignty, seeks out a POOR TINKER – gives him a lively imagination – a blessed participation – and sends him to prison to study, in preference to a University. In a later day, if a man who has an extensive acquaintance with the human heart be needed: if a bold defender of the faith be required, who shall neither covet the smiles, nor fear the frowns of men, He that in days of old summoned poor fishermen, will go down to the river's side, and take one of those rude, illiterate bargemen – A COALHEAVER – train him for his work – and make him a bright and shining light, not merely in his day and generation, but by his works, down to the latest period of time.[13]

Huntington's critics

Although Huntington was widely acclaimed as a faithful minister by most contemporary evangelicals who had kept to Reformed principles or been led to them by Huntington, there was a good deal of opposition in Christian pulpits and the secular press against him from semi-Arminians, and those who generally believed in a universal or conditional atonement. Perhaps the best known of these critics nowadays is Andrew Fuller, who snapped at Huntington's heels whenever he had the opportunity but never published anything against him of weight.

One scurrilous book against Huntington, however, has had lasting influence. This was an anonymous work of seventy-nine small pages which was published in 1814, the year after Huntington's death. Its title ran into fifteen lines but it is traditionally known as *The Voice of Years*. The author signs himself 'A Disciple of Jesus', which is useful information as one would not have realised this from reading the libellous book!

Traditionally the tiny volume is thought to have been written by a Mr Coucher, whose father and son were great admirers of Huntington. Coucher, however, chose to quarrel with his family's close friend. The

[13] Gospel Magazine, November, 1843.

author begins by telling his readers patronizingly that 'Mr Huntington's numerous congregation consisted mostly of working men and their families, persons of little education and reflection'. These hearers were so stupid in the author's opinion that 'A file of soldiers could not imitate their fugle-man with more exactness than inconsiderate hearers of Mr Huntington did his ignorant and anti-christian extravagances'. This point is laboured time and time again and those who know more about Huntington's hearers than the author evidently did are left wondering how he failed to notice other sections of the public amongst the worshippers at Providence Chapel. If he had used his eyes, he would have seen, besides the very poor, several members of the royal family, at least five baronets, a prime minister and a good score of well-qualified theologians, besides a fair number of authors, artists, skilled craftsmen, property owners and wealthy tradesmen, not forgetting the most famous architect in England at the time![14] Huntington's teaching obviously appealed to all social levels.

The poor in Huntington's congregation, far from being people of no sense and reflection, were mostly well-taught people of saintly character who had astute insight into scriptural truths. This will be made plain in my chapter on the Huntingtonians. The author of *The Voice of Years*, however, did not know the first thing about the membership of Providence Chapel, or about Huntington, for that matter. He says himself in his preface,

> It is not a history of his [Huntington's] private life, for I never was intimate with him, nor any of his family; nor is it a description of his private proceedings among his own people, for I never was a member of his community; nor a collection of stories that were circulated about him at different times and places. I never made any memorandums of such things, or received any written accounts of them from others; nor an

[14] Henry Peto. The story goes that the prime minister, the Earl of Liverpool, heard Henry Peto pray on laying the foundation-stone of the Custom House. This caused the earl to ask Peto where he worshipped. On hearing that it was Huntington's Providence Chapel, the earl began to attend the services there with several of his friends.

> enumeration of particulars obtained by enquiries about Mr Huntington, since I determined on writing this book. I have sought for no information whatsoever.

After blandly confessing his lack of research concerning his topic, the author proceeds to speak with authority on those very points on which he has admitted an absolute deficiency in knowledge. He explains, however, that his comments are based on what he has retained in his memory on occasional visits to Providence Chapel. These occasional visits must have been very few and far between as he first went to hear Huntington in 1793, in the later period of the pastor's life, and speaks of intervals between visits of up to seven years. He also confesses that he did not go to hear Huntington in the final years of his ministry. If then, the author heard Huntington over a period of, say, ten to fifteen years, with gaps between visits of up to seven years, it is very strange indeed that the bulk of his criticism and comments refer to events either outside of this narrow period or, indeed, outside of the goings-on at Providence Chapel. Many of the quotes he gives are taken completely out of context and he, on his own confession, cannot possibly have had first-hand experience of them. The kindest thing that can be said of the author is that he is a victim of hearsay which he has seasoned with his own spite.

The author's main view of Huntington is that, as a man from a lower working-class background, he ought never to have become a pastor, used learned books such as a concordance, owned a coach, which was only the privilege of gentlemen, etc., etc.. He should have lived in a manner 'consistent with his mean origin'. Apart from that, the anonymous and imaginative author says that, though Huntington had a few 'good' qualities (a point which he later takes back and argues that, in reality, they were all bad) he had many definitely bad qualities, as he was 'conceited, dogmatical, tyrannical, vindictive, infallible (or thought he was), inaccessible, political and anti-literal. The whole tenor of the book is one of lack of research, lack of sources, lack of proof, lack of theological insight, lack of knowledge and a lack of honesty served up with a great deal of snobbism and personal pride.

Why bother to mention such a book? Why, indeed? Especially as in 1909 Thomas Wright, biographer of Cowper and Toplady, published his *Life of William Huntington S.S.* and scattered all the arguments of

The Voice of Years to the four winds, vindicating Huntington finally from all such ludicrous criticism and demonstrating fully what a great man of God he really was.

Times change, however, and so do opinions. Once again, as in Huntington's day, Fullerism[15] is taking the place of Calvinism and Calvinists are refusing to believe that Arminianism, Amyraldianism and Neonomianism are illicit gospels. Huntington is once more forgotten, yet he holds keys that could open the doors to the fresh breeze of the free and unconditional gospel of salvation which is so much needed in present-day theology.

Proof of the low standards in doctrine of today's evangelicals, leading to low standards of Christian experience, is to be found in an anonymous article published in the Banner of Truth magazine for July 1988. The Banner of Truth has been the great bastion of Calvinism for years but, strangely and sadly enough, the article is a review of *The Voice of Years*, which has been taken out of oblivion where it ought to have stayed, dusted but not cleaned up, and presented as the 'voice of truth'.[16] This is all the more surprising as even those who were by no means Huntington's friends thought the book had severely bent the truth.[17] But now, one of Britain's most well-known Calvinistic magazines has taken the trouble to tar and feather the most important Calvinist figure in the late eighteenth century! No wonder the reviewer wished to remain anonymous!

It is true that, in the review article, the author presents Huntington's good points in rather a better light than does the work under review. When he comes to the more detailed bad points, however, he underlines them one by one and by taking half-quotes from various parts of the

---

[15] A combination of Amyraldianism and Neonomianism.

[16] See Henry Sant, 'A Vindication of William Huntington from the vicious calumny of the "Voice of Years", being an answer to the Banner of Truth's review of that book', May, 1994.

[17] Ebenezer Hooper, at times a harsh critic of Huntington's, yet says of *The Voice of Years*, 'We do not admire the spirit of the book, which evidences malignity, and the want of any spiritual esteem for his works' sake: for he seems to have attended the chapel rather as an observant and critical hearer, than as a sincere and devout worshipper' (E. Hooper, *The Celebrated Coalheaver*, 1871, p. 46).

book and placing them together as full quotes, or setting the quotations in quite a different context, he makes the bad points appear even worse. Furthermore the critic adopts the snobbish arrogance of his anonymous author and also reflects his complete ignorance as to what Huntington really taught and how he really lived. He makes bold assertions of what Huntington believed, or did not believe, although Huntington's own oral and written testimony prove the very opposite. This was the tactic of Huntington's Amyraldian, Neonomian and Arminian enemies and the reviewer has obviously taken over their arguments instead of taking first-hand note of Huntington's common sense and scriptural lucidity. In other words, the reviewer cannot possibly have given due consideration to Huntington's works, nor the scores of articles written by Huntingtonians, as they fully contradict every single criticism that he raises.

Furthermore it is extremely difficult to imagine that the writer of the anti-Huntington article had a complete copy of *The Voice of Years* in his possession. Instead it appears that he has used the various summaries which circulated for a time. This seems obvious from his misplaced quotes. The original author alleges in *The Voice of Years*, for instance, that Huntington's epitaph, written in 1813, was 'arrant nonsense'. The reviewer gives the impression that it was William Romaine who criticised the epitaph, arguing that 'Self must be abased'.[18] Now Romaine was a good friend of Huntington's and held him in high esteem. Whenever Huntington needed a comment on a Hebrew or Greek word, he would go to Romaine for it. When Romaine was asked to write against heretics, he humbly said that Huntington had done the work for him. It is thus extremely improbable that Romaine would ever use such language with reference to his friend. It is quite out of the question, however, that he could have called Huntington's epitaph 'arrant nonsense' as Romaine had been dead for eighteen years when Lady Sanderson penned it. Other, more serious and ridiculous 'howlers' in the review will be discussed in the course of this biography.

When analysing a book, an experienced reviewer usually looks at the good points and then the bad points, comments on these and then

---

[18] The words the author of *The Voice of Years* quotes as coming from Romaine refer to Huntington's work, *The Bank of Faith*. The author has obviously misunderstood Romaine.

comes to some kind of conclusion. In the Banner article, however, the reviewer accepts all the arguments of *The Voice of Years* with full approbation and offers not one single word of criticism against the book! The volume is, however, full of glaring historical and theological faults such as the author's view that Huntington was a false prophet because he taught that Rome would gain power once again in England. A Reformed reviewer could not possibly pass by such an accusation without comment. The reviewer, surprisingly enough, not only agrees with the criticism but adds his own words of strong condemnation, calling Huntington 'mad' into the bargain. Furthermore, his conclusion is merely a very garbled, and much shortened version of the one in the book under review, with the negative criticisms heightened. No critical assessment is attempted.

Moreover, the lengthy conclusion in *The Voice of Years* – wrong as it is – is a far fairer analysis of Huntington than that of the reviewer. Again, this is either a sign that the reviewer did not have a full copy of the book in his hands, or else evidence is being used with a lack of objectivity. Sadly there are many other signs in the article of unfair treatment of Huntington, coupled with dubious theological and historical insights. These call out loudly for correction and a more sympathetic appraisal of Huntington's life and teaching.

Huntington and the rise of Roman Catholicism

We must especially take issue with the reviewer on the way he deals with Huntington's presumed 'mad zeal' as a prophet. Not only were the churches earnestly intent on downgrading doctrine in Huntington's day, they were just as intent on upgrading Rome. The Reformers and Puritans had won the battle for doctrine by defeating the pope's tyrannical rule over popular opinion. In the eighteenth century, however, the unbelievable was happening. Calvinists and Arminians alike were openly campaigning for the emancipation of Roman Catholics and their freedom to exercise their rites and superstitions once again in Reformed Britain. This was closely coupled with the politics of Tom Paine. Huntington warned England of what was obvious for those who used their eyes and ears. Rome's power was increasing. For this stance, Huntington was ridiculed by the main body of evangelicals and called 'a false prophet' though he was merely pointing out what was happening for all to see. Moreover, whenever Huntington did use the term 'prophet' it was in the sense of one who speaks a word of God in due season to a rebellious people.[19] This was a legitimate New Testament usage. Huntington was most critical of 'modern prophets' who claimed to know exactly what was going to happen at the end of time.

So intent, however, were Huntington's radical enemies on maintaining that he was unsound, that they claimed that whatever he said was automatically wrong, without making any attempt to analyse it. Thus when Huntington said that Napoleon would fall, his enemies, including the author of *The Voice of Years*, immediately cried out, 'False prophet!' This was as illogical as it was unfair to Huntington who believed in 'fearing God and honouring the king'. It was this very aspect of Huntington's faith, however, which galled his enemies. Thus when Huntington said that the Church of England and King George III were the last bulwarks in England against the spread of Roman error, few took him seriously as they did not fear Rome and had no respect for the Establishment. Events, however, proved that Huntington had a far deeper insight into political and theological matters than the bulk of his contemporaries.

The reviewer in question takes sides with Huntington's scoffers on this issue. He judges Huntington's zeal to be 'mad' because he 'made absurd comments and glaring errors in prediction'. This is a reference, not only to Huntington's realisation that Napoleon was doomed, but also to a statement Huntington made, according to the author of *The Voice of Years*, around 1797-8 that in a short time popery would once again flourish in England. He said this in view of the growing pro-French and Jacobin sympathy amongst evangelicals in Britain, warning them that if France, aided by Italy and Spain, was allowed to dominate the world, Roman Catholicism would automatically spread. This was not a prophecy but sheer, obvious common sense and in keeping with the leading political theories of his day. The difference between Huntington and the politicians, however, was that Huntington feared the spread of Romanism and the politicians, many of them evangelicals, did not. Writing about 1813-14, the author of *The Voice of Years* says

[19] As in Ezekiel 2:5; 33:33.

that sixteen years have gone by and popery is still not flourishing in England. He thus concludes that Huntington was a false prophet. How wrong both author and reviewer were will be seen from the following account.[20]

In the summer of 1797 William Wilberforce introduced a bill in the Commons to allow Roman Catholics to serve in the militia. Backed by his Evangelical friends, this bill was carried through with little opposition. Britain at the time was at loggerheads with several Roman Catholic countries and her troops were ready to defend their country and their faith. Here, however, was an Evangelical who made it possible for a Roman Catholic general to command Protestant soldiers! The pope must have been the most delighted man in Europe and very grateful to Wilberforce for building a fifth column in Britain and Ireland for him!

In 1799 Wilberforce agreed to Roman Catholic Members of Parliament for Ireland. By 1802 evangelicals such as Henry Thornton, who was John Newton's patron (after John Thornton's death) and one of the most influential men in England, were loudly campaigning for full Roman Catholic emancipation. The result of this was that Pitt felt himself compelled to acknowledge the French conquests in Italy, the Ionian Islands and Belgium.

Worse was to come for traditional Calvinism. Holland had been a Calvinist stronghold for years and it is through the Synod of Dort, held there in 1618-19, that Calvinism was firmly established in England. But Holland was now firmly in French hands and both Pitt and the king, forced by their numerous Evangelical advisers, had to accept the occupation as legal. Calvin must have turned in his grave, as it was British nominal Calvinists, led by Wilberforce, that had linked liberty for Roman Catholics with equality between Protestantism and the papal system and fraternity with France.

20 There were very few Roman Catholic churches in London in Huntington's day. By 1829 there were 29 churches and by 1865 there were no less than 117 churches, 31 nunneries and 15 monasteries. Roman Catholics had entered the universities and were building colleges for Catholics (The Gospel Magazine, 1865, pp. 187, 188, 289).

Wilberforce, in fact, began to campaign that Britain should give up all of her colonies that had belonged to France and her allies as a sign of peace to the French. This would have meant that the French would certainly have regained possession of them. The French, rubbing their hands with success, now plucked up courage to demand of Britain that she should give up to them the Channel Islands, Canada, Gibraltar, Newfoundland and even India as a basis for talks.

It was only now that Wilberforce began to think he had been too hasty and said, 'I once was ready to give up all we have conquered, either from France or her allies; now, after the hostile mind she has discovered towards us, and our recent experience of the effrontery of her rulers, I would not make peace without reserving either Ceylon or the Cape [taken from the Dutch]; no both. I rather think of declaring this publicly. As for Trinidad [taken from the Spanish], it is not worth having'.[21]

This was short-lived remorse on Wilberforce's part, however.

Once the Christian politician had moved his left foot forward, his right foot had to follow. We now find Wilberforce and his friends saying that there is no essential difference between Roman Catholicism and the evangelical faith. He told Roman Catholics that they could believe the gospel and remain in the Roman church and he chose a Roman Catholic as a tutor for his grandson though he was surrounded by able Protestants who could have done the job just as well.

All this enthusiasm for Roman Catholics was against the will of the king, the Prince Regent and the bishops of the Church of England – just as Huntington had 'prophesied' – but the vast strength of those around Wilberforce won the day. By the time the author of *The Voice of Years* was writing to say that Rome posed no threat to England and Huntington was a false prophet, Parliament was debating the subject as if the Roman Catholics' regained political power was a foregone conclusion. Rome had already become a threat! From now on Roman Catholics received one concession after another until they achieved full emancipation in 1829. From that year on, new Roman Catholic

[21] See Robin Furneaux, *William Wilberforce*, Hamish Hamilton, p. 174. It is difficult to see why Wilberforce was ready to give up Trinidad so easily as the 10,000-11,000 slaves there were faring better under British masters than under their previous owners and legislation was under way to better their situation.

churches and monasteries in London alone sprang up at the rate of four a year throughout the rest of the century.

It is no coincidence that the Tractarians and Puseyites date their ideological birth from this time and J. H. Newman commenced leading the Church of England towards Rome. It is common knowledge that Cardinal Newman claimed it was the evangelicals who put him on the path to Rome. Huntington saw clearly what was happening and was a warning voice in a wilderness of ignorance, trying to make the blind see. He was laughed at for his pains by those who had forgotten the blood of the martyrs and he is still laughed at by them today.

Charges of heresy

The most serious criticisms the Banner article levelled at Huntington are still to be mentioned and, although they are wrapped up in an article supposedly based on *The Voice of Years*, they sail under a false banner as they have nothing whatsoever to do with that book. Those not familiar with *The Voice of Years*, however, would never have guessed this as it is not explained to the reader. Immediately below the title '*The Voice of Years*', there is a heading: 'An Appraisal of William Huntington'. Obviously the reader would expect this appraisal to refer to the contents of *The Voice of Years*. What comes next, however, are fifteen lines written either by the reviewer or the editor of the magazine, containing scandalous accusations against Huntington that overshadow anything that is quoted from *The Voice of Years*. The author states dogmatically that:

> William Huntington was an Antinomian who maintained the following doctrines:
>
> 1. The elect are justified from eternity, an act of which their justification in this world by faith is only a manifestation;
> 2. That God sees no sin in believers, and is never angry with them;
> 3. That the imputation of our sins to Christ, and of His righteousness to us, was actual, not judicial;

> 4. That faith, repentance, and holy obedience are covenant conditions on the part of Christ, not on our part;
> 5. That sanctification is no evidence of justification but rather renders it more obscure.
> These doctrines form the general creed of all theoretical Antinomians, more or less.

One might as well say on reading this. 'Think of any heresy you like and Huntington has got it!' Huntington, who was almost a lone voice in his day urging confused evangelicals to get back to the Bible as the whole Word of God, is now accused of rejecting God's holy law, believing in a faulty view of election, faith, the wrath of God, repentance, obedience, justification, sin, imputed righteousness, Christ's righteousness, the believer's righteousness and sanctification. This list of accusations would have left the author of *The Voice of Years* breathless! It is the most formidable broadside against Huntington ever targeted at him by an enemy but the charges made are totally without substance. Not a single word of proof is given for this scathing attack on Huntington, or for the attempt to disqualify him from being the saint that so many thousands have believed him to be. Those who know Huntington will only laugh out loud when they see such a shocking display of ignorance. But sadly, those who do not know him will be put off from reading him, thus missing a treat indeed.

Accusations against Huntington refuted

I am not a Huntingtonian by tradition. I came into contact with his books some ten years ago when attending a ministers' conference run by the Banner of Truth Trust. There were many who spoke with joy in those days about the 'Celebrated Coalheaver', as tradition calls him. I purchased several volumes of his letters from a friend at the conference and drank the pure honey of the gospel. Since then I have tried my best to obtain as much as possible by Huntington as it is all gold, with very little dross. Both the Collingridge collection and the larger Bensley collection have proved an enormous spiritual strength to me. Thomas Wright's biography has been a great blessing, as have also books by Huntingtonians such as Burrell, Rusk and Abbott, many of which, praise God, are being reprinted today. Reading how the Huntingtonians lived and died is like going back to the Spirit-inspired days of the early church. The many articles by and about Huntington in the Christian newspapers mentioned above have been thrilling indeed to read. Huntington, in my experienced opinion is an Owen, a Bunyan, a Gill and a Whitefield all rolled into one.

The Banner article shook me to the core. My one thought was, 'How are the mighty fallen!' This book is the product of my reaction.

Although I have written mainly in biographical form. I have been careful to take up all the completely false arguments both in *The Voice of Years* and the Banner review. *The Voice of Years*' arguments are based on pure ignorance; the Banner' arguments are more dangerous as they show a departure from the Reformed Calvinistic faith.[22]

This biography will show that Huntington, rather than being conceited, was a most humble man who was very conscious of his faults and continually brought them before the Lord. It is quite plain to see that where Huntington is accused of conceit, it is where he firmly rests on Reformed principles. Fuller, for instance, thought Huntington was conceited because he openly preached unconditional election and the perseverance of the saints.[23]

That Huntington was dogmatic was no sin. At a time when even so-called Calvinists were explaining away the doctrines of justification, sanctification and imputed righteousness, besides casting immodest glances at Rome, Huntington never swerved from true doctrine and was called 'dogmatical' for his stance.

The anonymous author of *The Voice of Years* obviously believed that Huntington was tyrannical and political because he would not tolerate the views of the so-called Enlightenment, whose Christian followers were supporting France and the revolutionary politics of Thomas Paine. We are talking of a time when evangelical leaders such as Rowland Hill and John Ryland preached revolution and bloodshed from the pulpit. Huntington reserved the pulpit for preaching and, though he occasionally condemned certain countries from that position,

22 Correspondence with the Banner editors confirmed that they stood fully behind the article and would not recant.

23 *Works*, vol. III, pp. 829-31. See Appendix I for a detailed analysis of Fuller's system.

it was because of their Roman Catholic intrigues rather than for their politics.

Huntington has been called vindictive chiefly because he was very quick to take up his pen and refute heresy. His enemies always felt free to spread the most evil rumours about him and when the saint showed the world that they were untrue – he was called vindictive! One leading Evangelical tried to trap Huntington in this way. He preached sermon after sermon against Huntington, hoping that he would react wildly in print so that he might take him to court for libel! Huntington did react in print, but with such biblical mastery that his tormentor, though not silenced, found he had not the inklings of a case against him.

The weakest argument ever put forward against Huntington was that he was inaccessible. He certainly did not suffer fools gladly and had a marvellous, God-given bluntness when dealing with hypocrites and the self-righteous. He was, however, hospitable to a fault, especially to those in spiritual and financial need. After sounding out his visitors, he usually gave them the run of his house and expected them to eat with his family. Huntington spent several hours a day writing letters to all and sundry. These letters are fine examples of good theology combined with a deep pastoral care of souls. It is difficult to imagine that a man who set apart so much of his time for counselling and always had a crowd of friends around him could be called 'inaccessible'. Even the author of *The Voice of Years* admits that there could be 100 people at one time in Huntington's house. Huntington's day, for the work he did for the Lord, never started later than four o'clock in the morning in the winter and he rose even earlier in the summer. His first callers would often be waiting to see him by then and would breakfast with him. Huntington reached more people in a week than other good pastors met in a month.

Coupled with the odd idea in *The Voice of Years* that Huntington was inaccessible is the even more grotesque claim that he was miserly towards the poor. It is obvious that the Banner reviewer has difficulty in accepting this, but it seems he cannot refrain from criticism and he says, 'Huntington spiritualised such Christian duties as feeding the hungry and clothing the naked'. There is no justification whatsoever for such a comment. Huntington was kindness personified. Even those who fell out with him usually acknowledged this and we have on record the honest testimony of not a few who hate Huntington's theology but who, nevertheless, admit that he was extremely kind to the poor. One such writer says,

> It [charity] forms the trait most excellent in his character, and ought to be proclaimed upon the house-tops, that the experience of necessity, instead of steeling, had softened his heart, which was ever alive to the distresses of those around him, and which more especially to those whom he believed to be of the household of faith, prompted him to be benevolent even to excess. In his disposition he was very humane, in all his dealings most just and conscientious.[24]

This biography will give the reader ample opportunities to see how benevolent Huntington was to the poor.

The accusation that Huntington was anti-literal is a blow below the belt indeed. The very examples which the above-mentioned review cites as proof that Huntington did not take the Bible literally in fact show Huntington at his most literal. It is not at all difficult to turn the tables on those critics who thought Huntington did not accept the plain meaning of Scripture and show that they themselves were the rationalists who argued away the literal meaning of the Bible.

A case in point is Huntington's doctrine of the imputed righteousness of Christ, which is mentioned in the review as being faulty. Huntington accepted this doctrine 'as written'. The Wesleyans denied imputed righteousness outright, whereas the Fullerites were more cunning. They paid lip-service to the doctrine, to keep up an appearance of Calvinism, but argued that its vocabulary must be interpreted metaphorically. They thus did not look on the doctrine of imputed righteousness as a literal truth but as a literary device. The review article's criticism of 'actual imputation' seems evidence enough

---

24 Quoted from *Memoirs of the Life and Ministry of the Late W. Huntington, S.S.* by Onesimus (G. Terry) found in Hooper, *The Celebrated Coalheaver*, p. 42. Huntington said of Terry that he was in theology what Tom Paine was in politics and Terry threatened to take Huntington to court. Nevertheless Terry wrote these kind words about Huntington.

that mere lip-service to the doctrine is being paid by the writer. The reviewer obviously implies that the term 'judicial' is the opposite of 'actual'. Is he arguing that a judicial imputation is not an actual imputation, but merely a metaphorical or a make-believe one? It would seem so. The reviewer accuses Huntington of being 'anti-literal' but who is being 'anti-literal' now? Opportunities will be taken to examine carefully Huntington's doctrine of literal, rather than metaphorical, imputation.

It was this unwillingness to take the Bible at its word that produced in Huntington's semi-Arminian and Arminian enemies a faulty view of the atonement, with a correspondingly faulty view of justification and sanctification. Their particular weak spot, as Huntington was quick to point out, was their doctrine of personal holiness. In rejecting a literal interpretation of the doctrine of imputed righteousness, they were forced to reject the truth of the literal outworking of the Holy Spirit and indwelling of Christ in the believer, creating a new creature in him. They could not accept that there was a literal justified and sanctified new man in the believer, but argued that salvation came through a kind of teamwork between the old man and God whereby the old man was gradually, more or less, sanctified. They agreed with Huntington that the Mosaic law had sentenced the old man to death, but they argued that the old man who strove to believe had the curse of the law taken from him and now lived under a less severe law which served as a pattern to be imitated. It is not open to doubt that the theological consensus amongst the vast majority of Christians in Huntington's day was: 'God will do his bit, if you do yours'. Oddly enough, it was these Neonomians (followers of the 'new law') who were most aggressive in calling Huntington an Antinomian although they were standard examples of Antinomians themselves!

Placing the old man under a new, modified Mosaic law which did not crucify, Huntington argued, was an alteration of the eternal, holy law. The only law-abiding Being in a believer's soul was the New Adam himself, Christ our righteousness, who alone was able to keep the true Mosaic law. All other humans, saved or unsaved, were law-breakers by nature, not law-doers. This is why Paul argued that in him the new man, made righteous in Christ, was at variance with the old man who was under the curse of the law. He knew, however, who had the victory, arguing that 'even so might grace reign [in the new man] through righteousness unto eternal life by Jesus Christ our Lord' (Romans 5:21). It would be very weak theology indeed to argue that Paul merely believed in a figurative indwelling of the righteous Christ in the believer. This topic will also come under closer scrutiny in later chapters.

Huntington's message for the church today

It is vitally necessary for the spiritual health of the church that Huntington should once again be allowed to speak freely against the downgrading which is taking place in doctrine and personal holiness today. After a revival of Reformed thinking in the late nineteen fifties up to the mid-seventies, we are once again lapsing into the low standards of doctrine and holy living that typified Huntington's day. We are reliving Huntington's age. Huntington, for instance, could not tolerate 'priests in petticoats' and 'cottish' men[25] and campaigned against immorality amongst the clergy, making himself unpopular with the highest dignitaries in many an evangelical denomination. Today, immoral movements of both sexes have open support from so-called evangelical churches who even go so far as to appoint 'priests in petticoats' over them, whilst powdered and perfumed male TV evangelists seem fated to open the floodgates to the world, the flesh and the devil.

Huntington campaigned against the worldly methods the churches were using to finance their work. One of them was to organise anti-Huntington demonstrations and charge sixpence a head for those who wanted to hear him ridiculed! In Huntington's day it was a common occurrence for evangelical ministers to be financed by the most unlikely benefactors. A few instances will suffice.

The Rev. Thomas Jones, sent down from university for 'methodist views', was a staunch evangelical but for years he had no qualms about accepting his patron Lord Peterborough's money. This earl, who went by the nickname of 'the Gay Lothario', did not make a name for himself, however, through his Christian giving but through taking other men's wives.

---

[25] Men who behaved like women.

John Newton had two evangelical patrons. One, Lord Dartmouth, made much of his money from a chain of public houses. The other, John Thornton, was shocked when the church of which he was patron refused to have Newton as vicar because they believed a New Testament church should call its own pastor and not have one thrust upon it from outside. John Thornton took the matter to the House of Lords, won his case, and Newton became pastor of St Mary, Woolnoth, although the church had not called him. Dartmouth, however, wanted to send him to America. It was extremely difficult for Newton to discern the will of the Lord as his patrons were continually coming up with new schemes they wished to finance under Newton's agency.

The Erskine brothers[26] fought against such patronages in Scotland and had a worthy ally in Huntington. One can thus understand that Huntington allowed no man to buy him.

The members of Huntington's congregations never resorted to such practices as holding raffles or collecting money outside of other churches when the worshippers came out. He would never send his members into the public houses or from door to door to beg money for the Lord's cause. Now, as then, these methods are still seen as acceptable by many an 'evangelical' church, whether established or free. But who is the better off spiritually for such methods? How can we expect the world to finance God's work? Huntington, as we shall see, had a good answer to these questions. Huntington campaigned against the use of musical entertainment, drama and concerts as a substitute for worship. Today one can hardly find a church, chapel or mission hall that is not thumping drums, scratching fiddles or banging banjos. It has once again become the fashion for clergymen who hold themselves to be anything to put down 'music' as their favourite pastime. No 'decent evangelist' would ever think of preaching for more than a fraction of the time he gives to his mixed choirs, soloists, 'converted' pop-singers and 'groups'. The word 'decent' has, of course, quite changed its meaning. It is worthwhile listening to Huntington's

[26] Ebenezer (1680-1754) and Ralf (1685-1752). Also like Huntington the Erskines combatted Neonomianism and claimed that the majority of the clergy had departed from the Calvinistic faith of their fathers. They were not able to go as far as Huntington in their condemnation of Amyraldianism.

reasons for keeping artificial noises outside when praising the Lord in church worship!

At a time when most evangelicals seemed to live in Old Testament morality with Old Testament conceptions. Huntington campaigned for the whole Bible, and nothing but the whole Bible, as the only rule of life. Anything less than this is Antinomianism indeed. When reading Huntington's books the earnest seeker will be surprised what hitherto hidden passages of Scripture he uses to illuminate his message. There was such a dearth of Bible knowledge in Huntington's day that when he used the image of the Suffering Servant to portray Christ, or the 'Desire of the nations' to point the way to the Saviour, or the wedding garment to illustrate Christ's imputed righteousness, people ridiculed him for being 'anti-literal' or for using unbiblical imagery. They just did not know the chapter and verse! Anybody reading Huntington today, in more ignorant times, must thus have a Bible and concordance at hand to assure him that Huntington is still wading deep in scriptural truths. Equipped with such aid and a prayer to God for guidance, he will have his soul filled with good things.

One of God's jewels

As you will have noticed, this book is highly biased. I need not apologise for that. After studying Huntington intensely for some eight years. I have come to regard him as the best of friends and the finest of pastors. Who would not valiantly defend such a man? It might be said in criticism of my book that I have left out the warts in Huntington's character and only shown him by his best profile. I would deny that vociferously but argue that I see Huntington's so-called blemishes in quite a different light. Personally, I find Huntington's warts and wrinkles all natural and beautiful. He never hid behind the face-lift and make-up of artificial mannerisms. The Lord had Huntington so much in his control that even the pastor's blemishes – and they certainly did not coincide with those listed in the Banner article – were used to his glory. Huntington's occasional grumpiness was used divinely as a weapon to disarm the haughty and the hypocrite. By God's grace, Huntington's carelessness with money almost always brought needed relief where it was so generously given. True, Huntington was bamboozled by many pastors who dragged money out of his pocket on false pretences, but so many more were genuinely in need and genuinely blessed. Huntington's stubbornness saved him from being blown backwards and forwards by the fashions in theology of his day. The many 'isms' of the time ran off him like water off a duck's back. His so-called 'working-class manners and morals', which so many of his ex-public schoolboy clergy contemporaries abhorred, saved him from the moral lapses which were, so often, part of their own upper-class lives. Sidney Smith and William Cowper both criticised the rich evangelicals in Parliament for having one law for the rich and one for the poor. Nobody could say that of Huntington and thereafter profess to be an honest man.

Again, it is interesting to note that it was ministers who freely propagated adultery who first raised the cry of 'Antinomian!' against Huntington. Horsemen say that the more nails that are loose in a shoe, the more noise the horse makes when it gallops. This is their way of saying that those who have something to hide usually accuse others the more to disguise it. It is no exaggeration to say that whenever Huntington was accused of heresy it was in fact almost always his accusers themselves who were guilty of it. Huntington was quite aware of this and it made him unconquerable in conflict, as he merely turned the tables on his aggressors.

Perhaps I have now said enough to tempt the reader to turn the next pages and enter deep into the amazing life of William Huntington. He was born under the worst social conditions possible, but at his death two noblemen were made his legatees. He came into this world a product of sin and shame, but lived to be the most successful pointer to the way of salvation in England. His life is truly similar to that of Pilgrim in Bunyan's famous book. There is, however, one important difference. Bunyan's tale, divine as it is, combines much fact with much fancy – Huntington's tale is all true. Read it, then, and find out how God can make jewels out of dross.

Chapter 1

Born Under The Law

William Hunt, alias Huntington, was born on 2 February, 1745 in a farmhand's cottage near Cranbrook in Kent.[1] No prayers of joy and thanksgiving went up to God at his birth. His mother, Elizabeth Hunt looked down on the baby placed in her arms with sadness and shame, knowing full well that her child was the product of her adulterous affair with her husband's employer, Barnabas Russel. Elizabeth's husband William, a humble, God-fearing man, stood by his wife's bedside fighting back the anger and remorse in his heart because of his wife's unfaithfulness. The fact that Elizabeth insisted on calling her child William after her spurned and rejected husband was a lasting insult to the man she had promised to love and obey. Huntington relates how William Hunt was banned perpetually from his wife's bed, yet Elizabeth had given birth to nine children before William was born and was to bear another child in 1751.

Barnabas Russel was a well-to-do farmer who was very conscious of his station in life and treated his labourers with cruel tyranny. He insisted that Elizabeth Hunt help in his household under the supervision of his wife, who was fully aware that her servant was her husband's bed-mate. Russel was especially beastly to William Hunt and paid him a mere seven or eight shillings a week to be at his beck and call at all times. Such a small wage was not nearly enough to keep a large family

[1] Early details of Huntington's life are taken from *The Kingdom of Heaven Taken by Prayer*, *The Bank of Faith* and *The Naked Bow of God*.

and the Hunts often suffered from hunger and lack of suitable clothing. William Hunt seems to have had little say in the management of family affairs and young William grew up in an atmosphere quite antagonistic to the gospel. A longing to live a life right with God was never quite wiped out from the Hunts' family life, however, and William was taken to be baptised in Cranbrook parish church on 14 November, 1750, when he was five years old.

The early years

Little can be said about William's education as there was very little of it. The young boy spent a few months at a dame-school but had to constantly help his mother and foster-father in their work and very soon left off going to the school altogether. Huntington never forgot this school, as its mistress impressed upon his mind the fact that God took notice of children's sins. William also learnt at school that sins would be punished after death. When people died, William's experience taught him, they were placed in coffins in the cemetery. Thus he reasoned that cemeteries must be the place of divine punishment. This caused him always to make a great detour around any churchyard for fear that he might be mistakenly punished with the dead.

William's conscience was also kept very active at this time by a strange, stern-looking character who troubled him whenever he entered the town. This person could be seen daily dashing in and out of shops carrying a mysterious stick covered in figures and an inkpot suspended on a string from his buttonhole. William was sure that here was God's bookkeeper at work recording children's sins. The fact that the character was always dashing around was proof to William's tender conscience that he had a host of children's sins to record. Whenever William saw him, the boy would flee in panic knowing his own heart. Actually the energetic old man was an exciseman who entered shop after shop with his huge yardstick to work out the taxes the shopkeepers had to pay.

After some time Elizabeth Hunt finally succeeded in persuading her employer-lover to send William to the grammar school at Cranbrook where he probably obtained a free place. Here again a Christian influence was put on William and he learnt to read and write through studying the New Testament. At the grammar school he also came to realise how unevenly wealth was distributed in the world. Russel's legitimate children went to the same school, well-fed and well-clothed, but poor William had to sit next to his half-brothers with an empty stomach and nothing but rags on his back.

Perhaps this was one of the reasons which drove young William to despair and tempted him to steal food. Late at night he would prowl through the fields on the lookout for ripe apples or turnips, or anything that would still his hunger. The poor boy did not really think of this as stealing because the fields he plundered belonged mostly to Barnabas Russel, his true father. Once, however, William was strolling over a sports-field when he met a French boy of his own age who was taking food to some enemy officers imprisoned at nearby Sissinghurst Castle. The sight of a large loaf sticking out from under the boy's arm proved too much for William, who had had scarcely anything to eat all day, so he pounced on the boy and succeeded in capturing a large piece of his loaf. This was his only attempt, Huntington later assured his readers, at 'highway robbery'.[2] Soon after, William was confronted by the French prisoners who were out on parole and the young French boy told them of William's attack. The Frenchmen, however, when they saw how destitute William looked, left him in peace. This incident happened at a time when William was so badly clothed that he hardly dared show himself.

It is sadly obvious that William's mother expected her son to steal and thus help support the family. Thus William was taught at a very early age 'the trade of pinching'. Looking back on those poverty-stricken childhood days Huntington wrote, 'I believe this way of bringing up poor children often drives them to steal until they become habituated by it. Many begin to steal to support life, and continue till they lose their lives for stealing'. It must be remembered that petty theft in Huntington's childhood was still regarded as a capital offence.

Whilst still struggling with the easier chapters in the New Testament and just as he had begun to learn 'proper writing', William was again taken away from school to work on the farm. Life in the Hunts' home was hard and the large family had only one cooked meal a week, which

---

[2] This was a dig at Huntington's 'Christian' enemies who often maintained that he had been a highwayman before his conversion.

was Sunday dinner, and at times a meal was given them by the farmer when they helped to thresh his wheat. William put up with this for about a year, after which he approached a wealthy yeoman and asked to be taken into his service. The yeoman, impressed by William's initiative, offered the boy a job as his page. He was to be fully clothed, receive full board and twenty shillings a year, not including gratuities. The yeoman explained that usually any tips in the household were to be shared by all the servants but he would make an exception in William's case. Unfortunately the generous yeoman forgot to inform his wife of this decision. At first William could not get used to having several square meals a day and his stomach rebelled furiously and he was ill for some time. After his recovery, William proved an able page and rose high in his master's esteem. One day the Kentish militia visited the area and William's employer decided to entertain them.

William was chosen to wait on the soldiers and he did so with such expertise that he was tipped profusely, gaining the equivalent of over six months' wages in gratuities. The other servants became jealous and complained to their mistress who insisted that William should give up two-thirds of his gratuities to the maidservants.

William went to his mother for advice, but she proved to be the wrong person to give him moral assistance. Mrs Hunt insisted that William should stick to his 'rights' and keep the money. He thus gave his mistress his mother's decision and was promptly dismissed on the spot. William was then further humiliated by having to go into the 'stripping room', take off his fine uniform and underwear and put on the rags he had discarded on first taking up the post. Thereafter William was obliged to return to working like a slave on Russel's farm and received a mere fourpence a day for his labour.

In spite of a life of poverty and misery, young William could not forget his Maker and prayed incessantly, soon receiving marvellous proof of the goodness of God. He had begun to imagine how fine it would be to live at the squire's mansion and be his personal servant. He therefore began to pray that God would open the door to such a post. William prayed vigilantly for several weeks, fully knowing that Squire Cook had a boy who was a very good worker. Just as William was getting weary of praying and beginning to doubt God's existence, a positive answer came. The Hunts had a visitor who told them that the squire was looking for a boy and suggested that William should apply for the job. The squire's previous page had been dismissed for thieving. Young William, still only eight years of age, went up to the mansion, applied for the post, was given it and started as the squire's page at twenty shillings a year with full board and lodgings and a clothing allowance.

William now lived through weeks of intense belief in God interspersed by equally intense moments of doubt. His faith was daily put to the test by a worldly-wise stable-hand who took a great interest in thoroughly corrupting him. The man's method was to argue how stupid it was to believe in a God who is at our beck and call. As further weeks and months went by, William gradually rejected any notion he had of a loving and caring God. As soon as William's advisor realised that his pupil's trust in an all-seeing God had gone, he began to teach William how free one could be in what one did as there was no God to control one's actions. Thus with his rejection of the God who sticks closer than a brother, William developed such a bad character that he was eventually sacked by his employer. Huntington says of this experience, '[I] went home as deeply stung with guilt for my folly as I had been before lifted up at the sight of God's mercy'.

The fear of God that had accompanied William's dismissal from Squire Cook's services stayed with him a short while but soon left him entirely as the precocious youth took to bad company and any other worldly occupation which his time and meagre wages allowed. It seems that he took to dancing at this time.

Death of his natural father

At the age of fourteen William obtained a servant's post in Battle Abbey where, however, illness trudged at his heels and at times he was near death's door. Thoughts of dying so young soon served to prick his hardened conscience. Death, however, came not to William but to his true father, Barnabas Russel, who died in agony of soul but unrepentant. He was nursed by Elizabeth Hunt and his wife and his last words to them were a pathetic, 'Do what you will to me, if you can but save my life'. Huntington was always conscious of the likeness he shared with his father, a likeness that was recognised by all who knew them both. During his childhood the neighbours had taunted the little boy by calling him 'Little Barnet' after his true father and it is obvious that William suffered terribly because of the knowledge that he was 'begotten by another woman's husband, and conceived in the womb of another man's wife'. Especially when saving grace began to make itself known to Huntington's penitent heart, he feared dismissal from God's presence because of his illegitimacy. When he was low the tempter would quote to him Deuteronomy 23:2; 'A bastard shall not enter into the congregation of the Lord; even to his tenth generation shall he not enter into the congregation of the Lord'. When these doubts assailed Huntington he would cry out, 'And is hell to be the reception of both progenitors and progeny? I see no way of escape. Oh wretched end! I shall hate them both to all eternity, for being instrumental in sending me into the world as the miserable issue of their lewd embraces; and to all eternity they will hate me as an aggravation of their heinous crimes, and as venom to their sting of guilt'.

A doomed love-affair

Huntington stayed at Battle Abbey until 1762 when he entered into the service of the Rev. Henry Friend who was Rector of Frittenden, near Cranbrook, at that time. It was at Frittenden that the seventeen year old Huntington fell into circumstances that were to hang like a millstone around his neck for many years to come. He had for some time been friends with a local tailor by the name of Fever who had made up clothes for him from time to time. This tailor had a daughter called Susan who was his only child. William continued to visit the tailor's home for several months whilst at Frittenden but had no romantic thoughts towards his daughter. Once, however, when William was lighting a lantern at the Fevers' home in preparation to set off to do some bell-ringing at the church, he exchanged a few jocular words with Susan. This made Mr Fever suspicious that there might be some sort of romance between the two and he told William to stop visiting his home. William could not understand the change in his friend's behaviour and left the house greatly offended. A few days later a boy brought a message to William saying that he was invited to visit the tailor's again. William refused to accept the invitation as he was still too upset by his friend's sudden animosity. Some time later Mrs Fever sought William out and confessed that she had been ignorant of the fact that William and her daughter were romantically involved with each other and she asked that William should accompany her home where her daughter was waiting for him. The youth replied that he, too, was quite ignorant of any romance between himself and Susan, but accompanied Mrs Fever. On reaching the Fevers' home, William found that Susan was much in love with him and that her parents were willing to back up the match for her sake. It was not long before William, too, was declaring his love for Susan which became so strong that he could hardly bear to be parted from her for a moment.

The two courted each another for a full year and made plans to be married. This spurred William on to look for better jobs so that he could keep a wife, but everything he laid his hand to failed. One promising post he obtained, for instance, was with a brother-in-law who agreed to teach William the trade of a gunsmith. His apprenticeship, however, was quickly brought to an end as his in-law was a drunkard and soon ruined his own business. Another job was with a sawyer as a pitman, but that business also failed. William was then out of work for some time and every visit to his sweetheart caused him grave anxiety as he had merely rags to clothe himself in and was very conscious of the critical eyes of Susan's parents. Soon Mr and Mrs Fever turned their backs on William completely and put their hope in a well-to-do cloth merchant whom they now wished to be Susan's husband. They encouraged the merchant in this matter, paying no regards to their daughter's own wishes.

At last, however, William obtained employment at Rolvenden in Kent as a carriage-driver, but this meant he would have to live a good way from Susan and only be able to see her occasionally. He thus formed a selfish plan which would either bind Susan to him for life or make sure that she would not 'drop as a pure maiden into the hands of another'. It has always been a worldly maxim that the only way to make obstinate parents change their minds towards their daughter's choice of a husband is to make sure she has a baby. Thus William called on Susan to say goodbye before taking up the Rolvenden appointment and asked her to join him on the first three miles or so of his walk to his new appointment During the walk both lovers promised that they would always be faithful to each other and united their bodies as a seal and token of this. They then parted, never to see each other again.

After some time in Rolvenden William managed to get a message to his loved one, arranging to meet her at a certain spot. Susan did not turn up to meet him. He wrote many letters to her, but they were not answered. What he did not know was that Susan had gone with her father to meet William but they had misunderstood his instructions and gone to the wrong place. He later found out that his letters to Susan had all been opened by her father and kept from her. Gradually William began to feel that it was a hopeless task waiting for news of Susan and in his agony he turned his attention to another young lady in an effort to forget his past. He found, however, no interest for the opposite sex apart from his love for Susan and he pined for her day and night.

This went on for some eleven months until one night William dreamt the same dream twice over. He dreamt that three men were chasing him and he slipped and fell, so they caught him. The dream so shook him that he decided to go out and take a walk to clear his head of the thoughts he associated with it. although it was still only four in the morning. As he opened the door he was hardly surprised to see three earnest-looking men waiting outside to see him. The three men brought the news that Susan had had a baby, that she would never be allowed to marry William and that he was called to stand before the parish officers' bench. The officers gave William a written order demanding maintenance payment. William argued that such a maintenance order was not necessary as he would be only too pleased to marry the girl. Mr Fever remained adamant against William, however, and so did the parish officers. Their first reason was practical though inconsiderate. They argued that if the two were married the parish would probably have to look after them, which would overburden the parish finances. They also stressed that Susan was too young to marry, although she must have been at least eighteen or nineteen years of age at the time. William argued reasonably enough, though in vain, that if she was old enough to mother his child, she was old enough to marry him.

Troubled times

Once back at Rolvenden, William went through months of turmoil. At times he suffered from a stricken conscience; at other times he tried to forget his worries by dancing well into the night. This means of killing time and conscience brought him into contact with the lowest of people and later Huntington was to criticise dancing severely, saying of it,

'[Dancing] is just as serviceable a net to ruin souls as devils could invent, or frail mortals drop into'. Working hard long hours of the day and dancing through the night began to ravage even William's iron constitution inherited from his father Barnabas Russel. Soon he became seriously ill again and once more the doctor gave him up for dead. After weeks of hearing 'Death's rattle' in his breath, as Huntington later put it, he once again began to look to God for help. He swore never to go dancing again and begged God's forgiveness for the crimes he had committed against Susan Fever. Within a month William was back on his feet, determined to live a life closer to God.

William was compelled to give up his post at Rolvenden because of his long illness and went to stay with his parents for some time in order to recover. He then heard that a servant's job might be available at Charren[3] in Kent and set off on foot to apply for the post. On his way William knelt down by a hedge and, acknowledging that he had deserved God's punishment, asked his Creator the favour of success in his new venture. He then took a stick out of the hedge, cut it half through and bent it. He promised God that if he returned after successfully applying for the job he would kneel down at the place marked and worship him for his favour. When William arrived at the gentleman's house, he found him in the process of signing on a servant for the vacant post. William felt that his prayers had been in vain but, to his utter astonishment, the gentleman broke off speaking with the man and asked William if he were married. When William replied in the negative, the gentleman said he would give him the job as the other man was married and he wanted someone with no family commitments. William, who bad wanted to marry so urgently, now found that God had answered his prayers and blessed his unmarried state. On his way back home William looked with tears at the bent stick and offered up his praise to the God whom he had offended yet who had shown him such favour.

As so often previously, William continued in his new position for a while, apparently strong in faith and upright in his way of life. Soon, however, all William's promises to God were forgotten and the young man again fell into bad company and followed the ways of his

[3] 'Charren' is the local name for 'Charing'.

companions rather than those of the Lord. As had also happened on several occasions before, once William turned from God he was stricken by a severe illness. During this time he was unable to pay the quarterly maintenance grants for Susan and her illegitimate child and he was in constant dread that he would be dragged into prison, sick as he was, for not keeping up the payments. When William recovered he became as sick in his soul as he had been in his body.

It is still a fashion amongst Huntington's modern critics to say they cannot accept Huntington's Christian testimony as being true because he never believed that a Christian could endure God's wrath because of his sins. Those critics are victims of their own fancy rather than the truth. Huntington was haunted by his sin for many years as a Christian and looked to many a setback in his walk of faith as a chastisement from God for the sins of his youth. Only after he had been converted for many years did Huntington gain peace and assurance that God would remember this special sin no more. Meanwhile, William's remorse and contrition at what he had done grew and the thought that he was justly living under God's wrath drove him almost out of his mind and rendered him as incapable of work as he had been when ill. In believing he could manipulate the decisions of others by taking Susan's virginity from her, he saw that he had been tempting God and defiling himself as well as her.

For the next four years or so William was to go through harrowing times of not being able to meet his commitments, of running away from responsibilities, of grave illness, of a troubled conscience and wrestling with God. During this time Huntington's dross was to be purged by the fiercest of fires and he was to emerge from this furnace fit for the work God had chosen for him to do.

Chapter 2

The Dawning Of Saving Faith

There were many reasons which drove Huntington throughout the next few years to wander from town to town and village to village like the travelling tinkers of old. He was still deeply in love with Susan Fever and his lovesickness caused him to be ever restless and constantly on the move. Ill health, too, clung to his footsteps wherever he went and no occupation that he turned his hands to, proved of a lasting duration. Another major reason for Huntington's restlessness was that the still very young man looked upon himself as a kind of outlaw with a price on his head. He was unable to pay for the upkeep of the woman who was denied him and the child he had fathered and the idea haunted him that the parish officers at Frittenden and Cranbrook would send magistrates out to arrest him and he would be made free game for anyone who cared to drag him off to the courts seeking a reward.

Even during this period of a sense of sin and shame and absolute poverty, Huntington saw signs that God was watching over him. Moving down to Maidstone in Kent, for instance, Huntington had his few effects sent on to the Star Inn whilst he made his way there on foot in the cold and sleet with only a shilling in his pocket. On arrival at the inn, Huntington found that his goods had been forwarded to a place two miles away so he had to brave the inclement weather again. His shilling was gone and it looked as though he would have to spend the night in the open. His thoughts turned to God, believing that he had lost contact with him because of his sin. Whilst meditating on his own worthlessness, Huntington started to walk down a horse-track instead of the footpath. After a minute on the new path a shiny sixpence glowed up at him from the dirt on the track and a few steps further on Huntington found a shilling. Huntington's later comment was: 'These manifold providences and answers to prayer did, at times, deeply impress my mind that God had some regard for me: but when sin was committed all these thoughts were blasted'.

A change of name

It was during this period of wandering from place to place that Huntington made a major decision which was to haunt him throughout life every bit as much as the way he had wronged and lost Susan Fever. Through his being an illegitimate child there had always been some doubt as to what Huntington should be called. This is reflected in the fact that, according to Church of England tradition, children are named on the day of their baptism, as soon after birth as is thought wise. It was not until five years after Huntington's birth, however, that his mother and foster-father agreed to give the sinfully conceived child William Hunt's name. Now Huntington began to hate the name that had been given to him at baptism – not because he had any hatred for his foster-father, but because it was a name too well-known amongst the Cranbrook parish officers for his comfort. Huntington began to argue that in reality his name should be Russel as his father was called Russel, so he could rightfully and legally call himself William Russel. He then considered the fact that his half-brothers on the Russel side were well-to-do and would object to Huntington's using their name, for obvious reasons, and take him to court over the matter. Huntington therefore dropped the idea of calling himself after his real father. He then argued that he had no true right to the name of Hunt so nobody could blame him for dropping that name. However, as he was actually recorded in the parish registers as William Hunt, he decided that a change of name was out of the question. He then thought, naively enough, that an extension of a name was not the same as a change of name and hit on the idea of adding the letters '-ington' to the name of Hunt. Thus the name Huntington was born.

From now on Huntington suffered from a very bad conscience for changing his name to avoid discovery by his debtors. This was the true and major sin attached to his name-change, as Huntington clearly recognised. The main thrust of the argument put forward by Huntington's many Christian critics, however, leaves aside his true fault and judges Huntington to be wicked for taking on a name which was not given to him at birth or at baptism. Huntington's act of deception, of course, cannot be explained away but a little Christian understanding would show that he can hardly be blamed for wanting a name of his very own which did not originate from the tragic circumstances of his birth. Years later Huntington used to play on the fact that his birth-name and baptismal name were dubious by saying that he was born again as Huntington and baptised of the Spirit in that name so he had no reason to change it.

With two great millstones of conviction around his neck Huntington struggled on, now finding work, now losing it through illness; now sleeping under hedges and in barns and now going for days without food. In a matter of months he had wandered through Tunbridge Wells, Arundel, Chichester, London, Epsom, Stratford, Low Leyton, Danbury, Chelmsford, Billericay, Tilbury and Greenhithe, to mention just some of the many places he visited.

At Danbury Park in Essex Huntington obtained work for a Squire Fitch. After only a few days in his new occupation, Huntington collapsed and was removed from the squire's house without any ceremony whatsoever and literally dumped in the village inn though he had only two shillings in his pocket. God's hand was on Huntington even in the Bell Inn. The proprietress of the inn was an old widow who, knowing that Huntington was virtually penniless still looked after him for weeks on end and showed him the same affection as she would have done to her own child. A few years later, when Huntington had a little money saved up, he went back to Essex to seek out the woman and reward her but was dismayed to find that she had recently died.

After Danbury things became brighter for Huntington and he obtained a post at Marden with a farmer he knew who was a professing Christian. Huntington confessed his whole story to the man who wept on hearing his tale of the Lord's dealing with his soul and promised Huntington he would help him. The only help that the farmer gave Huntington, however, was to call for the Frittenden parish officers, who made a post-haste visit to Huntington. Huntington had heard that Susan

Fever was married and thus he had no further commitments to her regarding the law alone. In spite of this, he insisted on paying all debts he would have incurred otherwise and after handing over £30 he received a receipt from the parish clerks exempting him from all further payments.

Soon after this event news reached Huntington that Susan Fever had died. Up to this time Huntington had kept his vows and promises to Susan, hoping against hope that she would be his again one day. Now he felt free to look for another wife and found such a person in Mary Short of Dorsetshire whom he married some time in 1769 and settled down with her in Mortlake, Surrey. Huntington was married under his new, elongated name and did not tell his wife that he had formerly been called Hunt until nine months after the marriage. Mary attached no importance whatsoever to the change.

Hard times in early married life

They say that burdens shared are burdens halved but Huntington found married life no bed of roses. He had always had difficulty providing for himself and now he had a wife and soon a daughter to provide for. Huntington had never learnt the basics of mathematics at school and he still had great difficulty in adding, subtracting, multiplying and dividing. This made it always difficult for him to plan ahead financially. To make matters worse, he became lame and was out of work again. Then one winter morning the couple found their five-months-old baby early in the morning lying cold, stiff and as black as coal. The young, undernourished child had apparently frozen to death. Of this time Huntington writes, 'My lameness, poverty, distress of mind, the sufferings of my wife, loss of my child, and the sense of God's wrath, were the most complicated distresses I had ever felt'. He goes on to write, however, 'From this time spiritual convictions began to plough so deep in my heart as to make way for the word of eternal life; which at length brought me experimentally to know "the only true God and Jesus Christ whom he hath sent"'.

Shortly afterwards, Huntington found employment again and his wife went to Barnes to nurse a lady who was lying in. Left to himself, Huntington became very dejected and blamed his own sin for the fact that he had lost his child. 'Why did not God take me instead of my child?' he constantly asked the heavens. For days Huntington wept when faced with his own wickedness but he wept, too, out of self-pity. It was then that he learnt to pray. He took portions out of set prayers he had read in books and he interwove them with pleas of his own and found ease for his soul in pouring out his problems before the throne of grace. Gradually his depressions and gloom left him as he found freedom in prayer.

Huntington had, however, made a number of very worldly friends and he realised that if he stayed at Mortlake he would never be free to have fellowship with God. He would commit sins as fast as he begged forgiveness for them. He thus journeyed over to Barnes to tell his wife that he had received a strong conviction from God that they must look for a new home. His faithful wife answered him, 'Do just as you will; I am ready to go with you to any place you choose'. This decision of Huntington's must have come as a pleasant surprise to his wife as Mary was a praying, Bible-reading woman who had been put off by Huntington's jocular worldliness and had secretly prayed for a change in her husband. This change was now taking place.

After his wife returned from Barnes, she had a terrible nightmare in which the devil took hold of her. Huntington immediately thought that the dream was directed at him, as he believed his wife lived too near God to be attacked in this way. The dream became a sign to him that 'death, judgment and eternal damnation' were now his portion. Shortly after becoming convinced that he was to leave his old friends and put down new roots, Huntington obtained employment as a nurseryman at Hampton Wick, near Kingston, and had to walk the six miles from Mortlake to Kingston and back every day for several weeks before finding furnished lodgings. At Kingston, Huntington determined not to form a friendship with anyone but professing Christians and kept up private prayer either alone or with his wife and went regularly to church. Now Huntington began to develop a very good opinion of himself as a Christian, particularly as his workmates daily teased him about his 'religion'. He tells us that his motto became the words of Isaiah 65:5, 'Stand by thyself, come not near unto me; for I am holier than thou'.

A stop was put to this self-praise when Huntington found himself slipping into sin as easily as ever. One of these temptations was due to his being out of pocket again. William and Mary now had another daughter, named Ruth like the first, and they were in danger of losing their second daughter the way they had lost the first. Huntington thus decided to go back to his childhood practice and steal turnips at night. He had been given a piece of bacon and felt that turnips would go nicely with it. Whilst climbing over the fence to the turnip-field, however, Huntington was arrested by his own conscience and stood for minutes on end not being able to move a limb. Finally he burst out with the words, 'What is it? What is it?' and heard the words ring clear in the cool night air: 'Thou shalt not steal'. Huntington assured his conscience that his employer allowed his men to pick a few turnips when they asked him politely if they could do so. Huntington had been too proud to ask but now, picking some choice turnips, he assured his conscience that he would ask his master for permission as soon as possible. The turnips were picked but Huntington 'forgot' to ask his master's permission.

Conviction of sin and a search for peace

Thus months went by and Huntington limped on under the burdens of legalism, always striving to live a life pleasing to God and always failing. One evening, he was sitting by the fireside reading his Bible when he came across the words: 'At that day ye shall know that I am in my Father, and ye in me, and I in you' (John 14:20). These words were at first incomprehensible to Huntington as he had not experienced being 'in Christ' and being thus a new creature. 'There must be some secret between Christ and those whom He will save, that I am ignorant of', he exclaimed. As he thought on these things all his sins paraded themselves before him and all his false hope disappeared in a twinkling. Great conviction came upon him and yet his first thoughts were ones of hatred to God for putting him in such a position. He shouted out to his wife with fear in his eyes and his hair standing on end, 'Molly, I am undone for ever; I am lost and gone; there is no hope nor mercy for me; you know not what a sinner I am, nor what I feel!' The amazed Mary tried to comfort her husband as well as she could but her Christian experience was weak and she did not know what was happening to him.

All through that night Huntington confessed his sins to God but dared not plead with his Maker for forgiveness as he was so certain that his own iniquities had damned him, cutting him off from God's mercy forever. He staggered to work the following morning looking at the horses and cows in envy, telling them that they would never be punished for their sins and they would never have to stand trembling at the judgment seat only to be cast into hell. Next came an overbearing conviction that he could escape all by taking his own life, but soon thoughts of the wrath to come after death drove him back to thinking more soberly. In this way Huntington lived through the days of the following weeks overcome with horror at his own self and at his hopelessness until he was completely run down and exhausted. But going one morning to work, Huntington suddenly asked himself which part of the world Christ was born in. He confessed that he did not know but judged it to be the East. He thus looked in that direction and began to daydream about Christ's name. Whilst his mind was fixed on the birth and name of Jesus he was suddenly overwhelmed with a spirit of love and meekness. Just as suddenly he felt like a bottle without a vent and began weeping tears of joy so loudly that he feared people must have heard him miles away. Huntington's thoughts progressed to the sufferings of Christ on the cross which made him 'melt, mourn and weep'. Huntington as yet had no doctrinal knowledge of Christ's death but he heard a voice distinctly say, 'He that overcometh shall inherit all things', a phrase he did not understand at the time, nor did he know that it was a passage from Scripture (Revelation 21:7).

Now for many days Huntington was as taken up with thoughts of God's lovingkindness in Christ as he had been by his own sin and earned destruction. Temptations came in an endless train but Huntington began to experience that God's grace was sufficient. He was rescued from perils into which he had fallen head first before. The more, however, Huntington praised God for temptations defeated, the more they came and still the inner voice told him, 'He that overcometh shall inherit all things'. It seemed, however, as if the Lord were showing Huntington that he could not overcome – at least not without earnest pleas heavenwards. Huntington found himself now at all times shaking his head against temptations, which came at the rate of five a minute, and opening his lips to praise God. This caused his workmates to think he had gone mad. So taken up was Huntington with the battle in his soul that he could not give a rational answer to a simple question as his thoughts were so strongly concentrated on the forces at work within.

Huntington continued to read his Bible earnestly but found he could only understand the passages that condemned him. As conviction and a thirst for God's saving grace grew in him, Huntington concluded that if he were to find an everlasting home in heaven the clergy would be the people to tell him how to get there. He thus called on the vicar time and time again but always discovered that he was 'not at home'. He then went to the vicar's clerk, who took him to a public house and invited himself to several portions of rum and water at Huntington's expense, but could only point upwards and say, 'Go there: look there. If I was in your case, I would always go there'. Huntington realised that the man meant, 'Go to God' but came to the conclusion that the clerk had not taken a step in that upwards direction himself although he had quite emptied the seeker's pocket.

Next Huntington felt that he might find peace with God at the communion table. Thus he went to the Lord's Supper honestly and contritely saying in his heart the words of the Prayer Book service: 'I do earnestly repent, and am heartily sorry for these my misdoings; the remembrance of them is grievous unto me, and the burden intolerable'. He was thus surprised to find that the suddenly very officious rum-and-water clerk told him to wait his turn until 'the quality had all done', meaning that the Lord's Supper was to be dealt out according to earthly rank and Huntington was obviously on the lowest rung in the social ladder. It is no wonder that Huntington came away from the communion table, not only with all his guilt and distress still intact, but also feeling peevish and fretful. He had asked for bread and had received a stone.

Back at work, the next day brought new anguish to Huntington as his workmates thought only of one thing – to pull his leg and mock him for his 'religious mania'. A break came soon after, however, when the foreman came to Huntington and told him a certain gentleman's gardener had cut his throat and his post was vacant. Would Huntington like the job? Huntington accepted the offer at once and whilst his wife went to visit relations in Dorsetshire with his children, Huntington moved home to Sunbury where he found a garden to look after and a large house, deserted except for a housekeeper.

Noting that Huntington made a 'serious' impression, the woman lent him her copy of *The Whole Duty of Man*, 'the best book', she informed him, 'that was ever written'. Thinking her to be a Christian, Huntington confided in her and told her of his heart troubles. The housekeeper appeared to sympathise in a Christian way at first but soon became very vulgar and contemptuous against all sacred things and plagued Huntington for months with her ridicule and vulgarity. The woman was obviously unbalanced and some time later she was strongly tempted to murder her own child and ran about the streets naked and finally died in a fit of madness.

Notwithstanding Huntington read *The Whole Duty of Man* several times but found no comfort in it. This was hardly surprising as the book is little more than a system of legalism. Henry Venn combatted the teaching of this best-selling book by producing his own best seller, *The Complete Duty of Man*, which put the whole matter on a more biblical footing. 'The best book' proved not good enough for Huntington, who found himself to be the worst sinner and *The Whole Duty of Man*, in his words, nothing but 'linsey woolsey manufactory'.

The next stage in Huntington's progress to faith was that he was tempted to shake off all sense of religion and believe that there is no God. Then all his terrors, he thought, would disappear. He thus went to variety shows and started to drink again and live as if he had no convictions. But the convictions remained as the best proof of God's existence that Huntington could have hoped for. 'If God does not exist', he argued, 'then who is condemning me? Why do I feel my sins so strongly? Why do I believe that I have angered my Maker? Whose wrath am I experiencing?' These thoughts drove Huntington anew to prayer one day and as he arose from praying, a beautiful rainbow arched itself across the sky. 'Look at that', said Huntington, 'That should be proof enough for me that God exists. He said in his Word that he would send the rainbow so that Noah might know that he kept his promise and there the rainbow is!' Now reverting back to pious efforts to ease his soul-ache, Huntington began to fast in preparation for receiving his next communion. Why fast? Huntington's answer was: 'What will not a guilty sinner do when he is at the gates of hell?' He was willing to try anything.

Fasting, however, did not help to take away Huntington's burden and his next vain effort to find peace was to go and hear preacher after preacher until he found one who could tell him the way of salvation. How disappointed Huntington was to become! One preacher preached about the fine Anglican churches, so sturdily built as a sign that the Church of England would never be forced out of existence by the Dissenters. Another minister – called 'the macaroni parson' because of his fine ringlets – thought too much about his rakish looks and his equally rakish friends to think much about his sermon. Another parson dressed up in his sacred robes on Sundays but spent the whole of the week hunting, so he had no time for sermon preparation. Yet another was downright filthy-minded and laughed over his own dirty jokes in the pulpit. Most of the sermons, Huntington found, were twelve minutes of 'incoherent odds and ends'. Huntington began to think that the clergy duped their congregations so that they would not become as wise as their priests. 'Alas!', he cried out, 'Where shall we look for Christians if the clergy are so destitute of Christianity?'

Whilst Huntington was in a turmoil about his unsaved soul, a friend invited him to go and see the new house and grounds which were being built for Lord Clive of India. He was amazed to find how thick the walls were and asked the reason. He was told that Lord Clive had commanded that the walls be built so solidly so as to keep the devil out. Huntington's immediate reflection was that the devil's possession was fallen man himself and the walls of his house could never protect anyone from Satan's darts.

After a fair quantity of beer Huntington started to discuss religion with his friend, who told him that man can do nothing to save his own soul. This was quite a new idea to Huntington, so he asked his friend how he could be so sure. The friend's reply was that he had heard Whitefield, Romaine and all the good preachers in London preach that the elect will be saved and none else. Huntington tells us that he protested strongly against this doctrine but his friend had learnt so many passages of Scripture from hearing Whitefield and Romaine that he was soundly defeated in the debate. Shortly afterwards Huntington found a copy of the Thirty-Nine Articles of the Church of England and was surprised to find that they agreed with what his friend had told him. No man can come to God unless God draws him. The mental and spiritual anguish that Huntington was in increased daily and he felt that he would either drop dead from exhaustion or have to take his own life. His employer complained that he could not get a civil answer from him and thought he was the worst-tempered man he ever saw. The employer's wife called Mrs Huntington to her to tell her that she was married to one of the most miserable men in existence and asked how she could possibly live with such a person. Mrs Huntington defended her husband as best she could but the couple now knew that they were not wanted.

After so many disappointments at so many different churches, Huntington decided he would be his own pastor and stay at home and read the Bible. Now, wherever he looked, he found passages telling him that only the elect would be saved. He thus took a piece of paper and a pen and read through the whole Bible, jotting down all the references to man's hopelessness and God's sovereignty. Such verses as 'No man can come to me, except the Father which hath sent me draw him' (John 6:44) and 'I know whom I have chosen' (John 13:18) fixed themselves so deeply in Huntington's memory that he never forgot them. After thus going through the entire Scriptures, Huntington concluded that, 'The doctrines of predestination and election reflect the tremendous doctrine of reprobation in many passages of scripture'. Now Huntington was in a worse dilemma than ever. What if he merely felt the condemnation that was common to all the non-elect? What if all his repentance and sorrow for his sins, however true, were in vain?

Such thoughts were plaguing Huntington one day whilst he was up a ladder pruning a large pear tree. He kept telling himself that though he strove to be holy, he was as worldly as ever. True, he was always trying to please God and appease his wrath, but it was without any success whatsoever. The doctrine of election, he told himself, is true. If I am not one of the elect, I shall never be saved, do what I will. When thinking along these lines all Huntington's bitterness concerning his illegitimate birth came back to his mind and he thought of the horrible life and death of his true father. He thought also of his mother, who took the Lord's Supper regularly but lived in open adultery. He thought of the Old Testament passages referred to earlier that pronounce condemnation on bastards and cried out from the treetop his horror at the thought that hell awaited both parents and child and that he could see no way of escape.

The light dawns at last

As Huntington was deep in self-pity and self-reproach, a great light seemed to shine all around him and swept all his anxious thoughts away.

As clear as a bell Huntington heard the words of John 14:26, 27, 'But the Comforter, which is the Holy Ghost, whom the Father will send in my name, he shall teach you all things, and bring all things to your remembrance, whatsoever I have said unto you … Let not your heart be troubled, neither let it be afraid'. Two sets of Scripture references poured into Huntington's now relaxed and receptive memory: all those which cursed the sinner and all those which spoke of the goodness and graciousness of God in salvation. Huntington climbed down the ladder wondering what was happening to him. 'What is it? What is it?', he cried out. He then distinctly heard the words that he never forgot: 'Lay by your forms of prayer, and go pray to Jesus Christ; do not you see how pitifully he speaks to sinners?'

Huntington was not disobedient to the heavenly vision and dashed into the tool shed with his apron over his head and face for fear of what was happening. He then knelt down and prayed extempore (his prayers up to now had been combinations of written prayers with his own comments): 'Oh Lord, I am a sinner, and thou knowest it! I have tried to make myself better, but I cannot. If there is any way left in which thou canst save me, do thou save me; if not, I must be damned, for I cannot try any more, nor won't'.

The very moment that Huntington said these words, he felt a freedom to unburden his soul before the throne of grace and prayed with a fluency in the language of Scripture that was quite new to him. All the blessed promises of God to a repentant sinner came into his mind and heart and he bombarded the heavens with all the biblical claims on God's grace he could muster. He then saw Christ crucified before him as in a vision and he had never felt his own sin so deeply as he did at that moment. He now prayed loudly, 'I did not know till now that I had been sinning against thy wounds and blood! I did not know that thou hadst suffered thus for wretched me! I did not know till now that I had any concern in crucifying thee! I cannot beg mercy of my suffering Lord and Saviour. No: send me to hell for I deserve it'.

The more Huntington denied his right to Christ's love, the more Christ seemed to approach him in love. Slowly but very surely, a conviction of God's forgiveness displaced Huntington's assurance that he was hell-bound. Thoughts of Satan, death, destruction, horror and despair fled as a composure, serene and full of new-born hope, replaced them. Huntington had met his Lord at the one place where all must meet him who are his – at the cross. There the farm-labourer met the King of Kings. He went, to use his own words, into the tool shed in all the agonies of the damned, and came out with the kingdom of God established in his heart. What a change!

Chapter 3

Preparation For Service

After this marvellous experience of conversion Huntington was so excited, he did not know what to do. He tried to work, but could not because of the joy in his heart. Every time he went to fetch a tool from the shed, he forgot what he wanted by the time that he got there. He laughed, cried and rejoiced in turn. It was just impossible for him to work, so he went for a walk across Sunbury Common, amazed at the change he saw in creation. Everything looked as if it were outlined in 'divine embroidery' as Huntington put it. It was as if he had grown up in the dark and now saw the light of day for the first time in his life! The thought of death had not left him but this time he wanted to die for joy knowing that if he died now he would be with his Saviour and never more be tempted to sin. Once back home Huntington reached for his Bible and was again amazed to find what sweet thoughts were revealed there. It was like reading a new book to him, as all the sting of death and sin had gone.

Huntington caricatured by his critics

William Huntington was to grow quickly in grace and a knowledge of the Lord Jesus Christ and to experience time and time again scenes such as that on his conversion day when he would find sweet communion with God. It is surprising, yet typical of doubting human nature, that Huntington has been criticised chiefly for the spiritual experiences he had and for his testimony as to how the Lord led him. Christian and non-Christian alike have often joined forces to 'prove' that Huntington's mountain-top experiences were nothing more than low-down efforts at deceit and hypocrisy. It is true to say, however, that Huntington's testimony always shines soberly, biblically and objectively in his telling of it, whereas the criticisms and interpretations of his many enemies abound with far-fetched phrases and non-verifiable hypotheses.

A typical example of this has to do with an incident described in chapter 2 shortly before his conversion. Huntington visited property recently built by Clive of India and described the incident in his own sober way, obviously without any attempt to exaggerate anything:

> However, on the Lord's day following, I had appointed to walk with a person to see Lord Clive's new house, then building at Esher. When I came there I asked the reason why they built the walls so remarkably thick? The person said that several had asked that question as well as me, and had received an astonishing answer from the owner; namely, that their substance was intended to keep the devil out! I replied, that the possession of Satan was the man, not the building; and that the walls would not answer the end.

Any ordinary reader would be forgiven for thinking this description to be a true account and a display of common sense. Not so the great Lord Macaulay, man of letters and son of an Evangelical. This famous person read Huntington's account in his book *The Kingdom of Heaven Taken by Prayer* and found it worthy of sarcastic comment in a most personal, immoderate way. This is how Macaulay reacted to and interpreted Huntington's plain words quoted above:

> The peasantry of Surrey looked with mysterious horror on the stately house which was rising at Claremont. and whispered that the wicked lord had ordered the walls to be made so thick in order to keep out the devil, who would one day carry him away bodily. Among the gaping clowns who drank in this frightful story was a worthless ugly lad of the name of Hunter, since widely known as William Huntington, S.S.; and the superstition which was strangely mingled with the knavery of that remarkable impostor

> seems to have derived no small nutriment from the tales which he heard of the life and character of Clive.[1]

How Macaulay deals with his source is symptomatic of the bulk of criticism which has been levelled at Huntington's testimony throughout the years. Macaulay says that it was the Surrey peasantry that thought the walls were there to keep off the devil. In Huntington's original he is told that Clive himself had spread the tale. This is fully in keeping with what we know of Clive's character. Huntington in no way refers to Clive as 'wicked', nor does he write that others did so. To describe Huntington as 'a gaping clown', 'a knave' and 'an impostor' is a serious breach of decorum and does not fit in with what we know of Huntington at the time – or afterwards – at all. He may have been a simple-hearted, unaffected soul, but calling someone a 'gaping clown' and worse is sheer bad manners if it cannot be substantiated. Yet Macaulay's *Essays* were translated into many languages and came out in numerous editions which were spread throughout the world, so that all the world could read that Huntington was a 'gaping clown'.

But there is more insult to come. Huntington is described by the man of letters as a 'worthless ugly lad'. Now Lord Macaulay, with all his fine titles and education, might have thought a man so low-born as Huntington was 'worthless', but Huntington was made in God's image, just as the noble lord was, and certainly lived a life which reflected divine values far more than did the scoffing Lord Macaulay, who rejected the scriptural teaching of his youth to poke fun at Bible-believers. Huntington might have been ugly, and, indeed, the portraits of him reveal no Adonis, but what has being as ugly as God has felt free to make a man to do with that person's integrity or value? Nor was Huntington a mere 'lad' at the time, but a married man in his middle twenties with a young family.

Macaulay has even got Huntington's former name wrong, or perhaps he used the name 'Hunter' merely to stress that there was something unorthodox about the man's lowly birth. Huntington was from now on

---

[1] Macaulay's *Critical and Historical Essays*, vol. i. p. 84 (my edition Leipzig: Bernhard Tauchnitz).

to increase mightily in God's esteem and become a preacher who drew in thousands to hear his sermons from all walks of life. Yet even his fellow-evangelicals were very slow to accept that a man of such lowly birth and such little education could be qualified for the pulpit and the sad truth is that it was professing believers who took the caricatures of Macaulay and used them as evidence against Huntington.[2]

Huntington explains his view of conversion

From his conversion on, Huntington became a writer of note. This is all the more extraordinary as he had never read a book at school apart from the New Testament and only learnt to write sentences to do with the Word of God. One of the first things Huntington formulated in writing was the doctrine of conversion, about which he had very fixed biblical beliefs. Because of this he always found it very difficult to enjoy any Christian fellowship with professors of religion who could not see eye to eye with him about conversion. In his defence, however, it must be stated that there was a general uncertainty about what true conversion was amongst the clergy and Dissenting ministry of Huntington's day. This uncertainty was not shared by Huntington.

First, Huntington argued that a man must be convinced of his sin. He must see that his life is a transgression against God's laws. There are three witnesses to show a man that he is such a sinner: his own thoughts, his own conscience and the voice of God in his righteous law. The voice of God may come via the Scriptures directly, or from the preacher, or from a Christian's witness.

Huntington maintained that conviction of sin does not necessarily mean that a man, once convicted, will confess his sin. The human heart is so wicked that even when it knows it is sinful it will not go to God for healing. The Spirit must enter the elect person's life and convince him of the goodness of God's law and show him that he is weighed in the balance and found wanting. The Spirit also shows the elect person that the balance can be regained by putting one's trust in a Saviour who keeps the law and has arranged that his keeping the law, his righteousness, will be acceptable to God on the sinner's behalf and, what is more, imputed to the sinner as if he had not broken the law.

---

[2] See *The Voice of Years*.

This early statement of Huntington's doctrine of conversion is very important as it is here, right at the roots of his theology, that Huntington is misunderstood.[3] In his work *The Kingdom of Heaven taken by Prayer* Huntington makes it quite clear that the sinner is always the debtor, God is always the creditor but Christ is always the elect sinner's security.

'How does this all work out in practice?', Huntington asks next. The Spirit's work in the heart of the elect is shown by the simple fact that they look to God for help, but the reprobate goes his own way. The elect not only look to God for help, they turn actively to God and confess their sins to him. Not all the demons in hell can stop this happening. A reprobate can confess that he has sinned, as Judas confessed that he had betrayed innocent blood, but he is not drawn to God by this, but rather established in his turning away from God. Judas confessed his sin to those around him but went and hanged himself instead of bringing his sins to God. The conviction of those the Spirit leads, however, is mingled with hope even whilst they acknowledge their legal hopelessness. They count themselves as dung and recognise that they have no righteousness whatsoever of their own. Most important, they submit themselves to the righteousness and justice of God and are prepared to do anything and be anything that God wishes. They come to him to be different. They come to him for a new life in Christ.

Disillusionment with the Church of England

After his conversion experience, Huntington could not wait to go to church but was quite surprised when he did so. People whom he knew to be unconverted were actually saying in the service that their eyes had seen the Lord's salvation and that God should not take his Holy Spirit away from them. Huntington found it a shocking mockery of sinners pretending to be saints. Then came the sermon – and that was even worse. The minister sought to show that all Jews were unbelievers but all the British who had been brought up in a Christian country were believers.

---

3 See comments in Introduction. The 'Banner' reviewer appears to think that Huntington trusted in an inherent righteousness transferred to his old nature at Christ's death.

On the way back home Huntington was accosted by a temptation of the worst kind. How was it, he wondered, that he who could not read a chapter of the Bible without great difficulty should be wiser than the learned clergy who had gone to college? How could he presume to believe that such men were ignorant as babes of the very fundamentals of conversion to Christ? Many Bible passages, however, came to Huntington's mind to show him that God can reveal to babes and sucklings what he withholds from the so-called wisest of men.

Once home, Huntington examined the doctrines of the Church of England and found that they resembled what he had come to believe himself rather than what he had heard from the pulpit. He was again amazed that a church that had such a statement of faith should be so slow to teach it to its members. He was himself twenty-five years of age before anyone told him that the Thirty-Nine Articles existed.

Huntington now told his wife that he feared the Church of England seemed to be full of people who were not born again but before giving them up for lost he would go and visit some of those who appeared the most righteous and interview them as to their faith. This was duly done and Huntington found out that the pillars of his church, although the kindest of people, had no idea whatsoever about what a true Christian was. Now Huntington was tempted again to think he was wrong, especially after he had visited another two Anglican churches and found the same ignorance there. He began to develop an Elijah complex, that he was quite alone with his faith and experience, and told his wife that they would stay at home on Sundays and read their Bible together.

Thus Huntington spent months as a pastor in his own house, reading and expounding the Bible to his wife. These hours together with his wife on Sunday mornings were a gold-mine of grace for the couple and Huntington especially grew rapidly in Christian strength and found cause to marvel at the richness of God's Word and its ability through God's grace to hold him up in the faith, though no one he knew, apart from his faithful wife, could share it with him.

Times of blessing and trials

One day, however, a friend invited Huntington to go to a Methodist meeting-house at Richmond. Huntington had always been shocked at what he had heard about the Methodists and did not really want to go but he finally let himself be persuaded. The usual preacher was not there and the sermon left Huntington neither hot nor cold. It seems however, to have made a better impression on him than those he had heard at his own church. He thus went on the following Sunday to the same meeting-house where the regular minister was to preach. The preacher was called Captain Joss, an ex-naval man, who spoke on Colossians 1:12-14: 'Giving thanks unto the Father ... who hath delivered us from the power of darkness, and translated us into the kingdom of his dear Son: in whom we have redemption through his blood, even the forgiveness of sins'. Huntington was deeply moved and uplifted. For the first time in his life he was hearing the Word of God preached in power and in the strength of the Holy Spirit. His comment was: 'This man handled his text like a workman, and reached my heart sweetly; and, through grace, I could see eye to eye with him in all he said'. Huntington needed no invitation to hear the preacher again in the evening and it was as if the old apostolic days of New Testament preaching had returned. Huntington returned home and informed his wife that he had at last found a man who preached the Bible and that the Methodists must be the Lord's elect. Mrs Huntington did not quite react as her husband had hoped and secretly thought that William was becoming 'righteous over much'. She had prayed for her husband for years and now Huntington prayed for her and was delighted to find a growing work of God in her soul also.

A week after hearing the Word of God, Huntington was invited to a testimony meeting at Kingston and was asked to relate how the Lord had spoken to his soul. He gave a mighty testimony, based on the fifth chapter of Romans, of the Lord's sovereign grace in his life. The leader of the meeting felt that such a babe in Christ could hardly have had such experiences and told Huntington to his face that he was suffering from a delusion and 'hardened under the deceitfulness of sin'. In his subsequent sermon he looked at Huntington coldly and told him he had got rid of one devil but seven had taken its place. Huntington did not even know what the word 'delusion' meant so he did not feel the whole force of the criticism until some time later. When asked by another person at the meeting if his soul were not troubled at what the preacher had said, Huntington replied that though the person would preach hell and damnation against him for twenty years he could not rob him of the fact that Jesus himself had delivered his soul.

Huntington now spent many weeks in true bliss, finding in every piece of furniture in his house and every tree and animal outside cause to praise God. He saw God's finger in just about everything around him. Out of work once more, Huntington now found a temporary job as a cherry-picker and soon began to see that a Christian life was not possible without experiencing the fiery darts of the Enemy. It was Saturday evening and the employer came round to tell the workers that they would have to report the following morning for work. Huntington promptly refused and the employer asked him if he were a Whitefieldite. Huntington replied that it was a sin to profane the Lord's Day and he would not do it. At this Huntington was laughed at, and even hooted at, by his twenty co-workers. Huntington had his way, however, and this meant that he suffered severe persecution from his fellow employees who felt that they had to work on the Sabbath and thus do more work. Huntington began to witness to the man appointed to work with him and he received half a promise from him that he would stop working on the Lord's Day. When that day arrived again, however, the man went off to work and Huntington went off to church. On the following Tuesday the man confessed that he had spent all the money he had earned on the Sunday on beer in the local pub, so the extra work had brought him no profit whatsoever. He added that he had also spent Monday's wages at the same place. After confessing this, the man fell from his ladder, probably due to the great amount of alcohol in his blood, and injured himself so badly that he was unable to work for the rest of the season.

Huntington continued to attend the chapel at Kingston but was far from happy there. Every time he tried to tell the members of God's dealings with his soul, they would go away and leave him or change the subject. Huntington at first thought it must be his very rustic language that put them off and tried his best, through learning Scripture off by heart, to be more articulate. This did not help matters at all and Huntington was now tempted to think he was a hypocrite and honest Christians did not want to have anything to do with him. Once back home, however, with his Bible and prayers, Huntington received new assurance.

There were other temptations that came Huntington's way that were less easy to bear. Huntington's second daughter became ill at five or six months and wasted away until she was a mere skeleton. The doctor gave her up for lost and Huntington went to his tool shed to pray. He prayed that if the child were to be healed and grow up to be a heathen and die only to go to hell then it would be better that she died as a baby and God should not grant Huntington's heartfelt wish. He went back into the house and his daughter grew better from then on.

As Huntington's employer at Sunbury had to reduce his staff, Huntington found himself without work again but after a few weeks found a job at Ewell as gardener to a manufacturer of gunpowder. A furnished room was provided with the job. Huntington still had lying-in expenses to pay for his wife and now had to finance the removal. All this was beyond his means so he had to pawn his best clothes. The couple moved into their new lodgings almost penniless and prayed to God that he would keep them alive and well. Day after day, relations of his new landlord brought Huntington and his family food and heard the gospel in exchange. Later Huntington was to pay the couple back fourfold for what they had given him in those early days at Ewell. In spite of the goodness of his neighbours, Huntington could not make both ends meet and often had an empty stomach. His constant prayer was for food and clothing, especially for his weak child. His wage was terribly small and a large portion of it had to go towards his furnished room.

Walking sadly to work one day, Huntington espied an eel lying in the mud. At first he thought it was dead but found it was only sleeping and caught it with difficulty. The next day he found a dead partridge, still warm, on the path going to work and this, too, provided welcome relief for his family. The next day Huntington found the nest of a large bird with four fledglings in it These also found their way into Mrs Huntington's cooking-pot. The very next day, Huntington was cutting grass near a pond and found several carp floating on the surface, fresh but quite dead. He discussed the matter with his employer and came to the conclusion that the heat had killed the fish. Huntington's boss had nothing against his taking the fish home and once again the Huntington family's hunger was abated. Now morning after morning Huntington found new dead carp floating on the surface of the pond. One day Huntington thought that he should try to earn a little extra money by mending shoes and soon became quite proficient in the trade. It was also gleaning-time so he and his wife used to glean in the fields, using their one-roomed lodgings as storeroom and threshing-floor. All in all, the couple now found that they could pay their way.

Preparation for entry into the ministry

Huntington continued to attend the Kingston meetings but also continued to have great difficulty in having fellowship with the members there. One Sunday the superintendent asked Huntington to lead in prayer before the entire congregation and he refused point blank. This annoyed the superintendent greatly and he said that anyone who talked about God as freely as Huntington did should be able to pray. The point was, however, that Huntington was ashamed of his language. His own prayers were formless, spontaneous utterings of the heart in his still very homespun dialect. In the chapel prayers were said that had a form and a build-up and a climax as if they were spoken essays to the Lord. Huntington went home and prayed in his own way that he would be able to pray for others in front of others and received assurance that he should do so. He thus prayed openly in the chapel when called upon to do so from then on. This was the first step for Huntington in his entry into the ministry. Step two followed soon on the heels of the first. A man and his wife at Ewell became very impressed with Huntington's testimony and invited him to come regularly to their home and expound the Word and pray. Soon young people were converted and Huntington found himself leading a small congregation.

This brought some harsh criticism from the chapel at Kingston and the Huntingtons were forbidden to glean in many fields, as the farmers thought it was beneath the dignity of a preacher to glean for leftovers. Persecution became so severe that Huntington felt he had been presumptuous in preaching and should not exercise a gift which was too high for his station. He thus decided not to go and preach on the following Sunday. When the day came, Huntington stayed in his room but soon heard a voice on the stairs saying that the church-singers had come to dispute with him and the house was full of people waiting to hear the Word. Huntington hid himself behind the curtains, telling God that he was terrified to death and dared not usurp the office of a preacher. Then the Lord spoke to Huntington in absolute clarity. The words came to Huntington's mind: 'He that is ashamed of me and my words, of him will I be ashamed before the angels of God' (see Luke 9:26). Huntington went to the crowded house and preached valiantly on the words: 'Upon this rock will I build my church; and the gates of hell shall not prevail against it' (Matthew 16:18). Of the row of choir-singers that had come to tear him to pieces Huntington said, 'God stopped their mouths, and opened mine'.

From now on Huntington was to preach several times a week but as he grew popular with his hearers, the chapels round about grew harsher in their criticism of him. Slowly, however, other churches began to open their doors to him and wherever he preached he was usually asked back to preach again.

Even the chapel at Kingston where Huntington often worshipped asked him to preach one Sunday morning when the preacher on circuit duty did not arrive. Huntington refused to climb up into the pulpit, but gave an exhortation in fear and trembling from the desk. The congregation asked Huntington to preach again in the evening but he refused, possibly because of the odd behaviour of the superintendent of the chapel, who seemed extremely nettled because of Huntington's sermon. In his exhortation he had spoken of pardon from sin and atonement from sin and he later found out that this gentleman, who had said that Huntington's own assurance of salvation was a delusion, did not believe that one could obtain such an assurance or in any way obtain a knowledge of pardon from sin. The work at Ewell continued to grow and in reality Huntington had now become its pastor. The members invited Huntington to their homes in other villages and asked him to preach there too. One day he was taken to a home in Horsham and asked to preach, when he found himself standing under a portrait of Whitefield. The thought that he was engaging in the same work as that great man not only humbled Huntington but terrified him and it was not until towards the end of his sermon that his bad nerves left him and he could preach freely. Gradually, however, Huntington realised that the Lord was calling him to the full-time ministry. One of Huntington's converts, John Pavey, writes how, when he was eating barley bread[4] with Huntington's family in their hovel of a home at Ewell Marsh, 'the glory was fresh' in Huntington and the budding pastor said that he believed God was calling him to preach to thousands. Any stranger hearing such words would have laughed out loud as Huntington, with his broad Kentish dialect, was sitting in his one and only shirt with trousers cut from an old pair of someone's larger ones and his feet were thrust into old, frequently patched shoes. At the time he was earning the grand sum of eight shillings a week.

After preaching two or three times every week, getting up early in the morning to glean before going to work and mending shoes, sometimes into the early hours of the morning, Huntington found his powers all gone and a deep melancholy overcame him. It seemed that the Holy Spirit had left him and taken all feelings of assurance with him. Huntington began to fear that he had sinned against the Holy Ghost.

It was then that a preacher named Mr Brookbanks turned up at the Kingston meeting and spoke, without knowing anything of Huntington's case, about those who had lost their first love and are tempted to think that they have sinned against the Holy Ghost. This was a sermon especially for Huntington's ears and he listened with rapture. The preacher outlined the way back to God for such a weary soul and Huntington was able to say, 'Thus he touched my case, and hit the right nail on the head. This I knew was from God, as I had not mentioned it to anybody. Satan immediately fled, my soul escaped, and I ascended the mount of transfiguration, where I had been before'. After this sermon Huntington was again to experience weeks of divine bliss in which he saw the New Jerusalem coming down from the skies and his work in the ministry progressing and bringing forth much fruit.

Further trials and temptations

It seemed that every time Huntington's faith soared up heaven-wards, circumstances altered so that he was surrounded with trials and temptations. Huntington had long been a source of envy to his fellow-

[4] Huntington and his wife could not afford to bake bread with wheat so they bought barley, reserved for animal food, ground that and made bread out of it. See Pavey's letter in *Epistles of Faith*, Collingridge, vol. vi, p. 244.

workers as his employer exempted him from working on Sundays but expected the other workers to work seven days a week. They complained about this so much that their master felt forced to tell Huntington that his services were no longer required as he refused to work on Sundays. As there was no work to be had at Ewell, Huntington had to preach a tearful farewell sermon to his flock there and move to Ditton, where he found a job as a labourer to a coal-merchant who professed with his wife to be a Christian.

Huntington had been praying at Ewell that the Lord would grant him a believing employer and now he had one, he thought life would be just one long time of bliss. Huntington was to be bitterly disappointed and to long for the rich time of blessing he had experienced at Ewell. His new master was a deep-grained Arminian who cavilled against the doctrine of election, rejected the imputed righteousness of Christ and did not believe in the final perseverance of the saints. These were all doctrines which Huntington had come to believe were essential points of the gospel – and here was a professing Christian denying them all! What grieved Huntington the most was that his employer's wife would talk to Huntington at every opportunity about 'religion', but all her 'religion' was composed of was tales about the tremendous feats she had accomplished in her service for God. As the good lady had only a mind for what she had done for God and Huntington could only talk about what God had done for him, Huntington said that they could 'no more unite in heart than the north and south poles'.

Huntington now entered into months of agonizing soul-searching and persecution. His master's wife would not leave him alone and followed him to all his private prayer corners at his meal times and even sought him out when at prayer after work and demanded that he pray and debate with her. She tried her very best to make him angry and on rare occasions she succeeded and then she claimed jubilantly that Huntington was not the man he professed to be. Hardly a preacher visited the area without this lady telling him the most atrocious tales about Huntington and she would send preacher after preacher to him, whether he was at work or at home, to speak to him about what they had heard from the untruthful lips of his employer's wife. This woman was such a hypocrite that every time anyone visited her house, she would quickly take out her Bible and open it on her lap and look as though she were reading it intently though she hardly read a chapter a year.

Soon her tales were joined by the tales of others and it was rumoured around that Huntington stole pigs in his spare time, and that he had entered a man's house and stripped it bare of furniture up to the last candlestick. He had supposedly robbed a starving man and his children of their last side of bacon and run off with his neighbour's goose. The stories came thick and fast and Huntington's enemies tried to outdo one another in the telling of them. All swore that there were dozens of witnesses to prove that all was true, yet none of these witnesses was forthcoming. Huntington had to be very careful to see that his testimony remained pure. Several people sent him money so that they could claim that Huntington was a scrounger but God gave him insight into these plans and he sent the money back. This did not stop the slanderers, however, from sticking to their stories. What upset Huntington the most was that at a time when he was literally starving, well-to-do people would write him letters deploring the fact that he 'preached for money', which was just not true. On the contrary, Huntington often walked up to fifteen miles to a chapel on an empty stomach, preached there, collected money for the pastor or for the building, and walked back home without receiving any hospitality or payment whatsoever.

Ordination to the ministry

Huntington's ministry, however, prospered and there were now many souls whom he could number as his spiritual children. The fact that a 'coalheaver' could preach the gospel was quite a sensation and large numbers gathered together to hear 'Dr Sack', which was another name given Huntington at this time. Soon Huntington was preaching five or six times a week and visiting with the gospel, mostly on foot, places as far away from Ditton as Mitcham, London, Woking, Kingston, Hammersmith, Horsham, Chelsea, Cobham, Worplesdon, Farnham and Petworth.

One church, however, valued Huntington's ministry above all. This was a tiny group of believers at Woking (or Wooking, as Huntington always spelt it), fourteen miles from Ditton, who had been hearing Huntington for about a year. This tiny church, who could by no means afford a pastor, yet felt moved of God to invite Huntington to take over their spiritual oversight in 1776. The Rev. Torial Joss, who was the first man Huntington had heard preach the true gospel, ordained Huntington and said in his exhortation, 'While I possess a Bible, I shall not be at a loss to prove that William Huntington has received from God a call to the ministry'. He then turned to Huntington and said, 'You may now take your axe and go to work'. Huntington took up that axe and used it so well that only a few years later he was able to fulfil his own heart's wish and calling and preach regularly to thousands in the capital, a feat hardly any other minister could perform at the time.

Chapter 4

Trials And Tribulation

It soon became obvious to Huntington that he could not exercise the oversight of a church which needed his full attention and be burdened down with the daily bickering of his master's wife. At the time a Christian shoemaker offered to teach Huntington how to make children's shoes, so Huntington handed in his notice to the coal-merchant and began to earn eight shillings or so a week as a shoemaker. Before leaving his employment as a coalheaver, Huntington had made sure that there was someone to take up his work after him. This did not prevent his master's wife from spreading the story that Huntington had left them without a substitute and thus caused the firm a considerable financial loss.

It might be asked why Huntington did not step out in faith and give up secular employment altogether. The newly-fledged pastor had thought and prayed on these lines but had come to the conclusion that while his church members were as poor as he was, he should be like the apostle Paul, who made tents so as not to be a financial burden on his flock. Soon Huntington's help-meet became his shop-mate, as Huntington put it and Mrs Huntington joined in the shoemaking.

Such a life was, however, far from easy for a pastor who had at least five churches to serve and rarely found time for studious preparation. He had also commenced as an author and had published a long poem comparing the Reformed Christian's life to a sea voyage and was now working on a treatise against Arminianism. Whilst working, Huntington kept a spare chair near at hand with his Bible on it so that he could peep into his Bible now and then and prepare for his five, six or more weekly sermons or find ideas for further publications. Much time was lost by his having to walk the fourteen miles and more to his congregations and back almost daily. He was also often detained away from home because of needy people he met on the way or the crowds who always flocked to hear him. When preaching at Woking, for example, he would prepare his sermon carefully but invariably find that the chapel was full and almost as many people were standing outside. He thus preached his prepared sermon to those in the chapel and then spent a few minutes of great anxiety wrestling with the Lord for a new text. He then went out into the street and preached a fresh sermon.

In these sermons Huntington was most intimate in his delivery and revealed his own trials and temptations to his flock whilst expounding God's Word. His hearers must have felt that a man was talking to them who stood with them in their daily cares. Huntington's letters from this time are also of this kind and read like an exhortation and confession in a prayer or testimony meeting. One letter, a very short one for Huntington, written at this time illustrates Huntington's manner clearly.

> Dear Friends,
>
> When may a child of God lie down? When he can get no higher in his spiritual mind; when no lower in humility; when no further in gospel experience; when there is nothing more new in the Bible; when he seeks Jesus in vain; and when he is the invisible image of Christ in full stature.
>
> I tell you when I intend to leave off prayer. When corruption is entirely destroyed; when my heart can no longer deceive; when I have done kicking at the cross, and never a cross to take up; when the world no more deceives my eyes; and when the devil is ashamed to shew me his face.
>
> Two ways I deceive myself, and two ways I am deceived. When I, to encourage pride, want to appear more gracious than I am; and when through fear I hide that grace I really have; when I thought I had strength for a great trial, and sunk at a small one; and when I sunk at the thoughts of a great cross, and when it came carried it boldly: one is strength in weakness, the other is weakness in strength.

I am always in fear. When comfort is gone I fear it will come no more; when I have got it I fear being robbed; when I am in trouble I am not easy; and when I walk long easy I am in trouble.

Two things I should like to pray for. To be saved from my good works, and to have the sins forgiven of my godly sorrow.

Two things I desire to see, which would strike me dead. To see myself as I really am in God's sight, as a sinner; and to see Christ as he is in glory, and that is the best sight of all; terror always hardens my heart, and to taste Christ's love coming out of a trial, breaks it all to pieces.

One way I commonly get a blessing at meeting. When the preacher has nothing of his own; when it comes hot from the Lord, given in as it is dealt out, and then it is wet; a discourse laid up in the head is mostly dry.

My dear C., and Mr and Mrs G., and all my poor dear souls, I wish you all the blessed Jesus; all is heaven with him, all is hell and damnation without him. O my dear, dear Lord, and God, and Saviour, Jesus, be thou my portion for ever, Amen.

W. Huntington[1]

After eight months the man who bought the shoes from Huntington went out of business and the ex-coalheaver was now an ex-shoemaker. Huntington tried to make both ends meet by repairing shoes but soon the whole family were almost starving, having nothing but barley bread to eat He then remembered that an old friend, a Mr Chapman, who was converted at the same time as he, had invited him to his home on Hounslow Heath. Huntington obeyed the impulse and set out on foot to visit his friend. He was given a very warm welcome and on parting he was loaded with gifts of food for his family. His friend walked some way on the homeward road with him and then offered him a guinea. Huntington, who had not a penny in his pocket, refused to accept it but said he would take half that amount providing his friend's wife was in agreement. Mr Chapman assured Huntington that his wife backed him

[1] W. Huntington, *Gleanings of the Vintage*, Letter VI, Collingridge, Vol. V, pp. 26, 27.

up fully. Huntington thus accepted the half-guinea and walked towards a toll- bridge which barred his way. His only problem now was how he could pay the penny toll as the keeper would scarcely have change for half a guinea. Huntington need not have worried. Looking down on the ground, he found a penny, paid the bridge-keeper and went on his way, loaded with provisions for his starving wife and children.

The onset of persecution

It was just when circumstances were at their lowest ebb for Huntington that acute persecution set in. Huntington lived in the worst part of the village and his house was adjacent to several slovenly homes inhabited by ne'er-do-wells and drunkards. These neighbours began to spread the most atrocious tales about Huntington and strove to harm him in every way possible, even to the extent that a neighbour would stand in front of Huntington's door and 'preach blasphemy', to the amusement of the passers-by. Huntington's chapel was a mere room adjoining a private house inhabited by a notorious drunken woman. Whenever Huntington preached, this woman used to invite a group of bargemen to her kitchen next door, where she would fill them with drink, then open her door and all would sing rude songs as loudly as possible to drown his preaching. If this had no effect she would go up to her bedroom which was above the room where Huntington preached and stamp hard on the floor, making as much noise as possible.

Soon she began to hatch a more devilish plan with her drinking companions. During the next meeting, Mrs Barret, as the woman was called, entered the room, went straight up to a lady who was listening intently and struck her with all her might. Several people dashed up to Mrs Barret to stop her doing further harm only to hear her shout, 'Murder!' at the top of her voice. This was the sign her drinking companions had been waiting for. They broke the outside door down in seconds in a pretence at rescuing their companion and proceeded to break up all the furniture. They then carried into the room a privy full of human excrement and emptied the lot onto the meeting-room floor. Not satisfied with this filthy behaviour, they burnt a huge portion of evil-smelling asafoetida and started to smash the windows.

As the meeting-room was licensed for preaching and Huntington held a preacher's licence, the church took the matter to the magistrates' court. The magistrates, whether out of sympathy or fear, it is difficult to tell, refused to rule against the mob. As this news spread the rioters danced for joy and rang all the church bells. They surrounded Huntington's house, in which the pastor was praying fervently for the rabble, and began to chant the Church of England burial service. They then lit a huge fire and burnt Huntington in effigy, shouting all the time that they were for the High Church.

Huntington's comment was: 'Indeed none could properly doubt of that, who saw the *height* of their wickedness; for had they been Turks or Pagans, they would have been ashamed of such conduct'. A few days later a friend of Huntington's spoke to Mrs Barret and asked her if she were not ashamed of herself and the way she was behaving. The woman answered that she knew that Huntington preached the truth but she had worse things in store for him. The very same night Mrs Barret went from public house to public house, drinking at each stop until she was so drunk that no public house would open the doors to her. She was found dead in front of a drinking companion's house at five o'clock the next morning. This house was very near to Huntington's and the cry went up amongst Mrs Barret's friends that either Huntington or his followers had murdered her. To strengthen their claim they said that Mrs Barret had left a track of blood from Huntington's house to where she was found dead. They demanded that a coroner's court be set up and a jury formed. The doctor, who examined Mrs Barret's body, testified to the court that there was no sign of violence whatsoever and the poor woman had obviously died as a result of alcohol poisoning. Nevertheless the persecutions went on and it became very easy to spot the meeting-rooms where Huntington preached. The windows were broken and the street outside was strewn with bricks and other debris, including large pieces of tin which the rioters used to make a great noise whilst Huntington was preaching.

Huntington's spiritual life was greatly affected by these persecutions. He seemed to be always reading Lamentations and preaching on the more melancholy passages of Scripture. Instead of his hearers sharing in his melancholy, however, they seem to have been lifted up by his discourses and there were many conversions. The more Huntington put his own soul troubles into his sermons, the more his people rejoiced and found strength against their persecutors.

Then 2 Corinthians 1:6 spoke to him: 'And whether we be afflicted, it is for your consolation and salvation, which is effectual in the enduring of the same sufferings which we also suffer'. He saw that the Lord was using his own sufferings as a comfort and strength to his people. Instead of rejoicing at this, however, Huntington was gripped by a spirit of envy. He was comforting others but found no comfort himself. He could only preach, as did the prophets of old, 'the burden of the word of the Lord'. He felt as though the Spirit of God was leaving Saul for David.

Up to this time Huntington had lived in spiritual harmony with his wife, but now she said openly that she doubted of his state. Huntington wrestled constantly in prayer about this matter but he gained no peace for some time, yet his work prospered.

Whilst walking home from a preaching engagement one day, praying on the way, Huntington felt that he had become a castaway and told God to his face that if he were at last to reach hell he would preach before all the damned and all the devils that God had called him by his grace, regenerated him, filled him with the Holy Ghost, justified and sanctified him according to his promise in his Word, only to cast him off. This thought was too strong, even for rebellious Huntington and, after this cry of helplessness and anger, God in Christ, in his mercy, appeared to him sweeter than ever.

Huntington then received a strong conviction that the Lord would rescue him from even the deepest gulf. He saw that it was a good work of God that had caused him to be low so that he could speak to those who were downcast. Now he was conscious of a powerful urge to bring words of comfort to those who were weary and cast down in their work for the Lord and he preached a whole series on the final perseverance of the saints which, he said, 'was cordially received by my flock as a most comfortable and soul-establishing doctrine'.

God's provision in times of hardship

Although Huntington always claimed that the Lord had given him the truest hearers possible, there were several gentlemen of independent means who accepted his ministry but could not accept their preacher's attitude to poverty. They did not know what it meant to pray for every loaf of bread, packet of tea or pair of trousers, and when they caught Huntington praying for his personal needs they told him not to be so carnal and to concentrate on 'spiritual' matters. Huntington, however, was weighed down with a tremendous burden of work and was battling with the decision to give up cobbling and occupy himself fully with the ministry. One rich man amongst his hearers warned him that it would be carnal to accept expenses for preaching and refused point blank himself to help finance Huntington's work, even when he found that the burden of building a new chapel fell mainly on the preacher's shoulders. Another very rich man called Huntington to him and spoke for a long time of his faith and hope and then with great ceremony he presented Huntington with *one shilling* for his Christian work! Huntington was thus more than once reminded of the saying of Jesus regarding the rich man and the camel!

The fact was, however, that Huntington could not live on the sixty guineas or so a year he now received in income. This was chiefly because he could hardly ever say 'no' to people in need and he was forced to pray, when he had given a beggar his last penny, that the Lord would not let any more beggars cross his path until he had some money in his pocket again.

One night Huntington and his wife were forced to put their children to bed on empty stomachs and wept for their loved ones and their own misery. In the middle of the night, whilst Huntington was weeping and praying, a man knocked at the window and said that there was a load of wooden hoops delivered to a nearby wharf and someone was urgently needed to unload it. Huntington set off at once and unloaded the goods. The owner of the hoops gave Huntington a meat pie and a flagon of cider. The preacher rushed home, knowing that his first child had died of hunger in the night, woke his children and fed them although they were too tired to know what was happening. At times Mrs Huntington, too, received marvellous answers to prayer and showed great faith. Once, when she was lying in and the cupboard was bare, Huntington's first convert, Anne Webb, was looking after her and told her that there was no more tea in the caddy. Mrs Huntington said that she should nevertheless put the kettle on to boil. Before the water started to bubble a complete stranger came to the door and said that she had brought some tea for the preacher's wife.

When the baby arrived, the Huntingtons wanted to have it baptised and as a sound minister was visiting Kingston, Huntington considered asking him to perform the ceremony. He hesitated to ask, however, as the minister was also to celebrate the Lord's Supper and Huntington never went to the Table unless he could take an offering with him. He had not, however, a penny to call his own. After prayer, Huntington became convinced that the Lord would provide and told his wife to get ready for chapel. A man rode up to the front door, gave Huntington three shillings as an offering to God and rode off without further ado. The child was duly baptised.

Huntington encourages others

Huntington's letters from this period show little of the spiritual troubles he was in. They are too centred on the needs of others. His words are plain, simple and to the point yet they do not in any way resemble those of a man who has had only a few months' school education. They are elegant and well chosen in their directness. To a married couple who were burdened by their suffering Huntington wrote:

> But say you, our souls have got many enemies; yes, I know it, and there is but one friend; I know the world, the flesh, and the devil are your enemies, and I am glad of it, for woe to your souls if you are at friendship with either of these three. We are to declare war with all Christ's enemies, and when you are nothing but perfect weakness in yourself, then you will beat every enemy you fight with, Joel 3:10; but when you are strong in the flesh, you are sure to be beat, Ezekiel 34:16. As for your enemies, Christ conquered them all for us, and when we come to Christ in trouble, then he imputes to us the victory, then all our enemies must hide their heads in a moment … But say you, the world hems me in, and I am afraid that it will draw me from Christ; I am glad you are afraid of it, for God says, he that is a friend of the world is an enemy of God, therefore faith looks to him that says 'Be of good cheer, I have overcome the world', John 16:33. Well, say you, but my own wicked, corrupted, deceitful heart is my worst enemy; yes, but says faith, God's word declares, he that trusts his own heart is a fool, a natural man, and not a saint … Well, say you, but if they cannot destroy me, they destroy my

comforts, and drive me from the sensible presence of God, into many misty clouds of ignorance, stupidity, and insensibility, and into many dark days of desertion: darkness covers my mind, so that I grope like one blind, quite without evidence: this is bad to be in, but, says faith, I must believe the promise, and look to the word of God, Ezekiel 34:12.

A good man once said, that God, when he converted a sinner, laid his Spirit in pawn to that soul, so the Spirit is the soul's earnest of its inheritance, and so when we die, Christ receives his own with usury. So, my dear souls, let your troubles be what they may, obey God's voice. God says, 'Give me thy heart;' let the blessed Jesus have it, and he says, Commit the keeping of your souls into his hands; pray let him have it, and he will keep yours as well as Paul's, till that day. He likewise says, Offer up your bodies, which is your reasonable service; pray, my dear souls, let him have them; and he likewise says, 'Commit thy works unto the Lord, and thy thoughts shall be established'. Obey his voice, for he gave himself for us; give we ourselves to him, and then says faith, 'You are not your own, you are bought with a price', 1 Corinthians 6:19, 20; then let what enemies will come against me, says faith, the battle is not mine but God's, and we must turn the battle to the gate, says David, and that gate is Christ.[2]

Attempts to discredit Huntington as a preacher

Huntington's enemies amongst the rabble and High Church ministers were constantly seeking evidence to unmask Huntington as the fraud they dearly hoped he was. They thought the ex-coalheaver was just too good to be true. A chance came at Sunbury where the rioters had been trying to stop Huntington preaching for some time. Amongst Huntington's hearers was a backslidden Christian by the name of Richard Hughes. This person contacted the ringleaders of the riots and told them he had a weapon with which they could silence Huntington for ever. Hughes then told them that he came from the same town as

[2] *Ibid.*, Letter III, pp. 18-22.

Huntington and had gone to school with him and that his real name was Hunt.

The rioters could not believe this at first as they had known Huntington by that name some years previously when he had lived at Sunbury. Hughes, however, hit upon a way to prove that he was telling the truth. He travelled over to Cranbrook where a poor sister of Huntington's lived and told her a pack of lies about her brother. He said that Huntington had come into money and would now like to get in touch with his sister and relieve her from all her financial burdens. All she had to do was write a letter to him listing all the things she wanted and Hughes would see that Huntington received the letter. The delighted woman quickly wrote a letter listing all her wants and addressed it to William Hunt. Hughes triumphantly took the letter to the leader of the rioters. Thus when Huntington next preached at Sunbury he found the meeting-place surrounded by a hundred of his enemies who, in mock ceremony, presented him with the letter.

Huntington read the letter inside the meeting-room and wept over it bitterly because he realised that he had brought reproach on the Lord's work. He prayed to God, asking him why he had revealed this to the world, but knew the answer already. In his book *The Kingdom of Heaven Taken by Prayer* Huntington refers to the incident and says,

> But all petitions could not prevail. Abraham's idolatry, Jacob's lies, Moses' murder, David's adultery, Solomon's apostasy, Paul's bloody persecution, and the Rev. Mr Huntington's forged name and first-born son, must all come to light; for all who trust in, and boast of a well-spent life must be cut off – that no 'confidence might be placed in the flesh' and that the world might see that the greatest of grace could condescend to an ingraftiture in, and thrive and flourish on, the basest of men. By this means grace appears in all her lustre, and nature in all her pollution.

The rioters' action in producing the letter brought immediate results in their fight against Huntington, who had applied for court protection for the Sunbury chapel. The letter was used in evidence to show that Huntington was a fraud and he was refused permission to preach and had to pay for all the costs arising from the court's proceedings.

The Vicar of Sunbury was not quite so successful as his allies in his antagonism against Huntington. On hearing the news about Huntington's name-change he immediately set off on a tour of places where Huntington preached and carried his gossip with him. To his chagrin, none of Huntington's friends seemed impressed with the news and, indeed, several said that they had known about it all along. The vicar finally visited Huntington's generous friend Mr Chapman. That good man proved the true friend he was and told the vicar straight that the devil himself had stirred him up to go about the country trying to make Huntington's work for the Lord useless.

It is an interesting fact that, at this time, those who were striving to have Huntington discredited for adding to his name were not reluctant to add to his name themselves. Thus from now on, Huntington was invariably referred to by his enemies as 'Doctor Sack' or plain 'Doctor' or simply as 'the Coalheaver'. It was most likely as a counter-action against all the 'titles' he was receiving that Huntington began to entitle himself 'W. Huntington S.S'., the double 'S' standing for 'Sinner Saved'.

Huntington had at first little success in the courts in his efforts to keep his meeting-rooms open. There were always influential people or clergy to side with the rioters. Even his preaching licence was no longer recognised by the authorities as they said that neither the word 'preacher' nor 'teacher' occurred in the text, thus making it void. This does not mean, however, that Huntington's work was stopped. On the contrary, the publicity which he won through the actions of the rioters caused him to be a well-known figure far and wide and he received invitations to preach from more and more churches, especially in the London area.

Very often, however, though Huntington's enemies were cleared by the earthly magistrates, they did not fare so easily at the hands of the Supreme Judge. The only true comparison with what happened to those who sought to stop Huntington's work is the fate of Uzzah, who put his hand on the holy ark. One by one Huntington's enemies either suddenly died, were sacked by their employers and left the district, or were stricken with some mysterious illness. Thus two young men who delighted in standing in front of Huntington when he preached and shouting out blasphemous words fell ill and died within days. Once a man entered Huntington's chapel dressed in women's clothing and with a blackened face. The next day the chapel-goers were taunted in the streets by the cry that the devil had visited their meeting in the form of the disguised man. The person who had performed the part of the devil was arrested for thieving shortly afterwards but the High Church clergyman and a few other influential citizens bailed him out. The man was next seen running around the streets and entering public houses dressed only in his shirt and quite out of his mind. He had to be taken home by force and strapped to a chair where he soon expired. Another man who taunted Huntington in the streets by shouting, 'Pray, are you born again, Mr Inspiration?' fell ill and had terrible dreams in which he was reckoned with the damned. Huntington went to pray for him and 'had some little hope of his soul's welfare'. Nevertheless, the man died. A local farmer encouraged the mob to persecute Huntington and he, too, fell mysteriously ill and died. Another mocker drove a heavy wagon under the influence of drink and met his fate in a terrible accident. One scoffer delighted in ringing the church bells whenever Huntington preached in order to drown his voice. One Sunday evening, after annoying Huntington as much as he could, he started wrestling with a fellow bell-ringer, fell and broke his leg. The leg refused to heal and the man died soon after. Yet another of the bell-ringers got caught up in the ropes and injured himself so much that he became a cripple for life. One rough fellow swore that he would 'pull the fellow out of his hole', meaning that he would drag Huntington out of the pulpit. He arranged for a great gang of rioters to surround the house armed with stones and organised a band to play music and had the church-bells rung. Huntington left his house and started to walk through the mob to the place where the faithful were to worship 'with no other armour than half a grain of faith in my heart, and a little Bible in my pocket', he tells us in *The Naked Bow of God*. The ringleader of the plot, however, was held up in London and galloped at top speed from his duties there to arrive at Huntington's meeting-room in time. On the way his horse threw him and he was taken to a public house where he lay, seriously injured, for many days. Meanwhile, the mob, finding themselves without a leader, soon dispersed and Huntington was able to preach unhindered.

So many of Huntington's enemies either dropped dead or were injured for life that the word went around that Ditton was 'a very unlucky place to live in'. Former persecutors of Huntington became wiser after the event and said of Huntington's hearers, 'Let them alone, they are wiser than we'. One of the persecutors who saw the folly of his way only came to this decision after a period of madness during which he tried twice to commit suicide. Of him Huntington said,

> Oh! it is awful to wage war against Christ, who is the Lord of hosts, mighty in battle; he is perpetually mounted on his white horse, and carries a bent bow against his adversaries, as well as a crown for his friends ... God grant that the poor man may find grace in his sight, as he has delivered him from pouring contempt on his word and commandment; and receive an answer to that petition which is often put up in hypocrisy, namely, 'Forgive our enemies, persecutors and slanderers, and turn their hearts'.

Help was to come for Huntington from a very unexpected quarter. Whilst the riots against Huntington's Methodists were in full swing, His Majesty King George III drove by in his carriage. On hearing the hootings of the crowd, he stopped his coach and asked what the matter was. He received the answer that it was merely a clash between the townspeople and the Methodists. This caused the king to leave his coach and in a very loud voice proclaim, 'The Methodists are a quiet, good kind of people, and will disturb nobody; and if I can learn that any persons in my employment disturb them, they shall be immediately dismissed'. This news travelled quickly around Ditton and the violence slowly died down. This incident may be the reason why Huntington had always a good word to say about the king. When he became a London pastor, the King's State Coachman, the Comptroller of the Household to Princess Charlotte, the Keeper of the Observatory in Kew Gardens and several servants from St James's Palace joined his church. Several princesses were regular hearers, especially the king's favourite daughter, Princess Amelia. King George regularly read the works of evangelicals such as John Newton and William Romaine and there is an interesting story of how he became a reader of Huntington's works.

One of his footmen was busy reading Huntington when he was called away to duties and left his book behind. The king passed by and picked up the book and took it with him to read, replacing it some days later. Hearing of this, the footman carefully left Huntington's books around where he thought the king might pass. They disappeared one by one and were all replaced later. Once when he had forgotten to leave a volume for the king to pick up His Majesty came to him and said, 'Where is my book, Saunders?'

The protests against Huntington's preaching were legion because people were flocking to his ministry and deserting the established churches. Drunkards were turning to 'Adam' s wine', which Huntington invariably now drank himself, and the many public houses were losing their customers. Thus the clergy in the district allied with the rabble and forced the parish officers to take action against Huntington. A large dinner was arranged at a local public house to organise the protest and give Huntington's various enemies a chance to say what could be done to rid the parish of such a disturbing influence. First, it was argued that as Mrs Huntington gave birth to a child a year (the Huntingtons had now three children who had survived and a fourth was on the way) and Huntington had only a meagre income he – as an intruder in the parish – was not the kind of newcomer the parish wanted. They then argued that such an intruder should try to make himself acceptable in the parish but Huntington preached against the parson, the church and all the parish.

It was also hinted at that Huntington refrained from paying the king's taxes. This latter point may have been true as he was not a member of the parish and thus did not need to pay the taxes. However, the local tax collector was one of Huntington's hearers and he warned him that he was to be summoned before the parish clerks as an unwelcome intruder in the parish and advised him to pay the taxes. Huntington did so and became thus legally a parishioner. Now Huntington's friends from all walks of life rallied round him with their support. The summons came and Huntington dressed himself as well as possible for the event as the parish clerks had emphasised his poverty. One gentleman who was quite well off promised to give Huntington any money that the parish officers demanded of him. At this time even John Thornton, the famous Russian merchant and John Newton's patron, came to Huntington's assistance giving him five guineas and later another ten. Two attorneys at law came up from London to support him and another gentleman lent Huntington his horse and carriage so that he could drive up to his appointed trial in style. The two lawyers soon made light work of the parish clerks' claims and showed that Huntington was a legal member of the parish as he paid his taxes and that he was a licensed minister of the gospel and had the authority to preach in any registered place of worship that opened its doors to him. This time Huntington returned home triumphant, gathered his friends around him and preached spontaneously on Lamentations 4:15, 'They said among the heathen, They shall no more sojourn there'. From this time on, Huntington's personal material sorrows lessened and he was able to concentrate more on the spiritual and theological problems of his ever-widening ministry.

Chapter 5

'Prophesying Upon The Thick Boughs'

Huntington's old home in Ditton was the worst place possible for his small children to grow up in. The windows came down to floor level and daily Huntington's enemies would come and stand in front of the windows and pull faces or utter curses at the top of their voices, or even hammer on the glass or smash it with stones.

One day a friend called to say he was leaving the town and suggested that Huntington take over his house which was in a much better area. Inside there were four rooms, a kitchen, two garrets, a parlour, a pantry and a cellar, and outside there was a large walled garden with a stable and a brewhouse in it. The rent was £6.10s per year but the fixtures in the house would cost seven or eight pounds. Huntington took the matter to the Lord but was greatly in doubt about the project because of the (for him) high costs involved.

Whilst he was searching for the Lord's will on the matter, a friend called and gave Huntington five guineas. That night he dreamt that his friend who was leaving the house in question told him that he would have to hurry and take over the house, otherwise someone else would snap it up. Huntington replied that he did not have enough money for the fixtures. In the dream his friend told him not to worry but go to a Mr Munday at Kingston who would lend him as much as he required.

The following evening the Huntingtons had a surprise visitor – one who had never been to their house before. It was Mr Munday from Kingston! Huntington told him about the dream and received a sum of money from the kind gentleman, who promised more to follow. The Huntingtons moved into their new home without further ado.

Huntington tells us that his family were no better off regards sleeping than the baby Jesus, who slept in a manger, as they, like him, slept on straw. The Huntingtons were to move up in the world in this matter, too. When on a preaching visit to Richmond, Huntington was invited to a home and presented with a huge bundle, tied up so that he could not see what was inside. When Huntington asked what it was he was told that he would find out when he got home. On arriving back in Ditton the Huntingtons and their four children opened the bundle and found enough bedding for them all. Now Huntington, to use his own phrase, took 'Gospel courage' and asked the Lord for a bed. Soon after, four people from London visited the Huntingtons and each left a guinea before returning home. Huntington thus ordered his bed, with a rug and a pair of good blankets to go with it When he turned up to pay for the goods, he was told to hand the money over to the clerk, who took it and gave Huntington a receipt. The gentleman who owned the shop then walked some way with Huntington deep in conversation but when the time came to depart, he gave Huntington the full amount back. More material blessings followed. Up to now the Huntingtons had been dressed in mere rags. Now they were to be fitted out with decent clothing. Huntington was measured up for a new suit by a wealthy friend and Mrs Huntington was presented with ready-made clothes and lengths of material to make up into clothing for herself and her children. 'We have more than enough clothing now', Mary happily told her husband.

There was still one thing, however, in which Huntington was in dire need, and that was a means of transport. It was no uncommon feat for him to walk well over a hundred miles a week, preaching as he went. One week he walked fourteen miles to Woking on the Lord's Day morning to preach there. He then walked three miles further on towards Worplesdon, where he took an afternoon meeting. After that he tramped another fourteen miles to Farnham, took the evening meeting there and then walked all the way back home. On the Monday Huntington walked thirty-five miles to another preaching engagement and then on the Tuesday twenty-five miles to Horsham to take a meeting there. On the Wednesday morning he got up early to walk to London but was so exhausted that his feet just would not move. Now the walking pastor went to prayer and prayed for one of three things: either more strength, or less work, or a horse. He hired a mount to take him to London and on arriving at a livery stables there, he found that the owner had been converted under his ministry. Huntington also learned that this very man and several others had clubbed together and had bought him a fine horse. That night Huntington rode back home praising God and yet feeling he little deserved all the benefits he was constantly receiving.

An invitation to London

Huntington had started to preach in London through a trick played on him by a well-meaning friend. This friend had invited Huntington to visit his London home and preach there and he had accepted the invitation. After the house-meeting was over, however, the friend told Huntington that he had also arranged for him to preach at the Margaret Street Chapel. Huntington was quite taken aback at this as he had heard that all kinds of heresies were preached there and, besides, he did not feel at all competent to preach before the more educated citizens of London. Not only had he no knowledge of Greek and Hebrew, he had no knowledge of English grammar either.

Nevertheless Huntington did not back away from the challenge and was rewarded by seeing a young man converted through his first sermon there. This young man became a minister himself some time after – the first of many of Huntington's converts who became preachers and pastors. The Londoners were so moved by Huntington's testimony that they begged him to preach weekly there. Huntington accepted but for a long time he had to put up with impolite people in the congregation who laughed loudly whenever he made a mistake in grammar or expression. Those who laughed the most were invariably those who were the most ignorant of the gospel.

It was not surprising that such ignorance existed in the chapel as invariably ministers of different persuasions were asked to preach and lecture on different evenings. Thus one evening a Deist would preach on the God that was far off and an Arminian would talk of God's supposed universal charity the next. This would be followed by an Arian, who would preach the humanity of Christ and nothing else and, the day after, an Antinomian would set the law aside and preach absolute freedom from its force. The chapel even had a regular speaker who taught that departed souls revisited the earth after death. Now Huntington knew the Arminians and had many conversations with a follower of John William Fletcher, John Wesley's right-hand man. This person had ridiculed the doctrine of imputed righteousness and – before he himself fell by the wayside – he had tried to put the veil of Moses back on Huntington's face. Arianism, however, was a new teaching for Huntington and he went through a period of much soul-examination before he could come to terms with it. Just as he had made a list of all the texts in the Bible that had to do with election to salvation, he now made a long list of all the Bible passages referring to the deity of Christ. The Antinomians puzzled Huntington the most as they also were new to him but he could not work out at first 'what to do with such a strange beast, which seemed all tongue, but no heart'. He soon came to realise that Antinomians were not of the Saviour's fold and warned his hearers against them, preaching on the status, function and scope of the law.

The Christian poet William Cowper always said that the main enemies of the church were to be found in it rather than outside of it. This was the view of the Puritans and most of the Christian writers of the eighteenth century. Nowadays evangelicals have found a common enemy in liberalism and most of their apologetic work is thus aimed at 'outsiders', and sorting out the heresies among the 'insiders' is neglected. Huntington was fully in agreement with his contemporary, Cowper, and sought to purify the church from within rather than to develop a Christian apology directed at those who were outside the fold. He saw that the great hindrance to the spread of the gospel was from Christians who either turned the eyes of the newly converted to Sinai rather than the cross, or trusted in their own personal holiness rather than Christ's imputed righteousness. He thus saw Arminianism as a great danger to the well-being of the church, as it included most of the heresies he was confronted with at the time.

It contained, for instance, the germs of Arianism, as Christ's once-and-for-all-time perfect sacrifice was thrown into disrepute. The Christ of the Arminians had died in vain for the majority of those whom he came to save, thus diminishing his power, sovereignty and Godhead. Jesus, to the Arminian, was a failure as God. Arminianism harboured Antinomianism, too, as it limited the laws of God to the Ten Commandments and preached that every man was free to seek Christ by his own effort, irrespective of the electing, sovereign will of God. They set aside the biblical teachings of grace and became a rule unto themselves. Traces of Deism could also be seen in Arminianism, as its followers did not believe in the inner working of the Spirit in the heart of the elect keeping him from becoming a castaway. They rather saw Christ's death as merely offering salvation, rather than procuring it, and the sinner was left to secure it for himself, as if the merits of Christ's sacrifice were not upon him and Christ's righteousness not imputed in him.

The 'Arminian Skeleton'

Huntington battled hard to find biblical teaching against these heresies and as he was taught himself by the Scriptures he wrote down his findings for general publication. The first of these doctrinal works was finished at this time and entitled *The Arminian Skeleton*. In his preface Huntington says,

> Every essential truth that we part with is an infinite loss; and we daily see an awful departure from the doctrines of the gospel. Errors gain ground; and champions for the truth are but few in number when compared to the other host. If thou art a child of God by Faith, see to the groundwork of it. Hast thou the faith of God's elect? Let election be its basis. Hast thou a justifying faith? Let imputed righteousness be its basis. Hast thou a victorious faith? Thy victory lies in a Saviour's arms. Hast thou a purifying faith? Then faith fetches its purifying efficacy from a Saviour's blood. Give up none of these truths; for, if we think truth is not worth contending for, we may expect the Spirit to clap his wings, and take flight from us.

Turning to John Wesley, who had shocked his fellow-Christians with absurd criticisms of the Reformed faith, Huntington called upon his readers to protect their faith so that 'God's decree shall not always be called horrible, nor an everlasting righteousness be called imputed nonsense'. He goes on to say,

> If God of his infinite mercy keep you from Arminianism, Arianism, and Antinomianism, I shall think you are Christians indeed. I rank the errors of Arminianism at the front, because the others are not so well masked. While the Arminian is robbing you of the doctrines of sovereign grace, he puts the fable of sinless perfection into your hand, as a rattle to amuse you, while he robs and plunders your conscience; and, while he is teaching you to resist the sovereign will of God, he endeavours to charm your ears with free-agency. But the Arian is more open; he proclaims to everyone that goes by that he is a fool. However, they are all three agreed against Christ; the Arminian cries down his merit; the Arian cries down his divinity; and the Antinomian cries down the revelation of him to the heart. May God turn their hearts to the truth, and keep your souls from turning to their errors!

Huntington stressed time and time again that though the believer was no longer under the condemnation of the law on tablets of stone, that same law had become part (part, not all) of his new nature and was written on his heart. This is why he argues that the Antinomian, in rejecting God's law revealed to the Christian's heart, rejects that which distinguishes the saved from the unsaved.

Like James Hervey, whose dying days were troubled with letters from John Wesley telling him 'for Christ's sake' not to talk about imputed righteousness, Huntington argued that Arminianism and popery were of the same root and one day would merge. One would expect Huntington to have ruled out the possibility of Arminians and Roman Catholics being of the elect. This he did not do, as his doctrine of God's sovereignty taught him otherwise. He writes in the *Arminian Skeleton*, 'Out of each host the elect of God will one day be called; and a light sufficient will be given them to discover the enemies of their liberties, to which, by a covenant of sovereign grace, they were predestinated'.

Huntington does not merely link Arians, Arminians and Antinomians together in the preface but comes back time and time again to this trinity of heresy, showing how they were united in turning true believers from the straight and narrow way. 'The Arminian calls upon you to forsake the strong food, or every essential truth in the Bible', Huntington goes on to argue, 'the Arian and Socinian want you to give up your God, and to bow your knee to a creature; the Antinomian calls upon you to give up the Spirit's quickening power, your daily cross, and a tender conscience'.

The *Arminian Skeleton* is really a public testimony of Huntington's own faith and doctrine in the form of personal autobiography and inner musings. He reduces the three major heresies he deals with to one basic doctrine. This is the belief in 'universal charity', or the doctrine that the gates of heaven are left wide open and unwatched for anyone to go in and out of at will. In the first two sections following the preface, Huntington shows how, as God's watchman on earth, the Christian should pursue, arrest and examine these heresies. In the final part Huntington takes up a literary device used by John Bunyan and Augustus Toplady and sets up an allegorical trial under the title 'Universal Charity Tried and Condemned'. Here the jury is composed of such men as Paul the aged, John the divine, Job the patient etc.; and the witnesses have names such as Mr Strong-in-the-Lord and Mr Dim-Sight. All in all this dramatization is harder to follow than the first two parts, which reflect spontaneous testimony. The main witness is the Queen, who signifies the church. She claims that the Arminian came to her in the garments of a chaplain only to tell her that the King's, her husband's, promises were not 'yea and amen' and that she ought to doubt his discriminating promises of love. The legal mechanism of the drama shows that Huntington is profiting a great deal from his experience in magistrates' courts and, after bringing all the biblical evidence to bear on 'Universal Charity', he shows how it is an impostor and to be condemned as an agent of the devil. The book, as a whole, is a fine exposition of the Christian gospel, nowadays called popularly 'Calvinism' or the 'Reformed faith'.

The call to London

Preaching Bible doctrine won the day at Margaret Street Chapel. As was so usual in the life of William Huntington, all his enemies fled before him. The Deist who preached at Margaret Street left off professing to be a Christian and turned outright pagan. The Arian, who was a shopkeeper, lost all his custom and had to shut down and leave the area. The Antinomian returned to Scotland, whence he had come, and the Arminian was put in jail! Referring to the fact that all opposition failed to overthrow him, Huntington said,

> I am a greater wonder to myself than to any other, considering myself as a person of neither parts, abilities, nor learning: nothing but a mere 'bruised reed', and yet supported by the omnipotent hand of a most gracious God! I have stood amazed to think that I have not hitherto fallen. Nay, at times I have thought it was impossible for such a defenceless worm to wade through such opposition, while so many, who seemed to be pillars, have given way. But these words have often been of great comfort to my soul, 'The law of his God is in his heart; none of his steps shall slide', Psalm 37:31. And again, 'If I fall, I shall rise again; and if I sit in darkness, the Lord shall be a light unto me', Micah 7:8.

In spite of all his success in London, Huntington was not satisfied with the way things were going. Margaret Street was a mere lecturing-place rather than a church and riding from village to town and from town to village each day was wearing him out. Knowing that God always goes before his own sheep when he takes them out of the fold, Huntington began to look for a sign whether the Lord had new fields to be harvested. Should he stay in Ditton, or was there other work to be done?

After preaching at Woking one evening, he returned home in the early hours of the morning quite exhausted. One of his children was ill and restless and his wife could not stay long in bed without having to get up and look after it. Huntington found a corner of the house where he could get some rest and fell fast asleep. He dreamt that the Lord spoke to him in a very loud voice saying, 'Son of man! son of man! prophesy son of man, prophesy!' Huntington answered, 'Lord, what shall I prophesy?' The voice replied, 'Prophesy upon the thick boughs'. Huntington woke up straight away and reached for his Bible. He found words referring to the 'thick boughs' in Ezekiel 17:23 and 31:3 but was quite at a loss as to their meaning. He went straight over to his wife and asked her what the words meant but together the two could find no solution.

During the following days Huntington asked his Christian friends what the words could mean but no one could help him. However, he was sure that they had something to do with his future calling. After days of intense journeying backwards and forwards amongst his flocks, Huntington fell ill and was confined to bed for several days. Gradually the command in his dream took on clarity. The boughs were people, or rather, sinners. The thick boughs were numerous people, numerous sinners. Up to then Huntington had been preaching on thin boughs (to small, scattered congregations) but he ought to settle down to a stable ministry in a place where he could preach to the thick boughs. Such a place could only mean London. But Huntington felt that his work at Margaret Street Chapel had come to an end. He contacted his Christian friends as soon as he was well and asked them for advice on the matter. They told him that a prophet was not duly honoured in his own country and that he should step out in faith to the capital, find a house there and see what the Lord would provide. Thus in 1782, Huntington, now aged thirty-seven, left Thames Ditton with his wife, two daughters, Ruth and Naomi, and two sons, Gad and Ebenezer, and settled down in Winchester Row, London, not knowing what the Lord had in store for them.

During Huntington's period of waiting a new venue opened itself to him. It was announced at his meeting-places that a London minister was to visit Moulsey on the Sunday morning and preach in the open air. Huntington had preached to his hearers standing outside his meeting-houses but he had never been a hearer at a proper open-air service before. He thus got up at three o'clock in the morning so that he could ride over to Moulsey in time for the six o'clock open-air service. As he was getting dressed and thinking with enjoyment of the treat which he was about to experience, he heard an inner voice say that he, too, would preach that day in the open air. His text was to be: 'Go ye therefore into the highways, and as many as ye shall find bid to the marriage'. Huntington had no idea where the text was to be found so he called on a friend who had a concordance and they found the passage in Matthew 22:9.

Huntington went to the open-air meeting and everybody waited for the minister, but he never came. Standing around, hoping that the minister would appear, were a group of men who had been very critical towards Huntington, and who were of the opinion that he had not the education to be a preacher and was running before he had learnt to walk. After waiting silently and with some embarrassment for an hour, these men looked round for a substitute preacher. Their eyes fell on Huntington and with one voice they asked him to preach. Huntington already had a finger in Matthew 22 and, trembling at first, was soon able to preach with power and conviction. Again this 'first' of Huntington's was favoured by a woman coming to Christ through his preaching.

Providence Chapel

Huntington had not been long in London before an influential friend of his started to make plans on his behalf. He sought out a site in the metropolis for a large chapel and when he was certain that he had found the ideal spot, he told Huntington of his plan. Huntington was to have his very own chapel in Titchfield Street and an architect had been found who was prepared to plan and supervise the entire construction free of charge. Huntington at once thought of his call to 'prophesy upon the thick boughs' and saw it coming to fulfilment. On being asked what name he wanted to give his chapel, he therefore answered, 'Providence Chapel'.

At first there was only £11 in the building fund that friends had scraped together but soon money and offers of assistance came in at breakneck speed. One timber merchant sent a load of building materials free of charge; another friend offered to do the interior decorating as a gift to the Lord; another provided furniture for the vestry; yet another furniture for a bedroom so that their pastor need not walk home on wintry nights. Many of Huntington's hearers brought numerous small gifts, such as cushions, a bookcase, a looking-glass and a pulpit Bible. The person who showed the most energy in fund-raising, was, however, Huntington himself. He went from friend to friend explaining what the costs of the chapel would be and later he was to say that not one single person whom he approached refused to support the project. Only a year after Huntington left tiny Thames Ditton to preach to his thousands in the metropolis his wish and calling came true. The chapel 'shot up', in the words of Thomas Wright, 'as if by enchantment' at a time when Huntington's fame as a preacher was spreading like wildfire. The way Huntington's friends gave was amazing, as no one was asked for money outside of his circle of friends and no one who had a shilling to call his own kept it from the building fund.

Providence Chapel had seats for a congregation of well over a thousand and was soon to be enlarged upwards by means of a gallery, to hold almost two thousand. Almost simultaneously with the opening of the chapel, Huntington published his work *The Last Will and Testament*, in which he relates what he has inherited from his heavenly Master and how he wishes to share it amongst his friends. At first he explains why it is biblical to publish such a will whilst still alive and goes on to deal with his responsibility to God, then his wife, then his children. He continues by turning to his congregation and chapel and, after quoting from Psalm 127:1 and Hebrews 3:4, writes:

> The Chapel which the kind, the undeserved, and unexpected Providence of God has given us, and on which account it bears its present name, I do commit the whole management of to the Lord Jesus Christ; likewise the management of the managers – the management of the pulpit – the management of the preachers – the management of the doctrines – the management of the flock – the management of their hearts – the management of their ears, and – the management of their manners. I do commit it solely to the all-wise Superintendent of all beings, and all things – the supreme Monarch of all that is visible or invisible; whether in the celestial or terrestrial worlds who is the omnipotent Creator of heaven and earth, and the absolute Disposer of all events. And now, O Lord, whom the heavens, nor the heaven of heavens, cannot contain, much less the little house which we have built, let it please thee to hear thy servant's prayer, and bless the house, and let thine eyes and thy heart be there perpetually, and make it a Bethel to thousands. Direct the steps of sabbath-breakers, blasphemers, and the basest of mortals to tread its floors; let sovereign grace and dying love be displayed in their greatest power, and in their fullest latitude; and grant that when thou writest up the people, it may be said, of millions, that this and that man was born of God there. O Lord, make the pulpit like Aaron's golden bell; and let every tried and faithful preacher's

> tongue be like a golden clapper; so that joy and gladness may be found therein, thanksgiving and the voice of melody. Let no dry formality ever be established in it. Let no ecclesiastical craftsman ever be heard there. Let no priestcraft ever prosper therein. Let no carnal inventions, however pleasing to flesh and blood, no human traditions, however ancient or highly esteemed; nor any doctrines of devils, however deep, or of whatsoever date, be ever heard in it But let thy truth be credited by that faith which is thy own gift. Be thou ever addressed and supplicated in the language of thy own most holy word, ever adored by thy servants in the happy enjoyment of thy own eternal love, ever admired in thy own illustrious and most glorious light: and be thou ever worshipped in thy own spirit. O Lord of all lords, be thou our *ALL* IN *ALL;* and grant that all preachers of every denomination, that preach thee as the sinner's only, present, and everlasting portion may be blessed with thy internal testimony, thy supporting hand, the unutterable comforts of thy Eternal Spirit, and crown their honest labours with ten thousand-fold success. Amen and Amen.

At first attendance at Providence Chapel fluctuated considerably. Huntington had prayed that non-church-goers should find their way to Titchfield Street as he did not want to be accused of poaching and he longed to see God's seal on his ministry in sinners being converted. Although Huntington's ministry drew in such people and there were many conversions, a large portion of his early congregations came from other churches. This caused their ministers to be jealous of Huntington's popularity and, in an effort to win their members back they did not shrink from very unkind criticism. Reports of heresy at Providence Chapel were quickly spread though no one could lay a finger on anything wrong in Huntington's life or doctrine.

The various denominations comforted themselves by the thought that Providence Chapel was built in a populous area and drew people from that area who had previously travelled a distance to church. Thus no less than three new churches of different denominations were built around Providence Chapel to tap off the crowds that went there. This in turn tempted a number of people to leave Providence Chapel to see what the new churches offered. Gradually, however, things settled down and

Providence Chapel was continually filled to bursting-point, providing Huntington with a church that remained faithful to his ministry.

This popularity, however, isolated Huntington from nearly all the evangelical ministers in London with the exception of William Romaine. The Rev. Thomas Scott, of the Countess of Huntingdon Connexion, for instance, suffered much from Huntington's proximity to his chapel at the Lock Hospital for vagrant women and wrote to his Baptist friend Dr John Ryland saying, 'When I think of such men as Mr Huntington, I often am ready to compare them to Samson, whose ingenuity was employed in catching foxes, and tying firebrands to them, to burn up the crops: but Samson used this stratagem against Philistines; they among Israelites'.[1]

Questions of finance

Providence Chapel paid their pastor a salary of £100 per annum at the beginning of his ministry but this was rapidly doubled. This was not an unusually large amount for a pastor of such a large church. Rowland Hill, the only London pastor with a comparably large congregation, always had a basic salary of at least £100 per annum more than Huntington. James Hervey (1714-1758) who, the church historian Balleine says, had the first evangelical parish in the Midlands, received £180 per year and also the profits from a farm which had been in the family for generations. In spite of his popularity, Hervey's congregations were much smaller than Huntington's though his wage was so high. Pastors in royal livings, however, often received between £600 and £1,000 a year. Many evangelical clergymen such as Moses Browne, Vicar of Olney when John Newton was his curate, pastored a number of churches on a sinecure basis which brought them in huge sums. Others such as Dr Cowper, William Cowper's father, combined a pastorate with a lucrative sinecure governmental position.

Be that as it may, when the news of Huntington's salary travelled through the London churches, pastored by ex-public-schoolboys and university graduates who were often paid far less, criticism grew. How could an untrained labourer earn as much as a university graduate?

[1] *Letters and Papers of the Late Rev. Thomas Scott*, L. B. Seeley, 1824, p. 129.

Thomas Scott, who always had difficulty making both ends meet, was scathing in his criticism. When he heard that Huntington was in financial difficulties, too, he boasted to his friends that if he had as much money as Huntington, he would know how to manage it better. This was the kind of unfair criticism that Huntington was reaping from all quarters. Most of the evangelical ministers in London, including Scott, however, were heavily patronised by such benefactors as the Countess of Huntingdon, Lord Dartmouth, John Thornton or Lord Carrington. Thus their basic salary rarely reflected their true income. When John Newton, for instance, was receiving a basic salary of a mere £60 per year, he was provided with over four times that amount annually by his patrons so that he could do charitable work in Olney. Huntington had no patron whatsoever. Most of his self-appointed enemies were ministers of churches which were either on freehold property, or belonged to those people who owned the living, or were supported by some trust or organization. Huntington's chapel was on rented land, the rent alone amounting to half of his annual salary. Huntington made all the debts of his church his own debts and if money for repairs etc. was not forthcoming from church funds, he provided the money out of his own pocket. Thus at times Huntington needed an income of thousands per annum, not a mere £100. That income was usually raised when needed although Huntington insisted that any gifts to the church or to himself coming from 'outsiders' would be sent back with thanks.

Huntington's method of financing his church and its works of charity was remarkable for its being no method at all. Other free churches at this time had contracts with their members whereby they paid so much money a week or a month. Huntington's custom was to wait until money was needed, then announce the exact sum from the pulpit and wait in faith until it came. 'Half a dozen words', he told one correspondent, 'brings in £60 or £70'. He went on to say that he never spent twenty minutes in the pulpit, 'pumping and squeezing a few shillings out of the pockets of worldlings'. Huntington was firmly against reaping where he had never sown and did not allow his people to collect from door to door as was the custom.

In spite of all Huntington's restrictions, very soon Providence Chapel was able to distribute three or four hundred guineas a year to causes which they felt were worthy, provide £700 for repairs and extensions to the chapel and £2,000 to support the building funds of other churches. Once when Huntington heard that there was acute poverty in Russia, he collected £200 for the Russian poor in a single short appeal. Whenever a member grew too old to work or was in honest financial straits, Huntington would remind his congregation of their responsibility towards one another and the person in question would go home with a plateful of guineas and half-guineas. Often, when Huntington had financial problems himself, they were due to his own generosity in not being able to keep a penny in his pocket whenever he felt someone was in need. He had experienced poverty too much himself to be deaf to the pleas of others. As everyone knew that Huntington was always approachable when money was needed, there were many who took advantage of this and fooled him into lending them money which they never intended to pay back, or asked him for money when there was no real need for it. This weakness was very apparent during Huntington's early days as pastor of Providence Chapel. Two businessmen, for instance, worth thousands themselves, fooled him into giving them £100, leaving himself penniless. Huntington said of himself at this time, 'Unremitted importunity dragged me like an ox to the slaughter, or as a fool to the correction of the stocks'.

Blessings on Huntington's ministry

Though not always successful, humanly speaking, in his stewardship of money, Huntington reaped blessing after blessing as a pastor and preacher. Usually some hundreds of his hearers would assemble outside the church long before the doors were open. They would take their seats in a hushed, disciplined manner and not chat with their neighbours before the service started but read their Bibles, Hart's hymns or a book written by their pastor. One clergyman who came out of curiosity to hear Huntington could only comment that the congregation was 'a people prepared for the Lord'. Huntington did not preach from a manuscript and his sermons which are extant were mainly written down *after* delivery, usually at the request of members of his church who had been particularly blessed by the sermon. As he often wrote the sermons down weeks and even months after delivering them, it is very difficult to imagine in what form they first reached the ears of his congregation.

The outline of one sermon has been preserved which, when preached, resulted in four conversions. The text is Romans 8:9. 'Now if any man have not the Spirit of Christ, he is none of his'. First, Huntington shows 'the insufficiency of a form of godliness without the power'; secondly, 'the necessity of regeneration'; thirdly, 'the operation of the Holy Spirit from the Word of God'; fourthly, 'that God seeketh spiritual worshippers', and finally that, 'The Holy Ghost is sufficient to work faith, to sanctify the soul, and prepare it for the reception of Christ; and sufficient also to lead the believer on in a course of spiritual devotion, as the spirit of grace and of supplication'.

Huntington had not been long at Providence Chapel before another nickname was added to the many he already possessed. He became known as 'the Walking Bible'. This was because he had no need to read a chapter from the Bible before preaching as he could recite it off by heart without making a single mistake. Huntington's prayers were almost fully couched in biblical language. This gift stood him in good stead as he quickly became so short-sighted whilst at Providence Chapel that he could only read with great discomfort.

Those who first came to Providence Chapel were quite surprised by the appearance that Huntington made in the pulpit and at his manner of preaching. He was tall and, in the early years of his ministry, very slim. He dressed all in black but did not wear a gown or clerical robes of any kind. It was the custom in those days for both Anglican and Dissenting ministers to wear long flowing wigs with two rows of dangling curls. The eccentric John Ryland Senior found a mere two rows of curls below his dignity and had wigs specially made with five rows of curls! Huntington thought this was being too fond of making a show in the pulpit. He shaved his head regularly for hygienic reasons and wore a small black wig which fitted his head closely. He would stand almost still for most of the sermon, simply talking to his hearers. He rarely raised his voice, nor did he use theatrical gestures, but his clearly spoken words were carried easily to all parts of his chapel. Though many have written about Huntington's behaviour in the pulpit, the only movement of their pastor they could remember was that he held a white handkerchief in his hand which he occasionally passed from one hand to the other whilst preaching, or wiped his mouth with it. The only time that Huntington was known to thump the pulpit was when he preached his last sermon after being in the ministry forty years!

Because Huntington was not tied down to notes he was always free to comment on what was going on in the chapel in front of him. When a hearer looked round at a clock on the wall. Huntington would tell him that he did not preach according to the clock but according to the word he had been given. Once he called out in the middle of the sermon, 'Watch that pickpocket!' as he discovered a thief making his rounds in the gallery. Often the neighbouring clergy in their full canonicals and flowing wigs would hide in the porch or a side-room, too ashamed to show themselves in the pews. Huntington had no sympathy with their behaviour and, when they were spotted, he would cry out. 'Come on out, you big wigs. There's plenty of room for you'. When one clergyman started to grin during the sermon. Huntington called out, 'What are you laughing at?' The clergyman replied, 'I smile, sir, with approbation at your discourse'. 'Oh, very well!' said Huntington and continued preaching. Another time Huntington stopped in his tracks and looked at a man who had fallen asleep. The order, 'Wake that man!' came from the pulpit.

One can imagine inattentive people falling asleep during one of Huntington's sermons as he seldom preached for less than an hour and very often for two hours, yet the bulk of the people heard him gladly and followed him with acute attention, often making notes whilst listening to him. One fellow pastor wrote of the experience he had at Providence Chapel:

> Only those who heard him preach can have any idea of the greatness of his mind in spiritual things, or can ever feel what those felt who heard the glorious truths of the Gospel from his own lips, for 'his doctrine dropped as the rain and distilled as the dew'. I shall never forget the impression I received under the first sermon I heard from him. I could only weep and pray, for at that time I knew nothing of the Lord Jesus Christ, but I felt an inexpressible awe, as if on hallowed ground, as if the Lord was there, and that it was 'the House of God and the Gate of Heaven'. His valuable and extensive writings give a faint idea of this truly wonderful and holy man, but his power as a Preacher was seldom

> equalled, if ever surpassed; he spoke evidently not his own words and thoughts, but as taught by the Holy Spirit.[2]

There was one very negative aspect of the services at Providence Chapel, or at other chapels where Huntington preached, against which even he was powerless. Hundreds of critics and scoffers came to listen to his sermons and scoff at them. These people, amongst them hearers such as Andrew Fuller and the author of *The Voice of Years*, not wishing to join in the worship at the chapel, waited until Huntington began to read or recite his text and then they would stride noisily into the building and sit down with folded arms and a defiant look on their faces. They would then stand up as soon as the preaching was over and march out whilst prayers were being said or a hymn sung. Many of these scoffers, however, came to criticise and remained seated after the sermon with tears of shame and repentance in their eyes.

In this way, William Huntington experienced the fruits of his calling whilst a poverty-stricken labourer living on scarcely anything else but barley bread. He lived to preach before thousands of 'thick boughs' in the metropolis and became so well known that his hearers were prepared to travel many miles to hear him. He was exceedingly happy at Providence Chapel and though opposition against him was immense, few who came to hear him because of his bad reputation continued to think of him in that way.

One such hearer, Thomas Burgess, came to hear Huntington because of 'his awful character', only to find that he announced the words, 'Judge not, that ye might not be judged', as his text. The critic got up and left in anger when he heard these words, wanting to judge rather than be judged. He came back on another occasion, however, in a different frame of mind. This time he stayed for the sermon and heard Huntington preach on Romans 8:2, 'For the law of the Spirit of life in Christ Jesus hath made me free from the law of sin and death'. Burgess saw his own soul condemned by the law and his inability to offer to God any righteousness worthy of God's favour. He also found hope in Christ, who was willing to accept him, sinner as he was. One can then well believe that Burgess, like so many others who had been in the same

[2] The Rev. S. Adams, The Gospel Magazine, 1850.

state, became a fervent hearer of the Word through the ministry of the one-time coalheaver.

Chapter 6

Life On The Good Ship Providence

Although Huntington was a landlubber by birth, upbringing and profession, he must have had some sailor blood in him somewhere. Whenever he spoke of his church and its members, he invariably used the jargon of the sea. The universal church to Huntington was a Noah's ark, fitted out to house and home all God's elect. Providence Chapel was 'the Good Ship Providence', her builder was God and Jesus was her Captain. The ship's heavy guns were spiritual prayer, her keel was election and faith her cable. Her anchor was good hope and her tackling truth. The three storeys of the chapel were the vessel's three decks. The lower deck was 'Contrition', the middle deck 'Adoption', and the upper deck 'Assurance'. The heresies abounding in London at the time were referred to as 'privateers', the worst being called 'Free-Will'. Others had such names as 'Feigned Assurance' and 'Pharisee'. Once they had signed on in Jesus' service, whatever storms prevailed, all crew members would reach the heavenly shores at last. Whenever Huntington took a breather between preaching engagements he would say he was 'lying at anchor'. Whenever he was in his study at the chapel, he would say he was in his 'Cabin'; in fact he had the name 'Cabin' affixed to his study door.

Thus it was quite common for Huntington to begin a letter written in his study with the words: 'From the Cabin, on board the Providence, bound for the Fair Havens'. At times he even gave the wind direction and the latitude! Sometimes it was as if he had quite forgotten he was not on board a real ship. When writing to a friend, he said once, 'Bad ink, small-table, no fire, the rolling of the ship, and the hopes of a rout, have rendered this scrawl very unintelligible'. When he made an exchange visit to another chapel, he wrote to his 'crew', 'I have heard by some that you have had a liberal boatswain in my absence, and plenty of fresh provisions, which I guess at by the corporations of the crew left here, who appear to be as robust as a penny whistle, and to waddle with fat like a beggar's dog'.[1]

Some of Huntington's most pastoral letters in this period abound in seafaring language. The following letter is not only an example of this but also an example of how he always wore his heart on his sleeve and shared his own spiritual problems with his friends.

> Sailing is often dangerous in fine weather when we are apt to get too secure. I had a sad storm yesterday, and difficult work to manage the helm. Satan stirred my old man up at a most awful rate; and they were raging and cursing below deck till I trembled above. I could not find my log-book, and visitors crowded in upon me continually, till I grew wretched, and Satan advised me to let down the boat under colour, and flee out of the ship, desert the service, and leave the crew without a pilot. O, what a creature is man! Of all the fearful conceptions that ever I have conceived of death, the king of terrors, and the worst imagination that ever imagined of ghosts, devils, savages, bears, tigers, lions, and wolves – put them all together, and paint them in the most fearful, frightful, or formidable light – all never terrified the doctor so much as a real sight and sense of William Huntington has done, when I have seen him in God's light. And I do believe that I can say with reverence, the Lord knows that I lie not in this confession. These views in the light of an angry God shining in a broken law send the vessel of wrath to the bottom. All false hopes, false faith, human righteousness, false notions of a God all mercy, etc., etc.. He goes through all these briers and thorns and burns them all together. This is the last gasp of free will, and the eternal death of legal hope. But this death is attended with

[1] See W. Huntington, *Posthumous Letters*, vol. I, Letter 20; vol. III, Letter 428 *Gleanings of the Vintage*, Letter 53.

new life; we rise to newness of life: 'the dead hear the voice of the Son of God and live'. After the sad storm of yesterday was blown over and I had been exercised with many texts striving one against the other, the last verse of the 25th of Matthew's gospel abode with me and I was long in it and led through with a high hand indeed. And now I am in a strait betwixt two, not knowing which to wonder at most; the badness of the doctor's heart, or the unfailing goodness of God's dear Son!

God for ever bless thee, fellow invalid. Adieu![2]

Huntington deals with visitors

In this letter Huntington mentions his many visitors who soon became a real problem. Whether in his 'Cabin' or at home, there was usually a steady stream of people who wished for various reasons to speak to him. Though most visitors were true seekers, many of those who knocked at his door came either to scoff, talk about their own righteousness, or beg for money for some weird scheme of their own. Huntington had, however, a God-given knack of assessing his visitors and in most cases he was able to separate the 'sheep' from the 'goats'. The fact that Huntington was rather brusque with a number of people, however, soon spread around and was used as ammunition by his enemies.

The anonymous author of *The Voice of Years*, whose book has been widely used as a basis for criticising Huntington, says that the preacher was 'inaccessible'. Only one example of this 'inaccessibility' is, however, given, together with a general statement that even Huntington's family were not allowed to disturb him. The fact is that Huntington's letters are full of his invitations to people to visit him and stay as long as they wish – his wider family not excepted! Many a pastor would be highly pleased to breakfast alone with the morning's newspaper but Huntington often sat at breakfast with enquirers whom he had invited. His letters are full of such invitations, or encouragements to have a chat with him after the services. It is, of course, natural that such a powerful preacher was in great demand after

---

[2] *Posthumous Letters*, vol. I, Letter 83.

a service, but it is just as natural to accept the fact that he could not deal with all the seekers and scoffers who sought his ear all at once. Often Huntington's home was crowded and he had as many guests in his home as other pastors had in their chapels.

It is true that a number of visitors found Huntington's tongue surprisingly sharp. One day he was visited by several 'Mumping Nannies', one after the other. He gave this name to those who were obviously more fond of talking about themselves than the Lord and those who professed to be Christians for some personal gain or other. Often these 'Mumping Nannies' came with a passage of Scripture to prove they were something special, such as the man who came to declare that he was none other than one of the two witnesses spoken of in the book of Revelation.

On this particular day, Huntington had been severely tried by such visitors when a woman was announced by Huntington's factotum. 'Have her up', Huntington said in a vexed voice. When the woman had sat down, Huntington told her, in none too friendly a manner, that he had just been visited by a woman who had wasted his time with 'passages' and he supposed she had brought some, too. 'Yes, I have', said the lady. 'As I came up the stairs to see you, I felt these words, "Cease ye from man whose breath is in his nostrils, for wherein is he to be accounted of"!' She then wished Huntington 'Good day' and got up to go. 'Here', said Huntington, 'Come back. You'll do!'

Another visitor called on Huntington after he had been severely tried. Before he sat down or could say a word, the pastor said, 'I suppose you want a lazy, easy life by becoming religious'. 'Ah', replied the visitor, 'if by God's grace the world, the flesh, and the devil are against us, they will not allow of much ease, I know'. 'There', said Huntington, quite transformed by the words, 'Sit down'.

Sometimes Huntington was in great danger through being alone with angry visitors and he was often given great grace to cope with them. One young man was persuaded by his wife to go and hear Huntington and did so for her sake. He wanted to leave the service before it ended but could not get out because of the throng. He swore, however, never to visit Providence Chapel again. The word preached, however, spoke to his soul and drew him a second time to hear Huntington. He was too ashamed to tell his wife, so he went secretly. Huntington preached as if he had only this one man in view and the young man became convinced that his wife had been talking to the pastor about him and this enraged him. After the service he gained entrance to the vestry and ran with his fists raised towards Huntington, shouting, 'I've heard of such wretches as you, sir, driving people mad, and your preaching has almost driven me so'. Huntington smiled at him and replied, calmly but firmly, 'Now sit down and be quiet, for I'm sure, young man, you'll come to me some day, with quite another tale to this'. When the young man found out that his wife had not spoken to Huntington, he began to listen to the pastor's words. It was not many weeks before he found peace and pardon in Jesus and became a regular member of Providence Chapel.

Huntington's generosity to those in need

True to his nature, Huntington was very often more than generous to his visitors and though he had a very busy schedule, he gave them all the time he could. Often seekers came for many miles to see him and very often they were people who could ill afford travelling expenses. Huntington always seemed to have silver in one pocket and a few guineas in another so he could help his visitors pay for transport back home.

One man in particular had real cause to praise God for William Huntington's generosity. There was a successful businessman in the leather trade called Wilshire who was a member of Providence Chapel but became discontented with life in general. Although his business was doing well, he felt he might do even better if he moved away from London. So he gave up his membership in a good church and his prosperous business and settled down in Kingston to make more money there. From then on, everything went downhill for him, not only financially but spiritually. When he had reached the bankruptcy stage, Mr Wilshire thought of his previous pastor, whose advice he had once relied on but had scorned concerning his move to Kingston.

Swallowing his pride, Wilshire walked to London, as he could not afford to ride, and knocked at Huntington's door. He was immediately invited in and found Huntington in deep discussion with two men. When Huntington saw Wilshire, he exclaimed, 'There, I would as soon have seen the devil walk into my room as see that man!' Nevertheless he invited Wilshire to take a seat until he had finished his business with the two men. Because of this very blunt reception, Wilshire was full of bitter thoughts concerning his former pastor.

Soon Huntington's conversation with the two men ended and as they left the room one of them said to the unhappy businessman, 'Don't be fearful'. Huntington then turned to Wilshire and told him that he supposed he had starved himself out at Kingston and had returned with Naomi's confession: 'I went out full, and the Lord hath brought me home again empty'. Wilshire had no other alternative but to agree with a sigh. He was then surprised to see his former pastor get up and put on his coat. Huntington invited Wilshire to follow him out of doors.

The pastor strolled through the neighbouring streets with Wilshire at his side, who was wondering what was going to happen. Huntington stopped outside a shop which was all boarded up and asked, 'Wouldn't this be a good shop for you?' adding that the area was very good for business. Wilshire agreed that the area was first class but said that it was no use his thinking on such lines as he had no money to start a new business with. Huntington, however, went into the adjoining shop to fetch a key and both men entered the empty store. 'What do you think to it?' Huntington asked. Wilshire could only answer that the premises were very good. His former pastor then told him to go home and ask the Lord about the matter and come back in two days' time. Huntington did not leave things at that but put into Wilshire's hand enough money to get him home safely.

After two days the man returned with a heavy heart to tell Huntington that he could not possibly take over the shop. Without seemingly being moved by Wilshire's protests, Huntington took him back to the shop. Great was Wilshire's surprise to find the shop open and fitted out with all the materials and tools needed for Wilshire's business. Huntington turned to him and said, 'There, now you can go on with your trade and may the God of Abraham, Isaac and Jacob, bless and prosper you'. Wilshire prospered from the start and his spiritual health was also restored under Huntington's ministry. After he had made enough profit to pay back part of the money he felt he must owe Huntington, he visited his pastor who refused to accept a penny from him

The man who published this story was none other than the Rev. Dr D. A. Doudney, an Anglican minister who was for many years editor of The Gospel Magazine and once a bitter critic of anything connected with Huntington. On publishing the story of Huntington's kindness to Wilshire, Doudney confessed, 'Ah, when I reflect upon my cruel aspersions poured out upon that dear man, and how my Arminian principles drove me to slander him and the precious truths which he preached, I am constrained to confess before the Lord, how grievously I have sinned by my hard speeches which I have spoken against him'. Doudney also wrote,

> At one time the writer took pleasure in charging this man of God with inheriting Ishmael's portion; his hand being against every man and every man's hand against him. All that he said or did was wrested, and made to wear the appearance of evil. And this was done because the great truths that he contended for clashed with the pride of my unhumbled heart; but, when I was brought to feel the transforming and renewing power of the Holy Ghost, then, to my dismay, I saw I had the letter only, but that Mr Huntington had the power. And, as I was afterwards obliged to confess, that while we were charging him with being an enemy to good works, and teaching his hearers to scorn them as beggarly things, yet he was far more zealous of good works, both in precept and practice, than many of us, who were his vile defamers.[3]

A busy schedule

As a preacher and a pastor Huntington could not have been more active. His week really started very early on Saturday morning when he would enter the 'Cabin' to do his sermon preparation. Huntington seemed to manage on far less sleep than ordinary mortals and, though he was often out until very late at night, he would get up regularly at four o'clock in the morning and in the summer even earlier. After working on sermons all day Saturday, Huntington usually preached in the evening, often invited to a distant chapel in the hope that he would draw a generous crowd, rather than be the blessing which he invariably was. He usually

[3] 'Personal Recollections of Mr W. Huntington', The Gospel Magazine, October, 1870.

took a service at seven o'clock on Sunday mornings at local lecture-rooms, or chapels such as Little St Helen's, and preached at his own chapel on Sunday mornings at eleven and in the evening at six. Saturday and Sunday nights, he slept in his 'Cabin' or at a house nearby where he also took his very frugal meals.

On Mondays Huntington carried out a widespread ministry through writing to enquirers and friends all day until the evening service at Providence Chapel. Tuesdays were spent visiting his flock, and especially the sick, but he also attended the morning lecture at St Andrew Wardrobe, where William Romaine spoke. Both men enjoyed sweet fellowship together and continually remembered each other before the throne of grace. Tuesday evenings would find Huntington preaching in one of the larger lecture-halls in London, but he gradually settled down to taking these midweek meetings in an old-established Dissenting chapel at Monkwell Street where over three thousand souls flocked to hear him.

At the beginning of his ministry Huntington found most of the large lecture-halls and meeting-places opened to him, but as his fame increased, opposition to him from jealous ministers increased also and several large assembly-rooms, such as the Tabernacle at Greenwich, closed their doors to him because other popular preachers refused to preach there should Huntington continue.[4]

Wednesdays were again visiting days and Huntington often took with him medicine for the sick. This caused his followers to alter the nickname 'Doctor Sack', which his enemies had given him, to plain 'Doctor'. Work on Wednesdays was rounded off by a seven o'clock service at Providence Chapel. Thursdays and Fridays were spent at Huntington's home where the minister worked alternately in his garden, growing vegetables for his ever-increasing family, and looking after the spiritual needs of a steady stream of visitors. Huntington's duties at home did not stop him from preaching on these two days, either; in fact he seldom took less than ten services a week.

Huntington's letters

Anyone familiar with Huntington's pastoral letters will be immediately struck with the excellent way in which he cares for souls. Thomas

---

[4] For instance, Rowland Hill.

Wright, who had already edited over a thousand of William Cowper's praiseworthy letters for publication, nevertheless says of Huntington in his biography that, 'Without a shadow of doubt he is the greatest religious letter-writer that England has produced'. Comparing him with Cowper, Wright says, 'If it is an achievement of Cowper to make interesting every subject he touched, it was also an achievement in Huntington to keep touching only one subject, and yet to make it constantly interesting as well as instructive'. That subject was God's care for his elect. J. C. Philpot, unlike Huntington, a man of learning, had the following to say of Huntington as a letter-writing carer of souls:

> His *Letters* are, we think, the most edifying and instructive of his writings. It is true they have not the grandeur of the *Contemplations*, or the details of personal experience as in the *Kingdom of Heaven*; but there is a freedom in them, an entering into many minutiae of the divine life and a drawing forth many sweet draughts from the deep well of his own gracious leadings and teachings, which makes them singularly instructive and edifying. There is also in them an absence of controversy, and therefore of that warmth which he sometimes displays in handling an opponent. The kindness, tenderness, wisdom, knowledge of his own heart, of the devices of Satan, of the consolations of the Spirit, of the word of God, and of the whole length and breadth of Christian experience displayed in them, is truly wonderful. Even as letters they are wonderful productions. Such originality of thought and expression, such variety of language, with occasional flashes of surprising wit and humour, with such freedom of style as if all he had to do was to write as fast as his pen could travel over the paper, stamp these *Letters* as most remarkable compositions. The wonder is whence he got his knowledge of so many things, his command of language, his ample and powerful vocabulary, and his dexterity in wielding his words and ideas. When we consider that he had no education but at a common dame school where he just learned to read and write, we stand surprised at his amazing genius. We do not say it in a boasting way, but it has so happened, from the bent of our studies

> in former days, that we have read some of the finest productions of human eloquence, in both ancient and modern languages, and therefore we know what we assert when we declare that, in our judgment, the description of his deliverance in the *Kingdom of Heaven*, apart from the experience there described, as a mere piece of eloquence, is one of the grandest and most beautiful pieces of writing that has ever come under our eye.[5]

In 1786, during Huntington's early period as a pastor in London, he started correspondence with a young woman which was to result in the publication of a collection of letters which must be unique in the history of the church. This young lady, by the name of Elizabeth Morton, was the daughter of a member of William Romaine's church and had been brought up as a Protestant. Her training as a governess took her to France where she boarded in a convent and, through the influence of the nuns, became a Roman Catholic. On returning to England she heard Huntington preach and began to realise that the gospel he taught brought one far nearer to God than all the rites and rituals of the Roman Catholic persuasion. She thus wrote to Huntington, explaining how she felt God had been leading her throughout her life. Letter after letter was exchanged with the pastor of Providence Chapel and in each of his letters, Huntington drew Miss Morton further into the arms of God and into a true and living faith. The final exchange of letters is truly remarkable. Huntington gives Miss Morton a long list of signs whereby she might know if she has truly left darkness for the light of saving faith and Miss Morton goes through them one by one, displaying what a true work of God has been wrought in her. The whole collection is a step-by-step survey of the way of salvation from start to finish and serves as a standard to all pastors who wish to point seekers to Christ and all seekers who are moved to approach God.[6]

Strangely enough, it was Huntington's eloquence in letter writing that earned for him the name of 'impostor'. His Christian enemies said

---

[5] Review of Huntington's *Posthumous Letters*, Gospel Standard, August, 1856.

[6] The correspondence between Huntington and Miss Morton has recently been republished by Focus Christian Ministries Trust under the title *Epistles of Faith*. This title should not be confused with Huntington's book *Epistles of Faith* in vol. VI of Collingridge and vol. V of Bensley.

that God had seen fit to create him a farm labourer and he had no right whatsoever to 'pretend' to be a literary man. His language, they argued, was thus 'borrowed' and not his own. Rowland Hill went even further and refused to believe that Huntington was anything else but a 'monkey', aping his betters. One high-born hearer of Huntington's who thought it was wrong of a man of low birth to appear as educated as himself in his writings, took his pastor to task for his 'borrowed' language. Huntington gave him a piece of his enlightened mind:

> The charge you lay against me of using a borrowed language in my writings stands on so weak a basis, that it may be blown away with the wind of a sparrow. Your letter that now lays before me, has not a word in it but was borrowed; you were not born a grammarian any more than I; nor was you born with any language at all; for had you been trained up from your infancy among the Arabs, you would doubtless have spoken Arabic; and if I had been trained up from five months old in Paris, I should have muttered something like French.
>
> But if your wealthy father had got his hundreds to spare, and put you to school at a great expense, to learn other people's language and words, this gives you no licence to reflect on the poverty of my progenitors; for it is God that maketh poor and maketh rich; he therefore that despiseth the poor, reproacheth his maker, Proverbs 14:31. But if I, by the dint of hard study and observation, am enabled to cope with you, my study and observation rather merit your praise than your derision. However, this charge of yours has no more weight with it, than that of the Jewish Rabbis against Christ, 'Whence hath this man all these things, seeing he never learned letters?' And the Saviour's answer may justly be turned on you, 'Whatever I speak, therefore even as the Father said unto me, so I speak'.[7]

[7] *Epistles of Faith*, Part I, Letter XV, Collingridge, vol. VI.

An anonymous gift

Huntington had not been in the full-time ministry long when he realised that he had no book-learning whatsoever and though he had developed a thoroughly biblical set of doctrines, he had not the views of others to compare them with and to check them by. He thus started spending a good deal of the extra cash he obtained on books until he came to see with Solomon that, 'In making many books there is no end', and that it would be too rash of him to spend all his pocket money in this way.

One day, however, he received an anonymous note saying, 'Mr Anti-Arminius's free-grace love to Mr Huntington, begs his acceptance of a dish of dead men's brains; he believes most of them are of the evangelical family; they will be with him in a day or two: he is desired to ask no questions of the bearers'. At first he thought the note must be a joke from one of his enemies as it was so oddly worded. A few days later, however, a gigantic packing-case arrived and the dead men's brains inside revealed themselves to be three to four hundred books on theology, history and geography. Shortly afterwards a similar case arrived, this time containing a large mixture of secular – even profane – works, mixed with some very sound ones. Huntington was shocked to find that such works as those by Joseph Priestly were bound in red morocco and embroidered in gold but many choice works were very cheaply bound. Huntington promptly cut the fine bindings from the worldly works and put them on the spiritual ones. Huntington never found out who his anonymous friend was but he had been graciously given enough good books to last him a lifetime.

A wider preaching ministry

All his life Huntington seemed to be only one step from becoming seriously ill and even though he ate better than in his youth and slept well and was well-clothed, he still had bouts of very serious illness. Soon after receiving the books he was stricken with such an illness and spent several days and nights in a coma, not knowing what was going on around him. During this coma he had visions of glory and it was as if he were already dead and in the presence of the Lord. This experience strengthened Huntington's faith no end, as he realised that God was with him in Spirit when his own flesh failed.

The reason for Huntington's illness was most likely that he was working too hard again. He just could not refuse preaching invitations, even when they came from very questionable sources. The 'Celebrated Coalheaver' had now a name as a crowd-drawer and crowds meant a higher income for the church in which Huntington preached. Thus many churches which were in financial difficulties did not find it too much of an affrontery to invite Huntington to fill their pulpit. Huntington found out, however, that he was preaching for pastors who stayed at home when he visited their chapels and were paid to do nothing whilst he took over their work. These pastors had the cheek to demand that when Huntington came to preach he should first announce the meeting at his own church and take a collection there for the cause he was about to serve. Furthermore, though the trustees of these chapels were quite willing to accept the extra income derived from Huntington's visits, they claimed that their constitutions prevented them from giving him a preaching fee and they even criticised his theology openly.

Other ministers were even more subtle and, knowing how generous the 'Huntingtonians' were, they would wait until the crowds came out of Providence Chapel and canvas for their 'good cause'. Rowland Hill, for instance, once sent his friends to make a collection amongst Huntington's hearers and they came back with a hundred guineas. All this money-seeking on the part of people who were by no means friends of Huntington's gradually began to wear him out, as it also curbed the spending of his members for their own church. After some five or six years of filling other churches' collection-boxes Huntington decided to do guest-preaching only in churches which could join with Providence Chapel in a united faith. Such churches were being opened throughout the country, so there was no danger of Huntington having nothing to do in his 'spare time'. In order to keep more of the members' money within their own church, Huntington hit on a method which was widely practised at the time but which caused his enemies to heap even more criticism on him. The pastor decided that as there was always a rush for seats in his church long before the service began, those who wanted to be sure of a seat should pay for one and have it reserved for them. Many 'free pews' were, however, reserved for the poor and for occasional visitors.

This method of private pews proved very difficult to maintain, as the following story shows. A Mr Eedes of Ramsgate had been convicted of his sin for many years and found relief in reading Huntington's books. He felt that if he could only hear Mr Huntington preach, he would find peace for his troubled soul. Mr Eedes thus decided to make the comparatively difficult journey (in those days) to London to attend Providence Chapel. He arrived in London early one Sunday morning, made a beeline for the chapel and, as soon as the doors opened, pushed his way to the front and occupied a pew as near the pulpit as possible. The pew-opener quickly went over to Mr Eedes to inform him that he was sitting in a private pew and that there were other places marked out for visitors. The man replied that he had waited to hear Mr Huntington for several years and had travelled over seventy miles to hear him. Now he was there, he would not allow himself to be turned out, either by men or devils! The pew-opener did not know how to react and hurried to meet the family who owned the pew to explain that it was occupied by a stranger who refused to move. Realising that the man was a genuine seeker, the family gave up their right to the pew for that day and sat elsewhere. Mr Eedes was not disappointed. Huntington preached the very words necessary to release him from his burden and he went home praising God, with whom he had found his peace. He remained true to his Lord and when Huntington was in difficulties because publishers were refusing to handle his books, Eedes used his own home as a distribution centre.

Huntington had started his preaching life as an itinerant preacher but had become convinced that the more scriptural form of ministry was the pastorate of a local church. As he became more well known, however, churches all over England who felt they were of one faith with him invited him to minister to them. Thus in the late autumn of 1786 Huntington received an invitation to preach at Bristol and Bath. He accepted with great hesitation, wondering whether he was the preacher whom they really wanted. His letter of confirmation that he would visit Bristol shows this trepidation:

> Reverend Father in the Lord,
> Grace, mercy, and peace be with thee. If God permit and you approve, I will honour your pulpit next Thursday evening; honour it I say with the person of *the vilest sinner that ever lived*, in the possession of a hope that can never die. If you want to know my pedigree, I am by birth, a beggar; – by practice, a devil;

– by trade, a Coalheaver; – by profession, and possession, a Sinner Saved; – by principle a stiff Dissenter, and one of God's own making, for it was He alone that *called, ordained me, and sent me out*; and He has been my Bishop, my Tutor, my Provider, and my Defence ever since, or else I had been killed or starved long ago. If you or your people are fond of the original languages, of eloquence, oratory, or grammar, – I am the man that can *disappoint* them all. But if Apostolic ignorance will suit them, they will go nigh to glean a few scraps of that sort; but my degrees will promise nothing further than that. But to inform my reverend father a little about my irregularities, I am in my prayers very short, in my sermons short also, unless the Master attends the feast. If so, and the cruse gets a spring of oil in it, then I generally stop all thoughts of working by the day, nor can I give it up until I have emptied the whole contents, though I know I shall get no more without much knocking and a deal of calling at mercy's door. This I call *liberality*, and am vain enough to think this is *fervent charity;* and that charity which, if applied, covers a multitude of sins; and no wonder, when we hold forth freely the blood and righteousness of Him that cleanseth from all the guilt of sin, and the robe that covers all the remains of sin.

Rev. father, God bless you; – abundant happiness, comfort and success attend both you, your family and your flock.

While I remain, though unknown, Affectionately Yours,

Wm. Huntington[8]

The Tabernacle at Bristol had room for a congregation of well over 2,000 and Huntington filled it to bursting-point on his first Sunday there. Even in his midweek services, Huntington drew between a thousand and two thousand hearers. Crowds waited to hear him a good

---

8 This letter appears in Huntington's works in various forms. Cf. *Posthumous Letters*, vol. III, Letter 449 for a shorter version. The longer version is taken from Hooper's *Facts and Letters*, p. 26.

hour before the doors were opened. This caused the church to beg Huntington to preach again and again until the few days he was supposed to stay there ran into six weeks, with Huntington never preaching less than seven times a week. A fair number of the more affluent and educated members of the Tabernacle protested when they heard that an ex-coalheaver was coming to preach but they became so impressed by Huntington that they apologised to him for their behaviour. Like Whitefield before him, Huntington preached for the miners at Kingswood and had a most blessed time there. Tempting offers were made to Huntington to keep him at Bristol but his heart was set on returning to his good ship Providence.

Once back in London with his home crew and the taste of success still on his lips, Huntington was suddenly to lose over half of his deck-hands. He was to be dragged into a storm of controversy which was none of his making and be smeared with a slanderous name which certainly did not fit him, yet which he was never fully able to rub off. He was also to play a unique part in the history of the church as a signpost away from what had become, on the whole, a man-centred evangelicalism, back to the Christ-centred faith of Paul and the teachings of the glorious Reformation.

Chapter 7

Huntington The Winnower

When summing up the strengths and weaknesses of the churches in England in the latter part of the eighteenth century, Thomas Scott wrote to a friend north of the border:

> Your account of the state of religion in Scotland, though rather discouraging, gives me the idea that far more regard has been, and even still is, there paid to the gospel than in England. Some years ago ... it might almost be said that the whole was here sunk into formality and self-righteousness. The irregular and desultory, yet zealous and honest labours of Mr Whitefield and his coadjutors produced great effects; and since he went forth there has been a great revival in the established church. Nor were the labours of Mr Wesley and his helpers without much fruit. Yet a great deduction must be made. A flashy, superficial, and immethodical style of preaching was rendered fashionable: gradually a view of the gospel rather tending to antinomianism[1] was introduced by the successors of the ministers that have been mentioned – that is, of Mr Whitefield and Co. An experience which admits of a great mixture of enthusiasm, and opens the door to delusion, was sanctioned: a bad taste, so to speak, was propagated: and the eminence of the men who set the example

[1] One who believes that a Christian may break God's laws at will. Do what he will, he is saved. A fuller definition will follow in the next chapter.

gave currency to these things; which became far worse in the hands of men in all respects their inferiors. In the Church of England, among those who are reputed to preach the gospel, many do comparatively little. There are, however, a considerable number of able, solid, and zealous men; and the expensive encouragement given by some superior people to the education of pious young men, of good abilities, for the ministry, presents the most pleasant prospect that the state of things affords. But, alas! our superiors in the church either oppose the most unexceptionable men who preach according to the articles and liturgy, or are afraid to countenance them ... Among the numerous bodies of the Calvinistic and Arminian Methodists, a considerable degree of fervour and earnestness is discoverable; and I trust there are many well-meaning people: but their religion is superficial; and they are easily deluded into pernicious errors, or unbecoming practices, for want of more complete and clear acquaintance with the system of truth, and the rule of duty. Though the two sects seem totally to differ, yet the same defect is visible in both; only the Arminians are more enthusiastic and joyful, the Calvinists more acquainted with their own hearts, and employed in escaping dejection by a low experience. But, in fact, superficial views of our obligations to holiness, according to the spiritual law of God, and an unperceived tendency to antinomianism, are too common in both – though the Arminians are thought to be in the opposite extreme. The Dissenters, both Baptists and Paedobaptists, are of various kinds. Some are of the methodistical cast, and have much life, and not proportionable judgment and depth: others are solid Calvinistic divines, but rather cramped by system and church order; and, with a few exceptions, useful only on a small scale. Others are dry systematics, with little life or unction: and, alas! no small number are avowed Arians and Socinians. A political spirit at present does considerable harm to the cause of vital godliness, and widens our divisions on religious points; an evil which the enemy promotes. In London and some other principal cities and towns, people have abundance of religious advantages; though I fear they do not proportionably improve them: but in many parts of the country gross darkness prevails in an awful degree.[2]

The need for a reforming leader

Scott was given a balanced insight into the state of the church which few ministers of the day shared. This was because of the peculiar state of evangelicals at the time who were split by a strong party spirit. A strong man was needed who could consolidate the positive teachings of the work of the great pioneer evangelists and root out the lax practices and weak doctrines that had sprung up in their wake. Scott could have been the man to do this. He stood four-square in Reformed traditions and looked upon the Amyraldian doctrines of Fuller and Ryland as false. In 1787 Ryland, a close friend of Scott's, had protested against a sermon Scott had published on election and final perseverance. Scott wrote to him to urge that the death of Christ was not intended to save those who eventually perish and that God has a particular purpose and special love for the elect. He added that God gives an appetite for the provisions he makes in salvation to none but those for whom that provision was specially intended. Elsewhere he argues against the commonly held fallacy that 'Christ and all his benefits are made over to everyone that hears the gospel'.[3]

Scott, however, argued that he had 'neither ambition nor expectation of proselytising the world'. He refused to take his doctrinal differences with Ryland and Fuller seriously and argued that there was only 'a little ditch' between them and, in principle, they had the same aims and argued for the same cause. He even said to Ryland, 'If you think yourself firmer on your ground, fight on, and the Lord prosper you!' This stance is all the more surprising as, in the very same letter, Scott criticises Newton for being 'too afraid of controversy'.[4]

Furthermore, Scott complained incessantly that he was unwanted as a minister. At Olney, he had taken over a church whose entire

---

2 Scott, *Letters and Papers*, pp. 180-182.

3 *Ibid.*, pp. 121-123, 200, 201.

4 *Ibid.*, pp. 123, 124.

congregation had joined the Dissenters owing to differences of opinions between them and their former curates Newton and Page. He was only able to build up a tiny following there and several of his church members strongly opposed him. On leaving Olney, Scott took over the Countess of Huntingdon's work at the Lock Chapel,[5] London, but his congregation remained very small, so that when he left the Lock to take over a parish with a mere seventy families in all, he said that his congregation was now the largest that he had ever had. Thus we find Scott complaining to Ryland, 'I believe no minister in London is so unpopular. Others may be more unknown, or have a less name, but none so ill a name, as to doctrine and preaching'.[6] Actually, Scott had a very good name amongst both evangelicals and Dissenters but with such an attitude one can hardly be a leader of men. Furthermore, Scott was continually being accused of Arminianism by his church people, probably because of his stress on a Christian's active duty and his calling those who stressed God's active grace 'Hyper-Calvinists' and 'Antinomians'. John Newton (1725-1807) was well known and respected throughout the country at the time but in the nineties he was too bowed down by the early onset of old age to set himself up as a reforming leader on a larger scale and he had his own personal battles to fight. Newton was never a controversialist in theological matters, believing that one should 'preach the truth in love' and the rest would take care of itself. In his old age, however, he became violently political and looked upon all Dissenters as traitors to their country. His outspokenness in this field caused great alarm amongst his closest Dissenting and Anglican friends who tried to persuade him to retire from the mid-nineties on.[7]

William Romaine (1714-1795) had certainly the gifts and the nationwide respect to lead a campaign to discipline the churches but he, too, was an old man by this time. Romaine's role in a reformation of doctrine in the eighteenth century was far greater than is generally realised by modern evangelicals. Romaine wrote at a time when the

---

[5] Martin Madan, though deposed, officially kept the sinecure post of chaplain until his death in 1790.

[6] *Ibid.*, p. 126.

[7] Newton told his Dissenting friend Bull that even orthodox Dissenters were enemies of the government. See *Memorials of the Rev. William Bull*, p. 221. See Bull's views in this book concerning why Newton should retire from the ministry.

doctrine of justification by faith was being heavily criticised by so-called Calvinists who were arguing that, 'The doctrine of justification is not the whole of Christianity; nor being justified the whole of salvation', and thus side-lining it in their teaching.[8] Scott, whose words these are, used them to demonstrate that those who stressed justification were Antinomian at heart. Romaine's trilogy *The Life, Walk and Triumph of Faith* (1771-1794) is a mighty demonstration of Reformed doctrine but no sooner had he written the work than his fellow-evangelicals accused him of being an Antinomian, too.

Rowland Hill (1744-1833) pastored a very large congregation, and had an enormous financial backing. When he refrained from controversy and kept to his pastoral work he was second to none. He was not, however, set enough in his character to be a stable leader of men and, though he loved controversy as much as Huntington, he was no apologist and when in fierce argument he tended to lose all his theological acumen, if not his head.

Huntington was really the only man of national influence, with a congregation of well over two thousand followers to support him,[9] and an urge to reform, who was given the courage and ability to stand out against the lax faith of evangelical churches and strive to show them a better and more New Testament way. It was thus no exaggeration when one writer in the 1850 volume of the Gospel Magazine, speaking of the religious zeal that had resulted from the preaching of Whitefield and the need for a true successor, stated that Huntington was 'a directing post fixed on an eminence, to which a traveller may direct his attention, and learn the road which leadeth to life'.[10] In fact in the nineteenth century many men of unquestionable Christian integrity and learning, such as Dr D. A. Doudney and J. C. Philpot, recognised clearly Huntington's work as a winnower of the churches left by the preaching of the eighteenth-century evangelists and revivalists. This led such men to compare Huntington with the very greatest of Christian men since the

---

8 Scott, *Letters and Papers*, p. 211.

9 I use the word 'congregation' here rather than 'church' as a great many of Huntington's hearers at Monkwell Street were in fellowship in other London churches.

10 'A Memento, J. T'., The Gospel Magazine, October, 1850.

days of Paul and to consider him well able to take his place in church history along with such names as Bunyan and Whitefield.

As indicated by Scott in his description of the state of the churches, Whitefield and Wesley had been instrumental in bringing the gospel to millions who were formerly at enmity with God. As old church buildings were once more filled to bursting-point, new churches and chapels were springing up all over Britain to cater for the spiritual needs of the new converts. John Wesley was still alive in 1783 when Huntington became pastor of Providence Chapel and he was to remain firmly in place as the leader of the Wesleyan Methodists until his death in 1791. Whitefield, who died in 1770, did not leave an organization behind him but had filled both church and chapel with believers eager to grow in grace. No one denomination took care of his converts at first but gradually the Countess of Huntingdon looked upon herself as the person who was to carry on Whitefield's work by providing ministers for, and financing churches in sympathy with, the doctrines that he had held. Those within what came to be known as the Countess of Huntingdon Connexion called themselves Calvinists[11] whereas Wesley's followers were out-and-out Arminians. The Countess founded a college at Trevecca in 1768 where, for a few years, Arminian and Calvinist Christians worked side by side under the presidency of John William Fletcher. Gradually, however, the two parties separated, which led John Berridge to describe the evangelical church as now being split between the followers of Pope John (Wesley) and Pope Joan (Lady Huntingdon).[12] If the only alternative had been between Wesley, who had revived Roman Catholic and Scholastic teachings and the countess, who rode roughshod over the biblical doctrines of womanhood, it would have been a tragic day for the church indeed. A leader of sterner theological and moral stuff was, by God's grace, at hand. He was neither an Oxford don, nor a noblewoman of the realm but a plain ex-odd job man and coalheaver.

Huntington sought to reform the churches by openly revealing their weaknesses both in character and doctrine. This caused him to make

---

[11] Traditionally a Calvinist is one who believes in five specific doctrines: man's total depravity, unconditional election, particular atonement, irresistible grace and the perseverance of the saints.

[12] Letter written 20 October, 1771.

very many enemies, although it won for him equally many friends. It was Huntington's heartfelt conviction that neither the Calvinistic churches loosely affiliated to the Countess of Huntingdon Connexion nor the followers of Wesley represented the true gospel church. He simply found them both too worldly and heretical for words.

Huntington and the Arminians

Huntington wrote off the Arminians at once as being a band of hypocrites. Their rejection of the doctrines of reprobation, predestination and final preservation, he found sub-Christian and their teachings regarding free will, 'sincere obedience', progressive sanctification and perfection quite foreign to the gospel. Furthermore, to Huntington's way of thinking, the Arminian attitude to the imputed righteousness of Christ was quite blasphemous.[13] The Wesleyan practice of 'love feasts' and 'holiness meetings' – even their prayer meetings – filled Huntington with horror as he thought of the experience meetings he had visited as a seeker. He had seen with his own eyes Wesleyans, with arms raised, eyes rolling, emitting deep groans, vying with others in their efforts to convince themselves, one another and God that they were having the correct soul-perfecting experiences. Wesley, of course, did not fully approve of such human displays but he was far from condemning them as unchristian, as his *Journal* shows. Whilst Huntington was extremely careful to see that worship was 'decent and in order', Wesley could write in his *Journal* after a visit to Derbyshire in April, 1786:

> It is chiefly among these enormous mountains that so many have been awakened, justified, and soon after perfected in love; but even while they are full of love, Satan strives to push many of them to extravagance. This appears in several instances:-

---

[13] See Wesley's letters to Hervey concerning imputed righteousness and Hervey's letters in reply. See *The Works of The Rev. James Hervey, A.M.*, Edinburgh, 1837, where these collections are to be found. See also my 'Whose Righteousness Saves Us?', Bible League Quarterly, July-September, 1991.

> 1. Frequently three or four, yea ten or twelve, pray aloud together.
>
> 2. Some of them, perhaps many, scream all together as loud as they possibly can.
>
> 3. Some of them use improper, yea, indecent, expressions in prayer.
>
> 4. Several drop down as dead; and are as stiff as a corpse; but in a while they start up, and cry, 'Glory! glory!' perhaps twenty times together. Just so do the French Prophets, and very lately the Jumpers in Wales, bring the real work into contempt. Yet whenever we reprove them, it should be in the most mild and gentle manner possible.

It is quite clear from the context that Wesley believes that all this screaming and indecent behaviour is performed by those who are 'perfected in love'. Huntington would have told them to shut up or get out and have thought them the worst of hypocrites.

The Countess of Huntingdon's Connexion and the law

Perhaps Huntington's criticism of 'Our Lady's Men'[14] and their churches was even more scathing than his horror at the antics of the Arminians. He believed Whitefield to have been a great man of God but saw little in the lives and work of his would-be successors to show that they were preaching the same gospel. The churches supervised by Lady Huntingdon were indeed going through a most unstable and difficult time.

The Reformers and Puritans had re-emphasised the fact that the just shall live by faith. This had been the orthodox belief of evangelical churches ever since. As hinted above in connection with Romaine, however, there was a shift in doctrinal emphasis in the middle of the eighteenth century. Evangelicals, and especially Calvinists, were being accused of believing in 'Sola-fidism', which was a misnomer to describe the idea that good works were superfluous items in a life of faith. The wheel gradually turned so that once again legalism began to be practised in churches that had formerly upheld the teachings of the

[14] Followers of the Countess of Huntingdon were generally called such by friend and foe.

Reformers. Two of the countess's leading preachers, Martin Madan and his assistant Thomas Haweis, were very zealous in working out to what extent the law and good works were morally binding for the Christian. The findings of both men were radically opposite and they were to create a major division within the connexion and also seriously challenge the doctrine of justification by faith alone. Both men came to the conclusion that the Mosaic law was still binding on the Christian, yet they disagreed as to what that law entailed. Martin Madan looked at the whole of the Old Testament as reflecting the wider law of God, whereas Thomas Haweis saw the law as being fully confined within the Ten Commandments. Both clergymen occupied themselves far too much with the Old Testament and apparently never thought of looking into the New Testament teaching concerning the function of the Mosaic law. Even their studies in the Old Testament were at fault, as they concentrated on the ethical implications of the law, to the detriment of its theological purpose.

Madan and Haweis were chaplains in the Countess of Huntingdon's chapel at the Lock Hospital for vagrant women in the West End of London. Their work was thus to reform prostitutes and help them spiritually, socially and financially, so that they could leave their lives of sin and take up an honourable occupation. Madan, especially, became so engrossed in his studies and in the plight of his wards that he began to think totally on Old Testament lines even though New Testament teaching clearly contradicted him. He noticed that Solomon, David and other great Old Testament figures had a plurality of wives and came to the conclusion that, according to 'the Divine Law', 'A man having more than one wife was allowed, owned, and even blessed of God: and in no one instance, amongst the many recorded in Scripture, so much as disapproved'. Madan thought that he had found out a solution to the problem of prostitution. Those men who committed adultery with prostitutes should be compelled to marry them and then there would soon be no prostitution left. This hare-brained scheme came from the pen of a man who was a brilliant lawyer, and who, after his conversion under John Wesley, was considered a brilliant preacher and honoured throughout the kingdom as a hymn-writer, musician, composer and classicist of great note. He was also Lady Huntington's right-hand man.

In 1781 Madan published his *Thelyphthora: or a treatise on Female Ruin, in its Causes, Effects, Consequences, Prevention, and Remedy; Considered on the Basis of the Divine Law*. That was just the title. The subtitle was: 'Shewing by what means, and by what degrees, the laws of Jehovah concerning marriage, were opposed and abrogated, and a new system invented and established by Christian Churchmen'. It came out as a three-volumed work and startled the whole church, pleased a great many, and shocked a great many more. It is obvious on reading these three tomes that Madan envisaged a New Testament church run fully on ancient Jewish lines. William Cowper, who was Martin Madan's cousin, playfully hinted in a satirical poem[15] that Madan had read his Hebrew upside-down and thus got the meaning wrong.

When Thomas Haweis found out what his senior chaplain's findings were, he broke with him completely and threatened to publish all the intimate confessions that Madan had made to him during their friendship to show the world what an evil person Madan really was. John Newton and William Cowper joined forces to persuade Haweis not to go to such an extreme himself.[16] Instead of being grateful to Newton for warding off a dangerous enemy, Madan, however, turned on Newton and accused him of not living up to his Christian duty as he had only married one wife, his beloved Mary, and ought to have more.[17] Newton reacted in verse:

> What different senses of that word, A Wife!
> It means the comfort or the bain of life.
> The happiest state is to be pleased with one,
> The next degree is found in having none.

To which Cowper added:

---

[15] 'Anti-thelyphthora: A Tale in Verse', published anonymously 1781.

[16] See my *William Cowper: Poet of Paradise* for a full account of Newton's and Cowper's opposition to Madan.

[17] There had been widespread, but completely unfounded rumours, that Newton had practised adultery as a slave-trader. Newton was able to prove that no such evil practice had occurred but the stain remained in Madan's confused mind.

If John marries Mary, and Mary alone,
'Tis a very good match between Mary and John.
Should John wed a score, oh! the claws and the scratches!
It can't be a match: – 'tis a bundle of matches.

Eventually Newton persuaded Cowper to take up his pen publicly against Madan. The poet did this with great reluctance as Madan had been instrumental in leading him to Christ[18] and was a near relative. For this deed many of Cowper's evangelical relations turned their backs on the poet. Instead of Madan becoming the laughing-stock he deserved to be, however, he was taken seriously by many clergymen and his book quickly sold out and a new edition was printed. This was all the more surprising as the book must have been almost unintelligible to anyone who was not highly versed in Hebrew and Old Testament law. Few Christians might agree with Madan nowadays but this sad story must be told as the Madanites, whose morals had become extremely questionable, were amongst the first to accuse Huntington of neglecting the law of God in his teaching. This was a great blow to a man who spent so much time preaching personal holiness and sanctification.

Perhaps it was a reaction against Madan that moved Haweis to insist that not the whole of the Old Testament way of life was valid for the Christian, but merely the moral law as given on Sinai. Thus Haweis and Lady Huntingdon, who was of his opinion, began to stress amongst their followers obedience to the Mosaic law as the only rule a Christian had whereby he could attain holiness. To Huntington, what they were really saying was that the just are justified by the deeds of the law and not by faith, which is God's gift to his elect. What both Madan and Haweis had overlooked in their Old Testament studies was that Moses was not alone in pointing the way to perfection. Abraham, who lived and died without the law of Moses, saw a more perfect way and had righteousness imputed to him through his faith in Christ, whom he foresaw. Moses' law condemned those who lived under it but Christ

---

18 See the story of Cowper's conversion and Madan's part in it in my *William Cowper: Poet of Paradise*.

took over Abraham's life and caused him to be a just man who lived by faith. Huntington could thus argue that it was Abraham, and not Moses, according to New Testament teaching, who was the great forerunner of all Christians. The purpose of Moses' law was to force upon fallen mankind the knowledge that it was impossible to live a righteous life by following moral principles alone. The purpose of Abraham's example was to bring hope of a more sure and better way of finding salvation. The big mistake of many evangelicals in Huntington's day was that, in their eagerness to set moral standards whereby a Christian could check and measure his walk with God, they paid little attention to the theological context of the law and even less to the new revelation in Christ in the New Testament.

It was not long before Lady Huntingdon's followers were making it seem that the whole will of God for the saved sinner was revealed in the Ten Commandments. Huntington saw in this a revival of the heresy of the 'Christian Pharisees' mentioned in Acts 15. These Christians could not accept a Christianity without a full justifying trust in the law of Moses – a heresy that the apostles rejected, telling them that 'By him [Christ] all that believe are justified from all things from which ye could not be justified by the law of Moses' (Acts 13:39). This justification, Huntington argued, resulted in the Holy Spirit occupying the believer and instructing and enabling him in the way he should go. This is why Paul and Barnabas rebuked those Pharisees by telling them that they put a yoke upon the neck of the disciples which 'neither our fathers nor we were able to bear'. The apostles thus argued that the just should live by faith, faith being an active intervention by God in the lives of believers, writing the law on their hearts and keeping them in mind of it – and the whole will of God – through the influence of the Holy Spirit. This was also Huntington's position in a nutshell.

Music and play-acting

There was another bone to pick with the Countess's men which shocked Huntington just as much and called out loudly for correction. The more Lady Huntingdon's followers looked into the ceremonies of the Old Testament, the more they introduced ceremonies of their own. The more they studied the cultic music of the Old Testament, the more they introduced instrumental music into their own services. Forgetting that these 'means', as they called them, were all shadows of better things to come, they emphasised not only the necessity of keeping the believer's gaze on Sinai, but also that of having music to accompany him on the way. Again the Countess of Huntingdon's chaplain Martin Madan was a pioneer in this respect. At first he wished only to liven up the worship by speeding up the hymn-singing. He then introduced musical instruments whose purpose was to keep up a faster beat. After this he introduced trained singers who were to 'lead' the congregation. Soon he dispensed with congregational singing altogether in many of his services and had music played without words and dramatized singing performances without the participation of the hearers.

John Wesley loved a melodious tune and was not averse to seeing a play now and then. He thus decided to pop in at the Lock and hear what was happening. They were performing Handel's *Judith* and had many singers, singing different words to different tunes in different musical renderings – all at once! Wesley came out shaking his head. He determined to stop such singing in his own churches, as he found it against all reason and common sense.[19] Soon oratorios were being held in the churches whose walls had once resounded to the preaching of Whitefield. John Berridge, who hated controversy, found himself compelled to write to Benjamin Mills at the Tabernacle to warn him that the music lovers were letting in the devil and all his works. This letter was circulated amongst the members and caused quite a negative stir. Berridge was worried that the churches would realise what a good income could be made by putting on concerts and begin to build places of worship financed by Mammon. Perhaps he had Rowland Hill's example in mind as Hill charged five shillings a head for his oratorios at Surrey Chapel, which was an enormous sum in those days for a mere concert – and that in a building dedicated to the service of God! Actually such concerts were quite a drain on the financial resources of the churches as they were performed by professionals who demanded payment for their work.

William Cowper was so shocked at this church worldliness that he wrote letter after letter on the subject and published verse criticising

[19] See Wesley's *Journal* entries for 24 February, 1764; 22 October, 1768; 9 August, 1778 and 6 April, 1781.

'fiddling parsons'. He thought that the new prayer of evangelicals was 'Tickle and entertain me, or I die!' John Newton preached no less than fifty sermons against the craze. Not content, however, with making music, some churches introduced play-acting and plays such as those written by Hannah More were performed. This was too much for Rowland Hill, who began to castigate ministers who put on plays. This earned for him the anger of Lady Huntingdon, who swore that he should never again preach in her churches. All this was the world, the flesh and the devil to Huntington. In his book *Every Divine Law in the Heart of Christ*, he deals with criticisms against his ministry raised by his contemporaries. After describing how his church is flourishing spiritually and materially he goes on to say:

> Nor can any of our evangelical slanderers charge us with making use of any carnal weapons, or popish acts, in order to gain proselytes. We have no gowns nor bands, nor do we make use of any forms which belong to the establishment. We use no empty oratory, nor earthly logic; we have no pipers or trumpeters; no viols, harps, nor organs; no choristers nor opera singers. We always consider that the glory is departed wherever these are introduced, and view all converts to be carnal that are converted by such carnal means; far enough beneath our notice, and not worth a penny a dozen.

These were sound words, written at a time of much ignorance in the church as to what true worship was.

The storm of controversy breaks

In 1786 the ex-coalheaver decided to tackle the problem of the moral life of the church in its correct biblical and theological context. He thus carefully prepared a Tuesday night lecture at Monkwell Street where he would be certain of finding hearers from all the different denominations in the city. On this particular evening the Rev. Thomas Haweis and the Countess of Huntingdon were present. Huntington expounded the Old Testament conception of the law as interpreted by New Testament writers and showed exactly what the law was intended by God to do and what it could not do. In so doing Huntington completely reversed the teaching of many of his contemporary evangelicals, including

Haweis and the countess. They, according to Huntington, preached the love of Christ to sinners to draw them to him and then, when they were supposedly 'converted', they gave their converts the law to show them how to live. For Huntington this was putting the cart before the horse, teaching that the law was superior to grace. If grace saves you only as long as you keep the law, grace is superfluous. Keeping the law would thus open heaven's doors, and not grace. This was sheer Judaism to Huntington, whose many writings on the subject show that he preached the law until the elect sinner was broken and saw how vile he was. He then preached the love of God in Christ, electing, justifying and sanctifying his church; establishing and fulfilling the law in the hearts of believers and granting them faith in him. Huntington taught that a life of faith in one who fulfilled the law was quite a different matter to earning one's own way via the law.

Haweis and Lady Huntingdon heard Huntington with dismay and anger on that fateful Tuesday evening and subsequently did all in their power to discredit him in their pulpits. Many of Huntington's Tuesday hearers came from other churches influenced by the Countess of Huntingdon Connexion and in those churches they learnt that Huntington was an arch-heretic and to be shunned by all and sundry. For the next few weeks, Huntington's congregation at Monkwell Street shrunk until the huge hall was almost empty. This caused him much heart-searching and prayer but also embarrassed him greatly financially as he had to pay for the renting of the hall and no income from collections was forthcoming. Everywhere Huntington went, he was met by jeering 'professors of religion' who mobbed him in the streets with all manner of abuse, blindly believing all that their law-bound ministers had told them. Scores of insulting letters were sent to Huntington and, as the recipient had to pay postage in those days, this was a heavy drain on his pocket. The word quickly spread that Huntington paid no attention to morals and lived a life of utter licentiousness. None, however, could place their finger on anything whatsoever of an immoral nature in his life, or in the lives of his faithful adherents at Providence Chapel, for that matter.

Whilst Huntington was going through such acute persecution from people professing to be evangelical Christians, he was often in bad health and was beset with great personal problems. Yet he remained firm to the calling he believed he had received, hardly ever wavering in the face of massive criticism. Though an unlettered man, Huntington was compelled to take up his pen against the numerous pamphlets that were written against him, sometimes by educated men of letters. Whether educated or not, Huntington's accusers were usually severely trounced by their opponent, who did not leave them a leg to stand on. Some of these controversial writings, such as those in response to Rowland Hill's attacks, are among Huntington's finest works. Others, such as Huntington's replies to John Ryland Senior, show Huntington at his worst as he merely takes up the vulgar accusations of his antagonist (and they were very vulgar) and proves that they apply to the accuser and not the accused. This difference in quality is probably because Huntington always respected Hill and thought that he was merely misled and misguided. He had, however, no respect for Ryland,[20] who in his opinion practised duplicity to a high degree and he could never excuse him for using as his spokeswoman Miss Maria De Fleury, who was as void of taste as she was of logic and a knowledge of the Scriptures. Thinking of Huntington's prowess as a controversialist Dr Doudney wrote:

> In his ministry and writings Mr Huntington wielded the sword of the Spirit with consummate skill, and in controversy, woe, woe to his antagonist! No combatant stood the slightest chance. Humanly speaking, right or wrong, none could wage war successfully with William Huntington. He had a clearness of apprehension – a scriptural knowledge – and a command of language, together with a fearlessness, that were sufficient to intimidate any opponent. He was, as a Controversialist, a Boanerges of the first order.[21]

---

[20] Ryland was notorious for his eccentricity in his dress and character and his uncouth and fierce language. William Jay relates in his biography of Ryland how, when he first met the 'awesome' man, Ryland told him that he would 'smite him to the ground' if he let the people of Surrey Chapel make him proud when he preached there. Dr Rippon, when Ryland's coffin was being lowered into the grave, declaimed loudly:

> Defects through Nature's best productions run, –
> Our friend had spots, – and spots are in the sun!

[21] Quoted from Hooper, *The Celebrated Coalheaver*, p. 60. Source not given.

This was a description of Huntington on the outside – the public man. On the inside, he was quite different, as he testifies in a letter to a friend:

> Could my bed, my curtains, my study, or my Bible speak for me, they would bear such a testimony of the unutterable felicity, foretastes, earnests, and celestial triumphs of my soul, that would prove to all that fear God, that I envied not the mansions of Gabriel. But I have done, and conclude with tears of gratitude to the God of Jacob, who condescends to give so much success to the worst of sinners; for as the Lord liveth, though I am clad with zeal in the pulpit, I seldom go one day dry-eyed to God; I am a Boanerges in public, but in private of a sorrowful spirit, not for fear of wrath, but under a daily sense of super-abounding mercy to the worst of sinners.[22]

Harassment by Rowland Hill

Though the reaction against Huntington's preaching and doctrine came initially from within the Countess of Huntingdon's Connexion, greater and unparalleled onslaughts were to come from one who had been banned from her pulpits.[23] This was Rowland Hill of Surrey Chapel. Humanly speaking, Huntington and Hill were similar characters with very similar beliefs. Both had a congregation of 3,000 hearers and more weekly. Both held to the tenets but not the forms of the Church of England. Both were paedobaptists. Both abhorred the prayer and testimony meetings of the Wesleyans and had very similar reasons for doing so. Both saw themselves as continuing the work that Whitefield had started although neither had known Whitefield personally. Both found themselves on the wrong side of the Countess of Huntingdon.

---

22 *Gleanings of the Vintage*, No. 169.

23 The countess soon realised what a mistake she had made as Hill always drew a crowd and was always sure of a good collection. Lady Huntingdon thus gave Hill permission to preach once a year at the Lock, providing that he gave all collections and donations to her cause! She then allowed Scott to preach a collection sermon at Hill's Surrey Chapel providing that the money gained there was also given to her work.

Both men rejected play-acting in the church although Hill did fit his chapel out with a large organ and paid professionals to look after chapel music. Both men were professing Calvinists and looked on John Wesley as a most misguided contender for the truth. Both men were very fond of animals. Both men were ridiculed savagely by the Sunday press. Both men were given numerous titles by their friends and enemies, several of which 'stuck'. Huntington became 'the Doctor' and Hill 'the Rector'. Both men were good preachers: Huntington, quiet, systematic and analytical; Hill with great fervour and passion, preaching without any apparent preparation as he was led, sometimes spoiling everything by a joke entirely out of place but often preaching with great eloquence and conviction. Both men could be extremely stubborn and they ruled their congregation with, at times, an iron hand. Thus, on a superficial level, the two men can be seen to have had much in common. Indeed, when one examines their works it would be a simple matter to gather together enough quotations from them to 'prove' that they held the very same beliefs.

There were, however, great differences. Hill was an Eton and Cambridge trained aristocrat and his self-awareness of this fact obviously coloured his view of low-born Huntington, as can be seen from the derogatory names he called the man he had chosen to regard as his rival. Huntington believed strongly in 'fearing God and honouring the king', and kept himself out of controversial politics. Hill was an ardent critic of the British government's policy in America and spoke often about this in the pulpit, which earned for him John Wesley's warning that he should preach Christ and not political revolution. Though Hill had friends and supporters amongst the Dissenters, he could never recognise their view of the ministry and considered Independency to be quite unbiblical although he was virtually a nonconformist himself! Even when Hill was honoured by being asked to speak at the Baptist Association at Bath he irritated and insulted his hearers concerning their Dissenting views of the ministry so that the host pastor felt compelled to stand up and walk out in protest during the lecture.[24] Even when administering infant baptism in a closed Anglican

---

[24] See William Jay's biography of Hill in *The Autobiography of William Jay*, 'Rev. Rowland Hill, A.M'., Banner of Truth Trust, 1974, especially p. 357. See also *The Life of the Rev. Rowland Hill, A.M.* by his nephew Edwin Sidney, (Seeley, Burnside and

circle, he would lash out at the Baptists, although his hearers were not interested in them at all and in no danger of going over to them.

According to William Jay[25] who knew him well, Hill's worst fault was that he was very quick to take offence or feel himself personally injured even when that offence was supposed rather than real. He would also fall out with people, says Jay, because 'some tattler, or busybody, who too often beset him, and was not sufficiently frowned off' gossiped about them and Hill believed their gossip. Huntington learnt this side of Hill after the Surrey Chapel minister had been so successful in collecting money for his own work amongst Huntington's hearers. The story goes that this moved Hill to buy a copy of Huntington's first book, *The Arminian Skeleton*. After a while a friend of Huntington's called on Hill to ask him what he thought of the book. When the visitor was announced, instead of receiving him, Hill took hold of the *Arminian Skeleton* with a pair of tongs and told his footman to put it in the fire and added, 'But first of all watch that man downstairs lest he should steal the silver or anything else he can lay hands on, for his master does not hold the law to be a rule of life'.

From then on, the story continues, Hill accused Huntington of being 'a vile, filthy, stinking Antinomian' as a result of reading the book. Now Hill cannot possibly have read *The Arminian Skeleton* as the book is distinctly anti-Antinomian. Its main thrust is against Universalism and uses arguments very similar to Hill's own reasonings against Wesley and his followers. Nor did Huntington change his mind. In later works he is just as firm in his condemnation of Antinomianism as witnessed by his *The Justification of a Sinner and Satan's Lawsuit Against Him*, where he argues that the Antinomian hates true Christian experience and talks of faith and religion but is a total stranger to the power of both. It seems here that Hill had merely been listening to rumours concerning Huntington's Monkwell Street lecture and how certain people had

Seeley, 1844) who goes into detail concerning Hill's relationship to the Establishment and Dissenters.

[25] *Jay, Autobiography*, 'Rev. Rowland Hill, A.M'.

reacted to it. He then allowed these rumours to go unchecked and influence his opinion of Huntington and his book.[26]

This kind of wild eccentricity was by no means uncommon in Hill's mental and spiritual make-up, as the poet Cowper had to learn. Cowper had shown Hill many acts of kindness and entertained him at Olney on several occasions. When Hill produced a large hymnbook, he felt that Cowper would be the best person to edit and revise it and add a few hymns of his own. Though he knew Cowper very well, Hill approached him anonymously via a friend and asked him to brush up his work. Cowper, wondering what all the secrecy was about, accepted the task for his friend's sake and put a great deal of work into the volume. Now Cowper was a strict Calvinist and a vociferous enemy of Universalism but Hill, probably irritated because Cowper had altered so much of his own work, openly declared that Cowper was a Universalist!

Be that as it may, Hill now doggedly persecuted Huntington as if his own Christian life depended on it. Wherever Huntington went to preach, whether at Deptford, Greenwich, Uxbridge, or even far away Bristol, Hill was sure to follow him and occupy a 'rival' pulpit near at hand to condemn him. Whenever he heard that groups of people were reading Huntington's books he would make a journey to that area, wherever it was, and rant and rave against the books he had never read. When one of Huntington's members went to live in Sheerness in Kent, Hill seemed to know of it immediately and visited Sheerness to preach against Huntington. Often he used the same sermon time and time again so that his arguments against Huntington became general knowledge. His story that if he saw the devil running away with Huntington, he would not find it in his heart to cry, 'Stop thief!' was just one sample of his pulpit jokes at Huntington's expense. Once a sermon was read out in his chapel and was praised by all until Hill found out who had written it – Huntington. He then banned all his sheep from having anything to do with Huntington's writings on pain of excommunication. When Hill heard that an Anglican minister, W. J. Brook of Brighton, believed as did Huntington, off Hill went at breakneck speed and preached against

---

[26] The only actual criticism Hill is known to have made of *The Arminian Skeleton* concerns Huntington's reference to God being our Father and the Church our Mother. For this statement Hill said, on referring to the matter in a burial service on Bunhill Fields, Huntington ought to 'put on a fool's cap'.

Huntington in Brighton although he was otherwise a stranger to the town.

Worse was to come. Hill dwelt on Huntington's life *before* conversion to 'prove' that he 'breaks commandments himself, and teaches men the same'. This was an inexcusably unfair assault on Huntington, but Hill was reported by his followers as wishing to provoke Huntington to wrath, await his reply and then sue him for libel. This is perhaps why Huntington merely replied to Hill's unbrotherly and unfair use of his pre-conversion biography with the words, 'If you were kept entirely free and pure from every vice throughout your childhood and youth, all the better: glory in this',[27] and assured Hill that he would not take him to court for *his* slander. Hill, like Haweis, was closely connected with the budding missionary movement and both men drummed it into the heads of their missionary candidates that Huntington was a heretic. Those who worked for the societies who went to hear Huntington preach were sacked without further ado. Huntington was surprised to find young striplings sent out to talk about the mission-field condemning him from pulpits although they did not know a thing about him and were quite ignorant of his works. Hill would try to elicit from the churches where Huntington had preached a promise that they would never allow him to return. Even when he obtained such a promise, as in the case of the Greenwich Tabernacle, Hill would never again accept invitations to preach there as he considered the pulpit defiled once and for all time. Hill thus became Huntington's shadow and stuck to him so closely that in 1800 Huntington could write,

> My venerable and most pious godfather has cleaved to me with full purpose of heart, and I question whether he has ever lost sight of me in any one sermon preached by him during the last twenty-six years; and I firmly believe that he has been forced to tell a thousand lies in the name of God, only to blacken my character and to render my labours useless. But what honour can redound to God, or what good can accrue to the souls of men by such ministrations is more than I am able to make out, and

[27] Preface to *The Moral Law not Injured by the Everlasting Gospel*, p. vii.

> therefore must conclude with David, 'Let him curse'. But I cannot believe that God has led my soul through the confines of hell, and then set me down on Mount Zion, and given me sight of the King in all his beauty, for no other purpose than to furnish pulpits with reproach, and fools with sport.[28]

Huntington always called Hill his 'godfather' because of the Anglican custom whereby the godfather gives the child a name at infant baptism. Hill was the first to give Huntington the name of 'Antinomian', hence Huntington, in return, called Hill his 'godfather'. All this must have been very trying for Hill's brother, Sir Richard, who heard Huntington gladly and often attended Providence Chapel. Sir Richard always strove to bring his brother's followers into unison with those of Huntington on the grounds that the difference between them was only a matter of words and not doctrine. Huntington was always courteous in his references to Hill and sought on several occasions to be reconciled to him. Hill, however, would have none of this and if he saw Huntington in the streets he would turn tail and run for his life as if a host of devils were after him. E. Hooper wrote of Huntington's antagonist:

> Hill was a mere child compared to him [Huntington] in spiritual understanding, – the knowledge and use of Scripture, or power of argument. Aware of his deficiency and inability to cope with him on fair grounds, and perhaps envious of his greater power, he resorted to the constant and unworthy employment of unmanly and calumnious abuse. Doubtless it *was* mortifying to nature's pride (but should have rejoiced a gracious heart) to observe the greater success attending a brother's ministry, though an unlearned, but Spirit-taught Coalheaver, in the West of London, than he with his high birth and college education (though very useful and diligent) could lay claim to in the humbler and more populous districts of the South.[29]

---

[28] *Posthumous Letters*, vol. I. LIII, Letter dated 4 September, 1800, pp. 144, 145.
[29] Quoted from Hooper. *The Celebrated Coalheaver*, p. 86.

Huntington asked Hill time and time again to come up with proof of heresy or immoral living or stop his harassment. Thus Hill and his accusers, assisted by the Sunday newspapers, expended great energy in trying to find weaknesses in Huntington's moral framework so that they could find 'proof' of his lax morals in allegedly not obeying the law. They argued that once they could prove that Huntington's *life* was wrong, they could prove that his *faith* was wrong. Such 'proof' was never forthcoming. The best they could do was to refer to events before Huntington's conversion, or make much ado about nothing concerning a small, straight, black wig that Huntington wore instead of the usual long, white, curly one. In spite of Hill's wild and unjust criticism of Huntington in the most slanderous language, Huntington's words to him in defence are very guarded. Hill had used, or rather misused, Matthew chapter 5 to denounce Huntington as a preacher sent from the devil. On sending Hill a sermon showing how Matthew 5 really ought to be expounded, Huntington signed off in the covering letter with a rebuke and best wishes in stark contrast to Hill's fiery language:

> That you may discover less pepper, and more purity; less heat, and more holiness; that you may perform more good works, and say less about them; that you may part with your tea-table stories for heavenly tidings, and your old wives fables for Gospel doctrines; that you may sound the Gospel trumpet more, and your own trumpet less – is the desire and prayer of him who frankly forgives you all that is past, and hopes to take patiently all that's to come.[30]

The trouble with Hill and his followers, Huntington argued, was that they neither believed the biblical doctrine of man's total inability to keep the law and please God nor the New Testament doctrine of sanctification. Huntington believed that no one could attempt to keep the law who had not the Holy Spirit dwelling in him and had thus become a new creature in Christ. Hill rejected this, believing that the fear of the consequences of the law could keep even an unconverted

[30] End of preface to *The Moral Law not Injured.*

man from sinning to some unspecified extent. Thus when Huntington preached a sermon at Deptford on Matthew 5, Hill occupied a rival pulpit close at hand and preached on the same text, emphasizing man's duty and ability, knowing full well that Huntington would be stressing man's inability and God's ability.

Hill proclaimed, 'Though a man, in his carnal, unconverted state, will hardly keep himself from anger; yet he can easily keep himself from murder'. When Huntington received a copy of Hill's sermon, he rejected this teaching flat and told Hill in a letter, appealing, as always, to Scripture:

> That a man can easily keep himself from murder, appears plain by Hazael. Elisha told him, that he should 'slay the young men of Israel, dash their children, and rip up their women with child': who answered – 'Is thy servant a dog, that he should do this great thing?' And the next day he killed his own sovereign; and soon after acted all the rest of the bloody tragedy (2 Kings 8). To make men their own keeper is a poor doctrine: they are better kept that God keepeth.[31]

Hill went on to argue: 'People, if they are ever so vile, can keep themselves from outward actions; and generally do, for fear of the consequences that attend them. The thievish man may keep himself from thievish actions through fear of punishment. Man may refrain himself from many acts of violence'. Again Huntington rejects this teaching as dangerous, especially coming from the lips of a gospel minister and says,

> This doctrine of self-keeping, Sir, has a tendency to keep men from looking to Him who is called Jesus, because he shall save his people from their sins. The Scriptures say, that 'the strong man, armed keeps possession of the palace'; and 'the Devil takes the sinner captive at his will'. If so, where is the sinner's power to keep himself, if God leaves him? And surely we have few empty gaols, maiden-assizes, or barren hanging-days, to prove the truth of this doctrine. 'Except the Lord keep the city, the

---

[31] *Ibid.*, Preface.

> watchman waketh but in vain': and if God takes off his restraint, the sinner runs to mischief; the fear of hell-fire is not enough to deter him, much less the fear of a gallows.

Hill was, however, not done in stressing the free will of man to keep himself from falling. He says, with his words directed at Huntington, 'A man may subscribe to his meeting, and come to his meeting; he may pay his tithes, and go to his church; he may go to a shop, and pay his debts'. Again Hill encountered a brick wall in Huntington who replied,

> I do not agree with my friend Rowland in these assertions. Providence must have a hand in all this. If a man subscribes to a meeting, God must give him the money and inclination. The gold and silver is the Lord's, and so is a heart to do good therewith. A man cannot pay tithes unless God enable him to keep a farm, give him crops, and a good market. And, if he pays his debts, God's providence must favour him; for Moses says, it is God that gives power to get wealth. Read Deuteronomy Chapter 8.

False views of the place of the law

It was very important for Huntington to clamp down heavily on Hill's teaching as he believed it led to four convictions that were widely held in one form or another amongst evangelicals, especially amongst supporters of Ryland Junior, Fuller and Dr Rippon, and that Huntington found heretical. The first was that the law alone was able to force a sinner to refrain from sinning and, indeed, cause a sinner to repent. The second was that every man felt it an inner duty to repent and believe the gospel irrespective of a previous work of the law and the third was a development of the second, believing that a general appeal to this sense of duty should be given in inviting souls to come to Christ. The fourth was that, 'Christ and all his benefits are made over to every one that hears the gospel'.[32]

---

[32] See Thomas Scott's able criticism of this teaching in his *Letters and Papers*, p. 200ff.

For Huntington these doctrines were a complete rejection of all that saints such as Calvin, Bunyan and Whitefield had shown to be gospel truths. They either gave the law a power which it never had or sidestepped the law completely by stressing the inner duty of every man to accept pardon in Christ before he even knew that pardon was necessary. This was Antinomianism at its worst for Huntington. These heresies led to the paradoxical situation in Huntington's day that sinners were invited to turn to Christ without any application of the law and then invited to become sanctified by closely following the precepts of the law (or rather a modified law). To Huntington this was preaching man's ability to save himself and make himself holy.

In his preface to his printed version of his sermon on Matthew 5 Huntington deals with man's presumed ability to repent on seeing his sin. Huntington quickly dispels such a theory by addressing Hill with the words:

> Repentance is not of the will of man, Sir; nor of the will of the flesh, but of God. Judas felt his sin detestable and damnable, and he repented himself, and hanged himself. Repentance is the grant of the Father, and the gift of the Son; and is produced, under the operation of pardoning love, by the Spirit; and it is a reflection with inward contrition on the long forbearance of God, that leads to it. Pardon must be sealed, love felt, God must appear pacified, (Ezekiel 36:31) and the sinner raised to hope, before any evangelical repentance, such as needs not be repented of, can take place. When God appeared to Job, in order to turn his captivity, 'he abhorred himself, and repented'. When God 'turned Ephraim, and called him his dear son' Ephraim repented: and when the prodigal got the kiss, the ring, and the robe, then he repented. Man is not driven to repentance by a sense of sin, but drawn to it by a sense of pardon. When man's misery and God's mercy meet together on the soul; when the self-despairing child and the loving parent meet; there is repentance indeed.

Thus repentance, in Huntington's eyes, is a sovereign act of the triune God whereby he grants his elect in love what they would never ask of him of their own free will. Repentance, in the same way as the forgiveness of sins, has thus nothing whatsoever to do with a human, selfish, feeling sorry for doing something which has harmful consequences, but it is a gift from God (Acts 5:31, 32).

Huntington is just as God-centred when dealing with sanctification as he is when dealing with repentance. In a 'Word to the Reader' which he prefaced to his published sermon on Matthew 5 he stresses all that he found lacking in Hill's remarks on sanctification in his anti-Huntington sermon. He goes through the scriptural use of the word, showing how it is God who sanctifies his elect, and not the elect who sanctify themselves. In the Old Testament God sanctified the seventh day (Genesis 2:3), the first-born of Israel (Numbers 8:17, 18) and also the sacrifices for sin which pointed to Christ our righteousness. In the New Testament we read that Jude writes to 'them that are sanctified by God the Father, and preserved in Jesus Christ, and called' (Jude 1). Here Huntington notes that Jude is referring to the predestination to adoption of sons through Jesus Christ and the fact that he makes his elect meet for glory. Huntington backs this up by quoting Hebrews 10:10, which tells us of God's will in Christ, 'by ... which ... will we are sanctified through the offering of the body of Jesus Christ once for all'. We read further: 'For by one offering he hath perfected for ever them that are sanctified' (Hebrews 10:14). These Scriptures are heavy reading for those who believe that Christ merely provided salvation so that the believer, by works of merit, could secure this salvation.

Actually all the criticism by the Connexion churches and by Rowland Hill and the Fullerites proved counter-productive to their own causes. Crowds left Huntington when the cry of 'Antinomian' was raised and flocked to the other evangelical churches. There, however, they found that though the law was preached, holier lives were not in evidence and those same crowds flocked back to Huntington after only a few weeks. Worse for Hill and Co., many souls who were 'in a profession', i.e., thought they were converted, went to churches such as Surrey Chapel and came under the law that was preached to supposed 'Christians'. This served as a school-master to really bring them to Christ. They found, however, that the grace of the Lord Jesus Christ, the love of God and the fellowship of the Holy Spirit were not applied as efficiently as at Providence Chapel, so many a member of these churches took a step forward in faith and joined Huntington's church.

Huntington's followers were also strengthened by those who were excommunicated from their churches for not believing that sinners could be turned to Christ by a mere appeal to their duty to believe the gospel. Huntington saw this development as natural because he felt that leaving a sinner without a knowledge of his own sinful self could never be a basis for preaching the gospel. On the other hand, pointing a Christian continually back to the law points him merely back to his old pre-conversion self. It does not point him to success in Christ but failure in himself. It makes the believer crucify Christ afresh as he is forced by his pastor to live his life as if Christ had not died for him but had left him under the law. This is why Huntington looked upon the Countess of Huntingdon's men and Hill as 'Law-men' or as 'British Pharisees'.

Whether it was the followers of the Countess of Huntingdon, Rowland Hill or the associates of Andrew Fuller and the Rylands, all these people were unanimous in calling Huntington an Antinomian. Huntington believed strongly that his aggressors were the Antinomians but he was never so vociferous in proclaiming this as his antagonists were in branding him with the infamous name. Thus the name of 'Antinomian' has traditionally stuck with Huntington today, especially in the minds of those Reformed believers who have adopted Amyraldianism and Neonomianism. It is now necessary to see if there is any truth in this allegation.

Chapter 8

The Antinomian Controversy

First of all it is necessary to examine the word 'Antinomian' and see if it could possibly be used to describe Huntington's theology. The word in its derivation means 'against law' and apparently Paul was the first Christian to be openly charged with Antinomianism, when he was accused of preaching righteousness without the deeds of the law (Romans 3). As he professed to have a righteousness that was not obtained by means of the law, his adversaries believed that he had no righteousness whatsoever and thus taught absolute licentiousness. Paul defended himself with the Christian gospel of the righteousness of Christ bringing justification to all believers, as the prophets and indeed the law itself had foreseen.

What is an Antinomian?

Historically speaking, the word was coined in the disputations between Luther, represented by Melanchthon, and Johann Agricola. Melanchthon taught that the moral law was necessary to promote a conviction of sin and repentance, whereas Agricola (termed an Antinomian by Luther) believed that repentance came by the working of the Holy Spirit in the sinner and is thus the fruit not of the law but of the gospel. The debate was never really settled and, by the eighteenth century, although the term had become a fashionable word, it was obviously being used with a great variety of unclear meanings.

Wesley, for instance, called all Calvinists 'Antinomians' and referred to their use of the phrase, 'the imputed righteousness of Christ', as 'Antinomian jargon'. In this connection he even argued that Abraham did not have Christ as the object of his faith at all when righteousness was imputed to him![1]

Augustus Toplady was equally sure that all Arminians were Antinomians saying,

> The Arminians have of late made a huge cry about Antinomians! Antinomians! From the abundance of experience the mouth is apt to speak. The modern Arminians see so much real Antinomianism among themselves, and in their own tents, that Antinomianism is become the predominant idea, and the favourite watchword of the party. Because they have got the plague, they think everybody else has.[2]

Scott, as shown earlier, believed that there were Antinomians both on the Calvinistic and on the Arminian sides. Calvinists even accused other Calvinists of being Antinomians. Scott himself criticised John Newton severely by stating that his ministry produced 'swarms of Antinomians' in Olney.[3] He wrote notes on Bunyan's *Pilgrim's Progress* for publication because he felt that those who had done such work before him were tainted with Antinomianism,[4] although the editors included several pioneers of the Evangelical Revival. The story goes that John Newton told William Wilberforce that William Romaine produced Antinomians by his preaching.[5]

It is extremely difficult to work out what exactly these men meant by the term or how serious they were in their use of it. Recognizing the confusion associated with the word, there were various attempts in the eighteenth century to give it a proper definition. The Rev. Richard

---

[1] See Wesley's *Journal* for 1 December, 1767; 9 October, 1777

[2] From 'Free Will and Merit Fairly Examined', *The Works of Augustus Toplady, B.A.* 1794, Sprinkle Publications reprint, 1987, p. 358. See also p. 319 and pp. 430-432.

[3] See Scott, *Letters and Papers*, pp. 315-317. Scott also accuses Newton of being an Eli and a gossip and not keeping his station, so losing all authority and influence.

[4] *Ibid.*, p. 133.

[5] Overton and Relton, *The History of the English Church*, Macmillan, 1906, vol. I. p. 175.

Cecil, Newton's biographer and member of the Eclectic Society thus defined Antinomianism as:

> An error which sets up the Grace of God, in opposition to His Government: according it makes light of the evil of sin – the necessity of repentance – and the evidence and excellence of holiness; and all this upon the specious pretence of exalting and glorifying the work of Christ. But his work was not only to die *for* the sins of His people, but also to save them *from* their sins, and to put his Law into their hearts. The truth therefore as it is in Jesus respects what he does *in* them as well as what He *did for* them; but as half of the truth is a lie, so is the lie of Antinomianism, that mystery of iniquity. Pride will lead the Pharisee to object to the humbling tendency of Gospel doctrines; and corruption will lead the Antinomian to resist the obligation of Gospel precepts. But one error is not to be cured by another error – but by Truth.[6]

If this be a true definition of the term 'Antinomian', then Huntington could never be called by that name by any stretch of the imagination. Writing to the Rev. J. Jenkins around 1796 about how God enlightens his people, Huntington says:

> I have no doubt but thy aims are right, for I am sure that that preacher that exposes the vileness of human nature, and preaches the purity, spirituality, and unlimited demands of the law; that sets forth the sinner's need of a Saviour, the suitableness and the worth of him, and that debases the creature; and who enforces the necessity of regeneration, spiritual fruitfulness, spiritual service, and a life and walk in faith, shall not err in these things.

Augustus Montague Toplady, who, like Huntington, was wrongly accused time and time again of being an Antinomian, defined such a heresy as teaching:

[6] Hooper, *The Celebrated Coalheaver*, p. 89.

> That believers are released from all obligations to observe the moral law as a rule of external obedience: That in consequence of Christ's having wrought out a justifying righteousness for us, we have nothing to do but to sit down, eat, drink and be merry: that the Messiah's merits supersede the necessity of personal inherent sanctification; and that all our holiness is in Him, not in ourselves; that the aboundings of divine grace give sanction to the commission of sin; and in a word that the whole preceptive law of God is not established, but repealed and set aside from the time we believe in Christ.[7]

Toplady concludes that if a man acts according to such principles, he must be a devil incarnate, yet such principles are attributed to Huntington. How different are Huntington's own testimonies of his own longing for holiness and his sense of being burdened by sin! After explaining to a correspondent the history of salvation, Huntington goes on to write:

> God has left in all his children the old crop, to remind us of our base origin, to hide pride from our eyes, to exclude boasting from our lips, and to keep us from putting any confidence in the flesh. It is to exercise our grace, especially patience; to make us watchful, to make us sensible of the depth of man's fall, and, finally, to exalt the grace of God; to make us sick of self, and sick of the world, sick of sin, and to teach us to prize the great Physician, and to make us long for that perfect rest which remaineth to the people of God.[8]

Speaking of the penitent believer's exercise of holy faith, Huntington says:

> Such a soul, hungering and thirsting after righteousness; fixing his longing eyes upon Jesus; mourning, sighing, and praying to him, with sincere and honest confessions; pleading the

---

[7] A. Toplady, *Complete Works*, 'A Caveat Against Unsound Doctrine', p. 319, 1794. Sprinkle Publications reprint, 1987.

[8] *Posthumous Letters*, Vol. III, Bensley, 1815, Letter CCCCLXIV.

> promises; loathing himself in his own sight; acknowledging his guilt before God; pleading the blood and righteousness of Christ; covered with shame and confusion; driven on by a sense of want, and encouraged by the kind invitations in the Word of God; such a soul, I say, is an army with banners.

It would not be easy to find in the writings of Huntington's accusers such vivid descriptions of a soul who hates sin and loves his Saviour.

Huntington's faithful biographer Thomas Wright must have the last word in this list of definitions. He wrote, 'An Antinomian, be it observed, is one who holds the opinion that Christians are freed from obligations to keep the law of God. He is supposed to say to himself, "I am one of the elect I am saved. Do what I will, saved I shall be. I may therefore indulge in what sins I please."' Faced with the evidence of Huntington's hatred of sin and love for all God's laws, he can only conclude, 'It need scarcely be said that Huntington held no such views'.[9]

Huntington, as always stressing the need to consider the whole Bible, felt himself that the run-of-the-mill definitions of Antinomianism did not go far enough. They were not specific enough in defining just which laws of God the Antinomian was supposed to reject and they were not New Testament-centred enough for his liking. They also gave the false impression that striving to keep the moral law was tantamount to keeping the New Testament will of God. He preferred to see a definition which showed up the Antinomian as rejecting in his heart the sum total of the counsel of God as revealed in the whole Bible. His definition also included those as Antinomians who believed that Christian ethics are merely limited to keeping the Decalogue as an outward ordinance. He thus wrote:

> A real Antinomian, in the sight of God, is one who 'holds the truth in unrighteousness'; who has gospel notions in his head, but no grace in his heart. He is one that makes a profession of Christ Jesus, but was never purged by his blood, renewed by his Spirit,

[9] T. Wright, *The Life of William Huntington, S.S.*, London 1909, p. 190.

> nor saved by his power. With him carnal ease passes for gospel peace; a natural assent of the mind for faith; insensibility for liberty; and daring presumption for the grace of assurance. He is alive without the law, the sentence of the 'moral law' having never been sent home to him. The 'law of faith' was never sealed on him, the 'law of truth' was never received by him, nor the 'law of liberty' proclaimed to him. He was never arraigned at, nor taken from, the 'throne of judgment'. He was never justified at the 'throne of grace', nor acquitted at the 'bar of equity'. The tremendous attribute of righteousness was never seen or felt by him. The righteousness of the law was never fulfilled by him; the righteousness of faith was never imputed to him; nor the fruits of righteousness brought forth by him. He is an enemy to the power of God, to the experience of the just, and to every minister of the Spirit; and is in union with none but hypocrites, whose uniting ties are 'the gall of bitterness and the bonds of iniquity'. He is one that often changes his opinion, but was never changed in heart. He turns to many sects and parties, but never turns to God. In word he is false to Satan, in heart he is false to God; false to Satan by uttering truth, and false to God by a false profession. He is a false reprover in the world, and in the household of faith a false brother. He is a child of Satan in the congregation of dissemblers, and a bastard in the congregation of the righteous. By mouth he contends for a covenant that cannot save him, and in heart he hates the covenant that can. His head is at Mount Calvary, his heart and soul at Mount Sinai. He is a Pharisee at Horeb, and a hypocrite in Zion. He is a transgressor of the law of works, and a rebel to the law of faith; a sinner by the ministry of the letter, and an unbeliever by the ministry of the Spirit. As a wicked servant, he is cursed by the eternal law; and, as an infidel, he is damned by the everlasting gospel. And this is a real Antinomian in the sight of God.[10]

What Huntington is saying is that a real Antinomian is such because he has a form of godliness but he denies the power thereof. He has a part-codex without the wherewithal to keep it. Though he might even

[10] *Moses Unveiled in the Face of Christ*, Collingridge, vol. v. pp. 557, 558.

profess to live according to God's laws, he rejects completely the soteriological purpose of the New Testament laws and empties the Old Testament laws of their theological and condemnatory content. His faith is thus just a bluff, or at the most a mere empty shell. He needs, according to Huntington, to put on the new man and, like Abraham, trust in Christ for his righteousness, having the law written on his heart and perpetually applied by the work of the Holy Spirit.

This was no new doctrine but had been taught by such Puritan writers as Walter Marshall (1628-80) in his work *The Gospel Mystery of Sanctification* over a century before. Marshall taught that nobody could ever hope to practise the duties of the law without first partaking of the comforts of the gospel. This was also the faith of James Hervey and William Cowper[11] but this kind of teaching had become unpopular with many of Huntington's generation. Scott, for instance, thought Marshall had been 'of very bad consequence to numbers',[12] believing him to give the Christian a false feeling of assurance. It seems that critics of Marshall, such as Scott, felt that his teaching was all too passive. There was not enough, 'Let us be up and doing', in his message.

Huntington would react to this kind of criticism by showing that only when a man has become a new creation in Christ and is empowered by the Holy Spirit can he be 'up and doing' in a real gospel sense. This being 'up and doing' in a real gospel sense was, however, quite absent from the Decalogue, which merely taught: 'Do this and live, or refrain from doing this and die'.

What Huntington teaches is really a solution to the Antinomian debate carried out by Melanchthon and Agricola which was never really settled. Melanchthon believed that the moral law produced conviction of sin and repentance. As we have seen in Huntington's words against Hill, the 'Coalheaver' rejected such a doctrine as incomplete. He pointed out how Judas was convicted of sin but instead of repenting in the New Testament way, he committed suicide and was lost. The law, of itself, cannot turn a man to God; it can only convince him of his fallen

[11] Cowper's *Works*, King and Ryskamp, 1982, letter to Martin Madan, p. 107.
[12] Scott, *Letters and Papers*, p. 202.

state. Agricola maintained that repentance was not the fruit of the law but the gospel, and the law has no relevance for the Christian. Huntington also rejected such a view as being unscriptural although most of his enemies, strangely enough, accuse him of adopting Agricola's teaching. Anyone who has read Huntington's works against John Ryland Senior and Miss Maria De Fleury will know how he trounced those fellows-at-arms for making light of the moral law in the lives of believers. He often spoke of 'being in the furnace', or 'tasting the rod', meaning God was dealing with him as a Christian for breaking the moral law. In a way, Huntington combined both Melanchthon's and Agricola's views. The law convicts the sinner of his sin and places him under condemnation of death. God's love draws him to pardon in Christ and grants him repentance and faith. The whole law is now written on his heart and the Holy Spirit, using Christ's righteousness as his pattern, coaches the saved sinner throughout his Christian life utilizing the moral law (amongst other biblical precepts) as a rod of correction.

To sum up the whole controversy from Huntington's point of view we can do no better than to quote Huntington's words in *The Law Established by the Faith of Christ*, where he simply says:

> The ten commandments, exclusive of other parts of Scripture, are not sufficient rule for the real believer's life, walk, and conversation. And that the will of God, which is the only rule, is not wholly revealed in the Decalogue is plain, for if it had, there would have been no more of it revealed in another dispensation. For if the first covenant had been faultless, then no place would have been sought for the second.

Thus William Huntington turned the tables on his critics saying in effect, 'Whom are you calling an Antinomian? If you do not believe as I do, you must be Antinomians yourselves as you reject the whole counsel of God as revealed in Christ, who fulfilled the law for his elect's sake'.

Huntington's high view of the Word of God

In his fight against poor teaching in the churches, Huntington stressed the need to base all doctrine on the whole of God's Word. He believed strongly that Arminianism had invaded almost every Calvinistic stronghold and brought with it an Old Testament interpretation of the believer's walk with God. This was to the detriment of the New Testament teaching of a life in the Spirit with Christ's own righteousness to guide the believer and God's own law imprinted on his heart. Writers who recognised Huntington's high position as a winnower in the history of the church stressed that he was one of the very few who preached the whole gospel from the whole Bible and could expound it in such a systematic way that each sinner and saint could see all of the steps necessary to find peace with God and live a life of holiness. Indeed it is Huntington's achievement that he took his hearers' and readers' gaze from the narrow doctrinal controversies of his age and spread before them the whole counsel of God for his whole church. This was an extremely urgent task for Huntington to perform as the churches and denominations of his days were rapidly being formed based on single doctrines, or ideas of church government, which were emphasised to the total exclusion of others.

Huntington had thus a very 'high' view of the Word of God and his eulogies of the way God has revealed his will to mankind make for the very best in Huntington's writings. His most thorough assessment of the Bible is to be found in his *History of Little Faith.* It is a rather lengthy passage but every word is deserving of being quoted as it is a wonderful compendium of true Christian discipline and turns the tables completely on all who wrongly charge Huntington with being an Antinomian and it shows clearly Huntington's contribution to doctrinal soundness in his role as God's winnower.

> I have sometimes thought, that a nation must be truly blessed, if it were governed by no other laws than those of that blessed book. It is so complete a system, that nothing can be added to it or taken from it. It contains everything needful to be known and done. It affords a *copy* for a king, Deuteronomy 17:18, and a *rule* for a subject. It gives instruction and counsel to a senate, authority and direction for a magistrate. It cautions a witness, requires an impartial verdict of a jury, and furnishes the judge with his sentence. It sets the husband as lord of the household and the wife as mistress of the table: tells *him* how to rule, and *her*

how to manage. It entails honour to parents, and enjoins obedience to children. It prescribes and limits the sway of the sovereign, the rule of the ruler, and the authority of the master, commands the subject to honour, and the servant to obey; and promises the blessing and protection of its Author to all who walk by its rules. It gives directions for weddings, and for burials: regulates *feasts* and *fasts*, mournings and rejoicings; and orders labour for the day, and rest for the night. It promises food and raiment, and limits the use of both. It points out a faithful and an eternal *Guardian* to the departing husband and father; tells him with whom to leave his fatherless children, and in whom his widow is to trust, Jeremiah 49:11; and promises a father to the former, and a husband to the latter. It teaches a man how to set his house in order, and how to make his will. It appoints a dowry for the wife, entails the right of the first-born, and shews how the younger branches shall be left: it defends the rights of all; and reveals vengeance to every defrauder, over-reacher, or oppressor. It is the first book, the best book and the oldest book in all the world. It contains the choicest matter, gives the best instruction, and affords the greatest pleasure and satisfaction, that ever was revealed. It contains the best laws and profoundest mysteries that ever were penned. It brings the best of tidings, and affords the best of comfort, to the inquiring, and disconsolate. It exhibits life and immortality from everlasting, and shews the Way to eternal glory. It is a brief recital of all that is passed, and a certain prediction of all that is to come. It settles all matters in debate, resolves all doubts and eases the mind and conscience of all their scruples. It reveals the only living and true God, and shews the way to him: it sets aside all other gods, and describes the vanity of them, and of all that trust in them. In short, it is a book of law, to shew right and wrong; a book of wisdom, that condemns all folly, and makes the foolish wise; a book of truth, that detects all lies, and confutes all errors; and a book of life, that gives life, and shews the way from everlasting death. It is the most compendious book in all the world; the most ancient, authentic, and the most entertaining history, that ever was published. It contains the most ancient antiquities, strange events, wonderful occurrences, heroic deeds, unparalleled wars. It describes the celestial, terrestrial, and infernal worlds; and the origin of the angelic myriads, human tribes, and devilish legions. It will instruct the most accomplished mechanic, and the profoundest artist; it will teach the best rhetorician, and exercise every power of the most skilful arithmetician, Revelation 13:18; puzzle the wisest anatomist, and exercise the nicest critic. It corrects the vain philosopher, and confutes the wise astronomer; it exposes the subtle sophist, and makes diviners mad. It is a complete code of laws, a perfect body of divinity, an unequalled narrative, a book of lives, a book of travels, and a book of voyages. It is the best *covenant* that ever was agreed on, the best deed that ever was sealed, the best *evidence* that ever was produced, the best *will* that ever was made, and the best *testament* that ever was signed. To understand it, is to be wise indeed; to be ignorant of it, is to be destitute of wisdom. It is the King's best *copy*, the magistrate's best *rule*, the housewife's best *guide*, the servant's best *directory*, and the young man's best *companion*. It is the schoolboy's *spelling-book*, and the learned man's *masterpiece*. It contains a choice *grammar* for a novice, and a profound *mystery* for a sage. It is the ignorant man's dictionary, and the wise man's directory. It affords knowledge of witty inventions for the *humorous*, and dark sayings for the *grave;* and is its own interpreter. It encourages the wise, the warrior, the swift, and the overcomer; and promises an eternal reward to the excellent, the conqueror, the winner, and the prevalent. And that which crowns all is, that the Author is without partiality, and without hypocrisy; in whom is no variableness, or shadow of turning.

There is an interesting sequel to Huntington's glowing testimony to the Word of God. During the Papal Aggression of 1851, churches true to the gospel were keen to promote the Protestant faith and show the value of God's Word in face of the superstitions of the Roman Catholics. The rector of a large town in the Midlands thus looked for suitable material which he could recommend in defence of the Bible as a sure guide to salvation. After some searching, he found a piece of writing under the title *On the Excellency of the Holy Scriptures* and was so struck by the truth it proclaimed that he decided to have it circulated and recommended it strongly from the pulpit, saying that he 'could not inform them who was the writer, but had no doubt it was by some Eminent Divine'. What the rector did not know was soon discovered by the editor of the Stamford Mercury, who published in his newspaper 'that the Author was a London Dissenting Minister named Huntington, once a Coalheaver, in whose works it could be seen as part of Dialogue XI, of the *History of Little Faith*'. The fact that this marvellous testimony to the all-sufficiency of God's Word was penned by an ex-coalheaver and not by an 'eminent divine' so shocked the rector that he stopped circulating the article and forbade his flock from doing so.

Chapter 9

The Law Established In A Life Of Faith

It is now time to look in detail at Huntington's doctrine of the Mosaic law in relation to a life of faith as it is central to his teaching concerning the redeemed elect of God. Most of his writings on the topic were published in the 1790s, works such as *Moses Unveiled in the Face of Christ* and *The Child of Liberty in Legal Bondage*, being originally lectures given at Monkwell Street to clear up points raised by Rowland Hill and his fellow-antagonists. These writings are mostly highly polemic and apologetic in nature. The reaction to Huntington's doctrine, arose, however, from his teaching in the mid-eighties and his views given then were expounded in a more devotional and practical atmosphere, devoid of the overtones of conflict and controversy.

The lecture which caused such a wild reaction on the part of Haweis and the Countess of Huntingdon was never published but before giving his lecture at Monkwell Street. Huntington had preached on the subject in his own chapel on 1 January, 1786 and this sermon was published under the title *The Law Established by the Faith of Christ*. In it Huntington expounds Romans 3:31, 'Do we then make void the law through faith? God forbid: yea, we establish the law'.

In his introduction to the text Huntington explains how Paul is defending himself against the accusation that the law of faith by which Christians live rules out the moral implications of the Mosaic law. These critics argued that as Paul did not believe he was under the law but under grace he could live an Antinomian life. Paul responds by saying that such a person would well deserve damnation (Romans 3:8) but living by the law of faith in no way makes the law of Moses void (Romans 3:31). Here, in a nutshell, is Huntington's own situation. Because he argued that the just shall live by faith and faith involves laws which go far beyond the Mosaic conception, his enemies falsely and quite illogically concluded that he reserved for himself the right to live a life outside of all biblical moral precepts. Paul explains in Romans 3:4 that, whether his critics believe him or not, his doctrine is God's doctrine and 'Let God be true, but every man a liar'. This was also Huntington's position.

Next Paul goes on to argue that the knowledge of sin comes via the law but righteousness and justification come via the grace of the Lord Jesus Christ (Romans 3:21-24). This righteousness and justification are won for the elect sinner by Christ's full obedience to the law and his righteousness is then imputed to the elect. Thus within the law every man is condemned but outside of the law those are justified who have Christ's righteousness put on them by a free act of God's sovereign grace. Thus the believer owes his allegiance to the law of faith which has saved him, and not to the law of Moses which had condemned him. Paul adds that this is no new doctrine, as the law itself and the prophets have already witnessed to its truth in the Old Testament dispensation (Romans 3:21).

After outlining this fact, Huntington says provokingly, 'Now I suppose you will run off, and declare, that we give a loose rein to all sin, corrupt the morals of the people, make void the whole law of God, and destroy all good works, by preaching free grace, and free justification by faith in Christ Jesus. But stop, do not conclude too hastily – we do not injure, nor make void the law through faith – God forbid: it is established this way and no other'.

After this introduction and as a first step in showing how the law is established in a life of faith, Huntington gives seven headings covering the ground of his study. First, he tackles what the law is and its lawful use. Secondly, he explains what the law can and what it cannot do. Thirdly, he deals with the meaning of faith and then goes on, fourthly, to prove that faith establishes the law. Fifthly, he shows who those are who make void the law and then, sixthly, he enquires 'whether the Law of itself, exclusive of the promise, be a sufficient, and a scriptural rule, for the real Christian's life, walk and conversation'. Lastly, Huntington deals with the question 'whether setting the law permanently before all ranks of Christians as a rule of life, can with propriety be called speaking the language or doing the work of an evangelist'.

The nature and lawful use of the law

Under his first heading Huntington limits his dealing with the law to the Decalogue as given in Exodus 20 and Deuteronomy 5. This is because the 'Decalogue is the main root from which all other trunks and branches were drawn by Moses and the prophets'. Also it was in relation to the Ten Commandments that Huntington's critics accused him of licentiousness. Huntington argues that the law reveals much of the perfect mind and will of God, but not all of it, as the mystery of his full mind and will is only revealed through the gospel of Christ. If the law had been the full revelation of the will of God, there would have been no need for a further revelation in Christ.

The law, Huntington argues, is holy, because it reveals the holiness of God and shows up our own filthiness by which we see that the carnal mind is at enmity with God. The law is good, says Huntington, because it commends only what we know to be good and forbids all evil. The law is immutable as it shows that 'God is one mind and no one can turn him'. The law too is just, according to Huntington, because in it we see how our good God shows his displeasure at our sin and also that we have not the least ground of hope in the law to escape God's justice. This makes the law also eternal as it shows God's eternal wrath upon sin and that its transgressors 'shall go away into everlasting punishment'. Huntington dwells some time on this point as some evangelicals led by Bishop Newton were teaching that God would call a general armistice one day for all those in hell, including the devil himself. Thus Huntington says, 'I know some of our troublers of Israel, who pretend to be famous Hebreians and Grecians, to support the new doctrines of a gaol-delivery for the damned in hell tell us, that eternal and everlasting in the original languages have a limited sense; but I have found none so daring as to affirm that it admits of a limited sense when applied to the eternity of Jehovah, or to the eternal happiness of the saints'.

Regarding the lawful use of the law, Huntington says that it is there to sound forth the dreadful alarm of God which batters down all self-righteousness and the false peace that attends it. The law is of the same nature as the Lawgiver, i.e., spiritual, just as the sinner is carnal. Thus when the law is enforced its spiritual meaning must be made clear. The conscience of the sinner must be laid open and his carnality must be disclosed. Likewise the unlimited demands of the law in all the characteristics mentioned above must be insisted on to put to flight any legal hope the sinner may have. He must see that the covenant of works is a killing covenant and places him under the curse of the law. Using the law lawfully is to stop all human boasting and present the sinner guilty before God.

Most of Huntington's enemies would have no quarrel with him concerning this usage of the law. They accused him, however, of going no further and refraining from using the Mosaic law at all in teaching Christians. Here Huntington says quite clearly that 'A gospel minister may gospelise any part of the law, and set it, disarmed of its curse and condemning power, in a beautiful light before the eyes of a real Christian'. He says this because such a divine standard appeals to the new man and is part – but not all – of the righteous will of God that the Holy Spirit testifies to the heart of a believer.

What the law can and cannot do

Going on to what the law *can* do, Huntington says that it can discover sin, as the knowledge of sin comes by the law. It can give sin an advantage, as 'When the commandment came, sin revived'. 'Sin, taking occasion by the commandment wrought in me all manner of concupiscence ... deceived me, and by it slew me' (Romans 7:8-11). The law can give strength to sin, which fixes itself on a man and delivers him up as a condemned criminal (1 Corinthians 15:56). The law can furnish the unjustified sinner with an accuser in the presence of God and the law can separate the sinner fully from his Maker. The law, however, *cannot* subdue sin or give the sinner any dominion over it. It can give man no quarters, no respite, no second chance. It cannot pardon a sinner or make allowances for 'giddy youth and doting age'. The law cannot quicken or give life and they that live under it are dead in a life of death. The law cannot justify any man nor, of itself, without God's effective call in Christ, bring a man to his Saviour. Thus it is quite scandalous, in Huntington's eyes, to say that the Decalogue is the only rule of life.

Huntington goes on to argue that, 'He that cometh to God, must believe that he is, and that he is a rewarder of all them that diligently seek him' (Hebrews 11:6). He points out, however, that it is not by trusting in the law that sinners come to this awareness, as those who 'stick the closest to the law are the farthest from God'. Such knowledge can only come by God's electing revelation. 'As many as were ordained to eternal life, believed' (Acts 13:48). In the Old Testament this assurance came through the covenants of promise which pointed the way to a better covenant, and not via the law (Ephesians 2:12). Thus, according to Huntington, the Old Testament ceremonial law is much more able to point a sinner to Christ than the Decalogue as in this law one finds the types of better things to come. Here Huntington takes John Wesley to task for so emphasizing the law that grace takes second place. Wesley called the imputed righteousness of Christ 'imputed nonsense', and the electing decree of God 'a horrible decree'. He looked on the doctrines of predestination and the eternal perseverance of the saints as 'the devil's law'. Huntington outlines how God's decrees were older than creation and thus older than the devil, so they could in no wise be called 'the devil's law'. He adds that in reality Wesley's doctrine of being perfected in love through obedience to the law must be 'the devil's law' as it teaches fleshly perfection which is denied by God's law. This is no exaggeration on Huntington' s part. Wesley had clearly argued that fleshly perfection was possible by telling Hervey that if sinless perfection came first in heaven, 'It would then come too late. If sin remains in us till the day of judgment, it will remain for ever'. In the same letter, he says, 'No one who is not conformed to the law of God here, shall see the Lord in glory'.[1]

---

[1] See Wesley's letter to James Hervey concerning his book *Theron and Aspasio*. My copy with Hervey's glorious answer is in *The Works of The Rev. James Hervey, A.M.*, Edinburgh, 1837, pp. 472-480.

The meaning of faith

Now Huntington expounds what faith is by dealing with the object of faith, the doctrine of faith, the grace of faith and the life of faith. The object of faith is the triune God, a fact that Huntington had to emphasise at this time as many Dissenting churches were turning to Unitarianism and Arianism. This he proves by Scriptures such as the reference to being baptised in the name (singular) of the Father, Son and Holy Spirit. Regarding the doctrine of faith, Huntington refers to Galatians 3:1-23 and Titus 1:1 saying that it is the faith of God's elect and thus, contrary to the faith of the Arminians, must include the doctrines of particular redemption, free justification and imputed righteousness. The grace of faith is shown in that only those who are given to believe these doctrines can really speak of 'the righteousness of faith'. The life and feats of faith are, according to Huntington, boundless as 'All things are possible to him that believeth'. Those who live this life and perform these feats, like Abraham of old, give God the glory as they now 'live by the faith of the Son of God', and not by their own powers. Faith is a grace that empties the creature and makes him cling to Christ and this will show itself by the faith-bearers being also fruit-bearers.

Faith establishes the law

Huntington has now reached his fourth point which is that faith establishes the law. By preaching the fact that Christ satisfied the demands of the law we show that the law is 'obeyed, magnified, and made honourable by one who is equal to the law-giver, and consequently equal to the law'. Thus Justice has received her utmost demands in Christ. As all believers are 'in Christ', they have satisfied the law solely through being in him. Clearly then, by preaching faith in Christ one shows how the law has been established and fulfilled in him. Those who share this faith believe in him 'whom God hath set forth to be a propitiation, through faith in his blood, to declare ... at this time his righteousness that [God] might be just, and [yet] the justifier of him which believeth in Jesus' (Romans 3:25).

Faith establishes the law by showing that the law, disarmed of its curse and condemning power, is in the heart of Jesus our Mediator (Psalm 40:8). It used to be shut up in the ark, which was a type of Christ, and now it is kept (in both senses of the word) in Christ's heart. Those who are 'in Christ', that is 'the children of the New Covenant', also have the law written in their hearts. This, according to the prophets, is the law's proper place. Thus the law is only truly established in the hearts of believers who are not without law to God but 'under the law to Christ' (1 Corinthians 9:21).

The law is also established by those in Christ when they show that a covenant of works demands the perfect obedience, on penalty of damnation, of all the unconverted offspring of Adam. The just Lawgiver is bound by his own law to pass sentence on all those who die under it. The law is established when God says, 'Depart from me, ye cursed, into everlasting fire, prepared for the devil and his angels' (Matthew 25:41). After showing how the law is established both in the hearts of believers and in the justice of God, Huntington can conclude that, 'We affirm, that though Christ has magnified the law, and made it honourable; yet he never abolished it; he fulfilled it but never repealed it or made it void in any sense whatsoever'. This was a very necessary statement in view of the many evangelical Neonomians of his day.

Huntington goes on to argue that faith establishes the law in every true believer by showing him what bounds have been fixed to prevent iniquity. If the believer steps over these bounds he will receive the rod of his Father's displeasure. But, 'If his children forsake my law, and walk not in my judgments; if they break my statutes, then will I visit their transgressions with the rod, and their iniquity with stripes. Nevertheless my lovingkindness will I not utterly take from him, nor suffer my faithfulness to fail' (Psalm 89:30-33). In the face of such evidence it is indeed surprising that a modern accuser of Huntington's can write that in Huntington's theology, 'God sees no sin in believers, and is never angry with them'.[2] What would this writer make of the numerous passages in Huntington's works where he speaks of God's 'threshing instruments having teeth' which he uses against rebellious Christians, dealing out 'reproofs and rebukes, judgments and calamities'[3] to purge the believer throughout his earthly life. This shows

---

[2] *The Voice of Years*, Banner of Truth magazine, July 1988, p. 8.

[3] See letter dated 9 February, 1795. See also letters written 10 October, 1808 and 4 July, 1802 which deal with God's purging of backsliders and his rebellious children.

the difference between those who die under the law and those who are dead to the law but alive to Christ. The law does not dominate the latter but the faithful rod of God is applied to them when they sin to keep them on course. The law is further established in that the child of God has now a friend in the law, and not an enemy. The law allows for a surety and finds no capital fault when the child of God is disobedient, as it balances off the debt with the imputed righteousness of Christ. Put more simply, when a child of God falls, he does not fall from grace.

Those who make void the law

Now Huntington looks at those who do not establish the law and thus make it null and void. The Deist, for instance, knows neither the Saviour nor the gospel. He is ignorant of the judgment to come and thus recognises no judge and consequently no law. Likewise the Universalist makes the law void because he believes all will be saved and there is no need for justice or judgment. Even the do-gooders who believe God will recognise their good works and reward them make the law void as they take away all its application to truth and justice. The blind guide who tells us that Christ mitigated the law and taught that one has only to follow his holy life and imitate him and that in itself will be acceptable to God makes the law void as it explains away the wrath of God and the sentence of the law. The Arian obviously makes void the law, as he makes Christ a mere man who would have been under the law like anyone else. Lastly, Huntington points out that those ministers who mix up preaching works with preaching grace are making the law void as they teach two conflicting ways of salvation both of which cannot possibly be true. They not only make the law void by giving it a function that God never intended for it, but they also make void the gospel by limiting its scope.

Huntington uses elsewhere the example of the seeker after holiness who went to a well-known London minister to ask how he should lead a true Christian life. The minister answered, 'Keep one eye on Christ and the other on the law'. Such a 'squinting' gospel almost amounted to blasphemy for Huntington as it suggested a dual way of salvation. Huntington always taught that the believer must keep both eyes on

---

Huntington taught clearly that God's 'threshing' of his children would only be completed when they reached glory.

Jesus, the Alpha and Omega of his faith, and that the law was a part of the whole counsel of God revealed in Christ, and not a rival source of salvation.

Is the law a sufficient rule of life for the Christian?

Huntington now takes up his sixth point regarding 'whether the Decalogue, of itself, exclusive of the promises and other parts of scripture, be a sufficient, and a scriptural rule for the real Christian's life, walk, and conversation'. His answer is a most definite, 'No'. For Huntington the only rule of conduct for a Christian is the whole will of God centred in Christ as revealed in the whole Bible. Many so-called evangelicals of his day tended to narrow down the whole will of God to the Decalogue alone, which was blatant heresy as far as Huntington was concerned. Even the Old Testament saints did not look to the law as their only rule of conduct, as hope in the Christ to come was an essential part of their teaching regarding righteousness. Huntington carefully shows how the law tells us nothing of our election in Christ, nor does it tell us anything about our redemption, justification and sanctification which come by Christ. The sweetest part of the will of God, the good news, is left completely out. Nor, according to Huntington, can the Decalogue sum up our 'conversation', or Christian witness to others. We must 'make known to the sons of men his mighty acts and the glorious majesty of his kingdom'.[4] Huntington accepts that the truths of the law should be part of our Christian witness, but we must also talk of everlasting love, blessed redemption, all-conquering grace, mysterious providence, the Spirit's work in our souls and a host of other gospel themes. All this, of course, is an exposition of Hebrews 7, which states that if the first covenant had been faultless, there would have been no need for the second.

The work of an evangelist

Huntington's final point is the question whether 'setting the law perpetually before all ranks of Christians as the only rule of life, can, with propriety, be called speaking the language, or doing the work of

---

[4] Psalm 145:12

an evangelist'. Again his answer is a most definite, 'Certainly not!' In his own clear way, Huntington says, 'That minister, that is always setting the law of Moses as a rule of life before all ranks of Christians, young and old, goes the ready way to bring them, whom God has justified, a second time to judgment, by setting the terrors of the judge before the child, instead of the bowels of the Father'. 'How can the law', Huntington asks, 'be preached to incline, reform, amend, convert, and bring to Christ?' It must be preached that 'God turns the sinner, makes him willing, puts his fear in his heart, and draws him to Christ, and by love unites him with him'. Of those ministers who always return to the law at the conclusion of a gospel sermon, Huntington says that they should leave their best wine until the last and adds tellingly that they are 'more like the profuse cow that gives a pailful of milk, and then kicks it over the milkmaid'.

Such preaching is not dealing faithfully with sinners, Huntington argues. When a soul, longing for redemption, cries out, 'Who shall deliver me from this body of death?' what evangelist in his right senses will point him to Sinai? He must be pointed to the forgiving love of God in Christ.

Again, however, Huntington emphasises that a believer has not done with the law after conversion and he argues, referring to the bounds set about us by the law, 'The man that breaks through these bounds, if he dies in the breach, God will break through upon him; and the believer that breaks through these bounds, God has promised to visit his sin with the rod, and his iniquity with stripes'. The believer is chastised in this way because he is God's own child who has been brought into a covenant of grace, and not of works. His minister ought to say to such a one, 'Christian, hast thou put on Jesus Christ? Then walk ye in him. Art thou in the race? Run it, looking to Jesus. Art thou in the love of God? Meditate thereon; "He will keep that man in perfect peace, whose mind is stayed on him"'.[5] Huntington argues convincingly that it is the blood of the Lamb that has brought such a sinner to God, and not the revelation of damnation.

Huntington explains that when Paul came to know God, he was told that God had chosen him so that he would know God's will, see the Just One, hear from his mouth and then be his witness to all men, telling

---

[5] Isaiah 26:3

them what he had both seen and heard (Acts 22:14, 15). When Paul wrote to the Galatians, his burden was to save them from merely having the law continually before their faces. Thus he used opposite characters from the Old Testament to show how much better the covenant of grace was than the covenant of the law. Abraham, Sarah and Isaac typified the new covenant, whereas Moses, Hagar and Ishmael illustrated the old. After showing the Galatians that not the rule of law but becoming a new creature and living a life of faith in Christ is God's will for the Christian, he concludes that 'As many as walk according to this rule, peace be on them, and mercy, and upon the Israel of God' (Galatians 6:16). It is thus obvious that the new Israel has a different rule to the old, and this rule of faith must always be put before the Christian.

Next Huntington gives a personal testimony of how the rule of faith works out in his own life by saying,

> God knows I am no scholar, nor am I endued with any shining parts or abilities; but I find, by happy experience, that the best rule to walk by, and try others and their doctrines by, is the revealed will of God, by the Spirit, in the heart, and in his word. And I believe to enforce the Spirit's work – to insist on a union in the bond of love to Christ; to declare the whole will of God as revealed in his word; to cry down priestcraft, and set up the gospel model; to preach down human inventions, and set up the will of God; to cry down the whole works of the flesh, and exalt the merits of Christ, is doing the works of an evangelist.
>
> And I believe, if God should use me as an instrument in bringing souls to the Lord, and keep me alive in my ministry; to insist on the enjoyment of a union with him; that I shall be able to bring forth as much fruit to God's honour, as those that produce them by fire; for all hot-house fruits have the worst flavour, though they always fetch the best price among the rich and the great.

Now Huntington takes those to task who say that the Ten Commandments are a schoolmaster that brings souls to Jesus Christ, thus by preaching the Decalogue, one is virtually preaching Christ. This is denied in the sermon on the grounds that Paul is here speaking of the ceremonial law whose sacrificial system was a type of Christ's sacrifice and pointed to him. Even before the Decalogue, from the days of Abel to those of Moses, the sacrificial system served as a schoolmaster to bring souls to Christ. 'Through faith he kept the passover, and the sprinkling of blood, lest he that destroyed the firstborn should touch them' (Hebrews 11:28). Again, the keeping of this law is not related to those who are under the law but to those who walk by faith. Earlier in the sermon Huntington says that even when the law teaches the way to Christ it is only because the arm of God has been revealed to them; otherwise they would not budge on their own initiative.

Fruit in the life of the believer

Huntington now goes on to argue that if the believer produces righteous fruits, it is not because he feels that Christ has begun a work in him which he should finish himself by returning to the covenant of works. It is by virtue of his union with the living vine. As the Scriptures say, 'The branch cannot bear fruit of itself, except it abide in the vine; no more can ye, except ye abide in me … He that abideth in me, and I in him, the same bringeth forth much fruit: for without me ye can do nothing'.[6] Of course, the new birth brings with it a new attitude to the law and a new respect for its standards but it is being a new creation in Christ Jesus that urges a Christian to produce fruit worthy of the Lord of the vineyard. God's word to his children is not the 'Do and live, transgress and die', of the covenant of works. In the new covenant, 'Do and live', is changed to 'Believe and live', and 'Transgress and die' has been changed to 'He that believeth shall never die'.

There is thus a mountain for Huntington which is far higher than Sinai. It is the mountain of the house of the Lord, which God has established and exalted above all mountains and from which Christ now reigns in glory. 'And many people shall go and say, Come ye, and let us go up to the mountain of the Lord, to the house of the God of Jacob; and he will teach us of his ways, and we will walk in his paths: for out of Zion shall go forth the law, and the word of the Lord from Jerusalem'.[7] William Huntington had a vision of the view from that

---

[6] John 15:5

[7] Isaiah 2:2, 3

blessed mountain which few have seen so clearly. He saw it because God's law was engraven on his heart and his trust was in Christ's love to him. Huntington's fierce enemies are sadly not able to focus their gaze on such a glorious sight because their eyes have become dim through perpetually looking backwards at tablets of stone. When Christ calls them forward, they cannot see him in his full light because the imprint of the stones is etched perpetually into their vision. Their life is a weary one indeed, struggling along in the promises of God in Christ but making Christ's easy yoke burdensome by striving to understand it by means of their capacity to keep to the letter of the law. To them Huntington has a message of hope and comfort from his Master but they will not hear it. To those who share the same vision of the glories of Christ and the glories in Christ, Huntington ends his sermon with the prayer: 'May the Father of all mercies, and God of all comfort keep us by his mighty power, through faith, to salvation; and enable us to give the world an account of the root in us, by the fruits produced by us! Thus God shall get the glory, and we the blessing. Amen'.

The doctrine reflected in Huntington's correspondence

Huntington's doctrine of the rule of faith proved to be a spring of hope and joy for his people. His letters to his correspondents are full of good counsel to stop looking to oneself for help and comfort in the trials of the old Adam but be renewed in strength in putting on the new man in Christ. 'God has founded Zion in the sacrifice of his Son', he tells one of his flock, 'and he builds her up, and establishes her by the faith of him, and faith feels all her springs of life in this city; salvation is her walls to all that are within, and all without the walls are dogs. "They that be planted in the house of the Lord, shall flourish in the courts of our God; their leaf shall be green, they shall bring forth fruit in old age to show that God is upright" (Psalm 92:13, 14)'.[8]

To another church member he writes when preaching away from home:

[8] *Gleanings of the Vintage*, Letter CLX.

I hope thou sharest in the rich repast, and sweet banquets, which (according to what I hear) you are entertained with in my absence. The good Lord is very kind and favourable to me, he hath not let me have one barren time in my soul in the pulpit, since my arrival here. Of all his creatures I am the least, and the most unworthy, and yet of all creatures the most indulged; but he will dwell with them that tremble at his word, he will love them that love him, and them that honour him he will honour. No state so safe, so sure, as that of being poor in spirit, and dependent on his fulness; he knows them that trust in him, and them that trust in themselves; he will humble the proud and exalt the humble.[9]

To one undergoing tribulations he writes:

Much tribulation must be the lot of all those who enter the kingdom of God; but the Captain of our salvation was made perfect through sufferings, and is touched with the feelings of our infirmities, being tempted in all points like as we are, and therefore able and willing to succour those that are tempted. If the dear Redeemer indulges thee with access to himself, with union, communion, and fellowship with him, this will keep thee out of the world, and from the company of it. It will be thy only refuge, refreshing, delight, and felicity in this world; your home will be a Bethel, your closet your banqueting house; and God in Christ, a fountain of living waters to satisfy every desire of thy soul. The blood of Christ cleanses us from all sin, the righteousness of Christ justifies us from all things, the Spirit of Christ makes us meet for the glorious inheritance, the grace of Christ is sufficient for us, and the strength of Christ is made perfect in our weakness. Therefore trust thou alone in him, for without him thou canst do nothing; for as the branch cannot bear fruit except it abide in the vine, no more can we except we abide in Christ.[10]

---

[9] *Ibid.*, Letter CLXXIV.
[10] *Ibid.*, Letter CXIII.

The tables turned on Huntington's enemies

As Huntington gave himself the same advice as he gave others, it is not surprising, that, try as they might, his enemies could never find room for criticism in his own moral life. They nevertheless did not stop accusing him of living as he wished and not as God wanted him to do. Huntington's 'godfather' went so far as to call him 'a vile, filthy, stinking Antinomian', a 'spiritual blackguard' and 'the property of the devil'. This moved Huntington to explain his position in *Moses Unveiled in the Face of Christ*. Taking up the accusation, 'If you are not under the law as a rule of life, you may live as you list', he says, 'I wish I could; for I would then be filled with the Spirit of God, and be free from all sin; and, if Paul could have lived as he listed, he would have been delivered from his "body of death"'. Of course, Huntington is referring to Paul's plight in Romans 7, 'For what I would, that do I not; but what I hate, that do I'. Huntington wanted to be free to serve God with all his heart but was kept back from doing so by his indwelling sin. Here, too, he is showing the difference between being under the law and being freed from the law. Those without Christ have no Holy Spirit to guide them and no imputed righteousness to make them want to live like Christ, though held back by the old Adam in them. Thus Paul argues in Romans 7, 'But now we are delivered from the law, that being dead wherein we were held; that we should serve in newness of spirit, and not in the oldness of the letter'.

Once again, as in Huntington's Ditton days, the most remarkable things began to happen to his fierce enemies on a very large scale. The facts are terrifying. One by one they fell by the wayside and either departed from the faith or were taken quickly from this world. Several ministers became mentally deranged after criticising Huntington; one of them went mad whilst listening to him at Monkwell Street. Two men who distributed tracts against him suddenly dropped dead at the same time. One preacher raved against Huntington until his church was empty and he became convinced that the Lord had never called him to preach. Another minister, who delighted in seeking out Huntington's friends and slandering their pastor, was thrown out of his coach and broke his skull. One minister called on a follower of Huntington's to persuade her against him. The good lady offered the clergyman a bed for the night, which he accepted. The bed being damp, he caught a bad chill and died. At least two of Huntington's fiercest antagonists hanged themselves. Martin Madan, whose followers had persecuted Huntington for years, suffered bad health and died in shame, and rumour had it that he had long dabbled in astrology. The Rev. Thomas Haweis was thrown out of his church and was not only banned from preaching there but also prohibited from entering the church as an ordinary worshipper. Haweis ended his life in a Baptist church but when he died, the Baptist pastor gave him one of the most negative write-ups imaginable for a man who had once founded missionary societies.[11] The Rev. Thomas Scott complained to his dying day that, though he preached the truth, he did so to continually emptying churches and always bemoaned the fact that he was extremely unpopular as a preacher. His enormous financial difficulties followed him up to the end of his life.

The antagonist who came off best was none other than the Rev. Rowland Hill, who had always been treated with respect by Huntington. Hill, however, was banned for life from preaching in the very churches where he found himself doctrinally more at home, and after he quarrelled with the General Assembly in Scotland, many churches there were closed to him. During one visit to Scotland, his second, wherever Hill went, he seemed to do nothing else but preach against the General Assembly as ferociously as he preached against Huntington in England. This led one canny Scotsman to say that the devil stood next to Hill in the pulpit, clapping him on the shoulder and praising him for his help in preventing sinners from turning to Christ.[12] Such criticism would have been timely in England to prevent Hill from wasting hour upon hour of pulpit time preaching against Huntington.

---

[11] See 'Practical Illustrations of Character' in *The Autobiography of William Jay*. The chapter entitled 'Rev. Thomas Haweis, M.D.' is the last in the collection.

[12] Edwin Sidney, *The Life of the Rev. Rowland Hill, A.M.*, pp. 201-204.

Chapter 10

The Pastor At Work

From 1786 onwards Huntington continued to expound the difference between life under the shadow of Sinai and life at the top of Mount Zion. This, to him, was the difference between living as a servant in God's household and living as a son.

Though his Monkwell Street lectures once again drew thousands and his Providence Chapel meetings were better attended than ever, life for Huntington was not without great struggles. Meeting the running costs of his two preaching venues taught him to seek the throne of grace daily for support. Whenever money came in, bills for double the amount would follow. An example of this was in 1788 when Huntington was preaching in Birmingham. He had £40 in hand but this was needed to pay back a debt. His chapel interior, however, needed a new coat of whitewash and better lighting. He then received the news that Providence Chapel had been badly damaged by fire. A building had begun to burn near the chapel and, to avoid having the large chimney fall in the wrong place, the stack was pushed down with long poles. It twisted round, however, and fell through the roof of the chapel, not only leaving the building open to all weathers but also damaging the gallery. The bill came to £80 and Huntington was at his wit's end. He had no alternative but to go to his creditor and say that he could not pay off his debt. Before he could say a word, his generous friend said, 'I shall never take that money again of you which you had of me, nor did I ever intend it'.

Domestic problems

Huntington's next problem was his house. It was only a rented dwelling and his host now told him that he would have to leave as he was putting the lease of the house up for sale. For months Huntington was disturbed daily at his work as would-be buyers were allowed full access to the building and inspected it at all times of the day. When the auction came, several friends of Huntington's put in a bid for their pastor's sake but the price was too high. As Huntington had added quite a number of fixtures to the house, including the paving all around, the auctioneer promised that he would be paid for this by the new lease-owner. The latter refused, however, to pay but had the audacity to send Huntington an attorney's letter demanding payment for a small bush that Huntington had taken to his new home although he had planted it at his own expense.

A new house was found very quickly in Church Street, Paddington and, although the rent was twice that of his previous home, friends told Huntington they would help provide the money. As the house was much larger than Huntington's former accommodation, he did not have enough furniture to fill the rooms, but his many friends soon came to his assistance. One gentleman gave him a writing desk and two mahogany elbow chairs, another sent him a large easy chair with a stuffed back and sides, with cushions to match, another friend paid for a carpet and yet another sent £40 to cover general expenses. Huntington did his part by digging out a cellar under the building.

Huntington found that he had been working too hard again and fell very ill and was in extremely poor health for the next four years. His whole family suffered from one complaint after another and tragedy struck his home with the death of no less than four of his children. This was a great blow to Mary his wife, who was having enough difficulty as it was, getting used to the new life of a busy London pastor. Mary had been a real strength to Huntington when they were poor and had to live on barley bread, but now they lived a more middle-class life she found herself less and less at ease. She could not cope with meeting people from all walks of life, managing a large household, including nine children and a number of servants, and entertaining guests who, at times, represented the cream of the London upper middle-class and gentry. Mary, in her sorrow, could no longer turn to the Lord with her troubles but turned to strong drink. In time this caused her to suffer from the gout which brought her great pain. After living for many years on a starvation diet, Mary could not get used to eating plentiful, regular meals and her appetite, for all that she could find in the way of food, grew and grew. This resulted in her putting on weight and it was not long before she reached an enormous size. Huntington was greatly burdened by this. He did not know whether his wife was the Lord's or not and when she was under the influence of the drink, he had to pass over her in chapel when administering the Lord's Supper.

An extension to the chapel needed

Meanwhile Providence Chapel had become far too small for the throngs that descended on the church building every Sunday. Many people came from miles around to attend the services and people from all over England, and even Scotland, moved to the capital so that they could take part in the worship there. Conditions in the chapel became unbearable as the crowds pushed and shoved to obtain seats and the heat of two to three thousand bodies packed tightly together was at times overpowering. As there was a spare piece of land next to the chapel, Huntington decided to take steps to buy it with a view to building an extension. The leaseholder was quite willing to sub-lease this part of his land, for which he paid the Duke of Portland a mere two or three pounds a year. By this time, however, Huntington's enemies had spread tale after tale about how the pastor of Providence Chapel was rolling in money and the leaseholder thought he had the chance of a lifetime to make some easy cash. He thus told Huntington he could sub-lease the thirty by twenty-five foot plot for a hundred guineas per annum. Huntington worked out that if the leaseholder were to sub-lease his whole property, for which he paid fourteen pounds a year, on such terms, he would make a net profit of ten thousand pounds per annum. Needless to say, Huntington thanked the man kindly with a firm 'No'! Having no success in buying 'earth', Huntington relates, he lifted his gaze up to 'heaven' and then had the idea of adding a storey to the chapel and running the gallery all round the inside of the building. A friendly builder said he could do the whole work for £400 so he was commissioned to start at once. Again, however, Huntington showed that he put too much trust in his fellow-men and let the builder tell him a pack of lies. Huntington soon discovered that the man had merely used the £400 as 'a shoe-horn to draw [him] on'. He had supposed, rather naively, 'As the person often sat under me as a hearer, I thought it was not likely that one who could face the rays of light, and stand the force of truth, would, or could, willingly and wilfully deceive a servant of Christ'. The £400 thus grew and grew until the final bill reached £1,230.

Again Huntington stressed that the money should only be raised amongst the friends of Providence Chapel and not a penny from outside sources. Letters are extant in which we read that poor people offered their last mite for the building but Huntington sent it back saying that those who were better off should pay for it. The ex-coalheaver was always on the side of the poor and, on the few occasions when he commented on the politics of the day from the pulpit, it was usually to break a lance for the poor. Once, when the price of bread was raised considerably, Huntington criticised the wealthy farmers and mill-owners severely. As he had a number of that class amongst his hearers he was hissed at from the pews for his pains. Several of these wealthy farmers stopped attending chapel, so Huntington let the poor have their pews. The result was that Huntington received several attorney's letters saying that the pews were the property of his clients and must be left empty when not occupied by their rightful owners.

When Huntington and his office-bearers counted the money that they had canvassed, they found they had only £700. Huntington thought he could add another £100 from his own pocket but on the next Lord's Day a 'friend' entered into his vestry and begged him to lend him £60, which his pastor did on the spot, adding another £40 to it. This man, however, though he was worth thousands, did not pay the loan back on the agreed day and, indeed, when he did pay, he offered Huntington only half of his loan back, saying he could never pay the rest.

Huntington took the whole responsibility of the chapel's debt on his own shoulders and soon thought he had found a solution. He had now written some eight or nine books, so he decided to sell off the stocks he had and his copyrights. These, he estimated, were worth £800, but he only managed to raise £400 on them and thus still had debts now amounting to £550 which he was able to pay off very slowly and which hung like a millstone round his neck and weighed heavily on his conscience.

Acts of kindness to those in need

It was around this time that Huntington met the Irishman John Bryan, who was to become his faithful factotum. Bryan was formerly a staunch Roman Catholic who worked as a bricklayer's labourer. One day he had an accident at work and broke both his legs. He was speedily taken to hospital but his legs were set so badly that he was never again able to work in the building trade. In hospital, however, Bryan became convinced of his sinful state though no one was available to point him to Christ. One Sunday he passed by Providence Chapel and decided to look in as a service was in progress. Huntington was preaching on Psalm 86:17, 'Show me a token for good; that they which hate me may see it, and be ashamed: because thou, Lord, hast holpen me and comforted me'. During the sermon, Bryan saw his need of Christ and was drawn to him and, like Abraham of old, he received faith which brought Christ's imputed righteousness to him and thus lifted God's wrath against all unrighteousness from him.

After this experience Bryan thought he had better call on Huntington and tell him what God had wrought in his soul. During their conversation , Huntington's heart went out to the man and he asked him what he intended to do for a living. The man replied that he was now physically unable to obtain a job as a bricklayer's labourer and there was very little else he could do. Huntington then asked Bryan if he would consider becoming his footman. Bryan replied that he was totally unfit for such a job. 'Oh, we will soon teach you', was Huntington's reply and employed Bryan from then on until his death. Such acts of kindness on Huntington's part must be borne in mind in face of the repeated scathing criticism from his enemies because a man of such low birth kept servants.[1] Those who were outraged at this were also outraged at the fact that Huntington was on very friendly terms with his own footman and gardener! On the one hand, they thought Huntington was acting above his class in keeping servants but, on the other, they thought that since he had servants, he must keep them in their 'correct' place.[2]

---

1 See *The Voice of Years*.

2 This is the view expressed by Huntington's reviewer and critic Ebenezer Hooper. See his *The Celebrated Coalheaver* and *Facts and Letters*.

Huntington was always ready to disappoint anyone who held to such prejudices. Thomas Haweis, Rowland Hill, Andrew Fuller and Dr John Ryland Junior were closely connected with several up-and-coming missionary societies.[3] These men, however, for various theological and political reasons, set themselves up as Huntington's fiercest enemies and warned their candidates against having anything to do with the ex-coalheaver on pain of expulsion from the societies or even excommunication from their churches. One member of a missionary society felt he should make his own decision concerning Huntington, so he went to hear him preach. That was enough for the missionary board and they sacked the young man as soon as this news reached their ears. This unwise move on the part of the society was reported to Huntington, who decided to help the man. In a midweek service Huntington told his congregation, 'I shall make no collection; you have kindly and liberally responded to several appeals I have lately made to you, that I am reluctant to ask, but I name this, and that a plate will be in the Vestry to receive the contributions of any that may feel disposed to help the poor man who is present, and in great need'. After the service, many a member went into the vestry and the young man received in one evening the sum of £40, which represented over a year's income for him.

Hymn-writing and verse

Ever since the seventies, Huntington had tried his hand at writing poetry and hymns, though most of his efforts were far from successful. His first book published, *A Spiritual Sea Voyage*, bears witness to this. It is supposed to be composed in rhyming couplets but Huntington's idea of rhyme differed vastly from the usual notion. The following 'rhyme' is quite typical:

---

[3] Huntington was dubious about the contemporary missionary movement as it was institution-centred rather than church-centred; it was supported by people of conflicting doctrinal opinions; it was not at all particular where the money to support it came from and it sent out striplings who had not proved themselves as missionaries at home. Another criticism was that pastors patronizing the movement fondly thought they could accomplish in Africa and India what they had failed to accomplish in their own churches and parishes. These were sober, serious arguments which the patrons of the young missionary movements laughed off and, instead of meeting Huntington's arguments fairly and squarely from the Word of God, they branded him as 'anti-missionary'.

The haven of rest now appeared in a *vale*,
From an easy descent at the foot of the *hill*.
Thus raptures of joy were balanc'd with *fear*,
For Death must engage us before we go *there*.

Huntington even tried his hand at hymns and prepared several for worship at Providence Chapel. One day he was visited by his son in law, Mr Blake who asked him what he was doing. When Huntington replied that he was writing hymns Mr Blake said, 'Then do you mean Sir, to have yours sung, and put aside dear old Hart's?'[4] After some thought Huntington replied, 'No, I will never do that', and threw his hymns into the fire. Two hymns of praise have, however, survived which might not be unworthy of a modern hymnbook. In 'Praise for Spiritual Mercies' Huntington writes:

Now, Lord, our hearts and voices raise,
In faith and love, while thee we praise,
For all the wonders thou hast done,
Thou undivided Three-in-One.

In 'Praise to the Trinity' he writes:

Praise ye the Lord, all saints of light,
Praise our Jehovah, day and night;
Praise him who gave you breath and birth,
Praise ye my Christ, both heaven and earth.[5]

All his Christian life, Huntington stressed the unity of the Trinity as Arianism was at that time rampant in the Dissenting churches and the works of Joseph Priestly widely read. Typical of Rowland Hill's attacks on Huntington was that he proclaimed publicly that he had three enemies: Joseph Priestly, William Huntington and the devil.

---

[4] Joseph Hart's *Hymns composed on various subjects, with the Author's experience*, first published in 1759.
[5] The complete hymns are to be found in Hooper, *The Celebrated Coalheaver*, p. 55.

Huntington, he added, was the worst of the three! J. C. Philpot used to say that of all Huntington's works, he preferred *Contemplations on the God of Israel* the best. This work is a glorious exposition of the Trinity.

Huntington's attitude to hymn-singing was very reserved and his toleration of it strictly limited. He believed with Romaine that when a church grew tired of hearing God's Word, they looked to the words of men set to music as a vain substitute. A clerk at Providence Chapel usually gave out the lines of Hart's hymns and led the congregation who sang slowly but with great feeling. One evening the clerk invited his son to lead the singing and introduce some 'livelier' tunes. After the service, the old clerk asked Huntington how he had enjoyed the singing. Huntington replied, 'Not at all. Not at all'. This surprised and disappointed the clerk who protested, 'Why, how so, Sir, it was good, and my son led, who is reckoned a first-rate singer'. Huntington replied, 'That may be, but second-rate suits us best'.

There is an amusing story of Huntington's knack of writing impromptu verse. Whilst walking through a churchyard in Sussex with some friends, the party decided to read the inscriptions on the tombs. One epitaph in particular caught the Coalheaver' s eye:

> Where I am now, you soon must be,
> Prepare for death and *follow me*.

Without a moment's reflection, Huntington took out his pencil and wrote out his commentary in verse directly on the gravestone:

> To follow thee, is that the cry?
> And not assert the reason why.
> To follow thee I'm not content,
> Unless I know *which way you went*.

Huntington deals with hypocrites

A close friend of Huntington's, the Rev. William J. Brook, once told him that he was surrounded by hypocrites. Be that as it may, usually Huntington could deal with false professors of religion. One of these was a scoffer who opposed the work in a chapel where Huntington often preached. The man was a wealthy property owner and a regular visitor to the chapel though he opposed the good teaching there. He used to wait outside the church and give Huntington his hand, stating how nice it was to see him again and how he hoped his visit would be profitable. Once Huntington's back was turned the man would change character and speak evil of the sermon. When Huntington heard of the man's two-facedness, he decided to expose him. The next time Huntington preached at the chapel, there was the man again, politely offering his hand in greeting. This time, Huntington did not give the man his hand but looked him straight in the face and said, 'Sir! What means this shaking of hands? You are an enemy to me and to my God!' The surprised man was at once convicted and repented of his hypocrisy.

Political differences with fellow-evangelicals

Many modern opponents of Huntington and his doctrines do not realise that much of the contemporary criticism levelled against Huntington by fellow-evangelicals was for political rather than theological reasons. Men such as the Rylands, Fuller and Hill were extremely critical of Huntington, and as it is taken for granted nowadays that these men were orthodox in their theology, it is also taken for granted that their criticisms were concerning matters of doctrine. This, however, was by no means always the case. Republicanism was growing rapidly in England and many evangelicals were openly taking sides with the revolutionaries in North America and France. As Anglicans owed their allegiance to the Crown, more and more evangelicals of republican sympathies were leaving the Church of England to become Independents or Baptists. John Newton's church at Olney, for instance, was composed almost entirely of republicans and most of these eventually joined the local Independent Church, or John Sutcliff's Baptist Church. There was thus some truth in Newton's exaggerated statement mentioned in a previous chapter that to be a Dissenter was to be an enemy of king and country. John Ryland, for instance, was openly taking sides with the Paineites from the pulpit and declaring, 'If I were General Washington I would summon all my officers around me, and make them draw blood from their arms into a basin, and, dipping their swords into it, swear that they would not sheathe them till America had gained her independence. And if after this anyone should turn coward or traitor, I should feel it my duty, a pleasure, a luxury, to plunge my weapon into that man's heart'. A King's Messenger was ordered to apprehend Ryland and warn him against rousing the populace to open revolution.[6] So great was the influence of the Paineites amongst the Dissenters that their teachings gradually made inroads into Huntington's congregation and eventually split the membership.

In 1796 Huntington was invited to preach at Plymouth Dock. The church there assured him that they were of one mind concerning doctrine and thus Huntington had no qualms about inviting their pastor, the Rev. John Wilkinson, to take his place at Providence Chapel. Wilkinson wasted no time in throwing the doctrines which he shared with Huntington to the four winds and concentrating even in his opening sermon on his own pet revolutionary politics. Many hearers were thrilled with Wilkinson's exposition of 'the rights of man', but one hearer was appalled and decided to make the long journey to Plymouth and warn Huntington of what was happening. Rumour has it that this messenger of bad news to Huntington was none other than Wilkinson's own son! The young man reached Plymouth in the middle of the night and woke Huntington to tell him the dreadful news. Huntington dressed at once, ordered a post chaise and four and dashed off to the capital as fast as the horses could gallop.

On his arrival back home, Huntington found that during the fortnight or so he had been away his church had split into two large factions with some hundreds of the congregation in sympathy with the rebels. Instead of gathering around the Word of God, they were meeting together to read Paine's pamphlets. Huntington sat in his 'Cabin' and wept for hours, pleading with the Lord to give him wisdom to tackle the problem. Wilkinson was sent packing at once but many hearers who were quite content to be ruled by King George had already scattered themselves amongst the other churches in London for fear of the influence the rebels had in Providence Chapel. Many refused to come back as long as the large faction of Paineites remained. 'Never did I see so evil a spirit so rapidly spread before', was Huntington's comment. He thus

[6] See Underwood, *A History of the English Baptists*, p. 143, Newton's *Autobiography*, Bull, p. 214, also *The Autobiography of William Jay*, p. 290. The Rev. John Martin preached at Broad Street Chapel in January, 1798, that, should the French land in Britain, they would find many British Dissenters to support them.

wasted no time in having the membership of well over a hundred cancelled and the other rebel members were asked to stop political agitation within the church or go and 'worship' elsewhere. From then onwards, Huntington did not rely on the testimony of his church administrators regarding candidates for membership but interviewed each candidate himself. Those who remained faithful to Huntington showed their allegiance by digging their hands further into their pockets and paying off the £500 debt outstanding on the building extensions. Gradually things settled down and Huntington pastored a larger church more bound to him in Christian love than ever.

When it became obvious that Huntington believed in 'fearing God and honouring the king', many evangelicals of republican sympathies banded together and formed societies with the intention of thwarting the great pro-constitutional influence they felt that Huntington was exerting on the nation. These societies met weekly with the sole purpose of preaching Huntington down. As they charged sixpence a head entrance fees Huntington wrote playfully about how he was helping these 'Evangelical Associations' to become rich. One society did indeed gain an average of £15 per weekly lecture for a period of no less than seven years. The wording of a placard announcing an anti-Huntington demonstration has been partly preserved and shows the importance Huntington's enemies attached to his influence pro king and country. The wording of the placard is as follows:

HYPOCRISY AND INFIDELITY – PAINE *versus* HUNTINGTON

In the WESTMINSTER FORUM held at the Assembly Rooms,
Brewer Street, Golden Square, the consideration of the
following Question is appointed for
MONDAY, JANUARY 22.[7]

'Which has been more injurious to the Christian Religion, the Publications and Preaching of William Huntington, or the writings of Thomas Paine?'

---

[7] 1798.

> The REV. MR HUNTINGTON, alias HUNT; alias PARSON SACK; alias THE ARCHBISHOP OF TITCHFIELD STREET; alias the COALHEAVER; alias ... &c, having preached and published what he calls a Sermon on his Majesty going to St Paul's (wherein he condemns the whole political world who oppose Mr Pitt, and abuses most of the great religious characters of this Metropolis) gave rise to the above question. That a man without learning should dare ... We thus publicly invite him to attend the debate, and not issue his opinions alone from the pulpit, where he is protected from replication. We hope those Ministers who have occasionally honoured this society by their remarks, will make a point of being present that should he attend ... His abuse of Mr Joss, Mr Rowland Hill, and the whole Missionary Society, will not be forgotten.
>
> Chair to be taken at Eight o'clock. Admittance Sixpence.
> No political remarks on the Government of this Country permitted.
> A good fire in the Assembly Room during Winter.[8]

Ebenezer Hooper, who reproduced the above placard, omitted words which contained 'shamefully scurrilous expressions' but enough has been given to show the line of attack Huntington's fellow-ministers took. He had 'abused the great religious characters of the Metropolis', which merely meant that the religious leaders preached against him and he wrote scriptural defences which they could not overthrow. To them the politics of Paine were more 'Christian' than the doctrines of faith and Christ's righteousness as Huntington saw them.

The big gun which Huntington's enemies always brought out to do battle with him was that he was 'a man without learning'. Anyone familiar with his exegetical works, however, must realise that here are the writings of a man who has walked with God and been taught by him. Even that arch-critic, Robert Southey, the Poet Laureate, confessed that he could only find one word that Huntington had used incorrectly

---

[8] E. Hooper, *Huntington: Facts and Letters*, 1872, pp. 31, 32.

in all his works[9] and that was the word 'promiscuously' which, of course, has meant different things at different times.

It is interesting to note that Huntington was simultaneously accused of siding with Pitt and opposing the missionary movement, but it was those who sided with Pitt, such as William Wilberforce and the Clapham Sect, who made sure that the missionary societies were tolerated by the government.

After issuing such a highly political statement against Huntington, it was sheer hypocrisy for the organisers of the debate to state that no political remarks were to be made concerning the government during the debate. In other words, Huntington was attacked politically but was not allowed to defend himself politically. It was thus reasonable that Huntington, always ready to debate for a cause he found good, refrained from attending such a meeting.

It was obvious that the Paineites were merely using Huntington's reputation to draw a crowd as the sermon referred to on the placard had only remotely to do with the American War. The King had visited St Paul's with the entire Parliament to thank God for the British victories over Roman Catholic forces in Spain and Holland which had been backed by the French. Huntington looked on these victories as God's defence of Protestant England from the pope's puppets on the Continent. These were only too willing to get their hands on the wealth of a growing, prosperous country, and to force their superstitions on a nation that had become strong through the Reformation. Huntington's sermon, entitled 'Watchword and Warning', was an exposition of Isaiah 51:20, 'Thou art my battle-axe and weapons of war, for with thee will I break in pieces the nations, and with thee will I destroy kingdoms'. Huntington was being heavily criticised for preaching that the nation should take heed to God's Word rather than Romanist claims, the so-called 'rights of man' and the voice of the mob. Hooper's comment on the atrocious conduct of the 'Christian' Paineites was: 'To compare a minister who had been instrumental in the conversion and profit of hundreds, to so notorious an infidel and hater of all religion and

---

[9] Robert Southey, 'Huntington S.S.', Quarterly Review, No. 48, April, 1821.

morality, was in the same spirit which called his Master, Beelzebub, and ascribed His works to Satan; in this he was honoured to share the reproach of Christ'.[10]

Around the year 1804 the government made an appeal to every church, chapel and congregation in England to make a collection to assist the king in carrying out the war against the French. Again we see how generous Huntington's church was in raising money 'for a good cause' as in one day (at the morning and evening services) Providence Chapel contributed the amazing sum of £250 to the appeal. The money was duly sent off with a covering letter from Huntington and his church officials which has been preserved:

> Honoured Gentlemen
>
> We, whose names are underwritten, and the congregation to which we belong, beg your acceptance of £250, as our mite towards the laudable design. It comes by the hands of Mr Joseph Aldridge, and Mr Thomas Green; which mite we send with our cordial respect and best wishes to our rightful Sovereign, and those whose hearts are with him at the helm; knowing that God hath not forsaken the earth, nor hath He left us without a token for good. For although He did not suffer us to ward off the blow of His hand on the continent, for reasons obvious enough to those who consider the operations of His hands and the justness of His judgments; yet He hath turned the scale in our favour, when engaged in behalf of our own country. Witness the many unparalleled victories He hath granted us, – the renowned courage He hath bestowed both on our commanders and men, the works of darkness He hath brought to light amongst us; and the many wise men that have been taken in the snare they have set for others. May we not view these as preludes of future success? We think we may; and confiding in our God, we do hope, pray, and expect that before our intended invaders swallow us up, or before the promised tree of liberty ease us of all money, our religion and our lives, that they may receive as many blasts and rebukes from the Lord God of Great Britain, as Balaam had, when going to curse the heritage of heaven for the wages of

[10] Hooper, *Facts and Letters*, p. 32.

unrighteousness. So pray the lovers of our God, our King, and our Country.
God save the King! God protect and prosper old England!
Signed, in the Vestry of Providence Chapel

William Huntington, Minister.
James Davidson, Stationer, Tower Hill.
Thomas Green, No. 93, Oxford Street.
Joseph Aldridge,
Edward Aldridge, 120, Aldersgate Street.[11]

A lone voice against Rome

In warning against Rome, Huntington was a lone voice in England and reaped the ridicule of Calvinists and Arminians alike. Evangelicals in Huntington's day were resting on the laurels of the Reformers who had put Rome to flight. Roman Catholicism had, for them, lost its sting and was to be pitied as a minority religion that had had its day. They went even further and argued that Rome was now the underdog and, according to British chivalry, a gentleman must be on the side of the underdog. Thus the most ardent of Calvinists became the strongest supporters of Roman Catholic emancipation. The poet Cowper felt this campaign for 'the rights of man'[12] was a betrayal of the Reformation and wrote *Expostulation* in the spring of 1781 which contained the following lines:

> Hast thou admitted with a blind, fond trust,
> The lie that burn'd thy father's bones to dust,
> That first adjudg'd them hereticks, then sent
> Their souls to Heav'n, and curs'd them as they went?
> The lie that Scripture strips of its disguise,
> And execrates above all other lies,
> The lie that claps a lock on mercy's plan,

[11] *Ibid.*, p. 41.
[12] A reference to Tom Paine's revolutionary book.

And gives the key to yon infirm old man,
Who once insconc'd in apostolic chair
Is deified, and sits omniscient there;
The lie that knows no kindred, owns no friend
But him that makes its progress his chief end,
That having spilt much blood, makes that a boast,
And canonises him that sheds the most?
Away with charity that sooths a lie,
And thrusts the truth with scorn and anger by;
Shame on the candour and the gracious smile
Bestow'd on them that light the martyr's pile,
While insolent disdain in frowns express'd,
Attends the tenets that endur'd that test:
Grant them the rights of men, and while they cease
To vex the peace of others, grant them peace,
But trusting bigots whose false zeal has made
Treach'ry their duty, thou art self-betray'd.

During this period, Cowper always placed his lines before what he called John Newton's 'tribunal' for scrutiny. Newton advised Cowper strongly not to publish the lines so the official first edition of Cowper's *Poems* was published with a very mild substitute. A later generation of Christians could not believe that their predecessors in the faith were so pro-Roman Catholic and sought refuge in invalid excuses. The Gospel Standard Supplement for July 1867, basing its notions on an earlier article by Philpot, argued that the suppression on Cowper's part was because of 'injury to his mind' and it was 'a blight upon his usefulness and peace'. They concluded that Cowper had written so because he had rejected Newton's influence and been influenced by his Roman Catholic landlord, Squire Throckmorton of Weston. It was, however, Newton who strongly urged Cowper to suppress the lines and Cowper formed a friendship with the Throckmortons some years after writing *Expostulation*. The Throckmortons had a wide circle of evangelical friends whom they often entertained, including the Rev. T. S. Grimshawe, Cowper's biographer, a professing Calvinist. Grimshawe dedicated his biography to the Throckmortons!

The Clapham Sect, with its devout Calvinistic spokesman Wilberforce, used their authority to campaign for 'equal rights' between

Protestants and Roman Catholics. John Wesley, of course, was not called the 'Methodist Pope' for nothing and his defence of Mary Queen of Scots and the Jacobites moved more than one leading evangelical to call him a 'papist' to his face. Huntington was amazed by these people who, with one voice, proclaimed the emancipation of the slaves from the tyranny of their masters yet also campaigned for the pope to be once again given the freedom to tyrannise the church. The same church mocked Huntington for not understanding that Rome was defeated and to be pitied. When he warned England about the whore on seven hills who would once again seduce England, he became the laughing-stock of evangelical and pagan alike.

Wilberforce's position here is extremely difficult to understand as judging by his speeches and writings, he seems to have abhorred Roman Catholicism. Yet he called people such as Huntington and his own good friend Milner 'sadly prejudiced' for objecting to absolute liberty for Roman Catholics. To be fair to Wilberforce, it must be stressed that by voting for a 'nominal emancipation' of the Roman Catholics, he believed he would help ordinary Roman Catholics free themselves from the authority of the priests by voting for Protestant leaders. In this way Rome would lose its power and its followers decrease in numbers. Never was an evangelical so deluded![13] Once, however, Wilberforce had decided to assist Rome, he became more and more influenced by its propaganda, as outlined in the introduction.

The move to Cricklewood

Huntington had signed a contract for an initial seven years with the lease-owner of his house in Paddington, but as he paid his rent regularly and had invested £300 of his own in the property, besides building cellars under it, he felt confident that he could stay in the house as long as he wished. His landlord had told him on several occasions that he had no wish to have anyone but Huntington in the house. Great therefore was Huntington's surprise to find that when he returned home from a preaching engagement one day in 1798 his wife told him that the

[13] See Robert Furneaux, *William Wilberforce*, Hamish Hamilton, 1974, pp. 319-331 for a thorough-going discussion of Wilberforce's stand.

landlord was about to sell the house. Huntington immediately told his landlord that he was interested in buying the property and arranged with him to have two builders call, who would represent both parties and evaluate the property. The landlord, however, returned directly with an auctioneer who set a lower limit on the house of £900 although it had been valued at £400 before Huntington had improved it. Meanwhile, Huntington's friends were actively looking for another home for him and found a house with some considerable farmland attached to it at Hendon. Huntington thought the property was too far from London and was against moving out of the capital. Mary thought the place was ideal, no doubt remembering her own origins and happiness when she had previously lived in the country.

The more Huntington thought of the size of the house and surrounding fields, the more he felt he would not be able to run it financially and he resolved never to make the mistake of getting into debt again. Huntington's friends, however, proved to be the only party interested in obtaining the house and the fifty-four acres attached and were thus able to obtain it at a very low rent. Finally they persuaded Huntington to take on the property. After some trouble with the former occupiers, Huntington settled with them to purchase by appraisement fixtures, tools etc. which could not be removed for the sum of £370. A pile of dung, valued at about £6, was thrown in free of charge. No sooner were matters concluded than Huntington received an attorney's letter saying that he had not been able to take part in the sale's proceedings but represented the previous occupiers and could not agree with the transaction concerning the dung. What, he asked, did Huntington intend to do about the matter? Huntington ignored the letter but shortly afterwards received a bill from the attorney for £40 for the dung. As Huntington ignored this demand, too, the attorney had him brought before the court at Westminster Hall.

Whilst the counsellor was busy stating his case against Huntington, the judge stopped him to tell him that his accusations were ridiculous and he had no case whatsoever to make. The attorney, however, obtained another court hearing on the grounds that he had come into possession of new evidence. A young man, one of the appraisers, was produced who swore that the appraisers had not settled the matter, which was between Huntington and his antagonist alone. The original appraisement, however, in the handwriting of this young man, was produced and in it the dung had been crossed out and the young man had written the words, 'This is to certify, that no one thing crossed out in this inventory is to be paid for'. This addition was signed by the young man himself. With a cry of 'Villainy indeed!', the judge closed the case and ordered Huntington's antagonist to pay all costs, which came to £270. It is obvious that the lawyer had believed the stories spread that Huntington was rolling in money and had hoped that he would be able to squeeze a considerable sum from the old coalheaver.

Now Huntington began to develop a plan whereby he could make himself independent (his aim had always been to be like Paul, who made tents so as not to be a financial burden on the church) and also help those of his fold who were out of work. He invited several poor families to take over the work in the fields besides the brewing, baking and dairy work. His trouble now, however, was how to get his own large family and the three or four families who helped him to Providence Chapel, which was over five miles away. Huntington rode to chapel on a little sorrel and had knocked together an old open cart to provide his families with transport. This did not prove to be an ideal solution in bad weather but a better was to come.

One Saturday, Huntington's private day, he was visited by two or three members of his church who presented themselves most formally to their pastor, so that he began to think a member must have died, or some such bad news was about to be given him. To his surprise, he found that the men had come to tell him that they had clubbed together and were about to buy him a coach and pair. Huntington protested that, taxes on coaches being so high, he would never be able to keep such an equipage but the men assured him that they had collected enough money to take care of the upkeep of the coach and horses, too.

Shortly after this a man called with a £45 gift for horses and another friend sent Huntington a gift of twelve ewes. After this, cows, bulls, sheep, horses, grain and farming equipment poured in a steady stream into Huntington's smallholding, which he called 'Cricklewood'. As soon as Huntington made a profit, or surplus calves, lambs etc. were born, a steady stream of animals and goods left Cricklewood for the homes of his poor neighbours and friends. Huntington was never to be in debt again and was to be a means of bringing material prosperity to a large number of people who already loved him for the spiritual help they had gained from him.

Charges of extravagance levelled against Huntington

Huntington's new affluence set all his enemies in a rage. It was soon rumoured up and down the country that Huntington, the ex-odd job man, had a coach with his initials painted on the door followed by the letters S.S.. These initials were repeated on the harness pads and even on the sides of the blinkers. Now there was nothing unusual about this at all. Almost every brewer, coal merchant and street hawker had such 'emblems' on his coach, cart and horse's harness and almost every clergyman, including Huntington's contemporaries Rowland Hill and John Newton, drove around in a coach and pair. A coach served the same purpose in the eighteenth century as a car or even an aeroplane does today. Yet the idea has stuck with Huntington's critics even in our day that low-born Huntington had no right to live as his fellow-ministers did and drive to chapel in a coach and pair. One modern critic still begrudges Huntington his coach and writes, 'In a time of great poverty, he lived in the style of foolish magnificence, somewhat resembling that of an Eastern Nabob ... he who before his arrival in London was a common day labourer was now trailing about in carriages with servants in livery'.[14]

This is criticism gone wild and comes after allegations that Huntington did not do his duty to the badly off. The author admits later that Huntington was benevolent in private life, so why this terrible exaggeration as if Huntington were living in the height of luxury and indulgence? The reference to Huntington being a 'common day labourer' shows that social prejudices die hard. The mention of a plurality of 'carriages', as opposed to a 'carriage', and of 'servants in livery' probably refers to the fact that in Huntington's old age the widow of a former Lord Mayor of London loaned out her coach and servant to help him in his work. In fairness to Huntington, it must be pointed out that Lord Dartmouth, the extremely rich Russian merchant John Thornton and William Wilberforce's aunt, Mrs Wilberforce, all loaned out their carriages to help such ministers as John Newton in their work without any criticism coming from any quarter against that saint.

---

[14] The anonymous reviewer of *The Voice of Years*, Banner of Truth, July 1988, p. 11.

Huntington certainly did not provide livery, but good working-clothes and tools, for those who helped him run his farm, as he treated them as friends and co-workers and not servants. Perhaps the myth that Huntington had as many servants as an 'Eastern Nabob' springs from the fact that his wider family carried many different appellations. Thus Clarke, a poor man whom Huntington chose to superintend his farm, served as foreman, steward, bailiff, coachman, jack of all trades and even as leader of the singing in Providence Chapel. In actual fact Huntington, who had perhaps the largest congregation in London and always had a house full of guests who had to be fed and accommodated, had fewer servants than most of his fellow-clergymen who had an income of far less. It is a pity that this critic did not reveal more of the contents of *The Voice of Years* from which he quotes as then the reader would see clearly of what spirit the author, whom he follows, really was. After criticising Huntington for having a carriage, the author goes on to say that this would not have mattered if he had been 'born and bred a gentleman'. As Huntington was not a gentleman, he should have dispensed with the coach and kept 'a comfortable apartment for the night, near the chapel, or a hackney coach kept in regular attendance'. Money was thus not the problem to the author as his alternative suggestions would have been far more expensive than Huntington's solution. It was plainly and simply the fact that Huntington belonged to a social class which the author believed should not travel by coach. It seems that George Orwell's quip that 'All animals are equal but some are more equal than others', really applies to humans after all!

Chapter 11

The Huntingtonians

No true assessment can be made of a pastor's life without taking into consideration the flock he shepherds. No matter how holy the man or how sound his doctrine, if his sheep are starved and stunted in growth, he is probably a hireling and no true shepherd. It is thus necessary to focus our eyes on the congregation at Providence Chapel and see if they show good growth through good spiritual management. In the case of Huntington's flock, such a scrutiny is a blessing indeed.

The Rev. Henry Cole, D.D., well-known for his English translations of Luther's and Calvin's works, wrote in Zion's Watchtower:

> It may be asked why, in my ministration, such as it is, I make frequent allusion to the ministry of that great and blessed servant of the Most High, the late Mr Huntington. The reasons are these, 1st, because I believe he bore and left in Britain, the greatest and most glorious testimony to the power of God's salvation, that ever was borne or left therein, 2nd, because I believe he planted the noblest vine of a Congregational Church that ever was planted therein, and 3rd, because I believe the Churches that maintain the vital truths he set forth form a very essential feature in the church-state of Christ in the land in these times, and perhaps will do so, to the time of the coming day of God's retribution.[1]

[1] Quoted from Hooper's *The Celebrated Coalheaver*, p. 35.

Thomas Hardy of Leicester shared Cole's view of the purity of the church as seen in Huntington's followers and said that 'The best Christians he met with in his travels were Huntingtonians'.[2] These men wrote so positively of the Huntingtonians over a hundred years ago because they were fully convinced that they would set the pattern of Christian living until kingdom come.

The late Dr Martyn Lloyd-Jones of Westminster Chapel has given a more modern testimony to the presence of Christ in the lives of the Huntingtonians. In a preface to *More than Notion*, J. H. Alexander's moving book on first, second and third-generation Huntingtonians,[3] Lloyd-Jones says that the moment he began to read the book, he was 'gripped and deeply moved'. He goes on to testify that, 'There are some books of which it can be said that to read them is an experience, and one is never the same again'. Such a book to 'the Doctor' was *More than Notion* because of its value to those who long for a vital Christian experience. Of it Lloyd-Jones adds:

> Many who have read it as the result of my recommendation have testified to the blessing they have received. In one church known to me the reading of the book by one man led to a prayer-meeting such as they had not experienced before. In these superficial and confused days I thank God for a book such as this and pray that He may bless it to countless souls.

In spite of such glowing testimonies to Huntington's flock and their spiritual offspring, the confusion mentioned by Dr Lloyd-Jones has stifled the optimism engendered by men such as Henry Cole and Thomas Hardy. Nowadays, the name 'Huntingtonian', rather than becoming more revered, is actually despised in many Christian circles. This cannot possibly be because those who have been brought to Christ and taught of God through the writings of Huntington have proved to be mere shadows of their brethren of two hundred years ago. This author's research has shown him that there are still some thousands of Huntingtonians who bear the same witness and testify to the same doctrines as their predecessors. The reasons for the change in general

[2] *Ibid.*, p. 53.

[3] The preface was written in 1965.

opinion amongst Christians today are to be found in the changes in doctrine which have occurred outside of Huntington's teaching since the seventeenth century: changes which Huntington saw coming and fought against during his lifetime. Just as there was a downgrading in doctrine amongst the Baptists in the time of Spurgeon, so there was a severe downgrading of Reformed, Calvinistic doctrines within all denominations during the time of Huntington, and it is still continuing in the present day.

The influence of Fuller

William Cunningham, in his book *The Reformers and the Theology of the Reformation*, shows how the British Reformers were, in the main, Calvinists and the Anglican clergy continued to be so throughout the reigns of Elizabeth I and James VI (commonly known as James I of England). Most Church of England clergy, however, Cunningham argues, dropped Calvinism during the reign of Charles I.[4] Independents, Dissenters and Baptists, on the whole, kept to their Reformed, Calvinistic persuasions for a further century so that Calvinists still remaining in the Anglican Church were prone to say that the Dissenters kept their Articles[5] for them. Dissenting churches, however, were not to remain untainted from Arminianism and its fellow-deviations Amyraldianism, Neonomianism and Baxterism, which were gaining ground rapidly by the time of Huntington. One of the most influential trailblazers in this downgrading away from the Reformed faith was Andrew Fuller (1754-1815), whose works are becoming increasingly popular.

Fuller, like Huntington, was a self-taught man and had been a Calvinist in his earlier Christian days. However, he gradually came to believe in a system of logic which was as highly rationalistic as it was unscriptural. He denied the penal, vicarious nature of the atonement, seeing it as a mere figurative, moral triumph over death on Christ's part

---

[4] Banner of Truth Trust reprint 1979. See especially Essay VIII, 'Calvinism and Arminianism'.

[5] The *Thirty-Nine Articles* of the Church of England which are basically Calvinistic.

rather than a literal substitutionary death on behalf of his elect.[6] All men have the natural ability to believe and all men, on hearing the gospel, know that it is their duty to accept it. The atonement, for Fuller, is conditional, depending on the willingness of man to embrace it.

No matter how flattering to man, or even logical, this teaching may seem, it falls far short of the plan and purpose of God as revealed in Scripture. Furthermore, it totally denies the teaching of the Reformers and the Puritans as documented in such confessional writings as the *Thirty-Nine Articles*[7] and the *Westminster Confession*.[8] In reality it is a red herring, drawing attention away from the biblical truth that God decrees mercy on whom he will and that the gospel can only be recognised and accepted by the elect. It presumes that not only the sheep hear Christ's voice, but also the goats, and that reprobate man has an awareness of gospel truths that Paul denies when he writes, 'We speak the wisdom of God in a mystery, even the hidden wisdom, which God ordained before the world unto our glory: which none of the princes of this world knew: *for had they known it*, they would not have crucified the Lord of glory ... But the natural man receiveth not the things of the Spirit of God: for they are foolishness to him: *neither can he know them*[9] because they are spiritually discerned'.[10]

John Adams and the problems with Ryland

The great gulf between the traditional Pauline faith of the Huntingtonians and that of Fuller is clearly illustrated by the trouble they had with Fuller's friend and supporter Dr John Ryland. Whilst on a preaching visit to Northampton Huntington met a Mr and Mrs John Adams with whom he started a deep friendship, calling them for ever afterwards fondly his 'Adam and Eve'. John Adams was an ironmonger, though he is also remembered as a hymn-writer. He was also an orthodox Calvinist and was very worried because his pastor, John Ryland Junior, had left the traditional Pauline and Calvinistic theology of his earlier days and adopted the position that later became

---

[6] See Fuller's book. *The Gospel Worthy of All Acceptation*, 1785.

[7] Article XVII

[8] *Westminster Confession*, XI, 3; XII, 1.

[9] My italics.

[10] See the whole of 1 Corinthians chapter 2.

known as 'Fullerism', after his friend Andrew Fuller, but which was really a combination of the old heresies of Neonomianism[11] and Amyraldianism, with a large measure of German Pietistic Liberalism thrown in. During his ministry he thus adopted the theory that all men everywhere are aware of their inborn duty to obey the gospel. Adams did his best to witness to his pastor concerning his departure from the orthodox faith and wrote a poem – not his best – which he entitled, 'The Lamentations', bemoaning the fact that true Calvinism was no longer preached in the chapel. Adams was also concerned that Ryland showed Antinomian tendencies by preaching Christ's love to the unconverted without first showing them that they had sinned and fallen short of the glory of God as expressed in his holy, eternal law. Thus Adams wrote:

> Calvin the champion's laid aside,
> Free grace is trodden down,
> And now we see Arminian pride
> In pulpits wear the crown.

He also protested in the poem that those who stressed God's grace in salvation, rather than inbred human duties, were given the name of 'Antinomians'.

One day Huntington visited the Adams, only to find them in tears and terribly dejected. When he asked what was wrong the couple told him that after the difficult birth of their son many years previously, the doctor had told Mrs Adams that she would never be able to have a child again. Since then she had had ten still-births, although the babies had developed normally in the womb. The time was now close for another child to be born. 'Nothing is too hard for the Lord', said Huntington and got down on his knees with his friends and began to pray. Mrs Adams protested that it was no use but Huntington stressed that it was no sin to try if they asked with submission to the will of God. Huntington prayed,

---

[11] The teaching that Christ atoned for all men in that he made salvation possible for all, giving converts a new and easier law so that they might remain in faith. Cf. Louis Berkhof, *The History of Christian Doctrines*, Banner of Truth Trust, p. 192 ('The Marrow Controversy').

'O Lord, if we have asked amiss, withhold; but if Thou art not displeased with our petitions, grant our request; not on the footing of our worth or worthlessness, but in the name and for the sake of Thy dear Son, who is worthy'.

Several weeks later, Huntington, now in London again, heard the good news. 'Eve' had given birth to a bouncing baby girl, full of health and vitality. Adams told Huntington that as the girl was a child of prayer, she would not be named until Huntington came and named her. This wish moved Huntington to pay the Adams a speedy visit and give the child of prayer the name of Mary – after his own wife.

When these joyful tidings reached the ears of the Rev. John Ryland, pastor of College Lane Baptist Church (Ryland called it a congregational church) instead of rejoicing, he was insulted. He protested strongly that a 'stranger' had been given a warm reception at the Adams' home – as if to say that he, the home pastor, had never been entertained so warmly. It is difficult to understand Ryland's thinking here as the Bible makes it a Christian duty to entertain 'strangers' and Ryland always stressed Christian duty. In his view, however, Huntington evidently deserved to be treated as an exception to this rule. This 'stranger', who was in fact no stranger at all, Ryland called 'a man with an envenomed tongue' and he started to campaign in his church for Adams' excommunication because of the mere connection he had with Huntington. Adams was not the first who had to go: Ryland had already excommunicated one member who had allowed Huntington to preach in his house – a house that was legally licensed as a place of worship. The fact is that Ryland was extremely sore concerning the trouncing his father had received from Huntington in his work *The Broken Cistern and the Springing Well* earlier in the year. This is why he called Huntington a man of 'envenomed tongue' and let his solidarity with his father get in the way of his fellowship with his church members.

The letter of excommunication was drawn up and signed by Ryland and nineteen members at a church meeting on the Lord's Day, 30 October, 1791. Excommunication was a most serious business in the denomination which Ryland represented and meant that the person excommunicated was now an outcast from Christ and his church. In the letter, terrible accusations are levelled at Adams' character. He is described as 'unruly', 'one who walks not in love', 'a little leaven that leaveneth the whole lump', 'bitter' and 'malevolent' and 'an enemy to our peace'. 1 Corinthians 5:6-11 is used against him: 'Purge out, therefore the old leaven ... the leaven of malice and wickedness ... not to keep company, if any man that is called a brother be a fornicator, or covetous, or an idolater, or a railer, or a drunkard, or an extortioner; with such an one, no, not to eat'. What, then, were the sins and calamities which had moved the church officers to compare Adams with fornicators, idolaters, drunkards etc.?

First, Adams was accused of withdrawing from the covenant he made with the church on becoming a member by turning from the doctrines then affirmed. Now this accusation was invalid from the start. In the letter of excommunication Ryland admitted that he himself had changed his own doctrine but he argued that as Adams had not been able to prove that this new doctrine was false, he was still under his obligation to support his pastor's teaching. Now Adams had shown Ryland clearly that his new doctrine was false but Ryland would not accept this.

The second accusation against Adams is that he alleges wrongly that his pastor has 'renounced the great doctrines of grace'. Ryland affirms that he himself maintains them as strenuously as ever. In the letter, however, Ryland admits in a very roundabout way that, after a 'neighbouring minister' (Fuller) published a treatise on the duty of sinners respecting faith in Christ,[12] he 'with some others, now considered the duty of the unconverted as extending further than they once conceived'. In his defence of Adams, entitled *Excommunication, and the Duty of all Men to Believe, Weighed in the Balance*, Huntington points out that Ryland's earlier writings, especially his hymns, were Calvinistic whereas his later teaching was that sinners should be pleaded with to accept Christ's love as a duty. In his defence Ryland claims that Adams' view that the law is not the rule for the believer's conduct was a 'new notion'. Ryland does not say what he means by 'the law' and misses out that very important word for Adams, 'sole'. Adams did not believe that the moral law, robbed of its theological

[12] Fuller, *The Gospel Worthy of All Acceptation*, 1785.

implications, was the *sole* rule for a believer, who was taught to live by the rule and law of faith.

Ryland's third point is that Adams remained in fellowship with an excommunicated member of the church. This member, a Mr Hewet, was the man who had allowed Huntington to preach at his licensed house and was thus excluded from fellowship at College Lane.

The fourth official point raised against Adams is that he attended Huntington's preaching one Lord's Day and then entertained him 'in such a manner as no other minister was ever entertained by you'. On this day, Huntington had asked for the use of the College Lane pulpit, had been refused it and thus preached at Mr Hewet's. Actually, Mr Hewet's house was very tiny and Huntington did not preach to a congregation inside it at all but stood inside the building, preaching through the open window to a great crowd outside. The whole street filled with hearers and they overflowed into a nearby churchyard. This caused the enraged Anglican clergyman to join with Ryland in condemning Huntington.

Ryland's final point in his letter of excommunication is that he hates 'sentiments that really tend to antinomianism, and to make professors set up privilege in opposition to duty' and he is sure that 'the Lord hates' these things, too. In this last sentence, Ryland laid his own faith bare. If Adams had spoken more of man's duty and less about God's grace, which Ryland termed derogatorily 'privilege', he would have been more acceptable to his pastor.

As Huntington was cited as one of the main reasons, if not *the* main reason, for Adams' excommunication, he felt he had a right to reply to Ryland, which he did in the above-mentioned work. First Huntington deals with Ryland's accusation that Adams had backed out of his covenant with the church. He shows how Ryland was a convinced Calvinist until he was influenced by Fuller, years after Adams joined the church. Thus it was Ryland who had changed his covenantal promises and not Adams. Huntington then concludes that it was correct of Adams to warn his pastor that he was departing from the 'old paths'.

Referring to the second accusation concerning Ryland's alleged rejection of 'the great doctrines of grace', Huntington points out that Ryland admitted that he had changed his opinions and followed Fuller who had, shortly before, changed his own opinions and argued in his works that, 'He knew not what he believed when he began to preach'.

Huntington remarks that through teaching that the children of Hagar should receive the gospel as their only rule of duty, whilst the children of Zion were to bow down their necks to the law of Moses, the children of wrath are sent to the promise (which was meant for the children of the promise) and the heirs of promise were sent to the law (which was meant to condemn the children of wrath). Huntington asked what Ryland's doctrine had to do with 'the doctrines of grace', when he taught that the duty of men whom God had concluded in unbelief was to believe the gospel. Since when had dead men duties? He thus argued that Ryland had stopped being a pastor to the sheep and had become a herdsman to the goats.

On taking up Ryland's third point concerning Adams' association with Mr Hewet, Huntington refers to his statement that Hewet had passed on 'slanderous insinuations' to Huntington, telling him that the gospel was not preached at Northampton and prejudicing him against his pastor. Huntington denied that Hewet had behaved in any way slanderously and said that the question of there being no gospel preached in Northampton had not been raised at all. Huntington was of the opinion that many good men preached there. He argued that Mr Hewet was a servant of Christ who was in his rights to protest against the everlasting gospel being used as a rule of duty for the unconverted and putting those who walk by faith again under the curse of the law. Hewet, it appears, had been excommunicated for alleged (but unproven) 'slanderous insinuations', rather than doctrinal abuse or a sinful life – again a very dubious basis for a swift excommunication. Huntington says that he preached at Hewet's house because he had received an invitation to do so. He went because Christ had sent him to preach to Hewet's household and did not know why Ryland felt he could deny him his calling and rights as a gospel minister. Huntington adds that Ryland's excommunicating Hewet 'did not expose him to Satan, nor make him cease from well-doing; nor abate his affection to Christ, nor his attachment to the truth; though he had been so roughly handled by one called a minister of Jesus'.

Huntington deals quickly with Ryland's fourth point, arguing that he is no 'stranger, nor a foreigner, but a fellow-citizen of the saints, and of the household of God: nor was he a stranger to many persons at

Northampton'. This argument of Ryland's is very odd indeed, if not a downright lie, as he knew Huntington very well – this is why Huntington had expected to be able to preach at his chapel – and was private tutor to Huntington's son Ebenezer. He explained to Ryland that the cordial reception and kind entertainment which he received at Adams' hand was no more than a servant of Christ expects when he visits a brother, so why complain about such good, Christian treatment?

In his PS Huntington concludes that:

> To censure, cut off, or excommunicate, a subject of grace, who is sound in the faith, and who loves and contends for the truth as it is in Jesus, without any charge of scandal in life, or error in principle, brought against him, is excommunicating Christ himself. Such proceedings are not agreeable to God's word, they are not allowable by the laws of Zion: the sentence comes not forth from God's presence; nor does God's displeasure follow upon such partial judgment. The process is against the truth; and springs from love to self, a zeal to be had in honour, and raging jealousy against the power of God attending supposed rivals. Mr Adams may enjoy as good a conscience before his tribunal as Paul did before Felix, when the supposed culprit, undaunted, reasoned of righteousness, etc. while the unjust judge trembled. The soul that will stand fast in the testimony of God, and not be moved away from the hope of the gospel, must separate himself from every false pastor, and from false doctrine, that he may enjoy the witness of God; and he that abides by such a pastor and doctrine, has the witness of men.

John Adams continued to walk with the Lord and died in 1835 at the age of eighty. He brought his children up to fear, love and honour God and his son became an Evangelical clergyman in the Church of England. Needless to say, it was William Huntington who led John Adams' son to a knowledge of the true and living way.[13]

---

[13] Some of the Rev. S. Adams' comments on Huntington's preaching are recorded in chapter 5 of this book. See Hooper, *The Celebrated Coalheaver*, pp. 31-33.

Fuller's criticism of Huntington

One day the Rev. Andrew Fuller decided to go and hear Huntington preach. This was not because he had seen the error of his own ways. He did not go to be edified nor to be built up in the faith. He went, he tells us,[14] because he was concerned for the spiritual welfare of those who sat under the ex-coalheaver's ministry. He went to criticise. As he was not concerned with sharing in the general fellowship of the meeting, he waited until it was time for the sermon and then rudely entered the chapel. Huntington had just begun his discourse and Fuller tells us that it was 'an abundance of misrepresentations and slander, too foul to be repeated' and that the preacher preached himself and not Christ. The sermon, according to Fuller, was a mixture of 'Billingsgate[15] and blasphemy'. The Baptist pastor apparently came to this damning conclusion for two reasons. First, Huntington did not believe in conditional atonement i.e., in an atonement which only becomes efficacious when the sinner exercises a presumed inborn duty to accept it. Secondly, Huntington maintained that the elect for whom Christ died could not possibly be lost. This latter criticism is surprising even for Fuller who normally professed belief in this doctrine. His hatred of Huntington obviously clouded his judgment.

When Fuller left the meeting, he was amazed. The Huntingtonians were praising God and exclaiming what a marvellous defence of the gospel they had heard. Fuller felt he had heard merely 'profane and vain babbling' and the crowds must therefore be seriously deluded. He confessed himself 'humiliated and distressed' that people should be deceived in such a way by the preacher. Giving himself a pat on the back, he concludes his report by saying, 'There must be heresies, that they who are approved may be made manifest'.[16]

It is obvious that Fuller believed Huntington's preaching was a slanderous misrepresentation of the gospel because it reflected a

---

14 'Picture of an Antinomian', *Complete Works of the Rev. Andrew Fuller*, vol. V, pp. 766-768.

15 A large London fish-market famous for the vulgar and ribald language used there.

16 This was a common saying amongst Huntington's enemies. See Thomas Scott's letter to Dr Ryland, *Letters and Papers*, p. 129.

completely different standard of holiness from that to which he was accustomed. Huntington had preached that the believer serves God, not because of an instinctive duty which forces him to do so in his own strength, but because the love of God is within him through the indwelling of the Holy Spirit and a Christian life and witness are products of this. Christian justification and sanctification are all of God and not of man's effort to fulfil supposed divine demands on him. This was the teaching of Paul, the Reformers and most of the British Puritans, but to Fuller it was downright heresy.

This inability to grasp the scriptural nature of Huntington's teaching has forced most of his critics to regard his hearers as deluded and deceived souls who have never learnt the first steps in Christian holiness. The truth, however, is quite different. It is no difficult task to show that the ordinary believers who worshipped at Providence Chapel and chapels in fellowship with them enjoyed a very high experience of God's power in their lives and were second to none in spirituality and daily witness to their Lord.

Huntington's major critic[17] has stressed that his followers were poor, ignorant, uneducated people – just the right kind of people to be deluded by a man like Huntington. This assertion, like so many made by Huntington's critics, was made by one who did not share in the fellowship at Providence Chapel and thus did not know the members. Actually Huntington's members came from a very varied cross-section of the public. Moreover, examining the spiritual lives of some of the poorest in pocket, who were also 'poor in spirit', in Huntington's congregation proves an enriching experience indeed.

John Rusk and his wife

Of these poorer members of Providence Chapel, John Rusk is not an untypical example. Rusk was a sailmaker by trade, as his father, a Dane, was before him. Yet the poverty which plagued his father was also his lot and he was often out of work for months at a time and did not know where the next crust of bread would come from. Often Rusk would not dare to go to church or chapel because of the ragged state of his clothing and he had to spend years with his family in a workhouse. The sailmaker had, however, been spiritually minded from his childhood and when he

[17] The anonymous author of *The Voice of Years*.

became an adult, he took it for granted that he was 'in a profession'.[18] When circumstances allowed, he went to hear many preachers, including Huntington, and came to the conclusion that the preaching of other good men 'appeared empty and had no weight' in comparison to that of Huntington. After hearing Huntington regularly over a period of several weeks, walking the five miles to Providence Chapel and back, Rusk decided to pay him a call.

Before going to see Huntington, he rehearsed a statement of faith with which he hoped to impress the pastor. Once seated in front of Huntington, however, Rusk lost all his self-confidence and could not explain his case to the preacher, who listened patiently for a while but finally said that he had some work which he needed to finish. Huntington, as was his custom with those of whom he approved, did not ask the man to leave but gave him the run of his house; however, Rusk had expected far more personal attention from Huntington and got up angrily to go. As he stood up to leave, Huntington said simply, 'God bless you', which angered Rusk all the more and he left the house feeling that Huntington was the worst of men. Rusk resolved never to go and hear the preacher again but before the week was out, he felt mysteriously drawn to hear him once more, realising that the pastor had shown him the pride of his own heart.

Now Rusk saw that there had never been a true work of the Spirit in his life and he had always been impressed with his own goodness, rather than conscious of his own sinfulness. He then began to fear greatly that he had sinned against the Holy Ghost, shutting himself off from true salvation. In this mood, he went to hear Huntington one day feeling 'nothing but sin, filth and pollution; a lump of putrefaction'. During that service, he tells us, he found 'the Lord Jesus as my Saviour, His blood to cleanse me from all things; his Spirit to regenerate me and make me meet for the inheritance with the saints in light; and at the back of this, sin, guilt, fear and shame were all removed'. A diary entry for 1 May, 1798, which was about the time of Rusk's conversion, shows what a work of grace was taking place in his heart:

[18] The eighteenth-century way of saying 'a born-again Christian'.

> *May, 1st, 1798.* Heard Mr Huntington from these words: 'The humble shall see this and be glad, and their hearts shall live that seek God' (Psalm 69:32). When he said that divine things would be uppermost in the mind, and described that it was life in a man that discovered his vileness, I was enabled to believe. Faith comes by hearing. And though before I was very unsettled and uncomfortable, yet I went away with a solid peace, and a secret pleasure, joy, and peace in believing through the power of the Holy Ghost.[19]

Rusk's diaries enable us to see how he lived with the Lord until his death in 1834 at the age of sixty-two. Often he is plagued with his own sense of unholiness and rebellion and often he is found praising God for victory gained. It is very evident when reading these lines that Rusk mostly grew in grace through an experience of Christ's presence during times of illness, acute poverty and affliction.

Whilst out of work, Rusk started to write down his experiences and advice to others and in time he produced a large number of books, though apparently without making much attempt to have them published.[20] Some forty-eight of these works were, however, published between 1845 and 1908 by the Gospel Standard and prove to be a mighty testimony to the grace of God in the lives of sinners. In *Sorrow and Comfort*, for instance, Rusk writes on the subject of righteousness in the typical Huntingtonian way:

> Righteousness. Ah! say some, my heart sinks when that word is spoken, for I feel so much unrighteousness. I always thought that when a sinner was converted to God, he would feel himself better and better – feel righteous, and that old things would pass away, and that all things would become new. But I feel quite

---

[19] Taken from *John Rusk, Sailmaker and Well-Instructed Scribe*, published by the editor, H. M. Pickles.

[20] It was long thought that Rusk published nothing in his life, but recent research by H. M. Pickles has shown that Rusk published three books: *Zion, the Peculiar People of God; Heavenly Treasure and Durable Riches Flowing from God the Father to the Elect* and *Scriptural, Experimental and Practical Remarks on the Lord's Dealings with his Poor Afflicted People* (See *John Rusk, Sailmaker and Well-Instructed Scribe*, Ed., H. M. Pickles).

> opposite to all this, and really get worse and worse. I well know where you are, and it is a safe, although a painful path. You must either go on in this way, or else in self-righteousness. But, after all, you do have these renewings, and then you can see righteousness. Now all this painful teaching is not because there is not provision made. O no – righteousness is as much ours as if we always felt it. But it is to keep us out of self and looking to Christ. See where Job got by admiring self, and so would you and I. But observe the blessed provision made. 'Drop down, ye heavens, from above, and let the skies pour down righteousness; let the earth open, and let them bring forth salvation; and let righteousness spring up together. I the Lord have created it' (Isaiah 45:8).[21]

On publishing Rusk's work entitled *Perilous Times* J. C. Philpot commented:

> We cannot but call the attention of our spiritual readers to the piece of John Rusk on 'Perilous Times' which we furnish this month. It is so scriptural, faithful, and experimental, and at the same time so simple, plain, and clear, that it seems to have been written with a special unction and under a peculiar power. Few writers in our judgment come up to Rusk. The concluding advice to believers we particularly admire, and have met with nothing for a long time that more falls in with our own feelings and experience, or has been more commended to our conscience, as full of holy wisdom and suitable instruction.

Rusk, like most Huntingtonians, died well. His widow, a woman who had witnessed much suffering in her life, wrote down every word from the mouth of her loving husband during the last few days of his life. Her last entry states:

---

[21] Gospel Standard, August, 1850, p. 255. Taken from *Sorrow and Comfort; or, Conflicts and Triumphs the Common Lot of all Real Believers.*

Tuesday, April, 22. After he had taken a little arrowroot I said, 'Could you bear me to read a chapter?' He said, 'Yes'. I said, 'Is there any particular place?' He said 'Awake, awake!' I read the 52nd chapter of Isaiah, then asked him if he heard it. He said 'Yes, that will do. Ah! I have no breath'. He lay still a while, and when I raised him a little higher, I perceived a change in his countenance. I asked him if he could take anything. He said, 'Yes', and took some sago with a little wine, which was the last thing he took. This was about eleven o'clock; he breathed very short and hard, seemed perfectly sensible, but not able to speak; his sufferings were very great, and he was much convulsed inwardly. About two o'clock the rattle was heard in his throat. Jane and I never left the bedside from the time he changed until he died. He had not power to speak; but when I asked him if he found peace, rest and quietness, he nodded more than once. He seemed very much in prayer all day; we could see his lips move, but not hear what he said, except, 'Blessed be the Lord! Blessed Spirit!' Jane, in great agony, took hold of his hand and said, 'Father are you happy?' He squeezed her hand and said, 'Yes'. O! it was truly afflicting to see him in that agony so many hours. We both earnestly prayed to the Lord to receive his spirit and release him. I was almost overcome. I do not think I could have stood it much longer. I was nearly fainting, but the Lord supported me, for I felt persuaded it was the last struggle, and he was entering into bliss. His breath got lower and lower, and just as he breathed his last, a pleasant smile came on his face, which continued. Thus he entered into peace, about half-past seven o'clock on Tuesday evening, April, 22nd 1834, aged sixty-two.

The next day Mr S. called to see my poor husband, and remarked how very pleasant he looked, and how much like himself. He repeated a verse of one of Berridge's hymns while gazing upon him:

> No more the world on thee shall frown
> No longer Satan roar,

Thy man of sin is broken down
And shall torment no more.[22]

After a long and severe illness, Mary Anne Rusk followed her husband to glory only a year after his decease. She was fifty-four years of age. Her last words were: 'My flesh and my heart faileth, but God is the strength of my heart and my portion for ever'. She then sang in a clear strong voice three verses of Cowper's hymn, 'There is a fountain fill'd with blood', and passed on to glory whilst singing the last verse.

James and Mary Abbott

Another poor Huntingtonian who was yet rich in heavenly blessings was James Abbott. He was a shoemaker and attended Providence Chapel with his brother William, who later became a minister of the gospel. We have no record of Abbott's conversion but, as in the case of Rusk, his diaries give us deep insight into his life and beliefs. Typical of these entries is the one dated 17, September, 1803 where Abbott writes:

> After having been for some time in a dark, barren state, much unbelief prevailing, and struggling of corruption, in reading Mr. Huntington's *Letters* these words – 'Ere long the remains of the veil that so often intervenes shall be done away, and we shall know as we are known', were attended with much sweetness, and brought much comfort to my soul, as set me down happy and humble in heart. Bless the Lord therefore, O my soul! and forget not all His benefits, Whose Name be eternally praised.

Abbott's writings are full of descriptions of absolute poverty made rich through the presence of God. Typical of such testimonies is his description of unemployment sent to his brother-in-law. Abbott writes:

> At a certain time, being out of employment, going from shop to shop in the city to no purpose, I made a stand at the top of

[22] Gospel Standard, August, 1861, pp. 232-236.

Cornhill, not knowing what to do, nor where to look for anything to do. Like one of old, I was ready to envy the prosperity of the wicked, and seeing many pass by in their coaches, who appeared to have plenty of this world's good things, I could not help thinking my lot rather hard, when these words dropped into my mind, 'Trust in the Lord, and do good; so shalt thou dwell in the land, and verily thou shalt be fed'. While musing a little on this, these words followed, 'Man shall not live by bread alone, but by every word that proceedeth out of the mouth of God'. This stopped my murmuring: for here I saw both temporal and spiritual bread promised. I was enabled to look up to the Lord, to keep me submissive to His will, and appear for me in His own time and way, which I now believed He would do. My heart glowed with gratitude for His kindness in sending such a timely word to stop my murmuring, and envying the prosperity of the wicked, and though things outwardly were just the same, yet the inward consolation was such that I went home satisfied all would be well. After I got home I walked up and down the room praising the Lord for His mercy, and a verse of Hart's came to my mind, with which I could make sweet melody in my heart to the Lord:

> My soul thou hast, let what will ail,
> A never-changing friend.

So I have found it to this very day; for though I have been in many straits, and had many trials, both outwardly and inwardly, yet He has always appeared sooner or later, and supplied my need; and hath not left me destitute of His mercy or His truth. I can set my seal to the truth of the promise, 'Seek ye first the kingdom of God and His righteousness, and all these things shall be added unto you'. So I found it now, for shortly after my wife called to see our niece, who lived servant to Mr Burrell, and when she left, Mrs Burrell to her great surprise put a one pound note in her hand; and not long after Mr Burrell came up to me when coming out of Providence Chapel, and put a one pound note in my hand, saying, 'It was impressed on my mind to give you this'. Soon afterwards the Lord's providence appeared in providing for me a shop of work, the best I ever had, which continued some years. Surely it is of the Lord's mercies that I am not consumed: 'they are new every morning; great is His faithfulness'. 'If we believe not, He abideth faithful. He cannot deny Himself'. Lord, increase my faith, that I may trust Thee at all times, and be truly humbled at the remembrance of and loathe myself for all my evil ways which were not good: for 'there is forgiveness with Thee, that Thou mayest be feared'.[23]

Mrs Mary Abbott, like Mary Anne Rusk, was a convert of Huntington's and she too had suffered greatly in her life. Before marrying Abbott she was the widow of a brutal Irish workman who had beaten her daily. In spite of her difficulties with her former husband, she had managed to visit Providence Chapel and found Christ there. After Huntington's death, the couple came under the ministry of another Huntingtonian of note, J. F. Burrell. Mary Abbott was the first of the couple to cross over Jordan and her husband wrote a loving account of her last few days, ending it with the words:

Towards the end she was so weak that it was great labour for her to speak so as to be understood. At times her senses were roving, but though she seemed quite insensible at those times to everything about her, and unconnected in what she attempted to speak of worldly matters, yet when I spoke to her of spiritual things she expressed herself correctly enough. The week before her death I wrote to my brother giving him some account of the exercises of her mind during the first part of her illness, and of the happy issue, that she now lay hoping and expecting soon to be released from all pain, sin and sorrow, that I was persuaded she was in possession of a good hope, a solid and settled peace in her conscience, founded upon what Christ had done, and revealed by the Spirit to her – that she had proved Him to be a sure Refuge, being the mighty God. I read to her what I had written, in which she agreed. This was her testimony so long as

[23] Taken from *James Abbott, A Witness of the Truth*, published by the editor, H. M. Pickles.

> she was able to speak, nor was there the least appearance of any terror or fear on her mind. Her countenance appeared to the last the index of a mind composed, which caused me to say to those about her, when I found she was gone, 'Mark the perfect and behold the upright, their end is peace'.

The writings of John Keyt and C. Goulding

Another member of Providence Chapel, John Keyt, has been called 'one of the choicest and most savoury of Huntington's hearers'[24] and there are many of his letters extant which testify to the truth of such an opinion. Once, when Keyt was going through a very difficult period, he picked up a copy of Huntington's *The Justification of a Sinner* and was so gripped by what he read that he stayed up almost the whole night to read it. This moved him, one day, to say to his wife that he would go to hear Huntington preach. His wife told him that Providence Chapel was far too far away but he replied that he would have to go or die. At the chapel, Keyt covered his face with a handkerchief, so as not to be recognised, and sat down in one of the free pews. Huntington preached on Joel 2:32, 'Whosoever shall call on the name of the Lord shall be saved'. Keyt was given grace to call. He was delivered from his sins and never looked back.

A letter of his, written in old age, is typical of the Huntingtonian experience of holiness showing the ups and downs of spiritual life. To a friend in Christ he writes:

> Dear and Well Beloved,
> A long season has elapsed since I received your valuable epistle, richly fraught with the various exercises of the wayfaring man, heaven-born and heaven-bound. When I venture to address a few lines to you, my desire was to draw out of your earthen vessel a portion of that choice treasure which I felt persuaded the Lord had deposited therein. This my desire was accomplished, and it proved sweet to my soul, seeing you have communicated to me things new and old, both in the heights and in the depths – the heights of God's distinguishing, discriminating, and sovereign

[24] Editor's comment, Gospel Standard, September, 1850, p. 322.

grace towards you, and the depths of human depravity innate in the recipient of his grace, as exhibited in the experience of your own soul.

Ah ! my beloved friend and brother, this chequered path is all the Lord's own work and way of acting with his redeemed family, and it is 'marvellous in our eyes'. Our dear Lord and Savour's great undertaking, when he humbled himself in the assumption of our nature, was 'to seek and to save that which was lost'. He came 'not to call the righteous, but sinners to repentance'; yea, the very chief of sinners. If this had not been his mission and commission, you and I should have remained for ever in the congregation of the dead. But God, who is rich in mercy, for his great love wherewith he loved us, even when we were dead in sins, hath quickened us together with Christ'; and all of sovereign grace and free mercy.

In the manifestations of his wonderful mercy and grace, the Lord Jesus Christ came where we were, sought us out, and gathered us up. He found us in a waste, howling wilderness, cast out to the loathing of our persons, in our blood, defiled, polluted, and lost; it was then that he passed by and saw us in this deplorable state, and said unto us, 'Live'. This was a time of love indeed, when in infinite kindness he thoroughly cleansed us; for 'according to his mercy he saved us, by the washing of regeneration and the renewing of the Holy Ghost'. This was all the Lord's own work, we had no hand in it; his divine power wrought it, and he continues to maintain it in the midst of all opposition, either from the devil or indwelling sin.[25]

This letter goes on for several pages more and is a feast of very good things. Such a letter is a far cry from the scathing words of *The Voice of Years*, in which the author quotes Dr Johnson's maxim that 'Wonder is the effect of ignorance', and applies this to the Huntingtonians who he believes to have been so ignorant that they allowed Huntington to dupe them through clever use of a concordance rather than words of

[25] *Ibid.*, pp. 319-322

true wisdom. He would leave us with the impression that the Huntingtonians had no knowledge of Scripture and, when Huntington reeled off verse after verse of the Bible which he had learnt off by heart, they felt he was a living wonder. The scores of letters which are extant from many Huntingtonians from all walks of life show that they, too, knew a great deal of Scripture off by heart and had also applied it diligently to their own lives. What would that disbelieving author have thought if he had taken the trouble to read the fine Scripture-based testimony of C. Goulding to God's power in Huntington and in the words he preached? Goulding is writing shortly after Huntington's death and says:

> It has proved an unspeakable mercy to me that I should have been brought under his ministry, the second Sunday after I arrived in London, twenty-one years ago, when it pleased the Lord, by his instrumentality alone, to strip me of all my false hopes and vain confidence, and to bring me down sensibly into the horrible pit and miry clay, where Christ, the door of hope, was opened to me; where the free unconditional promises in him to sinners were applied; which laid a sound, a solid foundation for a good hope to rest upon; and from thence God brought me, by his grace, his Spirit, and his power, to believe in his dear Son, to the salvation of my soul. 'And, when the Lord writeth up the people, and takes the account of them in perfect number', Psalm 87:6; 'maketh up his jewels', Malachi 3:17; and Christ, as the Mediator, great Shepherd of the sheep, and King of Zion, delivers up in full tale all the subjects of his mediatorial kingdom to his Father, 1 Corinthians 15:24; with a, 'Behold me, and the children which thou hast given me'; of Old and New Providence Chapel, as also of other places where our dear departed Pastor laboured, it will be declared, that no small number were born again there; for I believe few ministers will have a brighter crown, or rejoice more in it, 1 Thessalonians 2:19, when they deliver up their ministerial work to their Master, in the beginning of the thousand years reign, than William Huntington, S.S. And then every minister will appear at the head of his own work, that it may be known what every man hath gained by trading. 'He that goeth forth weeping, bearing precious seed, shall doubtless come again

with rejoicing, bringing his sheaves with him', Psalm 126:6; 1 Thessalonians 2:19. The parable of the talents (Matthew 25) will also prove the truth of what I here assert.

I believe in my soul that since the times of the apostles, there has not been a minister raised up who has been blessed with such an experience himself of the Spirit's work upon the heart, and with such abilities to describe it to others, as our late honoured pastor. Scoffers may rage at this; but his incomparable works, now he himself has gone, will indisputably prove what I now declare. No author under the sun can be produced who describes vital godliness, or saving religion, so experimentally, and so clearly, as he has done; and, for myself, I can say, that in him I have lost one of the best friends that ever I had in this world, or I believe ever shall have.[26]

Joseph Burrell

Huntington's critics continue to stress that the 'Coalheaver' only attracted those of his own social background who, because of their lack of education, were easily duped by his artificial display of knowledge. The fact that the Princess Amelia, Sir Richard Hill, Sir William Hay, Sir Ludlow Harvey and the Earl of Liverpool, afterwards Prime Minister of England, regularly attended Providence Chapel seems permanently to escape them. Henry Peto, the famous architect and builder of London Bridge, was a member at Providence Chapel, as was the king's printer and publisher Thomas Bensley, the Comptroller of the Household to Princess Charlotte, the Director of the Observatory in Kew Gardens and the King's State Coachman. At least two of Huntington's members became quite famous painters and still have their paintings on permanent display in London museums and galleries.[27]

---

[26] Taken from Goulding's preface to *The Substance of the Last, or Farewell Sermon of the Late Rev. W. Huntington, S.S.*, Bensley, 1813.
[27] Burrell and Bourne.

Joseph Francis Burrell was a Huntingtonian who, through the grace of God, never knew the experiences brought on by poverty. His story is really worth telling more fully. Burrell was born in Molsheim in Alsace, now part of France, and was brought up as a Roman Catholic. Under that faith Burrell learnt that if he died under the age of fifteen, he would be sure to go to heaven as all children are incapable of mortal sin. In spite of this, Burrell longed as a child to be saved from the penalty of sin which he knew was in his heart. His father had a comfortable pension as a retired officer but the Burrells were a sad family during Joseph's childhood as one by one sixteen of his seventeen brothers and sisters died mysteriously until only he and his eldest brother were left alive.

Joseph's mother had a well-educated sister in Paris who had come into a fortune, chiefly due to her son's brilliance as a diplomat and musician. This woman decided to take her sister's two boys into her care and give them the very best of education. Burrell's parents agreed, no doubt hoping that this would protect them from the fate of their brothers and sisters. Joseph's aunt sent the two boys to a top school and promised them a university education afterwards, expressing a wish that they would take on some high office in the Roman Catholic Church. Joseph's elder brother, however, proved too difficult for his aunt to manage and he was sent back to Alsace in disgrace. Joseph became the apple of his aunt's eye and learnt as a child that it is possible for a Jacob to be loved and an Esau rejected. Joseph's life, however, was not a bed of roses during the first few years of his stay in Paris. His aunt had also adopted her brother's son who was two years older than Joseph and an out and out rascal. This boy plagued Joseph with his lewd behaviour though Joseph was kept from joining in by his own abhorrence. After some time, however, the conduct of this child forced his aunt to send him back home and Joseph was left with his aunt and grown-up cousin. As a result of her deteriorating health, Joseph's aunt moved to Normandy where she hired a retired university professor as Joseph's tutor and managed to obtain for him access to the enormous private library of a local duchess. Young Joseph was thrilled at the chance to take in so much learning and voluntarily got up at four o'clock each day so as not to waste a moment's study. Soon Joseph was receiving promises of a scholarship to the Royal Academy of Paris.

Meanwhile Joseph recognised fully that his fortune was a gift of God and went to mass daily to give thanks. He had no knowledge of Scripture, however, or the way of salvation. He believed most sincerely that God must be very proud of him. He was also aware that if he was to enter on a brilliant career, he must prove that he was a faithful member of the Roman Catholic Church. He thus prayed and fasted, did penance, took the sacrament and learnt Latin psalms with all his young energy. Once at a midnight mass, his conscience was pricked and he realised what a mockery of true Christian living he was going through. Instead of changing his ways, however, Joseph, now fourteen or fifteen years of age, began to drift further away from God.

After doing brilliantly in his studies, Joseph Burrell was appointed as secretary to the Baron of Eskar, a member of the richest family in the kingdom. Burrell was only eighteen years of age. From now on he was trained as a courtier, learning to play the pianoforte, to paint and draw, to say the correct things at the correct time and to be very gallant to the ladies. The Lord, however, preserved Burrell from joining in the indecencies of court life. This caused his master's displeasure as he found his secretary did not even know the names of the filthy practices he loved to carry out. After Burrell had made it clear to the baron that he wished to live a life of cleanliness and decency, he was sacked from the rich man's services and he duly packed and left the 'sink of abominations and temptations', as he later called it, and returned to his aunt's.

Soon afterwards Burrell's aunt sent him to London, where her son was making a name for himself as a musician, and arranged that he should teach the pupils whom her son had not time to teach. Thus the one-time secretary to the richest family in Paris became a music teacher in the capital of England. The hand of the Lord in this soon became plain to see. The rich baron fell out of favour and soon after died of starvation in Germany. Other members of his court were put to death by the guillotine. Through going to London, Burrell found eternal life.

Though trained in the best Roman Catholic traditions, Burrell discovered that he was a total stranger to all gospel truths. He became involved with a young girl in a very dubious trade and in striving to reform her was himself pulled into sin, but eventually married her. One day a copy of Milton's *Paradise Lost* came into his hands and he read for the first time in his life of the origin of sin, the fall of devils and of man, of Christ's greatness and glory and what he had done for sinners. Burrell was amazed at this and wondered whether it was fact or fiction. Soon, however, the dreams of hell which he had so often experienced as a child came back to him and he laboured for many months under a conviction that God's wrath was upon him. In his misery he wasted away to a skeleton though an inner voice always told him that God would use this suffering to the good. At times Burrell had marvellous visions of the Lord being with him and gracious to him, though he still knew no Scripture and had never heard the gospel preached.

The house in which Burrell lived belonged to a Mr Legg whom he did not know personally. One day his wife found out that Legg attended Providence Chapel and regularly heard a Mr Huntington preach. On hearing this, Burrell was eager to hear this Mr Huntington. He thus visited Legg, who was a tailor, and pretended to be interested in ordering a suit. What he actually wanted was an invitation from Legg to go with him to Providence Chapel. The kind tailor lost no time in reading Burrell's thoughts and soon it was decided that the two men should go to hear Huntington preach the next day. As soon as Burrell entered the chapel, he felt he had found his true home. The very first hymn that was given out described the spiritual situation he had been in for some time. Burrell could do nothing but weep. He became alarmed, however, when Huntington got up to preach without any notes. How could a man preach 'a discourse out of his own head' without the assistance of notes? He found himself praying for the preacher that he would speak words of wisdom from God. At first Burrell was put off by Huntington's preaching as he did not know anything about the Scriptures and Huntington was quoting them non-stop. Soon, however, Huntington described in simple words how a sinner feels in his distress and the reception he meets with when Christ draws him. This Burrell understood and felt himself drawn to Christ, sinner as he was.

To cut a very long story short, Burrell was converted from his sins and found a home from home at Huntington's chapel.[28] He continued as a music and art teacher for some time but gradually became aware of

---

[28] For a very full account of Burrell's conversion read his *The Triumph of Christ*, London, 1819.

a call to the ministry. After his wife died, he married one of Huntington's daughters and became a notable preacher himself. After Huntington's death, a large number of those that had attended his ministry found a further spiritual home under Burrell's preaching.

Once Burrell realised that there had been a work of God in his life, he could not wait to tell Huntington about what had happened. He, like many others, was rather perturbed to be greeted by Huntington's gruff, 'What do you want?', but as Burrell outlined his story, Huntington showed great interest. When he heard that Burrell, in spite of his learning, had only read Taylor's *Holy Living* and the four Gospels, he advised him to buy a Bible as quickly as possible and also read *The Kingdom of Heaven Taken by Prayer*. Huntington then told Burrell how he himself had come to know the Lord and after the interview Burrell says, 'I went away well satisfied with my visit, blessing and praising God, who had graciously confirmed his own testimony to me by a similar experience in another'.

It is of great interest to note how this highly gifted man of great cultural abilities got on with a man who had hardly ever been to school and was as good as tone-deaf to the sounds of music. Burrell always regarded Huntington as a man of astute learning and spiritual powers and marvelled at the display of God's powers in him saying of him, 'The Lord having brought me under the ministry of that excellent servant of his, Mr H. he caused me also highly to esteem him for his work's sake; and the unfeigned love, reverence, and spiritual regard I had for him was truly wonderful. God had made him a nursing father to me indeed'.

Burrell was often vexed when he heard people criticise Huntington, and he noted that they were mostly people who had received advice from the 'Coalheaver' and had rejected it to their folly. Once when an acquaintance had raved about Huntington's 'temper, spirit and preaching', as well as his 'imperious natural disposition', Burrell told him:

> His infirmities, which I perceive as well as you, nevertheless lead me incessantly to pray for him, and the gracious Lord answers me with joy unspeakable, so that I seldom have a barren

> opportunity. Thus being enabled through the Spirit to mortify the prejudice of my carnal mind, (which overcomes you) I find life, love and power flow into my soul; which sweetly influences my life, walk and conversation. The pipe through which I suck these blessings at present, appears to be neither gold, nor silver; but the liquor is truly the new wine of the kingdom. Is not the excellency of God's power seen in his earthen vessel? If our confidence is never to be fixed till we see perfection in man, we shall never be at a point; but we are to stand, walk and live by the faith of the Son of God, whose perfect work the good man preaches. The Devil will not fail to magnify those evident blemishes in the real ministers of Christ, in order, if possible, to render their labours ineffectual; but God defeats his designs, by enabling his own people to cast their burden upon him: This I have been led to do times without number, and have escaped the snare of the fowler: and this blessing has come upon me, 'Blessed is the man that endureth temptation: for when he is tried he shall receive the crown of life, which the Lord hath promised to them that love him', James 1:12. Consider therefore, what loss you sustain by going after smooth preachers, and what I gain, by making the Lord my counsellor and guide.

Burrell tells us that this answer to the critic's complaints so moved the man that he became reconciled both to Huntington's person and his ministry.

Like most Huntingtonians of his day, Burrell departed from this life in deep harmony with God. One person who witnessed his end said movingly, 'I would not have been without that night for all the world', referring to the pastor's mighty testimony of the Lord's presence with him in the Valley of the Shadow of Death. Burrell was buried in Kensal Green Cemetery and a commentary on his work for the Lord is inscribed on his tombstone:

> In an age of erroneous and empty profession he preached the Word of God, its power and fulfilment, earnestly contending for the true faith of the ever-blessed Trinity and the Person of Christ: the fall of man, the redemption of the elect, their new birth, continual conflict and certain salvation; and enforcing the fruits,

inseparable from living faith – the fear and love of God. His ministry may be summed up in the Apostle's words, 'But ye, beloved, building up yourselves in your most holy faith, praying in the Holy Ghost, keep yourselves in the love of God, looking for the mercy of our Lord Jesus Christ unto eternal life'.[29]

Huntington's relationship with other ministers

Huntington must have been particularly thankful to meet up with Burrell as he was always on the lookout for a pastor-friend who held views similar to his own concerning the gospel and the all-sufficiency of the work of the Holy Spirit in the lives of the elect. This longing of Huntington's to have fellowship with like-minded ministers led him to be duped time and time again by those who could not have cared less for his doctrines but were eager to take advantage of his ever-generous hand in assisting fellow-ministers financially. In the early years of his ministry Huntington was approached by at least a score of 'poor' ministers who begged first his friendship and then the contents of his pockets, only to turn their backs on him when their need was satisfied. In a letter written to a fellow-pastor in 1805 Huntington tells how he had, in earlier years, collected well over £600 for pastors with whom he thought he would be able to work but he had to confess: 'I was for years a dupe and a tool to these men. Such deception made my soul sick'. The person to whom Huntington was writing well knew Huntington's knack of raising money quickly as he had himself benefited to the tune of some hundreds of pounds from Huntington's generosity.

Though Huntington was often deceived by false displays of friendship and fellowship amongst brother ministers, many of them in time became truly reformed as a result of his testimony and subsequently themselves witnessed to its truths in the pulpit. It must have been a great comfort to Huntington, as he preached in his midweek services, to see over a score of clergymen, pastors and ministers, representing several denominations, sitting absorbing every word with zeal for the Lord. When he opened his mouth to preach his first sermon

[29] Taken from Alexander, *More than Notion*, pp. 263, 264.

at the first Providence Chapel twenty-eight years before, his had been a lone voice against free-will, universal atonement, Roman tyranny, church musical and theatrical antics and a lack of strict adherence to the full Word of God. Now, one by one, ministers all over Britain were recognizing that Huntington was a bastion of strength in reviving the Reformed Calvinistic faith which had been so weakened by Fullerism and Wesleyanism.[30]

Men like the Rev. Thomas Burgess of Deptford had been highly prejudiced against Huntington because of the false reports of his free-will and Universalist enemies. Burgess thus went to hear Huntington preach in order to collect ammunition to use against him. Huntington spoke from Romans 8:2, 'For the law of the Spirit of life in Christ Jesus hath made me free from the law of sin and death'. Burgess was first struck down in his soul and then lifted up, enraptured by the biblical 'sweetness' of the sermon. Of his experience on that great day of enlightenment, he said of Huntington, 'He set forth all my experiences, from first to last, and my soul has been in union with him from that day to this'.

The Rev. James Bourne, who became a very successful minister of the gospel, first heard Huntington in 1807. Of this event he says:

> I well remember the first time I heard him, I thought him the most agreeable preacher I had ever heard, and was not in the least tired. I continued for two years to frequent his chapel, together with the Established Church. I now grew very anxious and much in earnest respecting the salvation of my soul, but had no

---

[30] As modern Fullerites stress that Huntington had no following whatsoever amongst fellow-ministers during the late eighteenth century and the first half of the nineteenth century, the following list of some of the eminent clergymen from at least four different denominations who were greatly attached to Huntington and his teaching may prove helpful: William Abbott, Samuel Turner, Joseph Burrell, James Bourne, Algar Lock, Jenkin Jenkins, William Brook, Isaac Beeman, Thomas Burgess, Joseph Chamberlain, Henry Birch, John Vinall, John Warburton, J. W. Tobitt, John E. Hazelton, W. Jeyes Styles, Mr Howells, Jonathan Franklin, A. J. Baxter, Dr Henry Cole, Dr Doudney, J. C. Philpot, Samuel Adams, Thomas Burgess, W. Sinden, Bernard Gilpin, J. K. Popham, Thomas Bradbury, Edmund Robins, George Holden, John Hervey Gosden, John Kershaw and William Gadsby. One could also include most of the large number of ministers connected with The Gospel Advocate, The Gospel Standard and The Gospel Magazine.

understanding what spiritual life meant, or what communion with God was. I used to pray as I thought but never waited for any answer, I supposed I should get that in heaven, not now; and though I found nothing in my heart to forbid the spirit of the world, or anything that was not openly flagitious, yet, I believed without doubt that all was right within.

Bourne then obtained Huntington's *The Barber*, which he had been told was a scurrilous book and ought to be on the heresy list. On reading the book, he realised that his own profession was vain and founded on sand, so he wrote to Huntington about it. Huntington replied on 13 May, 1807, saying:

Sir,
I have read your account over and over, and I perceive that it hath happened to you as to many others. You fell among thieves, and you have been joined to the citizens of this country, and you know what flesh and blood, voluntary humility and will-worship can do; and God has been for some time disciplining you with His holy law, that you may try your strength by that rule, and see your face in that glass; and when you have proved all these things, you will learn to hold fast that which is good. I have no doubt but you are under the tuition of God Himself, and in due time He will lead you to His dear Son. I have made use of my only, effectual, and never-failing means in your behalf – that is, prayer to God, and I shall continue these by the promised assistance of the Holy Spirit, not doubting but my Most Benign of all Parents will attend to them, and regard them in His own time and way.

Bourne is one of the central figures in J. H. Alexander's book *More than Notion* and his lasting work in evangelizing the great and small is for ever recorded there. This gifted painter-cum-pastor was the driving force in the founding of many a new work throughout England and his life, testimony and evangelistic work show how wrong is the criticism levelled against Huntingtonians that they felt no call to preach the gospel outside their own church services. They were church-founders of no mean competence. Bourne, however, campaigned strongly against the false assurance in evangelism given by Fullerites to sinners informing them that they could believe if they only willed themselves to believe according to their inbred sense of duty to God. Such pseudo-evangelism had nothing to do with the gospel in Bourne's opinion. Of this teaching concerning the natural man's ability to discern the ways of God, thus ignoring man's total depravity,[31] Bourne said:

> I have often pitied those for whom I have had great natural affection because I could not with all my attempts show to their understanding what the light of life is. God has been pleased to call it a mystery and a secret hidden from all but those to whom He is pleased to reveal it. The natural man cannot discern the things of the spirit. If a man truly taught of God is firm in his point he will find the close argument will arouse the secret enmity of any religious person who thinks he is right. The mere professor does, I believe, think he possesses all the essential points and that the difference is a mere quibble. Nor can he understand that what a real godly man knows is not from what he is determined to know, but it is the Spirit which is of God that makes us to know these divine things are really given us of God. The natural man (the Apostle insists upon it) receiveth not this truth. He cannot understand how it is and puts it down as a mere nothing but seeking to be contentious.[32]

Coupled with his awareness that the natural man has no knowledge of the light of the gospel was Bourne's conviction that no natural, fallen man had an awareness of any duties whatsoever that he owed to God. Nor did he believe in the Fullerite myth that sinners should be invited to repent, knowing that they *could* if they only *would*. Criticising the downgrading of the gospel in this way, Bourne wrote:

---

[31] For Fuller 'total depravity' does not mean 'totally unable to believe in Christ' in the sense of 'unable in every respect' (See Fuller's *Works*, vol II, p. 438).

[32] Quoted from Alexander, *More than Notion*, p. 237.

> Men may talk like fools and tell us it is our duty to believe; but, when the Spirit convinces us of our unbelief, then we perceive this unbelief is like gates of brass and bars of iron, and none can remove it but He who convinces us of it. And I am sure it is not in my power to repent though I would give ten thousand worlds to do so. I am taught that it is the gift of God in Jesus Christ. 'Him hath God exalted with His right hand to be Prince and a Saviour, for *to give repentance* to Israel and forgiveness of sins'.[33]

Another Huntingtonian of note was the Rev. Isaac Beeman. He came into contact with Huntington when he was a businessman and an inhabitant of Cranbrook, Huntington's home town. His business premises included a large warehouse which he often invited Huntington to use as a chapel when he preached in the neighbourhood. Soon quite a large congregation began to gather at these services and people were converted who belonged to no particular church. This moved Beeman to pray that a chapel might be founded in the vicinity to serve as a home church for these new converts and older Christians seeking fellowship with those of like experience. He thus wrote to Huntington explaining his thoughts and offered to erect a chapel at his own expense. Huntington, realising that Beeman could ill afford such a move, agreed that a chapel must be built but told Beeman that he would make collections to finance it, which he did without further ado. Whilst building was in progress, Beeman received a call to the ministry and became the new chapel's first minister. Speaking of his call to build a chapel years later, Beeman said to John Keyt, mentioned above:

> When my affection was set towards the house of the Lord, and my mind inclined to build, these words came, 'Go up to the mountain, and take wood and build the house, and I will take pleasure in it, and I will be glorified in it, saith the Lord', also, 'My Spirit remaineth among you; fear not', and again, 'In this place will I give peace, saith the Lord', and in the 18th and 19th

[33] *Ibid.*, p. 204.

> verses of Haggai 2, you will see what is there said. It was made out to me that, from the time I began to lay Christ as the Foundation of God's spiritual temple, I might look for his blessing. And blessed be the eternal God, I have ever since been kept looking, and to his eternal praise, have seen his blessing in many hearts. I know three at this time, who, I believe, are quickened souls; one has already gone very deep into soul trouble, and has had at times great encouragement by the application of God's word with power. I cannot doubt that they will all come out in God's good time. You know, at the finding of a lost sheep the friends and neighbours are called in to rejoice at the good tidings; believing it would be so to you, I have thus written.[34]

Beeman wrote this letter after preaching at Providence Chapel some years after Huntington's death. A real work of God seems to have continued there, as Beeman was full of tales of conversions. As one coming from the country to the capital, he could yet say in true Huntingtonian style:

> I am glad to find some in London that know the joyful sound, some to whom Christ is precious; indeed, it is he that furnishes the feast, and also is the feast of fat things upon Mount Zion. And where he is not, let whatever else be there, it is but as the mountains of Gilboa, without either dew or rain and of course, no fields of offering. But when Christ is the heavenly entertainment, there are dew, and rain, and fields of offering too; for at such times thanksgiving from the recipients goes up. It is at such times the Lord comforts Zion, making her wilderness like Eden and her desert as the garden of the Lord; 'joy and gladness are found therein, thanksgiving and the voice of melody'.
>
> These things have been most sweetly verified in the case of a person with us. Her deliverance came about three months since, after labouring in bondage (with a little help at times) for years. She received considerable help while I was speaking from Isaiah 44:21-23, and in that week she had a manifestation of Christ to

[34] The Gospel Standard, September, 1850, p. 304.

her soul, when all her bondage fled, all her sin was taken away, and the joy of heaven came into her heart; peace also flowed in like a river, and she was truly delighted with the abundance of Zion's glory, satisfied with the breasts of her consolations, and truly comforted in Jerusalem. She still continues on the holy mount, and her heart is filled with gratitude and her mouth with praise. I never saw a clearer deliverance. She loathes herself, and magnifies the Lord. So I hope the kingdom of God is amongst us, and does not stand in word only, but in power.

The 'Welsh Ambassador'

The Rev. Jenkin Jenkins was a Welshman who had studied at Lady Huntingdon's college at Trevecca but became drawn to Huntington through his writings and subsequently hearing him preach. It was through Huntington that Jenkins came to a full understanding of the gospel and a saving knowledge of Christ, although he continued to live through alternating periods of grave doubt and great assurance. Huntington became very fond of Jenkins and looked upon him as his son in Christ. The initials W. A., which Jenkins invariably used after his name, were given him by Huntington who called him Christ's 'Welsh Ambassador' to Lewes, where Huntington had a chapel built for him. Jenkins experienced much animosity from other ministers who delighted in telling the story that W. A. did not stand for 'Welsh Ambassador' but for 'Wonderful Ass'!

Jenkins was a good preacher and was capable of filling large churches and chapels, which he invariably did. His appearance, however, was very off-putting as he was unusually corpulent and his frequent serious illnesses did not improve his looks. He never married and lived in a large house with his niece and housekeeper, supplementing his salary by keeping livestock and doing gardening work, similarly to Huntington. In fact Jenkins invariably looked to Huntington as his example in almost all he did and his letters show how much he relied on the 'Coalheaver' for help and comfort. Jenkins visited Huntington and occupied his pulpit on numerous occasions. Huntington was equally at home at Jenkins' but always took care to take a large piece of cheese or a shank of bacon with him when visiting his friend as Jenkins' housekeepers had almost banned food from the house in order to bring his enormous weight down.

Huntington wrote more letters to Jenkins than to any other friend. These letters show how skilled Huntington was didactically in teaching his younger friend the doctrines of the gospel. Huntington's great book on the work of the Holy Spirit, *Contemplations on the God of Israel*, is really a series of letters to Jenkins on the subject and gives the reader some idea of the fine spiritual food the Welshman received from his English mentor. The volume must be considered as one of the most inspired of all Huntington's works and he was to say that he had never felt the presence of the Holy Spirit closer than when he wrote those letters. Of this collection of letters to Jenkins, William Stevens, a Huntingtonian of the first order himself, writes in his *Recollections*, 'The best work he ever wrote. There is nothing, I can say, that can fully set forth its real value … Whether for doctrine, experience, or practical godliness, I think it will be readily granted that this book cannot be excelled. Would that the Lord had given to all his opposers the heavenly wisdom its author must have been endowed with!'

Jenkins' letters are as good as his sermons and the following words to a friend show how deeply versed he was in experimental, doctrinally sound Christianity:

> The Lord upholdeth them that fall, and raiseth up all them that are bowed down. The first fall of an elect sinner is from his high-towering pinnacle of self-confidence, when the Lord comes to judge his house, and undermine his sandy foundation, for his foundations are in the dust. The arrows of the King of Zion are shot into the hearts of his enemies, whereby the people fall under him. But the Lord does not suffer them to sink, nor does the pit shut its mouth over them, nor are they left to despair of finding mercy. Here they are upheld; a secret confidence in the heart, a hope springing up therefrom upholds them. By these, with a ray of light that shines on their path, they get to a comfortable standing; but it is not long together that they are able to stand. Clouds and darkness come over them again; Satan besets them, fears lay hold of them, and down they go, and fall from all their sweet views, comfortable prospects, encouraging hope, and

> prevailing confidence; for the righteous falleth seven times and rises again. The Lord delighteth in the way of the righteous; when he falleth he shall not utterly be cast down, for the Lord upholdeth him with his hand. By the power of God he is supported, and the word of the Lord upholds him. 'Thy word upheld him that was falling, and thou hast strengthened the feeble knees'. The spirit of faith in the heart makes the application: 'Rejoice not against me, O mine enemy! When I fall I shall arise, when I sit in darkness the Lord shall be a light unto me'. And as he upholds them that fall, he raiseth up them that are bowed down. Heaviness in the heart of a man maketh it to stoop; oppression from the enemy, and depression through a sense of the plague of the heart make us to bow down. 'I am bowed down greatly; I go mourning all the day long'. Why? 'My loins are filled with a loathsome disease, and there is no soundness in my flesh, because of my sin'. But those that mourn are exalted to safety. He raises the mind, heart, and affections, with his presence; the power that attends his word raises up the drooping faith and languishing hope. This is the path, my dear brother, and these are the footsteps of the flock, and in these we must tread.

As the reader might have expected, Jenkins also died well. The Wednesday before he died, he knew he was going but said he had never felt so happy and resigned to God's will. On hearing that a friend had died, he prayed with great energy and earnestness that he might soon follow her. He was able to sing a Welsh hymn in the afternoon but became delirious and spoke half in Welsh and half in English so that his hearers could only catch the words: 'Blessed be his name. My warfare is almost over, and there is a rest remaining; but who are they that enter into rest? Why we that believe do enter into rest. I feel myself now on the borders of Canaan. And the ransomed of the Lord shall return, and come to Zion, with songs and everlasting joy and gladness, sorrow and sighing shall flee away', and similar words of hope and assurance. A visitor came in and asked Jenkins how he was. The dying man said, 'Here I am still, you see, and here I shall be till the glorious company from above shall be sent to carry me home'. That glorious company came soon after and Jenkins, after a time of great pain and vomiting but obvious joy in the Lord, was taken home.

William Brook

One of the closest friends of Huntington was a high-born minister of the Anglican Church by the name of William J. Brook.[35] This clergyman was widely known as a godly man before coming into contact with Huntington but it was through reading his books that Brook came to a deeper knowledge of Christ. Of this minister of St Nicholas Church, Brighton, and preacher to HRH the Prince Regent, it was widely said that, 'If ever the Lord made one man more honest than another, it was Mr Brook'. The Prince Regent, who was to become the notorious George IV, was once overheard to say to Sir Benjamin Bloomfield during a service taken by Brook, 'Oh, Sir Benjamin, if Brook is right, we are all wrong!' Once when Brook was preaching on the wages of sin, the Prince Regent was so struck by the message that he exclaimed, 'If what this man preaches is true – and who dares to say it is not? – we are all damned to a man!'

Humanly speaking, Brook was a 'made' man. His congregation in Brighton numbered princes, peers, judges, bishops, deans and members of the royal household and he was said to have an income of between £600 and £700 a year and was sure of a bishopric although he was hardly yet in his thirties.

The story of how Brook was moved to leave the Church of England is remarkable. A man who had become extremely rich in India travelled with his wealth and a guilty conscience back home to England and his ship docked outside Brighton. The man had been so plagued by the crimes that he had committed that on reaching England he had a mental breakdown and tried to commit suicide by slitting his throat from one side to the other. Friends found him before he bled to death and he was quickly treated and the nearest minister – Brook – sent for. Brook spoke to the man but found him lost in his sins. He strove to turn the man to Christ but this proved impossible. Faced with death and destruction, the man still could not repent. As Brook was ministering to him, the man's

[35] Brook's middle name is given variously as 'James' or 'John'. Huntington always called him 'James'.

wound, which had been stitched up, broke open and the rich trader bled to death in the arms of the young minister.

Brook was asked to take the funeral service and did so, remaining quite composed until he came to the words in the Prayer Book where thanks are given to God for taking a 'brother' to himself and the bliss of the deceased is described. Brook stopped in his tracks and could go no further. Afterwards he said, 'What could I think, but that if I insulted the Almighty, and told lies at this rate, he would cut me down and send me to hell, as I was fully convinced he had done this miserable man, as surely as ever a soul was sent to perdition?' He wasted no time in quitting the Church of England and saying goodbye to fame, fortune and his certain bishopric.[36]

The young ex-clergyman had been influenced in his thinking by reading Huntington's books and he now had time to visit London and have fellowship with Huntington, who gave his new friend the run of his house. Huntington soon set to work raising money and was able to contribute a large sum so that Brook could build a chapel in Brighton as many of his former parishioners wished to continue under his ministry. It says much for Huntington that as he was canvassing money for the new Providence Chapel, he still thought of others and raised money for Brook.

Brook often preached at Providence Chapel. This was an arduous task for any preacher other than Huntington as his congregation did not accept a second-best willingly. There was a remarkable dwindling in the congregation when Huntington had a guest speaker but at least 1,500 used to attend Brook's preaching, showing how much he had been accepted as a true 'Huntingtonian'. The following letter serves to show how deep was the young minister's fellowship with God:

> To the Wife of my bosom and the Daughter of my vows,
>
> Many changes and frequent are the lot of us both. A little measure of peace and rest in God, and great portions of darkness, deadness, unbelief, and distance from God; yet all these things serve as ballast to me and you too. We are highly favoured by the

[36] The Gospel Standard, 1 January, 1856.

Almighty himself in his kind providence as well as his grace, for it is his grace that directs his providence; and we need many, many changes to keep us in the fear of his name, and in that low place where his hand is much desired and sought. What we stand in need of is more life. I feel this sensibly. I want more divine life in my soul in secret with God; but I am exercised, not so much with the enjoyment of life as with feelings of life, if you can understand what this means. I am plagued with the corruptions of my heart, with much darkness of mind, and with much weakness of soul. Now life moves in all these things: in prayer, waiting, watching, confession, pleading, &c.; and we are to have 'the sentence of death in ourselves, that we should not trust in ourselves, but in God which raiseth the dead'. You have tasted that the Lord is gracious, but then you are a babe, and need more of the sincere milk of the word; and this can only be had by close waiting upon Him who has promised to give us another Comforter, who shall abide with us for ever. It is not looking to past experience, helps, and comforts, that will do to satisfy our souls in God; it is the express witness of the Spirit with our spirit which can alone do the business; and this witness is sure and certain in the court of conscience. It is not looking to a law work, nor to a gospel work that will stablish our hearts; but it is receiving the testimony of the Holy Ghost that seals us to the day of redemption. And how is this to be had? It is to be had from Jesus Christ. The Spirit is called the Holy Spirit of promise, the promise of God the Father, in and through Christ. To Christ we are directed to seek; and he has promised to give us the Spirit, to guide us into all truth. 'If any man thirst, let him come unto me and drink, he that believeth on me, as the Scripture has said, out of his belly shall flow rivers of living water'. But the devil's aim is to keep us from that fountain. He does not object so much to our looking at evidences, as our looking to Christ; there he makes the most desperate resistance, by darkening the mind, making the heart fearful, making us strong in ourselves, blackening God's character, and setting before us our own villainy, infusing pride, rebellion, unbelief, and hardness of heart. We are both tried in many and singular ways, I have sometimes thought; but it is a mercy that our faith in God increases, and the love of each other in Christ abounds. It is with me, for the most part, a hard service; but we are commanded to endure hardness as good soldiers of Jesus Christ. We both find God on our side; let us cleave close to him, and to those very few whom God hath joined together in our affections.

Kind love to yourself and the dear children.

W. J. B.[37]

Brook's death was also triumphant. Though he was only thirty-seven years of age, a long and serious illness had shown him that he was about to depart for glory. For two months previous to his death, his wife Anne wrote that he never lost the knowledge of the presence of God for a single moment. Three days before his death, he was able to say to a friend, 'I never till now could say with Paul, I am now ready to be offered, and the time of my departure is at hand; I have fought a good fight, I have finished my course, I have kept the faith: henceforth there is laid up for me a crown of righteousness, which the Lord, the righteous Judge, shall give me at that day'. The day after, he was seized with a paralytic stroke and the last words he said to his wife were: 'My dear Ann, you and I have but one Friend, but one Refuge, cleave close to Him, He will never leave nor forsake you'.[38]

Such recorded testimonies of Huntingtonians are legend and books could be filled with them. Far from being the poor, ignorant, deluded souls free-will critics force themselves to believe the Huntingtonians were, it can easily be proved that, on the whole, they practised a purity of faith and life that has not seen the like since New Testament times or times of great spiritual revival. It became quite a common practice at the death of Huntingtonians for those watching their departure to say, 'Mark the perfect man, and behold the upright, for the end of that man is peace'. So they lived and so they died.

---

[37] The Gospel Standard, June, 1850, pp. 202, 203.
[38] Taken from Hooper, *Facts and Letters*, p. 103.

Chapter 12

The Righteousness Which Is Not Of The Law

The lives of the Huntingtonians outlined in the preceding chapter were marked by a piety and holy walk that were second to none this side of glory. Their sanctification cannot be analysed in isolation from their beliefs. The particular doctrine which Huntingtonians treasured perhaps more than all was the doctrine of Christ's righteousness imputed by a gift of grace to them. For them rival doctrines of righteousness and the accompanying doctrine of sanctification were all man-centred. Sanctification could never come from within the old man. It was a putting off of the old man and a putting on of the new. The Huntingtonians, by means of their pastor's faithful preaching, had found the key to living a Christ-centred holy life, without which no man can face God. Thus we must look with extra care at the Huntingtonians' doctrines of righteousness, sanctification and holiness and go into greater detail in comparing them with the standards the Bible sets.

The historical background to the doctrine

The doctrine of the imputed righteousness of Christ which the Huntingtonians believed in has been held by the church in all ages and was the hope of all Old Testament saints even before the first advent. This was emphasised by the Waldensians who, as long ago as 1120, protested against the novel teachings of Roman Catholicism by affirming, 'Christ was promised to our forefathers, who received the law, to the end that, knowing their sin by the law, and their unrighteousness and insufficiency, they might desire the coming of Christ, to satisfy for their sins, and, by himself, to accomplish the law'.[1]

Calvin, in Book XIV of his *Institutes*, stressed that believers are 'justified solely by faith and the free imputation of Christ's righteousness'. The British Reformers held to this belief in the face of Roman teaching in favour of self-righteousness. Latimer proclaimed from the pulpit, 'When he [God] gave us his only Son, he gave us also his righteousness and his fulfilling of the law. So that we are justified by God's free gift, and not of ourselves, nor by our merits; but the righteousness of Christ is accounted to be our righteousness'.[2]

The Puritans, too, were, on the whole, relentless in attributing all righteousness to Christ. In the seventeenth century the Scotsman Robert Traill said:

> 1. That Christ's righteousness is the only plea and answer of a sinner arraigned at God's bar for life and death.
> 2. This righteousness is imputed to no man but a believer.
> 3. When it is imputed by grace, and applied by faith, it immediately and eternally becomes the man's righteousness before God, angels, men, and devils, Romans 8:33-39. It is a righteousness that is never lost, never taken away, never ineffectual; answereth all charges, and is attended with all graces.[3]

In the same century John Bunyan could affirm, 'There is no other way for sinners to be justified from the curse of the law in the sight of God, than by the imputation of that righteousness long ago performed by, and still residing with, the person of Jesus Christ'.[4]

The Welsh Calvinistic Methodist rules of 1742 required from their members that they accept 'the imputed righteousness of Christ in salvation, and that God's Spirit alone is the author of the faith whereby

---

[1] Article V, *Waldensian Confession.*

[2] Quoted from 'Excerpts of Latimer's Sermons' in *Complete Works of Augustus Toplady*, Sprinkle Publications reprint, 1987, p. 139.

[3] Traill's *Works*, 1795, vol. I, 'The Doctrine of Justification Vindicated from the Charge of Antinomianism', Postscript, pp. 338, 339.

[4] John Bunyan, *Justification by an Imputed Righteousness: Or No Way to Heaven but by Jesus Christ*, ed. George Offor, vol. I, p. 300.

you believe'. Augustus Toplady, writing in the eighteenth century, tells us, 'The justification of God's people, thus founded upon, resulting from, and secured by, the imputed righteousness of Christ ... is absolute and total'.[5] William Cowper wrote to his cousin Martin Madan concerning imputed righteousness: 'I plead guilty to the Doctrine of original corruption, derived to me from my great progenitor, for in my heart I feel the evidences of it that will not be disputed. I rejoice in the Doctrine of Imputed Righteousness for without it how should I be justified? My own righteousness is a rag, a feeble defective attempt insufficient of itself to obtain the pardon of the least of my offences, much more my justification from them all. My dear Martin, 'tis pride that makes these truths unpalatable, but pride has no business in the heart of a Christian'.[6]

The controversy between Wesley and Hervey

In the eighteenth century, however, this doctrine was to be seriously challenged by John Wesley, who emphasised that it was not enough to plead Christ's righteousness before the judgment throne: one must have a holiness of one's own. Such teaching moved James Hervey, the Evangelical pioneer, to write a book on the subject which he named after the two main characters in the work, *Theron and Aspasio*. It is the simple story of two friends walking together, contemplating the beauty of God's world in general and the doctrines of salvation in particular. To cut a very long story short (the final edition of the work ran into three volumes), Theron and Aspasio conclude that they can only be justified by faith which does not stem from themselves but is a gift of God. They also see that there is no righteousness in themselves apart from Christ's righteousness which is imputed to them. They thus conclude that Christ lives in them and that he alone constitutes their hope of glory.

Hervey sent John Wesley a manuscript copy of his book before publication and asked him twice for his comments. The Arminian leader praised many minor aspects of the work but his reaction was strong and

[5] *Complete Works of Augustus Toplady*, p. 140.
[6] Cowper's *Works*, Ryskamp and King, vol. I. p. 107

outraged against the main thrust of the book concerning imputed righteousness. He protested:

> For Christ's sake and for the sake of the immortal souls which he has purchased with his blood, do not dispute for that particular phrase, the imputed righteousness of Christ. It is not Scriptural, it is not necessary ... it has done immense hurt. I have had abundant proof, that the frequent use of this unnecessary phrase, instead of furthering men's progress in vital holiness, has made them satisfied without any holiness at all; yea and encouraged them to work all uncleanness with greediness.[7]

Here we are at the heart of Wesley's doctrine of progressive perfection. He earnestly believed that Christians could, by strenuous spiritual exercises, be 'perfected in love' or 'perfected in the faith', as he put it, here and now. Time and again we read in his *Journal* of his meeting such people, even naming them! Such a conviction led Wesley to make claims that ran head first against traditional biblical thinking. Perhaps the most outlandish of these claims is his emphasis that complete conformity to the law of God is possible here and now. Wesley thus accused Hervey of Antinomianism, believing his doctrine of imputed righteousness 'makes thousands content to live and die transgressors of the law, because Christ fulfilled it for them'. Anyone as familiar with Hervey as Wesley was must have been aware of the great emphasis Hervey placed on personal holiness. Wesley chose to ignore his testimony.

Wesley, seeing in the gentle Hervey's theology the very opposite of his own, condemned him ferociously from the pulpit and published his views on *Theron and Aspasio* and his letters to Hervey against it[8] on two separate occasions without taking Hervey into his confidence. He had, however, the audacity to warn Hervey that it would be unbrotherly of him if he, in turn, published an attack on Wesley's views! Hervey

---

[7] Wesley's letter is quoted in full with Hervey's answer in *The Works of the Rev. James Hervey, A.M.*, Thomas Nelson, 1837, p. 472ff.

[8] Wesley's first criticism was published in an abridgement of works by Watts and Hebden. Hervey was seriously misquoted in the work but Wesley said that the error was the printer's, not his own. The major criticism was published in Wesley's *A Preservative from Unsettled Notions in Religion.*

did prepare such an 'attack' during the last days of his life and it was published shortly after his early death.[9] Though Hervey's defence of imputed righteousness is fair, balanced and to the point and although Hervey died with God's praise on his lips, Wesley took it as a personal affront and reacted violently, telling his friends that Hervey had 'died cursing his spiritual Father' (meaning Wesley himself).[10]

In Wesley's correspondence with Hervey, we see that his great problem was relating imputed righteousness to Christ's person. He thought of it purely in relation to man. Righteousness, according to Wesley, is imputed to man because of man's faith. It is thus man's righteousness and not Christ's. Thus when Hervey writes to Wesley saying that Paul often mentions imputed righteousness in his epistle to the Romans, and adds the question, 'What can this be, but the righteousness of Christ?' Wesley denies that there is any reference to Christ here and writes back, 'Paul tells us quite plainly in Romans 4, "To him that believeth on him that justifieth the ungodly, faith is imputed for righteousness"', arguing that it was Abraham's active faith that secured righteousness for him, thus the righteousness was Abraham's own by virtue of his faith.

Such an exegesis is extremely questionable. The verse is dealing with the 'ungodly' who are justified, and not those who rely on their own inherent righteousness. Furthermore it is clear from the context and from our Lord's own commentary on what constituted Abraham's faith that Abraham was looking forward to the coming of one who could give him that which he could not achieve himself. Paul says in the same context, 'He staggered not at the promise of God through unbelief; but was strong in faith, giving glory to God; and being fully persuaded that, what he had promised, he was able to perform'. Paul then adds, '*Therefore* it was imputed to him for righteousness'. Here it is obvious that Abraham is trusting in something that God is to perform, giving God the glory for it. He is looking forward to a righteousness which is

---

9 *Works of the Rev. James Hervey, A.M.*, p. 481ff.

10 *Works*, vol. XIII, 'Remarks on Dr Erskine's Defence of Aspasio Vindicated', p. 123. See also my article 'Whose Righteousness Saves Us?', Bible League Quarterly, July-September, 1991.

not of the law. When we turn to Christ's words to the Jews in John 8:56, 'Your father Abraham rejoiced to see my day: and he saw it, and was glad', we see that it was truly the promise of Christ that spurred Abraham on to believe. This is why Paul in Romans 4 ends the passage on imputed righteousness with the teaching that Christ 'was delivered for our offences, and was raised again for our justification', and it is through Christ that we have 'access by faith into this grace wherein we stand' (Romans 5:2). Hervey thus argues that, seeing that Christ died in our stead, the just for the unjust, it follows that we are only counted righteous because God in Christ would have it that way. We are accounted righteous in Christ because we have had Christ's righteousness put on us. This is why Paul can write, 'For if by one man's offence death reigned by one; much more they which receive abundance of grace and of the gift of righteousness shall reign in life by one, Jesus Christ' (Romans 5:17). Righteousness therefore, like faith itself, is a gift and is of Christ's nature and not man's.

Why the doctrine was neglected

Although Hervey had merely stated what was Pauline theology and the teaching of Calvin, the doctrine of Christ's imputed righteousness made little headway in the teaching of the churches after Hervey's death in 1758 at the age of forty-four. There were two reasons for this. The first was the enormous outreach, success and influence of Wesley's preaching. His followers ran into hundreds of thousands. These were people who were obviously professing Christians, though they questioned one of the central doctrines of the Bible! These Wesleyans exercised a tremendous influence on the theology of the eighteenth century and made almost a cult figure of Wesley, presenting both him and his views as if they were virtually infallible. Hervey's teachings, in comparison, were looked upon as Antinomian. He could make no headway here, especially as it became a commonly held opinion that Hervey had tried to denounce the Methodist leader.

The anti-Hervey myths grew and reached ridiculous proportions, so that later Methodists began to look on the gentle Hervey as a deluded man and a heretic, if not something of an ogre![11] So we find that learned pro-Wesley biographer, the Rev. L. Tyerman, writing in his 'life' of Hervey that, 'His theory, that, the death of Christ bought the sinner's pardon, and the righteousness of Christ procured for the sinner the privileges and rights of justification; or, to speak more precisely, of adoption into the family of God, was a speculative distinction, without Scriptural authority, and pregnant with Antinomian heresy. He meant well; but he missed the mark'.[12]

The reason Tyerman says this – apart from his strong allegiance to Wesley – is his belief that the doctrine of imputed righteousness rules out personal sanctification. Hervey was well aware that such a criticism might arise and, even before the publication of *Theron and Aspasio*, he had planned to write a sequel showing how only those who had Christ's righteousness imputed to them could ever hope to lead a sanctified life. Hervey's early death intervened and the sequel was left unwritten. Far from being an Antinomian, Hervey had a hunger and thirst after righteousness second to none. John Ryland Senior testified to this by writing, 'Hervey was no Antinomian. He loved and practised every branch of moral virtue in the best manner, and on the purest and most noble principles. No man upon earth exceeded him in love to holiness, in heart, lip, and life'.[13]

The second reason why a trust in Christ's imputed righteousness was seldom required of preachers and believers in general was that there had been a steady shift in emphasis away from the Christ-centredness of the Reformers and Puritans to a man-centred emphasis in theology. During the so-called Restoration period, the Reformed teaching of justification by faith as a complete and eternal act of Christ's had been toned down to an emphasis on Christian duty towards the gospel, moral living and good gentlemanly manners. Such teaching was outlined in the book *The Whole Duty of Man* which Whitefield called sarcastically 'England's

---

[11] See Frederick C. Gill's *The Romantic Movement and Methodism*, Haskell House, 1966 p. 78ff. for evidence of the extent to which this anti-Hervey propaganda has reached amongst Wesley's followers.

[12] L. Tyerman, *The Oxford Methodists*, 1873, p. 298.

[13] John Ryland, *The Character of James Hervey, A.M.*, London, 1791, p. 103.

greatest favourite' and Cowper called 'that repository of self-righteousness and pharisaical lumber'.

This is the very same book that Huntington studied in vain in his pre-conversion days to find the way of salvation. Coupled with this emphasis on the duty of man was the teaching that Christ's atonement had only paved the way for man's legal justification according to the old law which had now to be worked out in the believer's life through the new law of repentance, conversion, faith and sincere obedience.[14] Christ's atonement thus made it legally possible for all men to approach God by doing their level best to serve him. This doctrine, given the name of Neonomianism by theologians, was refuted by Puritans such as Traill in the seventeenth century but became popular, especially in Scotland, in the eighteenth century. Thomas Boston and the Erskine brothers, Ebenezer and Ralf, combated this and, as Traill had been before them, were labelled as Antinomians for their pains.

At the same time a movement was gaining ground which had been started in the days of Moses Amyrald (1596-1664), a French Protestant. Amyrald rejected the Calvinistic teaching that Christ died for his sheep alone and argued that the merits of Christ's atonement were sufficient to save the whole world on condition that they believed. This virtually ruled out the doctrine of Christ's vicarious suffering, as it teaches that Christ died for a non-definable number rather than for his sheep and that he had died in vain for some and, theoretically speaking, he could have died in vain for all! It seems, however, that Amyrald realised that mankind was so corrupt that no one would wish to fulfil God's condition, so he argued that God saved a select few so that Christ's death would not be altogether in vain. The Calvinistic systematic theologian Berkhof called this view 'an untenable position', but it was widely held in Huntington's day and was the belief of at least two of his most vociferous enemies, John Ryland Junior and Andrew Fuller. These two men challenged the Calvinistic doctrine of the discriminating and electing love of God by teaching that it was the duty of all sinners to believe the gospel and that the atonement was sufficient for all men on condition that they believed. Thus the substitutionary death of Christ,

---

[14] This is why Huntington accused Ryland Senior of changing the law and then having the cheek to call Huntington an Antinomian for not following his changed law! See *The Broken Cistern and the Springing Well* and *An Answer to Fools*.

who died for his sheep alone, was called into question and a feeling of duty in all men substituted for the sovereign, discriminating love of God. The emphasis was removed from God's sovereign mercy and placed on man's duties as a fallen creature.

A by-product of Fullerism, as this theory became to be called, was that the doctrine of the imputed righteousness of Christ was robbed of almost all its Pauline meaning. This was mainly due to Fuller's idea that it was 'improper' to look upon redemption as a legal or commercial transaction between a creditor and his debtor with Christ as our surety.[15] With such a conviction, it is no wonder that Fuller viewed both Hervey's and Huntington's teaching as being the very opposite of his own. This led him to deny that Huntington had any Christian doctrine or testimony whatsoever.[16]

Huntington takes up the mantle from Hervey

Huntington realised early in his ministry that a too worldly, Romanist and rationalistic view of justification, sanctification and personal holiness was rampant in the churches. This was, in his opinion, because the biblical doctrine of imputed righteousness was either paid mere lip-service, robbed of its direct connection with the person of Christ, or denied altogether. Thus Huntington, who was familiar with Wesley's attacks on Hervey and suffered personally at the hands of the Fullerites, decided to take up Hervey's mantle and complete the work he had begun to do, stressing especially the part personal sanctification played in the lives of the elect. In his first prose work, *The Arminian Skeleton*, Huntington attacks both Arminianism and Fullerism by emphasizing the traditional tenets of Calvinism and stressing that only when these tenets are accepted can one begin to understand the biblical doctrines of imputed righteousness, sanctification and holiness.

---

[15] My remarks on Fuller are based on a detailed study of his *Works*, in particular, *Answers to Queries; Miscellaneous Tracts etc; Reviews; Figurative Pieces; Agnostos' Letters* and *The Gospel Worthy of All Acceptation.*

[16] See Fuller's review of *The Voice of Years* in his *Works*. Huntington's works are not searched for 'proof' of the wild accusations made and the article descends to the level of 'mud-slinging'. See Appendix I for Fuller's criticism of Hervey.

For Huntington, both the Arminians and those influenced by Fullerism believed in a universal atonement. Fuller differed from Wesley merely in his belief that God applied the universal atonement to whom he would, whereas Wesley emphasised that the atonement was efficacious to anybody in general and nobody in particular. Huntington, though he rejected Wesley's theology, felt at least that it had an inner – human logic, whereas Fuller's doctrine was quite self-contradictory. What Fuller was actually saying was that though the atonement was universal in its scope (Christ's atonement was accomplished for everybody), it was only particular in its application (only the elect will be saved) – and this, to Huntington, was blasphemy. It would mean that Christ shed his blood in vain for all the sinners in hell. He was unsuccessful in redemption and his sovereignty had been thwarted by man's refusal to do his duty.

In its place Huntington argues from such texts as Revelation 14:4; John 10:15 and Acts 13:48 that those whom God redeems are redeemed from amongst those who will not be redeemed. God loved Jacob but hated Esau and Christ's ransom is in line with God's discriminating love and is for the elect only. When God gave Egypt for Israel's ransom, he gave no ransom for Egypt. Christ lay down his life for his sheep and not for those who were not his sheep. Jesus is quite explicit on this theme as he tells the Jews in John 10:26, 'Ye believe not, because ye are not of my sheep'. He could say this because, 'As many as were ordained to eternal life, believed'. Thus 'Christ prayed not for the world but for them that God had given him out of it'.

In refuting the idea that every man knows it is his duty to believe the gospel, Huntington uses the story of Lazarus. Christ commanded him to come out and live – but Lazarus was dead and stank. Thus any efficacy in Christ's call must have come from Christ and not from Lazarus' supposed duty, obligation or inclination to wake himself from the dead. This is the case with all who are 'dead in trespasses and sins'. Huntington refutes such heresy with Christ's words: 'No man can come to me except the Father ... draw him' (John 6:44). He argues that those who are thus drawn by the Father are equipped with a new righteousness: 'even the righteousness of God which is by faith of Jesus Christ unto all and upon all them that believe'. This, argues Huntington, is Christ's imputed righteousness. This argument was expanded and built on in later letters, sermons and writings as Huntington himself grew in knowledge and as the circumstances demanded.

Writing to a friend who had just recovered from an illness, Huntington turns to the fight with the world, the flesh and the devil and deals more closely with imputed righteousness, showing how it relates to the old and new man:

> My poor soul still aspires, still ascends; but, after all, it is but free in part – free to hope; but it is hope in a prison; 'Turn to your strong hold, ye prisoners of hope'. But ere long this clay cottage, with all its daubed walls, decayed timbers, and infected materials, shall come down and dissolve, and leave its loathsome leprosy in the dust, when corruption shall be no more. This will be the ruin of the whole usurped empire of Satan; and he will be buried in its rubbish; for, as sin and death came in by Satan, sin and death shall reign in and rule over Satan, and he shall suffer eternal torment and destruction by his own inventions. This work is already begun in us, and God will perfect that which concerns us. Thus our guilt and filth are purged out and destroyed by the blood of Christ. The remains of sin, or the old man, are condemned in Christ's flesh, and crucified with Christ, that it should not live – 'the body is dead because of sin'. It is counteracted by grace, that it should not reign. 'Sin shall not have dominion over you', being justified from it by an imputed righteousness, that it should not condemn; and a new man is put in us, that sin should not be imputed to us. The Holy Ghost is given unto us, that we might serve God under its influences, and not be reckoned as servants of sin. At death we shall get rid of the inbeing of it, and at the resurrection it will be confined in hell, and the Canaanite shall no more dwell in the house of the Lord of hosts. The uncircumcised and the unclean shall pass through Zion. This is the good work begun in us, and it shall be performed and perfected in us at the

grand assize; 'faithful is he that hath promised, who also will do it'.[17]

The old man and the new

Robert Traill, in his *The Doctrine of Justification Vindicated against the Charge of Antinomianism,* looked upon the Neonomian and Arminian heresies as arising from a too limited, merely judicial, 'as if' view of the imputed righteousness of Christ and a tardiness in accepting the traditional Christian teaching of the two Adams and the old and new man. The old man is totally depraved but the new man is indwelt by Christ. Huntington avoids both pitfalls by showing that Christ's imputation of righteousness is not merely 'legal' or 'as if' but actually at work in the believer's new nature.

On Sunday, 18 December, 1800, Huntington preached a morning and an evening sermon on 1 Corinthians 15:49, 'And as we have borne the image of the earthy, we shall also bear the image of the heavenly'. These sermons he entitled, 'The Loss and Restoration of the Image of God in Man'. In the morning sermon he outlined how the image of God in man is utterly defaced and eternal life, which was part of the divine image, lost. He then went on to argue that, 'The incarnation of Christ, his sufferings and death, the proclamation of the gospel, and the mission of the Holy Ghost, are to restore the lost image of God [the Saviour] to God's elect among the sons of men'. These elect-and only the elect-are predestined to be conformed to the image of God's Son. Thus nothing shall thwart God's purpose in carrying out his plan of restoration.

After dealing with a number of 'divine features' which man has lost in the Fall, Huntington turns to man's lost righteousness and how it may be regained. He shows that Christ, who alone is righteous, grants his elect 'abundance of grace and of the gift of righteousness'. This is why Christians call their Saviour 'the Lord our Righteousness'. Thus without being linked to Christ, or, to use biblical language, grafted into the vine, there is no holiness. As Paul says, 'According as he hath chosen us in him, that we should be holy and without blame before him

[17] *Posthumous Letters*, vol. III, Letter CCCCXXX. It is of interest to note that this Pauline teaching of the old and new man is quite absent from Fuller's theology when referring to imputed righteousness.

in love'. Any true holiness that is produced is experienced and enjoyed in Christ Jesus and must come from him as his gift to his elect. Any other form of holiness is make believe imitation and a stumbling-block to true Christian growth.

This is no new 'Huntingtonian' doctrine, as his enemies supposed,[18] but a belief that the Puritans held dear. Traill writes, 'That God justifieth the ungodly, Romans 4:5, neither by making him godly before he justifieth him, nor leaving him ungodly after he hath justified him; but that the same grace that justifies him, doth immediately sanctify him'. He goes on to say, 'If for such doctrine we be called Antinomians, we are bold to say, that there is some ignorance of, or prejudice at the known Protestant doctrine, in the hearts of the reproachers'.[19] Huntington was thus in very good company!

Huntington now shows how Adam was created in righteousness and holiness but he fell and lost these features of God's image. Our old man – that part which is derived from Adam – has now no righteousness and holiness to offer. Paul, however, speaks of a 'new man' and says, 'And be renewed in the spirit of your mind; and that ye put on the new man, which after God is created in righteousness and true holiness' (Ephesians 4:23, 24). In other words, a Christian is a person working under two influences. He has his old man, which is derived from fallen Adam and is under the law as it can produce no righteousness to fulfil the law. He has also the new man which is given him by Christ and which is a re-creation in righteousness and true holiness. This is why Paul can say, 'So then with the mind I myself serve the law of God, but with the flesh the law of sin' (Romans 7:25).

Thus, according to Huntington, just as the old man witnesses to God's lost image in man, so the new man witnesses to God's regained image in Christ. But how does this come about? How is the change made? This is where the doctrine of imputed righteousness comes in. Keeping close to Scripture, Huntington starts by showing the

---

[18] This biblical teaching of Huntington's has been completely misunderstood by the Banner of Truth reviewer of *The Voice of Years* who argues that sanctification for Huntington obscures justification.

[19] *The Doctrine of Justification Vindicated*, p. 320.

importance of the incarnation in re-creating the image of God in his elect, who are predestined 'to be conformed to the image of his Son' (Romans 8:29), and refers to Hebrews 2:14-17, which says, 'Forasmuch then as the children are partakers of flesh and blood, he also himself likewise took part of the same; that through death he might destroy him that had the power of death, that is, the devil; and deliver them who through fear of death were all their lifetime subject to bondage. For verily he took not on him the nature of angels; but he took on him the seed of Abraham. Wherefore in all things it behoved him to be made like unto his brethren, that he might be a merciful and faithful high priest in things pertaining to God, to make reconciliation for the sins of the people'.

Christ, however, did not merely become a 'partaker of flesh and blood', Huntington argues. That would never have rescued the elect. The law had to be dealt with and this demanded the death of all sinners. So Jesus had also to take on 'the likeness of sinful flesh' in order that he should be 'like unto his brethren'. To prove this Huntington quotes Romans 8:3, 'For what the law could not do, in that it was weak through the flesh, God sending his own Son in the likeness of sinful flesh, and for sin, condemned sin in the flesh: that the righteousness of the law might be fulfilled in us, who walk not after the flesh but after the Spirit'. God wished to condemn sin in the very nature that Satan had ruined.

Now what part of man was fallen and had lost the image of God? It was the old man in Adam. This old man was crucified with Christ. Huntington says:

> He made himself of no reputation, and took upon him the form of a servant, and was made in the likeness of sinful flesh; and, being found in fashion as a man, he humbled himself, and became obedient unto death, even the death of the cross', Philippians 2:7, 8. There was a union which took place between Christ and his elect from everlasting: they were chosen in him and loved in him, and given to him; and he was set up and appointed to be the head and representative of them; in pursuance of this he takes their nature, and their sins, and dies in their room and stead; and they all die and suffer the law representatively in him: 'if one died for all, then were all dead', and at conversion we become dead to the law, dead to sin, and dead to the world;

this is called a likeness in their sufferings, 'For if we have been planted together in the likeness of his death, we shall be also in the likeness of his resurrection', Romans 6:5.

Huntington goes on to expound how:

When Christ was condemned and crucified we died, being crucified with him; and when the law enters at our arraignment and conviction, sin revives, and we die, like Christ: this is being planted together in the likeness of his death: but when faith comes, and we are delivered from sin, and from the law, we rise to a lively hope under the operation of the Spirit of God; and so serve God in the newness of life: this is called rising, with our risen Head under the operation of the Spirit of God, 'Thy dead men shall live', saith God, 'with my dead body shall they arise', saith Christ.

This Paul calls being 'planted together in the likeness of his resurrection', 'Knowing this, that our old man is crucified with him, that the body of sin might be destroyed, that henceforth we should not serve sin. For he that is dead is freed from sin. Now, if we be dead with Christ, we believe that we shall also live with him', Romans 6:6-8. In Christ we die representatively; and in our own souls when the law is applied, and we are condemned and die by it. By faith we pass from death to life; and, having obtained justification, we become freed from sin: freed from every stain of sin in Christ, being complete in him; freed from sin with respect to the book of God's remembrance; they are blotted out, and God will remember them no more: freed from sin as considered in the putting on of the new man; for he is created in righteousness and true holiness: and freed from sin in the covenant of grace: 'Blessed is the man to whom the Lord imputeth not iniquity'. And, though sin be in us, and work in us, yet it is condemned; it is crucified with Christ. And, the Lord Jesus Christ being put on, the old man is put off; and, as Christ is dearly beloved by us, and the old man perfectly hated (although we do at times that we would not, and do not what we would), it is no more us, but sin that dwelleth in us: thus we become dead; and, in the above sense, freed from sin.

This sound biblical teaching of the utter deficiency of man and the utter sufficiency of Christ raised the ire of Huntington's so-called evangelical contemporaries. They could not believe that man was so void of natural abilities and that the change in him, if he wished to become a Christian, must be so radical. Out came Fuller's pen and he wrote reams against these doctrines, claiming that the only difference between fallen man and regenerated man is in the realm of 'inclinations'. Arguing against the Arminian Dan Taylor, who thought Calvinists believed that man has no ability or power to believe in Christ before the saving work of the Spirit commences, Fuller says he believes no such thing. He argues that there are no natural impossibilities in unsaved man and that he has the same rational and moral powers to believe before the Spirit works savingly in him as after.[20]

The imputed righteousness of Christ

In face of such contemporary error amongst his fellow-ministers, it is obvious that Huntington was nowhere more misunderstood than when speaking of Christ's imputed righteousness. The sad tale is, however, that though we modern believers have Hervey and Huntington to build on, the doctrine of imputed righteousness is still gravely misunderstood by many believers of today who have obviously built their doctrines on the views of Huntington's erroneous critics rather than on the old coalheaver himself. There is no other way of explaining why a modern critic can claim that Huntington is heretical in his teaching concerning the imputed righteousness of Christ because he believes that, 'The imputation of our sins to Christ, and of His righteousness to us, was actual, not judicial' and can conclude thus that Huntington must be an Antinomian.[21] This is the Hervey-Wesley controversy revived. Or perhaps it was never dead?

If Christ's imputed righteousness is merely 'judicial' and not 'actual', what purpose has the Holy Spirit in working in the life of the

[20] Fuller, *Works*, 'The Reality and Efficacy of Divine Grace', vol II, p. 546.
[21] *Ibid.* p. 27. Banner of Truth review of *The Voice of Years*, July 1988. This criticism is to be found nowhere in the book under review.

believer? Why do the Scriptures tell us that we 'put on Christ'? Is his work merely a formality that does not attain to true 'actual' holiness in the believer's life?

The Scriptures make it plain that without holiness no man shall see God. 'Actual' righteousness is obviously meant here and not merely 'judicial'. There is no 'make believe' along the path of holiness. But where does this 'actual' righteousness come from? It cannot come from man, as the Scriptures tell us that man has no righteousness of his own. This question seems hardly relevant to the critic. He appears to take it for granted that Christ's imputing of his righteousness to his elect is solely a 'judicial' or 'pro forma' transaction, i.e., a mere legal matter of form. Such a teaching is no help to a repentant sinner whom God requires to partake of the divine nature.

On looking at Huntington's 'proof texts' for his doctrine of imputed righteousness, we find that when Christ was condemned and crucified, we died and were crucified with him. Now obviously the Bible teaches that Christ *actually* bore our penalties and died. His death, however, was twofold in its application to man. The elect were killed *judicially* as, of course, all Christians did not physically die when Christ *actually* died physically. As regards the old man's hold on the new man, however, the old man did *actually* 'die', as he has no longer the power to send the new-born Christian to hell. The old man has thus no *judicial* hold on the new man whatsoever, and his *actual* hold is severely restricted because of the *actual* work of Christ in the believer and the *actual* indwelling of the Holy Spirit. The imparting of Christ's righteousness is thus not merely *judicial* but *actual*, as the righteous Christ *actually* indwells the believer. This is why Paul can say, 'I am crucified with Christ [the old man]: nevertheless I live [the new man]; yet not I, but Christ liveth in me: and the life which I now live in the flesh I live by the faith of the Son of God, who loved me, and gave himself for me' (Galatians 2:20). Thus through the vicarious death of Christ, all who are 'in him', that is all the elect, are not merely *judicially* alive for evermore but *actually* alive for ever as 'Death shall have no dominion over them'.

The sinlessness of Christ

Huntington is not only criticised for seeing an actual application of Christ's righteousness in the believer, but he is also accused of teaching that, 'The imputation of our sins to Christ ... was actual and not judicial'.[22] The critic appears to believe that this implies that Christ's character was defiled. Nothing could be further from Huntington's teaching.[23]

During his lifetime Huntington was certainly no stranger to criticism, yet very few ever suggested that his view of imputation demanded a Christ who profaned himself. Although he received stacks of letters over many years, mainly from Arminians and Fullerites, criticising his beliefs, he only ever received one letter which accused him of teaching that Christ became sinful. This was a letter which could hardly be taken seriously. A minister wrote to Huntington anonymously saying that he had fallen asleep during one of Huntington's sermons and had dreamt that Huntington had taught that Christ assumed sinful nature. Furthermore, though Huntington had a steady stream of callers, some seeking his advice and others wanting to give him theirs, he had only one caller in forty years of pastoral service who accused him of teaching that Christ was defiled.

Early in 1786 three of Huntington's members wrote to him to tell him that the 'malicious report' was being spread that their pastor had said Christ 'was a sinner in the same sense that we are, either by birth or practice'.[24] This corruption, Huntington was reported to have preached, was derived from fallen Adam through Mary his mother. In Huntington's reply, he refutes the allegation completely saying it is 'a doctrine which the Bible never mentions, a doctrine that never escaped my lips. Therefore, Woe, unto him through whom the offence or slander cometh'. Huntington mentions the anonymous letter and the visitor and goes on to say, 'In him was no sin, yet he bore our sins in his own body on the tree, and by paying the price of his blood the debt was discharged'. He also argues that though Christ was made sin for us he

---

[22] *Ibid.* p. 27.

[23] This may be confirmed by reading Huntington's sermons on Romans 6:7 and John 17:17 published under the title, 'A Short Discourse on Sanctification' (1 and 2) in The Gospel Standard for 1850 pp. 228-232, 369-373.

[24] *Epistles of Faith*, Letter XX.

knew no sin himself. Christ is depicted in the Bible as a surety and not as debtor. He showed 'perfect and perpetual obedience' and was a 'perfect sacrifice'. He was 'without spot and blemish'. He washed away 'our sins', i.e., he had none of his own to wash away. Huntington goes on to say, 'The law is an adversary, and must be agreed with by a perfect righteousness; without this, it will not agree with anyone; but will hale the unjustified sinner to the judge, and the judge will deliver the self-righteous to the officer, and the officer will cast him into prison, until he can pay the utmost mite, Luke 12:58'. Jesus always had that 'perfect righteousness' according to Huntington, which certainly proves that he did not teach a doctrine of a defiled Christ. In the same letter Huntington argues that if anyone thought that he erred in his doctrine, he should be approached in the correct biblical manner, according to 1 Timothy 5:19, 'Against an elder receive not an accusation, but before two or three witnesses'. Huntington's church members, however, were quite satisfied that their pastor did not believe that Christ was defiled and never sent him such a delegation. It is only logical that Huntington argued in this way. Just as any righteousness attributed to man is Christ's and not his own, so any sins borne by Christ are man's and not his own. Christ's righteousness in man is, however, real, just as man's sins were real which Christ voluntarily bore. Furthermore, Christ left our sins at Calvary so that we might have his righteousness imputed for ever after Calvary. What seems so illogical is that so many of Huntington's evangelical contemporaries reacted to this teaching with the cry of Fuller: 'I never read anything more void of true religion'.[25]

The practical outworking in the life of the believer

Another criticism raised against Huntington concerns his doctrine of the practical outworking of Christ's righteousness within the believer. It is alleged that in his view, 'Faith, repentance and holy obedience are covenant conditions on the part of Christ, not on our part', and that 'Sanctification is no evidence of justification but rather renders it more obscure'.[26]

---

[25] Fuller, *Works*, vol I. p. 74.

[26] *The Voice of Years*, Banner of Truth, July 1988.

Thomas Scott once said to a Fullerite that, 'No man can know his election, except by the evidences of regeneration, especially repentance and its fruits, and faith in Christ working by love to him, his people, and his commands',[27] and it has always been a tenet of the Reformed faith that the elect are predestinated to faith, repentance and holiness. Calvin is quite explicit in Book III, chapter 22 of the *Institutes*, where he says that holiness of life springs from election and Christ's flock are not elected because God foresaw that they would be holy, but they are elected *to be* holy. He has similar arguments concerning faith and repentance, stressing that only those repent whom God turns. Furthermore, as we have already seen, sanctification did not at all obscure Huntington's view of justification, as he believed, 'Whom he called, them he also justified' (Romans 8:30), and 'By the which will [God's will] we are sanctified through the offering of the body of Jesus Christ once for all' (Hebrews 10:10). Justification and sanctification, to Huntington, are both gifts of God. Thus it would not seem unbiblical for Huntington to stress God's side in these matters rather than man's side.

What the critic seems to mean by 'holy obedience' and 'sanctification' is the believer's own effort in taking up Christ's cross and following him. He seemingly believes that Huntington made no such active effort and was content to passively accept his salvation but not to reform his life. This was also Fuller's unfounded argument against Huntington whose 'bad points', he argued, were all unchristian and all his 'good points' had nothing to do with Christianity![28] Now, if ever Huntington was really and deeply misunderstood, it was on this point. Much of the trouble here is due to a common phenomenon that Thomas Scott takes up in a letter to Dr John Ryland written in 1797. Scott is emphasizing the fact that Christians tend to 'judge of their feelings by certain rules', and set up patterns of doctrine and behaviour to be followed which are different from those in other denominations. Thus, he says, all Arminian Methodists tend to think alike, as do Calvinistic Methodists and 'Huntington's disciples'. He stresses that this is also true of the 'New England divines'. This tendency has often

---

[27] Scott, *Letters and Papers*, p. 174.

[28] See Fuller's slanderous comments on Huntington's faith and Christian morals in his review of *The Voice of Years* (Fuller, *Works*, vol. III, p. 762f.).

led to 'Huntington's disciples' being misjudged by those in other denominations. Whereas the Arminians emphasised their way to 'perfection in love' and the Fullerites stressed reprobate man's 'duty', we find Huntingtonians often either bemoaning their corruption, being chastised by the rod of God, going through the furnace, or confessing that they are the chief of sinners. Where Huntington's critics tended to stress their positive, active faith, Huntingtonians tended to bewail their weaknesses in their negative, active walk with God. When a professing Christian gave Huntington his testimony and there was no confession of contrition and vileness on seeing his own sinful nature, Huntington feared that there had been no full work of God in the soul. Thus Huntingtonian testimonies tend to be more of a 'God be merciful to me, a sinner' than a display of personal triumph or the 'victorious living' of the Keswick conferences. This has led many an Arminian and Fullerite to have a superior feeling tending even to snobbishness over Huntingtonians. It also led Huntington to tell Arminians and Fullerites that they should blow Christ's trumpet the more, and not their own, and do more good works rather than talk about them. In other words, Huntington was moved to brand his enemies' idea of sanctification as self-praise, self-keeping and self-effort which seriously set their justification in question.

In *The Justification of a Sinner and Satan's Law-Suit with him*, Huntington takes up this different attitude amongst Christians to their own holiness. In the volume, which is a dialogue between Ahimaaz and Cushi, the latter speaks of one who 'preached up holiness likewise to a very high pitch; insomuch that you would have thought at times that he had been perfect'. Cushi answers,

> If that was the case, poor broken-hearted sinners, and those buffeted by the devil, could get but little sympathy from him. For tempted souls that are labouring under the plague of their own heart, think themselves as far from holiness as Satan himself; when at the same time it is the quickening and illuminating power of the Holy Ghost that makes them feel and see the evil of their hearts. I have heard men preach as if divine holiness were to be produced and put in practice by flesh and blood. They call for

> heart-holiness, family-holiness, life-holiness, insomuch that I have gone groaning home, and crying out, 'I have no holiness at all'.

Calvin, like Augustine long before him, taught exactly the same sentiments as Huntington, believing that the mark of a Christian's perfection is that he sees that he has no human perfection at all.[29] Just as Calvin and Augustine did, Huntington also emphasised that sin still dwelt in the old man, but the new man, indwelt by Christ, provided the Christian with a righteousness and true holiness which is not of the law (Ephesians 4:24). The more Huntington stressed this, however, the more his enemies argued that he was hiding behind God's promises of what he would do and not stressing what was Huntington's own Christian duty in living a holy life. Quite simply, they wanted to know whether Huntington kept the Decalogue or not and whether he was charitable or not. They believed that he neither kept the Decalogue nor did he see any use in charitable acts.

This moved Fuller to blatantly declare of Huntington that, 'It is an unhappy circumstance, however, in a case wherein the good and the bad are to be weighed one against the other, that his good qualities as a minister should prove nothing for him as a Christian, while his bad qualities as a minister prove everything against him as a Christian. His good qualities contain nothing decisive of his goodness; but his bad qualities are indications of the predominancy of a spirit which is not of God'. He goes on to say that he cannot perceive what else Huntington could be but a man who 'lacked virtue, temperance, patience, godliness, brotherly kindness, and charity' and was a 'lover of his own self, covetous, a boaster, proud, a blasphemer, unthankful and unholy'. Huntington, he sums up, was a man 'not allowed by the Scriptures to understand or believe the truth' and should have remained a day-labourer rather than become a preacher.[30] This he said of a man who always bemoaned his being the chief of sinners, lived a moral life after conversion that nobody was able to objectively criticise, spent thousands of pounds in providing homes for the homeless, pensions for

---

[29] See Calvin's use of Augustine's teaching on holiness, *Institutes*, Book I. chapter 5; Book III. chapter 22.
[30] See Fuller's review of *The Voice of Years*.

the aged, work for the unemployed and church buildings for those without a place of worship and gave many thousands of pounds to charitable appeals not directly associated with Providence Chapel.

Although Fuller was vitriolic in his condemnation of Huntington, nothing of this dirt-smearing vocabulary came from Huntington's pen concerning him. Fuller always dealt with Huntington in a snobbish way, as seen by his reference to Huntington as a 'day labourer', yet Fuller's background had hardly been more sophisticated than Huntington's. Fuller made a name for himself as a young man as a wrestler of note. Huntington never told him that he ought to have 'stuck to his trade' and remained a public pugilist.

The example of Huntington and his flock

Huntington's life and teaching and the lives of his own flock stand in stark contrast to the mean accusations levelled at him by such controversialists as Fuller. A useful test in finding out how Christians react to the need of others is to apply the words of our Lord in Matthew 25 regarding feeding and clothing the needy. Here the anonymous Banner reviewer is adamant that Huntington 'spiritualised' away any social duty referred to here. It is true that in several expositions of this text Huntington applies it to a far wider area than the mere clothing and feeding of strangers, but this does not mean, as the reviewer takes it to mean, that Huntington sees no literal application necessary. We only need to read his *The Justification of a Sinner*,[31] a book that stresses holy living and fruit-bearing, to find Huntington applying the text to Christian duty of a very practical kind. The rich shepherd Nabal refused to give David and his men food though they were in great need. When commenting on Nabal's punishment Huntington says,

> Even so the Saviour will one day punish the covetous worldlings as God punished Nabal. 'I was an hungered, and you gave me no meat'; this was the crime of Nabal, who refused to relieve the Lord's anointed; and the indignity done to His servants, so will the Lord say, 'As ye did it not unto these my

[31] Collingridge, vol. II, p. 44.

> brethren, ye did it not unto me'; and these shall go away into everlasting punishment.

Here, of course, Huntington draws a spiritual moral from Nabal's refusal to help a person in need – so does the Bible – but Huntington, nevertheless, also gives it a very practical application, which the author of *The Voice of Years* and his reviewer have missed.

It is interesting to note that in the early sixties, Dr Soper and those who practised the social gospel were heavily criticised – rightly so – by evangelicals for taking Matthew 25 merely literally and not spiritually. Now Huntington is criticised by an evangelical for taking this passage spiritually and not literally. Actually Huntington did both. He drew spiritual truths from practical applications of Matthew 25.

In *The Justification of a Sinner* Huntington says, 'The glory of all good works wrought in men ought to be attributed to God, from whom every good and every perfect gift cometh'. He goes on to say that he usually finds his flock:

> ... employed like the blessed Lord; sometimes weeping and carrying the cross; and at other times employed in acts of charity to the utmost of their ability; at other times at war with some sore temptation, besetting sin, or spreading error; at other times opposing the wise disputers of this world, who oppose the sovereignty of their Maker, and justify themselves; sometimes I find them at the work of self-examination; at other times citing themselves before the tribunal of God for some misdemeanour, fighting against the flesh, confessing their faults, justifying their God, imploring forgiveness, and seeking reconciliation with him, as the summit of all their happiness; sometimes I find them bemoaning the loss of their Lord, and earnestly seeking his face; at other times, with the state of some poor sinner on their minds, travailing in birth until Christ be formed in him; at other times I find them condoling the miserable, or weeping with them that weep; and sometimes holding forth the word of life, as good stewards of the manifold grace of God, 1 Peter 4:10. In short, I never could apply the Lord's divine salutation of 'All hail',

> Matthew 28:9, to any but to these; for these, in the strictest sense of the word, may be called holy workfolks.[32]

Those who accuse Huntington of teaching lasciviousness and being tardy in doing good could do no better than read his distinction between 'legal workmongers' and those Christians who 'mortify their members' in *Contemplations on the God of Israel*, another of Huntington's very best books. Here we see Huntington at work seeing that his flock obey all God's precepts in leading a holy life. Lying and covetousness are two breaches of the Decalogue that he particularly refers to as he argues that the old man must be put off and the new man put on.[33] In Letter 19 of that work he tells his friend, Rev. J. Jenkins, 'Let us not be weary in well-doing; for in due season we shall reap, if we faint not. As we have, therefore, opportunity, let us do good unto all men, especially unto them who are of the household of faith (Galatians 6:7-10)'. Elsewhere he urges, 'And above all things have fervent charity among yourselves; for charity shall cover a multitude of sins. Use hospitality one to another without grudging. As every man hath received the gift, even so minister the same one to another, as good stewards of the manifold grace of God, 1 Peter 4:8-10'.[34]

In *Every Divine Law in the Heart of Christ* Huntington argues how he has nothing against his enemies' preaching the law but they ought to be telling their flocks how to fulfil it and how to apply it in practice.[35] Huntington considered that his enemies who accused him of being an Antinomian were often worldly themselves in their attitude to the law and to everyday Christian living. Here we see a parallel between Huntington and John Witherspoon (1723-1794) of Scotland who, like Huntington, campaigned against the Moderates who wished to water down Calvinism by calling it Antinomianism. Witherspoon attacked the 'paganised Christian divines' and told them that, though they preached good works, they leave practising them to others. Huntington was thus

---

32 Collingridge, vol. II, pp. 118, 119.

33 See Letter XV.

34 Collingridge, vol. III, *Every Divine Law in the Heart of Christ*, p. 531.

35 See Collingridge, vol. III, pp. 516, 517

especially critical of John Ryland Senior, whom he accused of changing and emptying the law of its legal and theological implication to believers, making it an easier, mere moral rule.[36] This was, of course, nothing but Neonomianism. For Huntington the law was to stand unchanged until the Day of Judgment, when God would use it to measure the righteousness of the sheep (in Christ) and the goats (in Adam).

Huntington was far more meticulous in holy giving than most of his evangelical contemporaries. He would not accept a penny that was raised through musical concerts, drama and oratorios.[37] Nor would he accept a penny from sources which he felt gave a dubious Christian testimony. Thus he was amazed at the way the so-called 'work of the Lord' was being financed by Christians who believed that the end justified the means. He was particularly astonished at the collections taken up by such people as Fuller, who had no qualms in going to churches with whom they were not in fellowship and collecting money from them for their missionary societies and other works.

Thus Huntington could say in face of criticism,

> Nor are we afraid to meet any of our accusers upon the footing of good works. We have collected within these few years more than two thousand pounds, to assist others in building places of worship in the country, and seven hundred pounds to enlarge our own place. And in none of our collections do we go from house to house, much less send to beg a guinea of those who make no pretensions to religion, which many do. No, nor do we even go among any of the evangelists, nor to any other but to those, and only those, who are often seen attending the worship of God

---

[36] See *The Broken Cistern and the Springing Well* and *An Answer to Fools*. These are perhaps Huntington's least edifying works as he merely takes up the vulgar arguments of Ryland and his spokeswoman De Fleury and turns them on their authors. Critics who object to Huntington's language in these works often forget that be is quoting his assailants. Ryland did not go quite as far as Fuller, who completely reversed the law and the gospel and saw the former (in its moral sense alone) as revealing Christ and the latter as convicting of sin (see *The Gospel Worthy of All Acceptation*).

[37] Huntington was by no means alone in his view. See Grimshawe's *Memoir of the Rev. Legh Richmond*, p. 382ff for a lengthy condemnation of such 'Christian concerts' by a near-contemporary of Huntington's. Richmond, an Anglican, calls them 'prostitutions of religion'.

among us. We do not give the hand to the Assyrians for bread, Lamentations 5:6; nor call to the Egyptians for help, Isaiah 30:7. And many pounds that have been sent to us when collecting for places of worship, I say many pounds have been sent us unasked for; and, because we did not like the profession of the givers, we have always sent their money back to them again. If we sow spiritual things in the souls of any, it is a light thing if we reap of their carnal things, 1 Corinthians 9:11. This is the apostolic rule; and we think it is wrong to reap where we have never sowed.

We keep a bank of charity among ourselves, to relieve our own poor; and this is supported, not by a two-penny rate, much less by the Arminian tribute of a penny a week. We do nothing in this poor, low, mean, contemptible, pitiful way but rather despise it. Ours is supported by subscriptions and voluntary contributions; and we seldom distribute less than three or four hundred guineas per annum. And, if at any time the bank gets low, half a dozen words from the pulpit brings in sixty or seventy pounds to recruit it. Nor do we spend, as many do, twenty minutes or half an hour in pumping, pressing, squeezing, and extorting a few shillings out of the pockets of worldlings, who appear in a sheep's skin. We seldom or ever spend two minutes at this labour. A gentleman, not long ago, to whom we gave a collection, with a few words, got one hundred and forty-five pounds under one discourse; and, had he mentioned it in the evening, I doubt not but it would have amounted to upwards of two hundred pounds.[38]

Huntington's attitude to prayer

In evaluating Huntington's view of practical holiness one must pay due attention to the pastor's attitude to prayer. Whatever else Huntington was, he was a true man of prayer and it was well known amongst his people that he often spent five or six hours at a time on his knees. The Rev. S. Adams, who knew Huntington closely, writes, 'His prayers

[38] *Ibid.*, pp. 495, 496.

were as special addresses to the Father, as a man speaking to his friend, and almost entirely in the words of Scripture – one passage after the other flowing out in confession, supplication, or thanksgiving; he frequently used the words, "If it please the Divine majesty"'.[39] It was in prayer that Huntington confessed his sins, felt the rod of God chastising him and God's holy furnace cleansing him. It was here that this man of once very humble means was qualified to shepherd one of the largest churches in the country and present a bold face against the criticism of a large number of enemies that exceeded, if possible, the scorn that Whitefield received from those who scoffed at him for similar reasons. Huntington was always careful to pray for his enemies and repeatedly urged his congregation to do the same. Thus he could say:

> We are commanded to pray for them that persecute us, not knowing but there may be some like a persecuting Saul among them. And many of the saints' prayers have been heard in behalf of persons that never will be saved; as when prayers have been put up for people sick, afflicted, or in poverty: God has raised them up, delivered, and relieved them. The whole ship's crew that sailed with Paul reaped the benefit of his prayers, and so did many sick in the isle of Malta.[40]

Writing to a friend in 1806, Huntington tells him:

> The life and soul of real religion lies in being alone with God, and in seeking his blessed face by humble prayer: The little cabin, and my own bedchamber at Cricklewood, are the two favourite and consecrated spots for this business. Seek his face, my dear friends, and let no reproofs, no rebukes, no chastisements, no crosses; no discouragements, damp your spirits at this; remember, the rod of God is not upon the wicked; it is those whom God loves that he chastens; chastisements are the lot of sons, not of servants. God bless you! I do not, I cannot forget you in my poor prayers.[41]

---

[39] Hooper, *The Celebrated Coalheaver*, p. 31.
[40] Collingridge, Vol. III, *Every Divine Law in the Heart of Christ*, p. 530.
[41] *Posthumous Letters*, Letter XXXVI.

Elsewhere on the subject of prayer, he says:

'By the increase of his lips shall he be filled'. Godliness with contentment is great gain, having the promise of the life that now is, and of that which is to come. Solomon prayed for wisdom, and he got riches and honour into the bargain, which is what he did not ask for. This increase of the lips mentioned in my text is *answers to prayer;* which consists in an increase of knowledge, of experience, of faith, of life, of peace, and of love, comfort, joy, and strength. Some folks make many long prayers, and think that they shall be heard for their much speaking; but, if God gives no answer, there is no increase; and, if no increase, how can they be filled? Great is the delight of the Lord in the prayers of the faithful. 'Let me hear thy voice, let me see thy face; sweet is thy voice, and thy countenance is comely'. The prayer of the upright is the Lord's delight. 'Ask and ye shall have, seek and ye shall find, knock and it shall be opened unto you; for he that asketh receiveth, and he that seeketh findeth'. And again, 'Call upon me in the time of trouble, I will deliver thee, and thou shalt glorify me. Open thy mouth wide, and I will fill it'. O how great is the condescension of God to listen to the prayers of such poor rebels! and how sweet and savoury are those blessings and gracious answers, that are obtained by much importunity in prayer! Reader, as long as one doubt remains touching the goodness and safety of thy state, if suspicions are working, if any fears are cherished, if any pro and con in the court of conscience, if any jealousies; let these things be manifested, let them be sifted to the bottom, let them be canvassed over, and set to rights; make straight paths for thy feet; remember that thy belly is to be filled, and thou art to be satisfied with the fruit of thy lips; there is a great gain in godliness, a choice revenue in wisdom, and a blessed increase in prayer. Begging is the most profitable branch of all the heavenly trade. 'He raiseth up the poor out of the dust, and lifteth up the beggar from the dunghill, to set them among princes, and to make them inherit the throne of glory', 1 Samuel

> 2:8. But without prayer what can be expected, when God hath said that, for all the spiritual and temporal blessings promised, he will be inquired of by the house of Israel to do these things for them? Read Ezekiel 36.[42]

Prayer for Huntington was one of the means used by the Holy Spirit to work out and secure the sanctification of the believer. He could thus advise his flock that:

> Prayer, my dear friends, is a blessed means which God hath appointed to bring every grace from Christ to us. We are to let our requests be made known to him; and for our encouragement he tells us that the prayer of the upright is his delight; yea, that he loves to hear it; 'Let me hear thy voice, let me see thy face; for sweet is thy voice, and thy countenance is comely'. Prayer is casting of our cares and burdens on the Lord; it is pouring out the soul before him, and shewing him our trouble; it is communing and corresponding with Christ, and receiving grace from his fulness to help us in every time of need; it is keeping the intercourse open between the Lord and us; it is our way of paying morning and evening visits to the King of kings and Lord of lords; it is going to court, and shewing our respects and royalty there; it is keeping our debt-book clear, and cultivating and keeping up perfect friendship with a friend that loves at all times; and therefore should never be neglected. Prayer is God's appointment, the Spirit's gift, the saint's privilege, and Satan's scourge; therefore prize it, and use it.[43]

A positive note

The enmity against Huntington and the harsh voice of his fierce critics must not be stressed too strongly. Thousands and thousands saw Huntington as a holy man sent from God and words quoted in The Gospel Advocate in 1873 must also be quoted as an example of how deep was the love and respect shown by a large number of Christians

[42] Collingridge, vol. III, *Light Shining in Darkness*, pp. 98, 99.
[43] *Posthumous Letters*, Letter CCCCX.

for the 'Old Coalheaver'. A Mr C. Willingham of Richmond wrote to the Rev. Samuel Turner of Sunderland and said of Huntington, 'I know he is but a man, and man may err; but I do conceive him to be a partaker of a larger measure of the Spirit than any other man on earth'.

But we shall give Huntington the last word from his book *The Bond Child Brought to the Test*. Defending the doctrine that God upholds his people with his free Spirit (Psalm 51:12) and arguing that he knows of no other help when trials come along, he says:

> For my part, I never found any doctrine that would beget souls to God, keep them alive, make their minds heavenly, their conversation pure, keep their conscience tender, or make their lives exemplary, but that of enforcing regeneration, or a spiritual birth; justification by faith; union and fellowship with Christ by love, and a walk in the testimony and liberty of the Holy Ghost. However, this I can say, that the religion that God has taught me has been sufficient to make me industrious and willing to live honestly; and I must declare, and will with my dying breath, that I never knew what happiness, peace, rest, quietude, comfort, joy, or pleasure meant until Jesus Christ appeared to my soul. In him I have seen the perfection of all beauty. I have felt him to be the foundation of all real happiness. The light of his countenance, and the anticipation of his love, is the quintessence of all that is called pleasure; and to have him is to be possessed of an immortal, incorruptible, undefiled, and never-failing inheritance, which has so crucified me to this world and to the pleasures of it that I have just as much desire to return to it again as Abraham had to return to Ur of the Chaldees, when God had promised to be his shield and everlasting reward in the land of Canaan.

In the introduction to this work Huntington says, 'I wish everyone that calls me an Antinomian had got the same hope!'

Chapter 13

An Old Tree Bearing Much Fruit

Early in July 1802, Huntington received a letter from a thirty-seven year old woman who was in great soul trouble and needed spiritual assistance. He wrote back, explaining to the lady her condition and what she ought to do about it. It turned out that the woman was the widow of Sir James Sanderson, M.P., a former Lord Mayor of London, and daughter of Alderman Skinner, who had also been a Lord Mayor of London. Lady Elizabeth Sanderson was so changed by Huntington's Christian advice that she bought as many books of his as she could find and read them diligently, corresponding with Huntington throughout the next year or so. She remained, however, in deep bondage, mainly because of her rich friends who abhorred the very idea of leading a Christian life. She also suffered very much as a result of her tiny stature.

One Sunday morning in July 1803, Lady Sanderson plucked up courage to go and hear Huntington preach. Much that he said caused her to tremble but, on the whole, she was greatly blessed by what she heard and sent her servant to ask Huntington for an interview. Huntington invited the lady to breakfast with him and soon was well on the way to leading Lady Sanderson into gospel truths. On hearing that she had contacted Huntington, however, her father and sisters were wild in their protests and the clergy with whom she had been in contact warned her urgently to have nothing to do with the ex-coalheaver. Lady Sanderson also had Quaker friends who echoed the Church of England ministers' warnings.

Ever since he was fifty-three years of age, Huntington had felt that he had prematurely become an old man. In 1796 he started to make arrangements for his own decease and bought a plot of land with a few of his closest friends where they hoped to be buried. By 1803, although Huntington was still only fifty-eight years of age and preaching five to ten times a week, he felt he was a wreck physically and at the end of his usefulness. In his youth. he had been plagued with illness which at times lasted several years. His health improved somewhat when he was settled in the ministry with a steady income and good food but he was continually plagued with headaches, severe colds, bouts of fever, asthma and severe rheumatism. Very often he found it extremely painful to walk short distances and it was impossible for him to climb even the smallest hills. Mary, his wife, was no help to him as she had been drinking hard now for some seventeen years and was still putting on weight so that she was hardly able to move. She suffered from the gout in both feet, which meant that she could not walk far and grew even fatter through lack of exercise. She was often in great pain besides not being quite in her senses through the influence of alcohol.

Lady Sanderson's help becomes a source of gossip

Lady Sanderson came to Huntington's assistance in his ill-health and put a coach and driver at his disposal, accompanying him at times on his various preaching engagements. This, however, caused tongues to wag and soon the satirical newspapers were telling dirty stories about Huntington's imaginary escapades with young ladies. They did this knowing full well that Huntington was crippled with rheumatism and could hardly walk and the amorous feats they accused him of were sheer physical impossibilities besides being anathema to one of Huntington's spiritual status. These journeys have been highly exaggerated as Lady Sanderson was only one of very many friends who assisted Huntington in this way and Huntington was rarely alone with her as others rode with them. Often Lady Sanderson rode to the services in another coach with other members of Providence Chapel. Whenever Huntington preached away, a whole convoy of friends – male and female – would accompany their pastor in various coaches, but whenever Lady Sanderson did this it was the talk of the town! Critics also forget that Lady Sanderson did not only drive Huntington from place to place but put her coach at the service of the poorer members of the chapel.

Huntington's letters to Lady Sanderson at this time have been preserved and they are highly pastoral and spiritual. Soon the opposing clergy, however, always willing to believe anything bad which was said of Huntington, started to outdo the newspapers with their stories. Thus rumours were spread that the former labourer was now the protégé of the idle rich and was driven around in the coaches of the gentry and served by liveried lackeys. It was pointed out, quite wrongly, that Huntington was always ready to grant interviews and write letters to the rich but he would not do the same for the poor.[1] This is a ridiculous accusation as it was commonly known that Huntington set apart four consultation periods a week where the poor who were spiritually or financially in need were sure they would find a sympathetic listener and helper. These critics forget how strong Huntington's feelings were towards anyone who tried to patronise him. In point of fact, the coach which Lady Sanderson put at Huntington's disposal was not her own but belonged to Alderman Skinner. Huntington wasted no time in making a deal with the alderman and bought his coach cash down.

It is very evident here what a disgraceful strategy Huntington's 'Christian' critics practised. When it served their purpose, they emphasised that Huntington was merely the pastor of the ignorant poor. Equally, when they thought it would help their arguments against Huntington, they would quite illogically accuse him of being the pastor of the idle rich.[2] Actually Lady Sanderson's income was very small for a member of the 'gentry' and was certainly far less than that of Huntington, who now had an income of some £2,000 per annum. Even Hooper, who is so critical of Huntington's apparent regard for the rich, admits that Sir James Sanderson was a *distinguished* rather than a *rich* man, thus admitting that there would have been little to inherit from him. Furthermore, from the start of his correspondence with Lady Sanderson, Huntington wisely and categorically refused to accept any financial gifts from her for his work.

---

[1] See *The Voice of Years*.

[2] This is the dubious stance taken both in Hooper's *The Celebrated Coalheaver* and in the anonymous *The Voice of Years*. Sadly, it is reflected in The Banner of Truth review of *The Voice of Years*.

Be this as it may, numerous friends and foes of Huntington have been unanimous in condemning Lady Sanderson and her presumed influence over him. Ebenezer Hooper, a descendant of a Huntingtonian family, devotes seven pages of absolute vitriol to her in his *The Celebrated Coalheaver* and a further nine pages of severe criticism in his *Facts and Letters*. These two books have greatly influenced the secular and Christian readership in forming an opinion of Lady Sanderson. Reading between the lines, however, shows that Hooper's completely negative picture of Lady Sanderson was built more on prejudice and misunderstanding than on evidence. It is extremely difficult to obtain a balanced view of her ladyship from outside sources although her correspondence with Huntington is of the highest spiritual kind.

Hooper accuses Huntington of 'great weakness' in allowing Lady Sanderson to help him as she did. It may have been unwise of Huntington to accept Lady Sanderson's practical help, although the fact that she did her level best to serve the Lord by escorting the ailing Huntington from preaching engagement to preaching engagement can hardly be called scandalous. When there is no proof whatsoever to support a scandalous theory, Christian men should be the last to defend it.

One day J. C. Philpot was travelling to London in a coach when he found himself in conversation with a chatty, well-dressed old man who seemed a stranger to the gospel. As the conversation came round to religion, however, the old man suddenly said to Philpot, 'Did you know the celebrated Mr Huntington, the Walking Bible, as he was called?' Philpot replied that he was too young to have known him personally. The old man then said that he had known Huntington well as he was his lawyer. After praising Huntington for his uprightness and integrity and knowing that this had been challenged by Huntington's unjust critics, he told Philpot the following anecdote. One day the lawyer went to Huntington concerned about Lady Sanderson. He told Huntington that he believed she had a good deal of property and as she attended his chapel and there were several young men there who might become interested in the widow for her property's sake, he asked, 'Would it not be desirable to tie up her money and settle it upon her in such a way that it could not be touched?' The lawyer argued in this way as in those days any property belonging to a woman was automatically transferred to the name of the husband unless other measures had been taken previous to marriage. Huntington replied, knowing full well what was being said about him and Lady Sanderson's fortune, that the lawyer should tie the money up so that he, too, would never be able to touch it. Thus Huntington had Lady Sanderson's five to six thousand pound income from her father's property and that of a male relative 'tied up' in her name at a good interest. When Huntington died in 1813 Lady Sanderson's fortune had risen to £8,600, which meant that Huntington's stewardship had increased her investments by some £3,000 not counting the withdrawals of well over £1,000 her ladyship had made during this period.

Huntington's portrait painted

During 1803, Huntington's friends, probably alarmed by their pastor's talk of death, plagued him continually to have his portrait painted. There were scores of portraits, or rather cartoons, in existence at the time but these were all drawn by newspaper cartoonists who delighted to portray Huntington as a blue-beard, or as a fat glutton or a salivating monster. Each friend wanted a portrait of his own to remember Huntington by and he envisaged days and weeks of sitting for portraits if his friends had their will. Eventually he agreed to have one – and only one – portrait painted. An eminent Italian painter by the name of Domenico Pellegrini was hired for ninety guineas and he started work on what he assured Huntington would be one picture only. Huntington's friends, however, were guilty of a mild deception. They had arranged with Pellegrini to change the canvas as often as possible without Huntington noticing the fraud. The 'Coalheaver' soon got tired of sitting for the artist but not until Pellegrini had clandestinely finished three portraits.

Death of his wife

By mid 1805, it became obvious that Mary Huntington would not live long. She developed the dropsy and her liver started to decay rapidly because of the large amounts of alcohol she consumed. The gout in her feet grew worse. Her size by this time was enormous and she could not stop eating. Huntington was heartbroken, chiefly because of her spiritual state. He was very critical of himself as he had not been able to keep her from falling. Mary Huntington died on 9 December, 1806 and was buried in the vault Huntington had prepared for himself. There was no great gathering of mourners at the funeral and Mrs Huntington just faded away without much notice being taken of her. Huntington, however, took Mary's death very hard and suffered greatly because of it.

Huntingtonians were used to discussing the death of fellow believers in great detail because of the support and comfort they received from believers gladly crossing Jordan. Shortly after Mary Huntington's funeral, a well-meaning but blundering visitor said for all to hear, 'Oh, Mr Huntington, I have never heard you mention your late wife, nor have you ever given us any account of her end'. This was too much for even the iron-willed Huntington, who burst into tears before all present and rushed from the room.

Huntington and the poor

Many of Huntington's friends, such as John Ring and George Lansdell, were so generous with their gifts to the work of Providence Chapel that they caused Huntington a great deal of embarrassment. On several occasions around this time we read of their pastor sending money back and giving them a piece of his mind. He told Ring that it was wrong to impoverish himself by giving money to one who was better off than he was. Huntington was even sterner with Lansdell, who had several young children, and told him that he should show more piety at home and spend more money on his children rather than starve the whole family by giving so much to charity and to his pastor. 'He who does not provide for his own family denies the faith', was Huntington's wise comment. Lansdell did not merely receive good advice from Huntington but also good works. When the 'Coalheaver' thought his friend was in need, he would send him a cow or two and would lend or give him money whenever he was in debt.

Lansdell thought the world of his pastor and would have done anything for him, knowing that Huntington was a friend indeed. Once in January, 1807, however, his demands on his pastor left the realms of reason. Lansdell's young daughter Sarah died and he was out of his mind with grief. He wrote several letters a day to Huntington, begging him to bring his daughter back to life. He seemed to believe that this would move the masses to trust in Christ. His pastor replied quickly, calmly and soundly, writing:

> Your letter rather surprised me. To raise the dead in sin to a life of faith is most certainly a work that I am called to and engaged in, and in which I hope and believe I have some small success, but to raise dead bodies to a mortal life is not in my commission, nor will I ever attempt it, unless God Himself should make it known to me that it is His divine will that such a miracle should be wrought in answer to the prayers of such an unworthy sinner as me. It is at this day more satisfaction to me to follow my poor children that are gone before, than to have these that may stay behind. As to the raising of your daughter being of any use to infidels is talking nonsense. Abraham's answer to the rich man in hell is sufficient upon this point, 'They have Moses and the prophets'. Yea more, we have Christ and His apostles; let them hear them. and if they believe not these, neither will they be persuaded, though one rose from the dead.[3]

It is Huntington's great generosity and his continually refusing gifts from those who could ill afford to make them that has fuelled the fire of his critics. They argue, quite illogically, that as Huntington gave so much money to some friends, and refused gifts from others, he must have had huge sums left at his own disposal. These critics do not realise that Huntington often gave his last penny to needy people when he and his family were living on almost starvation level. Oddly enough, the anonymous writer of *The Voice of Years* tells us that Huntington refused to look upon it as a Christian duty to 'relieve the afflicted and oppressed', mentioning that other pastors had 'impoverished themselves' by doing so. Huntington, he argues, was only generous to the rich. Nothing could be further from the truth. There were few pastors in Huntington's day who were able to raise so much money so quickly for the assistance of those in need. But Huntington also kept his

[3] *Letters of William Huntington: Further Gleanings of the Vintage*, editor and publisher H. M. Pickles.

own pockets empty that the pockets of the needy might be full. Whenever Huntington gave, however, he soon found that he was abundantly rewarded for his giving. The writer of *The Voice of Years* just could not see that it was Huntington's Lord who kept him 'in pocket'. There are many anecdotes to show the truth of this; the following will suffice.

One day a person called on Mr Over, a close friend of Huntington's who helped manage the affairs of Providence Chapel, and gave him a £10 note, telling him that he was to give it to Mr Huntington as soon as possible but not tell him who the donor was. Although the next day was Huntington's day of rest (in which he usually worked in his fields) Mr Over decided to call at Cricklewood and give his pastor the money. He found Huntington talking to a gardener and waited until he had an opportunity to speak to him alone. When the gardener had gone, Huntington greeted Mr Over in his usual brusque way and was given the money. Huntington could only comment, 'Well, how marvellous is the providence of God! There is poor White just recovered from a fever that has afflicted him and all his family; I was about to give him £2, but recollecting it was all the money I had, I resolved not to do so; but directly I had so thought, these words came to my mind, "The liberal deviseth liberal things; and by liberal things shall he stand" (Isaiah 32:8). I instantly gave him the money, little thinking that you stood at my elbow with five times the amount which God had sent me.'

His generosity to his family

Huntington had a large family of thirteen children and when they were young he had to scrape together the pennies in order to feed them. Seven of these children survived to adulthood and all but one professed faith in Christ. Huntington never forgot the hardships they had suffered and was exceedingly generous to them. Several of his children failed in their occupations and callings, most likely for the simple reason that, whenever they were in financial difficulties, they expected their father to help them out. This caused them to be extremely careless in how they managed their own financial affairs. Thomas Wright, in his excellent biography of Huntington, says that Huntington invested over £4,000 in his children's businesses but they allowed the money to slip through their fingers. The money that Huntington invested in his in-laws also went into several thousands of pounds and when Wayte, the husband of

Huntington's daughter Naomi died, his large debts were paid by his father-in-law. The 'Coalheaver' was just as generous with his grandchildren. Once, for instance, Huntington was walking in the garden at Cricklewood when he saw one of his grandchildren (Ruth's daughter) at play. Remembering that it was her ninth birthday, Huntington called the little girl to him and told her to stretch out her apron. The girl obeyed at once and was rewarded by seeing her grandfather empty the contents of his pockets into her apron. She counted out no less than nine golden guineas which her parents invested for her until she came of age.[4]

Huntington has been severely criticised for leaving little money to his own relations in his wills. These critics do not take into account that when Huntington wrote his last will in 1810, he had hardly any funds left through being over-generous to scores of people, including not only members of his own family but also in-laws whom he considered to be proper objects of charity. Apart from paying all the debts of his son-in-law Wayte, Huntington was also very generous to his other in-laws. Two of Huntington's sisters had married two brothers, Tom and Daniel Young. The latter was the gunmaker mentioned in an earlier chapter to whom Huntington had been apprenticed but who had to give up his trade because of his love for strong drink. Daniel Young was one of the many relatives who believed Huntington was a never-ending source of financial assistance. A letter has been preserved which shows how concerned Huntington, his sister and brother-in-law Tom Young were for Daniel. The letter also shows what a faithful witness Huntington kept up in his dealings with his family.

---

[4] Such stories ought not to be forgotten as modern critics of Huntington echo *The Voice of Years* by saying that Huntington was inaccessible to bis own family. On the contrary, there were almost always members of his family staying as welcome guests in his home. He often wrote to his family and was exceedingly generous to them.

Post Mark, June 29, 1790
Dear Brother and Sister

I received your letter and the Register of my age, and thank my brother for his trouble in procuring it; but am sorry to hear of the life of old Daniel. Daniel will be the death of Tom, if Tom do not see the death of him.

There is no happiness my dear friends, but in Christ Jesus, he is the Fountain of Life where a man may drink and forget his poverty and remember his misery no more; the spirit of love in a broken heart is the best new wine in the new bottle, both these 'shall be preserved', when thousands shall be dashed to pieces like a potter's vessel.

This better banquet – better part – and better portion, through matchless grace is mine: this flagon shall be supplied in endless bliss, when those who add drunkenness to thirst (Deuteronomy 29:19, 20) must beg water in hell. O Dog! what has grace done for us? I look forward to death, the grave, the day of judgment, and to heavenly glory, with unutterable delight; and by the eye of faith, often see my carcass in a tomb and my soul in heaven.

This is living dog, Ecclesiastes 9:4; there is no man on earth whose happiness I envy, or whose state I covet; I know in whom I have believed: and am fully persuaded that He will keep that which I have committed to HIM against that day.

The good work of God still prospers in the hands of the Coalheaver, this is the Lord's doing, and it is marvellous in the eyes of many; but fools must confound the wise, the base must debase the honourable. God will have it so, and the bond children must be content.

Tender my love to Mr Lloyd, Goudhurst friends, to Tom the elder, and Tom the junior, and accept the same

From a double Brother, in the double bond of the Brotherly covenant,
W. Huntington.

P.S. I will send you a pot of Spruce by Tye's waggon

Tom Young was soon to see the death of Daniel before Daniel became the death of Tom. Daniel often visited Huntington when he was in London, usually in an intoxicated state and in need of money. On this last occasion he was fed, entertained and given a bed for the night and on the following day received a dressing-down by Huntington who gave him a new silk scarf for himself and a guinea for his wife. Huntington's last words to his brother-in-law were: 'Now mind Daniel, and be sure you do not spend this, but give it to my sister, or else never see my face again'. On his way home Daniel could not fight back the longing for alcohol and spent the guinea on drink. He never arrived home but was later found dead in a wood. He had hanged himself with the scarf he had received from Huntington.

Marriage to Lady Sanderson

Although there are no signs in Huntington's letters from this time that anything was afoot, many of those who were close to him were very fearful that Lady Sanderson would now exert more influence on him. Others, however, equally believed that Lady Sanderson would be a good match for their pastor whom they felt needed a wife to help him with his pastoral duties and to support him in his ill-health. The gossip grew and grew and it seemed that every single adviser Huntington had could not wait to broach the matter with him until he was sick and tired of the subject. Brook, though he held Lady Sanderson in great respect, sided with those who were against a match and told Huntington that those who told him he should marry Lady Sanderson were hypocrites. Up to this time, two things are certain: Huntington had no thoughts of marrying Lady Sanderson – or anybody for that matter[5] – and the gossip was causing serious strife amongst the members of Providence Chapel. Soon a large faction, including Cornelius Tozer, Ebenezer Huntington and Brook, had formed who were against Lady Sanderson and a smaller faction including Thomas Bensley were for her. The church, however, did not openly split as both sides loved their pastor too much to desert him.

---

[5] Huntington told a friend at this time, 'I no more want a wife than a toad wants side-pockets'.

Lady Sanderson now paid Huntington more and more attention. She moved home so that she could be near Providence Chapel and made herself in many ways useful in the affairs of the church. She looked upon Huntington as her 'invaluable friend' and always referred to him as if he were a prophet of old. She started to manage his household and gradually became a kind of personal secretary to him. About a year and a half after Mary Huntington's death, Lady Sanderson as good as proposed to Huntington, telling him that the whole world had already concluded that they were one. Huntington was cut to the quick at first but – for reasons that might never be known – acceded to her wish, officially proposed, was accepted and the two were married on 15 August, 1808, by the Rev. Benjamin Lawrence, a curate of the Church of England. Huntington signed the register in a very small and shaky hand, most unlike his previous bold signature. Rumour has it that he was quite lost in meditation whilst waiting for the bride and absent-mindedly suddenly asked Bensley, his best man, 'What wait we for?' Bensley replied, 'For the Lady, Sir!' and Huntington commented, 'Oh, indeed!'

Soon tongues were wagging more than ever. One half of the chapel members were saying that Huntington had come down in the world and had married a spiritually inferior being. The other half were saying that Lady Sanderson was a true child of God, led a profound Christian life and was a gift of God to her husband. The secular press and many Christians outside of Huntington's influence said that the marriage was one of convenience so that Huntington could tap off Lady Sanderson's fortune.

There was soon no doubt, however, that a new broom was sweeping in Huntington's household, and it swept hard. Huntington always ate frugally and took toast and water to his meals. His pantry and kitchen, however, were always well stocked because of the eating habits of his former wife, Mary, and the fact that the house was always full of guests. Soon, like Mother Hubbard's cupboard, Huntington's kitchen was bare. Lady Sanderson, possibly owing to her tiny size and slimness, took no more than a morsel for her meals and expected her husband and his guests to do the same. Often there was no food whatsoever in the house. Huntington soon realised that he would have to put his foot down but could not talk to Elizabeth as openly as he had spoken to Mary.

Once, on returning home with an enormous appetite after a long journey, Huntington dashed into the kitchen to make himself a meal. To his great disappointment, not a crumb was to be had. The hungry pastor thought a moment about what course of action he should take and then picked up a plate and smashed it to pieces on the kitchen floor. Lady Sanderson rushed in wondering what on earth was happening. Huntington pointed to the broken crockery and calmly told her that plates were to put food on and if there were no food to put on the plates, they were quite superfluous and could be discarded. After that, the kitchen was restocked but Lady Sanderson still managed to puzzle the guests by filling old wine bottles with cheaper brews of her own concoction which bore no resemblance to the commodity represented on the labels.

Lady Sanderson's new broom next went to work on Huntington's finances. He was too generous and too indulgent by far, in her opinion. She was especially shocked by the amount of money he gave his children and their families and managed to persuade him to change his policy towards them. Her main energy was directed against Ebenezer, who was one of the saintliest of men. Ebenezer had inherited much of his character from his father and was known far and wide for his generosity to those worse off than himself. His house was always full of guests and his particular concern was for new visitors to Providence Chapel and those who came from outside London. Ebenezer would collect these numerous people together after the services and take them to his home where they were entertained cordially.

After being tutored by Dr John Ryland, Ebenezer learned the trade of a coachmaker and practised it until his marriage in 1804. As he suffered from epilepsy, he had great difficulty in continuing as a craftsman. Huntington thus set him up in business as his personal publisher and printer. As Huntington's books were now selling very well indeed, Ebenezer's success was assured. This was particularly the case as four 'friends' decided to invest capital in his business. This, however, came to Lady Sanderson's ear and she was shocked that, in her interpretation, Ebenezer had got himself into debt. Business-wise this was not at all true as, though Ebenezer had debts of £700, his stock was valued at around £5,000. Lady Sanderson now thought it her duty to put Ebenezer back on the 'right path' and organise his finances. She made it quite clear to Huntington that he should drop his son entirely until he mended his ways. She also got in touch with Ebenezer's creditors and told them that Ebenezer was a bad investment. This made them demand their money back. As Ebenezer had no ready cash, he could only hope to sell off his stock quickly. Lady Sanderson came up with what she thought was a solution and insisted that it should be carried out. Huntington was to make Mr Bensley his official printer and Ebenezer should sell him his stock. This would, of course, have helped Ebenezer pay his debts but ruin him as a businessman. According to Ebenezer's friend, Cornelius Tozer, this is exactly what Lady Sanderson wanted to do. Bensley caused difficulties by saying the stock was not worth much and bid next to nothing for it. Lady Sanderson and Bensley eventually agreed that Ebenezer would sell his stock at two thirds less than the production price and Lady Sanderson would give Bensley £1,200 security. Hands were shaken and Bensley, instead of passing the reduced price of the books on to the public, promptly put the price of Huntington's books up by as much as 700%, and began to make an enormous profit. Ebenezer's many friends believed divine justice was enacted when shortly afterwards Beasley's stock and premises were destroyed by fire.

Both Bensley and Lady Sanderson now found themselves very unpopular amongst the members of Providence Chapel. The truth was that Lady Sanderson had done everything according to the best principles but she had even less knowledge of business than Huntington and his son. Her husband, she thought, needed all his strength for his pastoral work, so she should take charge of other duties. Though Lady Sanderson strove to be very thrifty and business-like, and not make the financial mistakes she believed her husband made, nothing was saved by her efforts; indeed, she lost her £1,200 as Bensley never thought of paying it back. Moreover, Huntington had always been divinely favoured by having his right pocket filled whenever he emptied his left pocket to help the poor. Now that he was forced to keep his hand on his left pocket, his right pocket remained empty. The result was that Huntington was able to do less good works and his cash in hand did not grow. The poet Cowper once said of the Olney poor, 'With all their thrift, they thrive not'. This could well be said of Lady Sanderson's management.

The members of Providence Chapel tried to get in touch with Huntington on the subject of Ebenezer but Lady Sanderson either blocked them at the door or gave them scandalous reports of Ebenezer's behaviour which were completely untrue. She told an official delegation of chapel members, for instance, that Ebenezer had an expensive country house on the sly and this had absorbed much of his funds. Lady Sanderson had misunderstood the fact that a good friend of Ebenezer's in the country had put a room at his disposal where he could rest after the fits from which he suffered. Other arguments Lady Sanderson used were that Ebenezer spent more money on his small household than his father did on his much larger one and that he kept 'an old woman' in charity which was a drain on his resources. These arguments were as fanciful as the first. The fact that Ebenezer spent more money on his household than Lady Sanderson was hardly a criticism as her ladyship was becoming a real skinflint and spent next to nothing. The 'old woman' Lady Sanderson referred to was not that old at all and assisted Ebenezer in his bookshop. The lady was the mother of Cornelius Tozer, whom Ebenezer employed to take down his father's sermons in shorthand for publication. The Tozers were well-loved at Providence Chapel and when the delegation heard these feeble and unjust accusations against their friends, they realised that they could get nowhere by arguing for Ebenezer.

Huntington's new wife further upset many members of Providence Chapel by keeping her former name. Instead of being plain Mrs Huntington, the pastor's wife, she insisted on being treated as a gentlewoman and would not adopt Huntington's surname. There was, of course, some stigma attached to the name but Huntington had made it honourable throughout his blameless years as a pastor and there was many a woman at Providence Chapel who would have been proud to be called Mrs Huntington. Her ladyship thought otherwise and did not become the more popular for doing so. Actually, she made things worse by continually referring to Huntington in her usual way as 'our invaluable friend' or in terminology usually used for Bible characters such as 'the Prophet' or 'the Apostle'. Many of the mistaken criticisms levelled at Huntington for supposedly calling himself a 'prophet' are traceable to Lady Sanderson's usage of the term. She never seems to have referred to Huntington as simply 'my husband'.

In January, 1810, shortly before his sixty-fifth birthday, Huntington decided to make his will. After committing his soul into the hands of Christ his Saviour, he expressed the wish to be buried near Jenkins. The chapel, which was Huntington's property, was to be given to the trustees, who were asked to pay a quarterly sum, at their discretion, to his widowed daughter Naomi, and to Ruth, now Mrs Blake. Naomi was also left a cottage adjoining Providence Chapel. Huntington also mentioned other members of his wider family who were 'objects of charity' and again committed them to the care of the trustees. Huntington bequeathed £3,000 to his wife which they had invested in stock and all other money which was in joint accounts or in accounts under Huntington's name alone. He also granted his wife £5,000 inherited from Lady Sanderson's father and which Huntington had refused to touch. His son William was left £300, Ebenezer £30, Benjamin, for reasons unknown, was left a mere £5 to buy himself a mourning suit, Gad was to receive £70, Lois £100 and his four grandchildren were to receive £50 each on attaining the age of twenty-one or on getting married. It was stressed in the will that the amounts to his children, apart from Naomi's cottage, were approximate as they were to be paid from the sale of Huntington's personal effects, the value of which he could only estimate. Huntington made such careful provision for his wife as he now genuinely believed that should the money fall into the hands of his children, they would squander it and leave his widow penniless. Lady Sanderson was still relentless in accepting any concessions from her husband concerning Ebenezer. Huntington, however, gave him a great number of letters to publish and made him one of the chapel trustees.

At this time, though in very bad health, Huntington was still preaching almost daily. Nevertheless he was more convinced than ever that the time to end his pilgrimage had come. He had lost his appetite completely in January and was continually troubled with fainting fits coupled with violent coughing and attacks of asthma. It was also evident that lengthy discussions with his wife concerning his children were getting him down. One day in February, during a violent fit of coughing and dizziness, Huntington caught hold of a wardrobe to steady himself but fell unconscious to the floor. When he came to himself, he became very conscious of death and was filled with a love for God and sweet expectation of his coming deliverance from his 'body of flesh'. Huntington quite obviously longed to be with the Lord and told one of his workers that his family life had become a hell. Little did Huntington know that God had planned that he should be more fruitful in his old age than ever before in his prime of life. At first, however, all the signs suggested to Huntington that his life's work was done.

Fire at Providence Chapel

On Friday, 13 July, 1810, Huntington's newly married nephew Thomas Young was doing some repair work at Providence Chapel when he saw that some houses were burning at quite a distance from the chapel. Suddenly a flame shot through the sky and landed on the chapel roof, immediately setting it alight and spreading rapidly to the galleries. Soon huge crowds gathered and made any attempt to stop the spreading of the flames impossible and shouts were heard saying what a pity that the pastor and his entire congregation were not in the building, which rapidly burnt to the ground.

When he saw that it was not possible to save the chapel, Thomas managed to borrow a horse and galloped off to Cricklewood to tell Huntington the bad news. On reaching his destination, he dashed into the room where Huntington and his wife were sitting. Thomas was unable to speak for a time as he had been in such a rush but Huntington realised something terrible had happened and said, 'Why Tom, what's the matter? Is your wife dead?' He still could get no words from Thomas and asked again, 'What is this all about?' 'Oh, Sir', said Thomas, 'your chapel is burned down to the ground!' Huntington was speechless for a time but Lady Sanderson exclaimed, 'Oh dear! Oh dear! What shall we do?' Huntington went over to her and said, 'Now do be quiet, what's the use of all this to do, sit down, we are not bankrupt yet, nor our God either'. He then turned to Thomas and said, 'Well Tom, God gave Ziklag to David, and he took it away by fire. He also gave me Providence Chapel, and has seen fit to take that also away by fire; I must not complain, for it is His doing'.

Huntington was in a very mixed state of mind about the fire. Knowing it was a sign from God, he was uncertain at first what God intended by it. Was this a sign that he ought, indeed, to give up his ministry? Did this mean that he should leave London and return to country areas, where he felt there was a great need? Huntington just did not know. The thought of his large Providence Chapel flock without a shepherd, however, constantly drew him back from such thoughts. Though we find that Huntington's letters from the days and weeks after the fire reflect his strong trust in God, they also show that he did not know what the future would bring. Writing to Isaac Beeman about his dilemma, Huntington says:

> Dear friend,
> Hope and her anchor are both within the vail, and therefore far enough above brick walls and deal boards. The man after God's own heart lost Ziklag by fire, and the best saint in all the east lost both sheep and shepherds by a fire from heaven; then what may not a despicable, sinful Coalheaver expect? My God has not suffered my mind to be moved, nor one moment's sleep to depart from mine eyes, on account of the chapel. God satisfies the desire of every living thing, Psalm 145:16. Numbers have long, wished, and expressed their wish, that the chapel might be burnt down, and God has fulfilled their desires. But will he not much more fulfil ours? Not a few have heard me as long as they could; till, having received their sentence, they are become desperate. Such have but one sort of food; namely, 'except we eat of their flesh we cannot be satisfied'. The burning of the chapel was not sufficient; they lamented aloud because we were not in the place when the fire began.
>
> I am no enemy to their joy, nor could I help laughing when I heard of it. I thought of the old story – 'When the Philistines saw the ark, and heard Israel's shout, they cried out, These be the gods that smote the Egyptians with all the plagues in the wilderness; be strong, and quit yourselves like men, and fight', And, when they took the ark, they set it before Dagon, as a trophy of Satan's victory, ascribing the glory of the conquest to him. But the fall of Dagon, the loss of his head and hands, the emerods and the mice, made their joy but of short duration; and the triumph of these will be but for a moment. At first I thought this was intended to drive

me into the country, which I have long wished, and had set my mind on Suffolk and Ely. But it is not so to be.

God Almighty for ever bless thee, my dearly beloved in Christ Jesus!

W.H. S.S.[6]

The fire occurred on the Friday and Huntington was out preaching at Richmond on the following Sunday. His text summed up his own situation, 'What I do thou knowest not now; but thou shalt know hereafter' (John 13:7). He preached around the country for three weeks until a suitable substitute for Providence Chapel was found in London. Such a building was eventually discovered in Grubb Street and was let to the Huntingtonians by a friendly clergyman. Two days later, on 9 August, 1810, Huntington preached there and in spite of the difficulty in informing all his old friends at such short notice, over 2,000 hearers filled the building and many hundreds had to remain outside. As soon as Huntington's 'god-father', Rowland Hill, heard of this, he dashed off to the Grubb Street area to campaign amongst the neighbours against the 'Antinomian'.

Huntington preached unhindered week after week to growing numbers at Grubb Street, although it was a most unsuitable spot. This was because of the nearby Fore Street Market which was open on Sundays. At times Huntington could hardly make himself heard above the noise of the traders. Once, in the middle of a sermon, he had to give up preaching for a few moments because of the din and exclaimed, 'A man might almost as well try to preach in the belly of hell as in all this uproar and confusion!' He outlined his feelings to a friend in October, 1810:

I am now preaching in a place most disagreeable to me; the way of access, and everything belonging to it, is unpleasant yet there I am fixed, and there I must abide: and by the continual and various exercises which I pass under previous to my preaching,

---

[6] *Posthumous Letters*, vol. III, Letter CCCCLVI.

> and the uncommon zeal and energy with which I am influenced in the work, especially on the Lord's day, convince and assure me that God has a work to do in that place: and I suspect that the old Chapel was burnt down in order to remove the camp to another spot, where more work, and a fresh soil to work upon, may produce such fruit as shall in due time make this manifest. But we are called to watch and to wait; and, if the Lord's footsteps were always plain, we should follow by sight and not by faith.[7]

There was a general rejoicing in the Arminian and semi-Arminian churches in the district when Providence Chapel was burnt down. They felt they had now lost the warning finger that had been pointing at them for twenty-seven long years. Day after day Huntington's enemies visited the site of the fire and celebrated its destruction. During one of these gatherings of scoffers a man was heard to cry out, 'Where is Providence Chapel now?' He was quickly answered by another voice in the crowd which said, 'I would lay the world if I had it, that Huntington gets a better chapel and a larger one. You see if he doesn't!'[8]

Whoever he was, that man was right. Before the glowing embers of the fire had cooled down offers of money came in from all quarters to help finance a new church building. It was rumoured that one wealthy Christian offered to build a new chapel entirely at his own expense even if it would cost £10,000. Huntington refused the offer but accepted £1,000 and added £1,000 of his own to it. Soon after several gifts of £500 came in and Huntington realised that the Lord wished him to build a new chapel. He made it quite clear, however, that if his congregation wanted a new chapel and wanted their old pastor back, then the chapel would have to be built without incurring a penny in debts.

Writing to a generous giver whom he had not solicited for help, Huntington gives some insight into his feelings concerning the burning of the old Providence Chapel. He tells the lady, a sea-captain's wife who had been converted on a sea voyage by reading Huntington's books, that the new chapel had to have a deep foundation and now the walls were four feet above ground. He continues:

---

[7] *Posthumous Letters*, vol. III, Letter CCCIX.

[8] *Posthumous Letters*, vol. I, p. 241.

I know not what to say, nor how to express myself, for your kindness and generosity to me, and towards our new chapel. I never asked it, nor could I find a heart so to do, knowing the expense you have been at in raising your own. At the first news of it being burnt I was unmoved, not knowing what was the mind of God, and believing that this was among the all things that shall eventually work for good, I found my mind composed. But, when I heard of the crowds and public newspapers ridiculing Divine Providence; and of such a triumphant mob assembling daily round the ruins, that the peace officers were obliged to go in person to disperse them, I could not help feeling; however, considering that triumph of the wicked is but short, and the afflictions of the just are not for ever, I bore it pretty well; but not so as to exclude the voice of Satan, of murmuring, or of unbelief; for, if I take counsel in my own heart, these are sure to be heard. I verily believe that neither Satan, nor hell itself, are half so detestable, in the conception of sinners, as that chapel was. But the standard is now removed from that spot, and 'Woe unto them, (says God) when I depart from them', Hosea 9:12.[9]

The building of the new chapel

Finding a site had not been easy as Huntington was confronted with so many eager helpers who claimed they knew of a variety of places. This caused much time-wasting discussion as each praised his own choice. After several months Huntington had eliminated most of the more absurd offers and there remained four men who had sensible suggestions so he formed them into a building committee. Several West-Enders, however, tried to use their influence to persuade the men to build in their various neighbourhoods. Their interference so angered the committee that they eventually refused to carry on and no progress was made. Huntington reacted by saying that the members were obviously not serious about having a new chapel and he would send the

[9] *Posthumous Letters*, Letter XCIII, p. 240.

money back to the donors. This sobered them up wonderfully and in a very short time a new committee was formed and a site in Grays Inn Lane was found which had formerly been a farmyard pond. Because of the swampy nature of the land, the builders had to dig very deep to find solid ground, and amused onlookers thought that Huntington was going to build an under-ground church! The foundation stone was laid on 21 November, 1810 and, as the winter was very mild, building went on at full speed and was more or less completed by the following spring.

When the building work was nearing completion, Huntington heard that £6,000 had been raised but a further £500 would be needed to pay off the last bills. He immediately called on John Over and Edward Aldridge, two of the chapel's trustees, and told them that they were to accompany him on a fund-raising tour and they would not come back until they had enough to pay all bills. Call after call was made amongst the membership. One gave £20 and another topped it by donating £50 and so it went on for a few hours until the money had quickly been raised. As soon as the chapel was opened, however, bills came in that apparently nobody had thought about and another £3,000 was demanded. Huntington was able to pay this within days, his only trouble being in sorting out what money had come from the membership and what had come from outsiders. All the money from outsiders, no matter of what faith and persuasion they were, was politely sent back. Here again, we see how Huntington kept himself above reproach. Few indeed of his evangelical critics in the ministry thought twice about accepting money from unbelievers and strangers or from non-churchgoers who attended their concerts. Huntington was made of sterner stuff.

The opening service

At the opening of the new Providence Chapel on Sunday, 23 June, 1811 Huntington preached one of the mightiest sermons of his life to over three thousand hearers. He chose as his text the most appropriate words from Haggai 2:7-9: 'And I will shake all nations, and the desire of all nations shall come: and I will fill this house with glory, saith the Lord of hosts. The silver is mine, and the gold is mine, saith the Lord of hosts. The glory of this latter house shall be greater than of the former, saith the Lord of hosts: and in this place will I give peace, saith the Lord of hosts.'

Full of the Holy Spirit, the old coalheaver, crippled with rheumatism and breathing with difficulty, told his loved ones of his glorious hope that Christ, the Desire of all nations, would shake the world's empires one by one until they bowed down before him and the knowledge of the Lord would cover the earth as the waters cover the seas. As he preached, all signs of age and infirmity left him and every ear was able to catch his words spoken with youthful vigour and power. Sinful man confronted with a view of Christ's holiness which would shake him to the quick was his theme as he preached, 'I that am the high and lofty One that inhabiteth eternity, whose name is Holy, I dwell in the high and holy place, with him also that is of a contrite and humble spirit, to revive the spirit of the humble, and to revive the heart of the contrite one'.

Using Christ's picture of foundations of sand and stone, Huntington outlined how God strips his elect of their shaky foundations of legal hope, fleshly confidence and self-righteousness and sets them on the Rock of Ages cleft for them, and them alone. How different was this message to that of his enemies who had hired churches in the vicinity that day to combat Huntington and preach another gospel! Theirs was the gospel that God stood helpless on the shores of the great lake of hell and saw souls perishing for whom his Son had died. It was as if he could not swim and therefore could not save them. What a blasphemous picture! These ministers were not honest enough to put it quite like that. They were telling their hearers that Christ's atonement was universal but one could accept it or reject it as one felt fit. They did not realise that they were thus denying the sovereignty of God and Christ's words that only his sheep hear his voice and that Christ had given his life for those sheep, and not for the goats that would be separated from his sheep at the Day of Judgment. Huntington abhorred the heresy of a Christ who had died in vain.

Many who came to hear Huntington had been in difficulty in understanding to what extent a person may come to Christ, motivated by his own longing. They had been led to believe that everyone felt an inborn duty to obey the gospel. For such seekers after the truth, Huntington's sermon on the glories of the second house is full of choice morsels. Here is one of them:

> Take notice of this, there never was any intense, real, or spiritual desires in a sinner's heart for a whole Christ, till God himself put it there; for all our feeling sense of want, our hungerings and thirstings after the grace of God, and the righteousness of Christ, do spring from the quickening influences and operations of the Holy Spirit of God. And whenever that blessed Spirit does enter the heart, and begin his work, he will not suffer that man to settle on his lees; he will not suffer him to rest in his own performances; he will empty him from vessel to vessel, till he makes him a vessel of mercy, and fills him with his own treasures.

Huntington's sermon gained general acclamation amongst true Reformed men. It was quickly printed and put on sale in London, Lewes, Bristol, Battle, Grantham, Ramsgate, Leicester, Sunderland and Penrith, where the largest concentrations of Huntingtonians were to be found. Just as the news that, 'Winston is back' spread like wildfire at the beginning of the Second World War, so the words 'Huntington is back' were echoed throughout the country. Just as Churchill was of retiring age when he began to lead Britain against the pagan terrors of the Nazi regime, so Huntington, at the same age, became undoubtedly the greatest preacher of the day[10] and the most able man to lead Christian Britain against the regimes of British heathenism and false thinking.

Times of blessing in the new chapel

Huntington's success surprised him greatly although he had always been sure that he was in the Lord's will in his ministry. More than three thousand souls heard him gladly on every occasion and often, especially when he preached elsewhere, many longing to hear him had to stay outside. Converts were made weekly and had Providence Chapel been in other hands, one would have spoken of revivals going on there. For

[10] Thomas Wright wrote, 'That Huntington was the greatest preacher of his day is indubitable. His one serious rival, Rowland Hill, was far less effective in the pulpit, and certainly less popular.' He adds, 'Still it is as a writer that Huntington has obtained most fame, has effected most good' *(The Life of William Huntington, S.S.*, p. 186).

Huntington it was normal pastoral work. Writing to some friends a year after the opening of the new chapel, Huntington stresses both his own weakness and the power of God.

> My Dear friends,
> I received yours yesterday in the Chapel, and thank you for it. Our new place is remarkably attended, and God owns and honours his own work, and gives testimony to the word of his grace. I think I never had the success that I have had in this place; it has been the wedding chamber, the banqueting house, and the nursery to many; and I may say that I bring forth fruit in old age, to shew that the Lord is upright. I am grown old, and have many infirmities that stick close to me; a bad cough, the rheumatism, and the gravel in my loins; so that it is with difficulty I can walk; and I find that these daily increase upon me, insomuch that, after having finished my labours on the Lord's day, I do not recover myself before Tuesday; and therefore I conclude that my travelling times are over. I suffered much in my younger days, and I now feel the effects of it; yet in the pulpit I forget and lose all my complaints, for there I am really more than myself. The Lord is very indulgent to me in the decay of strength and health; he is my great physician, my healing balm, my saving health, my life, and the length of my days. For, although my outward man decays, the inward man is renewed day by day. I have been enabled, through rich grace, to hold fast the truth which the Lord hath taught me, and now I reap the benefits of it; my Saviour has been my all in all, and I now feel and enjoy his all-sufficiency, for he keeps me low and little in my own eyes; often sweetly meekened, softened, and melted, with much nearness to him and freedom with him; with the sweet enjoyment of solid peace, and the aboundings of a good hope. My enemies wonder much that a place should be built by the congregation, at an expense of £9,000, without collecting or even begging of others. It has been done by the subscriptions of our own friends, which astonishes all our evil observers, who leaped for joy at the burning of the old chapel.

> You inform me that you are as speckled birds, and dwell alone; and you do right: the Lord has chosen us out of the world, and has made us to differ; and he tells us to come out from among them, and to be separate. If there is any happiness to be found in this world, if any joy, comfort, or peace; if any rest, quietude, or satisfaction; they are to be found only by faith in Christ Jesus; must lie between him and our own consciences; all besides is vanity and vexation of soul. Even our former days of vanity and folly tell us, that destruction and misery are in all the ways of sinners. You are right; I believe Mr C. will be a good minister of Jesus Christ. The Lord bless you. Grace and peace be with you! so prays your affectionate friend,
>
> W.H. S.S.[11]

Huntington continued to be lame in body but not in faith. Soon he was writing to friends on numerous occasions to say that conversions of both the old and young were increasing and New Providence Chapel, although much larger than the old chapel, was crowded to bursting-point. Huntington was continually being criticised by other evangelical churches who had their bands and their classes, splitting their churches up into boys' clubs, girls' clubs, men's fraternities and women's unions. They warned that Huntington would never hold the young people unless he held special meetings for them. Huntington abhorred the thought of children being separated from their parents and put into classes where they learnt a milkier version of the meat their parents were receiving. He thought all this was a Wesleyan invention to make organization look like spiritual life and he would have nothing to do with it. He seemed to be right, as the members of his church proved to be one large family and as fast as old members died, young members joined the chapel.

Some few of Huntington's members had requested that the singing should be improved in the chapel and an organ installed. Huntington discussed the matter with the Rev. Joseph Chamberlain and, after speaking of another seven conversions in the chapel, goes on to say:

---

[11] *Posthumous Letters*, Letter CCCCLXIII.

> Our chapel is amazingly filled, without an organ, without fine singing, and without schools. Christ, all in all, needs no addition. The finished work of the cross is all-sufficient, and where our salvation was wrought out, there the offence is taken. On the cross our sins were expiated, and wrath appeased; truth was cleared, judgment executed, and justice satisfied; God was reconciled, man redeemed, peace was made, and everlasting righteousness brought in; which is an eye-sore to the devil, and the stumbling-block of sinners. This work, proclaimed and applied by the Holy Spirit, brings on all that malice and reproach that is called 'the offence of the cross'. So that our glory is their offence; our foundation their stumbling-block; our altar and table their snare; and our welfare becomes their trap. See then the goodness and severity of God, and sing we of mercy and judgment; for God will not lead us to Sinai the second time, seeing he has said that we shall go that way no more.[12]

A modern reader might wonder what all this theology had to do with organs and fine singing, as such 'additions' have become part and parcel of modern worship and few believe that they deter from the gospel but rather promote it. Huntington, like many of his contemporaries including Cowper and Romaine, saw an undue emphasis on singing and any playing of organs as superficial substitutes for true Christian worship.[13] Where the Bible was not honoured, they argued, man's words in hymns were substituted for God's Word. Where the Holy Spirit had withheld his inner working resulting in spontaneous worship and praise in the natural human voice, synthetic musical

---

[12] *Posthumous Letters*, vol. I, Letter CLVII, pp. 397, 398.

[13] It may be argued that, as Cowper was a hymn-writer of note, this could not possibly be the case. Cowper did not write his hymns to be sung in church services – he did not write them to be sung at all! His hymns were set to music outside of his influence. When Olney Parish approached him to help raise money to have an organ put in the church, the poet said he would not have anything to do with such folly. See my *William Cowper: Poet of Paradise*, Evangelical Press, 1993, for further discussions on the subject. Romaine called Watts' hymns 'Watts' whims' and insisted that only the biblical psalms should be sung in church.

substitutes were invented to make a show of religious worship that was merely human entertainment. This is why Huntington could say, 'Pompous appearances and public parading to assemble and excite the curiosity of a multitude, with the assistance of an organ and such trumpery rattletraps, may serve to charm fallen nature, lay carnal prejudice in a trance, and fill a house with hypocrites; but conversion to God is another thing'.[14]

The move to Hermes Hill

Huntington was not only forced to leave his old chapel for a new one during the years 1810-11 but he was also obliged to seek a new home. His Cricklewood landlord suddenly told him in the autumn of 1810 that he wanted his house and land back and the pastor would have to go. As Huntington had invested a great deal in the house and had hoped to live the rest of his life there, this was quite a blow. The old coalheaver could not help thinking that landlords let their buildings to him so that he could do them up and they could then re-let them at a greater profit! Used to such ups and downs in life by now, Huntington did not get downcast but merely said patiently, 'I bless God for burning down the chapel; I thank Him for turning me out of this house; and I bless Him for all the plague, trouble and opposition we meet with in the new chapel'.[15] Soon, however, Huntington found a new home on Hermes Hill, not far from the Pentonville Road. It was not much to look at but was spacious, commodious and belonged to a good friend of Huntington's who had proved his faithfulness for a good number of years. Cautious by this time, and knowing the brevity of life, Huntington rented the house on a yearly basis.

Though now an old man with the heavy burden of building a new chapel on his shoulders, Huntington started to build a new wing onto the house. Necessity drove him to it, weak as he was. Lady Sanderson took a keen interest in playing the harpsichord, or 'the devil's rattle' as her husband called it. This made it impossible for Huntington to concentrate on his sermon preparation or talk with the many who came to seek his help. To Huntington, Lady Sanderson's noise was unbearable but in marriage one must bear and forbear, so Huntington

---

[14] *Posthumous Letters*, vol. IV, p. 429.
[15] *Posthumous Letters*, vol. II, p. 121.

built a soundproof room so that he could work in peace and his wife could play with her 'rattle'.

To tell the truth, the heavy farm work at Cricklewood had become too much for Huntington and he needed to settle down to a more leisurely kind of life. He had received blow after blow during the past few years, what with his best friend Jenkins dying and his next best friend Brook falling out with him (temporarily) because of Lady Sanderson. This, coupled with the fire, work on the new chapel and the new house, would have been a great burden indeed on any man past retirement age. Life at Hermes Hill, however, made Huntington very happy. He got on very well with his wife when she was not playing the harpsichord or telling him how to manage his money. He had a beautiful garden and large greenhouse and he was in easy transporting distance from the new chapel.

Though everything in the garden was lovely, Huntington was still not in paradise, as he was soon to find out. Hermes Hill was not in the very best of districts and there were many loafers and ne'er-do-wells in the neighbourhood. These grown-up ragamuffins found a new pastime when Huntington settled in at Hermes Hill. They would throw stones through the glass roof of his new summerhouse and listen with delight to the noise of broken glass and enraged occupants. Once Huntington was sitting in the summerhouse, having a quiet chat with Mr Over when a large stone flew through the window. Up jumped Huntington and rushed out on his stiff legs and was able to grab hold of a man who was about to throw another stone. 'Got you, at last, you villain!' said Huntington, forgetting his age, status and calling, and knocked the man down with one blow. The man got up and disappeared like lightning but Huntington, slowly coming to himself, was full of shame. He told Mr Over that the moment he struck the man the Word of God had struck him from 1 Timothy 3:3: 'The man of God must be ... no striker!' Huntington dug into his pocket and gave Mr Over two guineas, telling him he should find the man and give him the money on condition that he threw no more stones. Mr Over found the man after some time (some sources say he was sitting behind a pint at the local) and told him what Huntington had said. The man promised to obey, took the money with thanks and said, 'You tell Mr Huntington he may knock me down as often as he likes provided he gives me two guineas every time'. When Mr Over got back to Hermes Hill, he found his pastor on his knees confessing his sins.

That was not the only trouble Huntington had with his neighbours. The poor people around obtained their water from a public well called the White Conduit. This well was extremely dirty and unhygienic so Huntington had it cleaned at his expense. As soon as it was finished and the poor neighbours were able to drink without detriment to their health, a group of thugs emptied a whole load of dung and tip refuse into the well one night making it unusable.

Even when married to the wife of a former Lord Mayor of London and able to drive in his own coach the old coalheaver never forgot the poor. One evening he was riding through the countryside with Bensley, who knew no poverty and lived in Dr Johnson's fine old house off Fleet Street. Far from home, the coach broke down. Huntington suggested to Bensley that they should go to a poor man's cottage by the wayside and ask to be sheltered whilst the coach was being repaired. He asked the lady of the house if she could make a cup of tea but the woman answered that she had not enough tea to go round. Huntington told her to give them what she could and, though they received next to nothing, Huntington put a guinea in the poor woman's hand on leaving. Bensley, the businessman, objected at once and told Huntington he was too liberal with his money. The pastor replied, 'Tom, I never forget the time when I stood in need of such a gift'.

Longings for the glory to come

In spite of seeing his flock grow and flourish, the old pastor was longing to move to new heavenly pastures and be with his Great Shepherd and be done with the cares of this world. Writing to Mrs Duncan, the sea-captain's wife, about this longing, Huntington says:

> But there will be an end to this misery of miseries, and to this world, which is the sinner's portion and our bane; – a world wherein the devil reigns and rules; to whom his children pay implicit obedience, and in whose works they boast, exult, and triumph, all the day long, till, by a sad translation, they find that 'the wages of sin is death'. And here we must look to the balance of the sanctuary, and weigh both the duration of time and the

substance of eternity. But this is already done to our hands, as Paul says: 'Our light afflictions, which are but for a moment, work out for us a far more exceeding and eternal weight of glory'.[16]

Just four months before his death we find Huntington mourning because of his sin but now looking steadfastly for God's chariot to come and take him. Expressing similar thoughts to those in the above letter to Mary Duncan, he goes on to outline to the Rev. Joseph Chamberlain what is his hope for the future:

> Never right, dear Joseph, nor can be; something will ever be out of joint, off the hooks, unpinned, or displaced; something wanted, something missing, something deficient; until that blessed period arrives when we shall see him as he is, be changed into his likeness, bear his image, be clothed with his immortality, shine in his rays, swim in his pleasure, burn in his love, triumph in his victory, bask in his glory, and be filled with all his fulness; made perfect in one, see as we are seen, and know as we are known; then shall the high praises of God be in our mouth, and eternal joy upon our head; and our sweet, unwearied, unmolested, uninterrupted, and unceasing employ, be celebrating the perfections of God and the Lamb forever and ever! This, my dear brother, is the glory set before us, for which we must endure the cross and despise the shame.
>
> The great God and our Saviour, who only hath immortality dwelling in the light, shall be revealed; his glory shall cover the heavens, and the new earth shall be filled with his praise; he shall come to be admired in his saints, and to be had in honour of all that are about him; then will the marriage of the Lamb take place, and the long loved, long looked for, long espoused bridegroom appear, with all the angels following him; and the bride, made ready, go out to meet him, with all her train of virgins and companions following her; these shall be brought; 'With

[16] *Posthumous Letters*, Letter CLXXVII, p. 449.

> gladness and rejoicing shall they be brought; they shall enter into the King's palace', Psalm 45:14, 15. Then shall the wedding garment of an imputed righteousness adorn us, the Holy Spirit shall make us all glorious within, and the atoning blood of Christ purge us from every corruption, stain and wrinkle; peace shall adorn our feet, and life, righteousness, glory and honour, shall crown our heads.

Huntington closes his letter with the words, 'I am at present very weak and low in body; but blessed by my God, who favours unworthy, sinful me, with heavenly rays, distant views, and budding hopes'.[17]

After writing this letter, Huntington was still to see God work mightily through him in the last months of his earthly pilgrimage but two expressions were continually on his lips, 'Why does the chariot tarry?' and 'There are no ifs and buts', concerning his future hope.

[17] *Posthumous Letters*, Letter CLXII, pp. 405-408.

Chapter 14

Why Does The Chariot Tarry?

During the years 1811-1812 Huntington's ministry produced more conversions than ever, but popular and useful as he was, it was evident to all that his earthly pilgrimage was drawing to an end. Work in the pulpit was demanding all his energies. After a sermon he was so stiff with standing in one position and his legs ached so much that he could do no more physical work until the time for the next sermon came along, usually the day after, although now Huntington strove to keep Mondays free from preaching as his Sunday services exhausted him so much. The old coalheaver was, however, never idle and continued to rise at four in the morning, or earlier, to commence a working day of fifteen hours.

When confined to his chair because of stiffness, Huntington could still write, although his handwriting was now very shaky. In 1811 he produced at least five books, followed by another four in 1812. He also began to re-read and edit letters which he had received from those who had come to know the Lord through his ministry or had been blessed by it. Huntington called such letters *The Lamentations of Satan* and published them under that title in two volumes. He called them such because, 'The conversion of sinners is the lamentation of devils', and the letters show how greatly blessed Huntington was in reaping souls and how ridiculous the constant cries of 'Antinomian!' against him were. *The Lamentations of Satan* is a final vindication of the gospel that Huntington preached faithfully for so many years. It reveals Huntington in the final months of his life still displaying man's unworthiness and God's righteousness, which had always been his theme:

> God himself, in his divine person, is the sole moving cause of every good motion and good work in us. He is the only stimulator, inspirer, animator, instigator, influencer, and director in all real worship. All the light, the life, the truth, the integrity, the honesty, the sincerity, and the uprightness in all heavenly devotion, are of him, who is the grand object of them, to whom they ascend, and on whom they terminate; and he is the exceeding great reward of all his heavenly worshippers. Every good and perfect gift is from him, and by him is the man of God furnished for every good work; for what has man that he has not received?[1]

During the last year of his ministry Huntington was only able to take the Sunday services and one midweek service and was often obliged to let his assistant take the services when his strength failed.

Standing firm to the end for the truth

During this time. Huntington meditated much on the doctrine of the Trinity. He used to say that he would never think of giving up hope for the salvation of a soul until that person started to deny the triune God. One of his last works, *The Doctrine of Garrett Refuted*, shows what a low level of theology prevailed amongst the evangelicals of his age. Through the teachings of Joseph Priestly, and his worldwide recognition as a great scientist, many had come to accept his Arian beliefs. Some evangelicals were so engaged in fighting this paper tiger that they built up a false defence of their own and went to the extreme of denying Christ's humanity. Christ's blood, they argued, must have been divine as no human could suffer as the just for the unjust. They taught that God requires an infinite sacrifice, but if Christ died as a human soul, his was only a finite sacrifice and not sufficient to pacify a just God.

A London pastor by the name of Jeremiah Learnoult Garrett had gathered quite a crowd around him, all intent on denying the humanity

[1] *Lamentations of Satan*, pp. 113, 114.

of Christ. A woman called Elizabeth Cotton had belonged to his 'church' for some four years before she moved to the Providence Chapel district and decided to go and hear Huntington preach. She quickly discovered that Huntington was a Trinitarian, but thought it wrong of him to stress the point as other 'Christians' begged to differ. Huntington had warned his hearers against the doctrines of Garrett and this annoyed Mrs Cotton no end. She thus wrote a haughty letter to Huntington telling him that she was only a poor weak woman but she felt she had been chosen to confound the mighty and strong! Her argument was that it is neither here nor there whether Christ was human or divine: the 'essential point' was that God in Christ has reconciled us to himself and made us one in heart. This was taught, she maintained, both by Huntington and Garrett, so why quarrel? It was obvious to Mrs Cotton, however, that Christ shed divine blood on the cross. Mrs Cotton seemed to be under the impression that she only had to call on Huntington and she would be led of God to put the pastor right.

In Huntington's reply, he told Mrs Cotton what he thought of 'women clergy', quoting 1 Timothy 2:12, and then, in his own forthright way, he outlined the biblical doctrine of the dual nature of Christ, showing how both natures are 'essential points' in the sinner's salvation. Looking at the divine side, Huntington explained that to talk of the blood of God who is Spirit and not flesh and bones, was nonsense. Looking at the human side he asked, 'Did not Christ tell the apostles that they should handle him and see "for a spirit hath not flesh and bones, as ye see me have"?' (Luke 24:36-39).

Mrs Cotton, with her emphasis on 'essential points', illustrates how Huntington could not help making enemies, as, do what he would, there was always someone who thought he was doing the wrong thing and preaching on dispensable doctrines. When, for instance, Huntington was attacked by another woman, Maria De Fleury, for being an Antinomian, he could have remained quiet but as he realised that De Fleury and her backer John Ryland were teaching sheer Neonomianism he defended the truth. Ebenezer Hooper, though often very antagonistic to Huntington, nevertheless agrees that Huntington turned the tables on De Fleury and Ryland concerning Antinomianism and proved that 'What he was in name only, they were in fact'. But this awareness leaves Hooper cold. Huntington was still to blame, he thought, because he let himself be lured into controversy. Hooper could not understand why good men should grieve and astonish the church though they 'agreed on important and essential points' and differed merely 'on minor and immaterial ones'. He apportions the greater blame to Huntington as De Fleury and Ryland were 'not equal to an encounter with so powerful an opponent'. Huntington should have known better! To Hooper, it is immaterial whether a man is saved by free grace and Christ's imputed righteousness, or by his Christian obedience in keeping to an easier law than that given on Sinai. Such points are merely 'minor'. For Huntington, however, they drew the dividing line between Christianity and heathenism and he counted it a great sin to remain silent in the face of such glaring errors.

This stance for the truth which Huntington adopted was, according to the Rev. A. J. Baxter, editor of The Gospel Advocate, one of his greatest virtues. Baxter wrote, 'There are hundreds who will both speak and write with respect of such men of God as Owen, Bunyan, Romaine, Berridge and Newton who would recoil at the mention of the name of Huntington. And why? Because his conduct was less consistent than theirs? No: but because in depth, closeness, and discrimination of vital realities he excelled them all; and was therefore the least comprehended, 1 Corinthians 2:15.'[2]

The final months

Huntington's final months were made more peaceful to him by the fact that his enemies left him very much alone, which meant that he need not write controversial letters and he had now a host of friends who believed as he did. He always felt free and relaxed to discuss true Christian experience with such believers and his best practical theology is reflected in the letters he now wrote to them. Writing to Isaac Beeman in December, 1812, seven months before his death, Huntington reflects over his life as a Christian, saying:

> Happy, thrice happy are we who have the God of Jacob for our help, who makes us wonders to the world, – the admiration of angels, – and riddles to ourselves. I am now an old man, and

[2] The Gospel Advocate, 1872, pp. 27-31.

yet a new creature; I totter and tremble, and yet am a brazen wall and an iron fence; nothing but frailty, and yet possess everlasting strength. A bruised reed, and yet an invincible column; stark-naked, and yet adorned with seven robes: divorced for spiritual adultery, and yet a chaste virgin: near seventy years old, but only forty years of age; a condemned criminal, and yet just before God, conscience and men. Less and worse than nothing, and yet more than a man, often ill, yet possessing saving health, and never sick; Isaiah 33:24; thrice dead and four times alive.

A polluted leper, yet without spot: an enemy to God, and yet in the highest friendship with Him, a vile sinner, and yet a thrice-sanctified saint; a beggar and yet an heir of three worlds: a worm of the dust and yet an heir of God. An awful rebel and yet an Ambassador of peace; nothing but evil, yet filled with all goodness; a mass of corruption and yet incorruptible; a child of wrath, and yet a child of God; a cloud of darkness, and yet a shining light. An ignorant fool, and yet a wise spiritual teacher; naturally barren, yet the father of a hundred sons, the last of all, yet few before me; a servant of servants, yet crowned and anointed king; in the lower room, yet in the highest seat.

A native of Cranbrook in Kent, yet born and brought up in the city of Zion; ever from the dunghill, yet always filling a throne of state, Job 36:7. The offspring of a thief, yet the son of the King of kings; an incarnate devil, but a temple of the Almighty; a smutty Coalheaver, but a priest of the most high God; a labourer in the vineyard, and a ruler in Israel. A condemned heretic, yet a teacher of the Gentiles in faith and verity; a man of a bad spirit, yet blessed with a holy one; an Antinomian, yet influenced with truth and power; the offscouring of the earth, yet the treasure of heaven; the bane of mankind, and the delight of the Almighty, an ill savour to sinners, and yet salt to preserve them. The Kentish man sends to the man of Kent the compliments of the season, to wit, 'a comfortable Christmas and a peaceable New Year'.

W.H., S. S.

During the spring of 1813, Huntington's health grew worse and he found it almost impossible to hold a pen in his hand owing to severe shakes. He realised that his work as a writer was at an end but told friends that though his quill had finished, his tongue would go on working for the Lord.

On Sunday, 6 June, 1813, Huntington preached in the morning on 1 Corinthians 8:3, 'But if any man love God, the same is known of him', and in the evening on l Corinthians 10:16, 'The cup of blessing which we bless, is it not the communion of the blood of Christ?' After expounding the institution of the Lord's Supper and explaining its purpose and the qualifications of a communicant, Huntington administered the bread and wine to his large flock. The effort was obviously too much for his declining strength and he had to sit down twice whilst a few verses of a hymn were sung until his strength returned. He told his hearers that the religion he had received from God was not worn out but he felt his work was almost done and he must leave them soon. This was Huntington's last Sunday service.

Huntington's last sermon

On the following Wednesday, he preached on Revelation 3:3, 'Remember therefore how thou hast received and heard, and hold fast, and repent'. Huntington preached at great length and with great power showing no signs of weariness. The whole congregation listened, however, with great attention, conscious that they were probably hearing their pastor for the last time. Mr C. Goulding, writing a few days later about the event said, 'I am certain also that, if ever one man in this world was influenced with an abundant measure, and an abundant influence, of the Spirit; as a spirit of life, of power, of love, and of a sound mind; our invaluable and irreparable Minister was, on that occasion, so influenced'.[3]

In his farewell sermon, Huntington outlines to his flock what a pure church is, as opposed to national, provincial or parochial churches. He quotes the Nineteenth Article of the Church of England that, 'The visible church of Christ is a congregation of faithful men, in which the pure word of God is preached, and the sacraments be duly ministered

[3] *The Substance of the Last, or Farewell Sermon of the Late Rev. W. Huntington, S.S.*, Bensley, 1813, p. v.

according to Christ's ordinance'. He shows that though the English Reformers received and held fast every truth essential to salvation they erred in their doctrines of church discipline and government. He points to John Owen and Thomas Goodwin, who he believed had founded churches of the type that the established church taught in her articles but did not practise in her church government.

Next Huntington deals with the doctrines this pure church should believe and teach. He begins with the Trinity, a belief in which, he argues, is essential to salvation. He proves this by showing how saved sinners are those who 'experience the pardoning, justifying, sin-subduing grace of our Lord Jesus Christ; and the inward renewing influences of the Holy Ghost in their hearts, giving them a meetness for heaven, such have an experimental, and a saving knowledge of God in three persons, and are sure to hold fast the doctrine, as Paul wished the Corinthians to experience. "The grace of our Lord Jesus Christ, and the love of God, and the communion of the Holy Ghost, be with you all, Amen." And this is an experience that belongs exclusively to the children of God.'

Next Huntington goes on to stress that a belief in Christ's divinity is necessary to salvation. He goes to great lengths to quote Scripture and the Reformers on this topic and concludes that those who do not believe in Christ's divinity will die in their sins.

The third doctrine essential to salvation for Huntington is the doctrine of God's eternal election of his people. A Christian is chosen before the foundation of the world to be holy and without blame before him in love, having been predestinated unto the adoption of children by Jesus Christ to himself, according to the good pleasure of his will, to the praise of the glory of his grace (Ephesians 1:3-6). Huntington concludes that 'Eternal election secures faith, the forgiveness of sins, and a meetness for the kingdom of heaven, to all the objects of God's choice; and therefore it leads us from and not to, licentiousness'.

Huntington's fourth point is that the doctrine of particular redemption is essential to salvation. He notes that the Reformers held fast to this belief but it was almost lost in his day. The subjects for redemption are the elect of God and Christ secured this redemption by his atoning death on the cross. Those who teach universal redemption must argue away the fact that Christ redeemed his elect 'from among men' and that he separates the sheep from the goats. Thus particular redemption implies particular rejection. Those who preach that numbers for whom Christ died will perish and be damned contradict the Redeemer, who said, 'They shall never perish', for whom he died.

Fifthly, Huntington argues that an essential doctrine to salvation is justification by faith or by an imputed righteousness. As the Bible tells us that no flesh shall be justified by the deeds of the law and also that there is none righteous and that a corrupt tree cannot bring forth good fruit, just as a leopard cannot change its spots, whence comes our justifying righteousness? 'Now to him that worketh is the reward not reckoned of grace, but of debt. But to him that worketh not, but believeth on him that justifieth the ungodly, his faith is counted for righteousness. Even as David also describeth the blessedness of the man unto whom God imputeth righteousness without works' (Romans 4:4-6). 'Here', concludes Huntington, 'is righteousness by imputation; and it is thus that all the elect are made righteous'. Thus no child of God can boast of his righteousness, as it is a gift of God which he ever holds as a debt to the divine Giver.

Sixthly, Huntington preaches that the doctrine of the inhabitation of the Spirit and regeneration by him is essential to salvation. Thinking of his fellow-ministers who had banned the teaching of the new man indwelt by the Spirit from their pulpits, Huntington argues:

> There is no doctrine that gives more offence than this; and yet it contains every branch of saving knowledge or experience that ever has been, or ever will be, enjoyed in this world. Where the Spirit of God does not inhabit; where his influence and operations are not experienced; all such are servants of sin, and free from righteousness: 'the strong man armed keeps possession of the palace', and, having no spiritual understanding,[4] 'he that made them will have no mercy on them, and he that formed them will shew them no favour', Isaiah 27:11.

---

[4] This is against Fullerism which teaches that the reprobate must have spiritual understanding otherwise God would never judge them for what they did not know and could not do. See Appendix I.

Now Huntington is at the heart of his doctrine of holiness, arguing that:

> All those whom the Spirit inhabits he influences and operates upon, to deliver them from the reigning and destroying power, both of Satan, sin and death, that they may be brought to enjoy proper meetness for heaven; and his work upon the soul accomplishing this is thus described – 'Not by works of righteousness which we have done, but according to his mercy he saved us, by the washing of regeneration and renewing of the Holy Ghost', Titus 3:5. It is a precious exchange that the saints experience in this washing, when their old things are washed away, the things common to us in a state of nature, and the new things come which the Holy Spirit is the author of; for our being renewed must imply a restoration to something that has been experienced before; and this is the image of God, lost by the fall; but we are restored to it again by the washing of regeneration and renewing of the Holy Ghost.

After the service the congregation stood in groups outside the chapel, discussing what they had heard. The sermon had touched the very roots of their faith and had drawn them closer to their Lord. They all felt that there had been a special unction on their pastor and none but the Holy Spirit had spoken to them that evening. A good number of the congregation gathered in groups at the various members' houses to speak in hushed and solemn voices of what they had heard. Many, assisted by their friends, began to write down what they could remember of the sermon, urgently wishing to preserve every memory they could of their faithful pastor's testimony.

Huntington's last illness

Four days later, on 10 June, Huntington's son Gad visited his father and found him cheerfully and calmly waiting for his home-call. The day after, Huntington was severely ill and Lady Sanderson refused to allow his children to see him. On the following Sunday the pulpit at Providence Chapel stood empty until Huntington's assistant, Algar

Lock, sadly rose to preach after informing the members and guests that their pastor was exceedingly ill. Lock's text that day was John 6:17, 'It was now dark, and Jesus was not come'. For the next week a stream of visitors called at Hermes House to pay their respects to their beloved pastor but Lady Sanderson kept a firm hand on the door not even letting Huntington's children in. Huntington was obviously not told that his children had wanted to see him.

Realising that her husband's illness was terminal, Lady Sanderson suddenly whisked him off to Tunbridge Wells at six o'clock in the morning on Friday, 18 June. It was a seemingly senseless thing to do as Huntington was so very ill and by no means fit to travel. It was with great difficulty that Lady Sanderson and Mr Bensley were able to lift him into the coach and prop him up comfortably on the seat. Feeling the discomfort, Huntington said that he had begged the Lord to make it his last journey on earth. As he was so ill, the travellers had to make many stops on the way and did not reach Tunbridge Wells until late the next day.

Soon Lady Sanderson's plan became evident. Their destination in Tunbridge Wells was a house called Mount Ephraim which was situated next door to her solicitors, Messrs Morgan and Stone. Lady Sanderson had carted her husband off from the neighbourhood of his family so that she could, without any interference, persuade him to make a new will for her benefit and to the detriment of his seven children. It was a callous move and obviously speeded up Huntington's decease and it made Lady Sanderson a spiritual outcast from then on in the eyes of most Huntingtonians.

Without wasting a minute at Huntington's last earthly home, Lady Sanderson let Mr Stone the solicitor in. He had obviously rehearsed with her what he had to say and do. Now there was no talk whatsoever of shielding Huntington from visitors. There was a coming and going of legal advisers from then on until his death, so that a solicitor was present in the house at all times until Huntington frustrated their wicked plans by dying without giving in to their demands.

Huntington, weak as he was, took the initiative and explained what should be done with the chapel and his cash in hand and property. Mr Stone, however, told the pastor that because of the law of mortmain, he would have to live twelve months and one day, otherwise his wishes would have no standing in law. Huntington replied, 'Twelve months! I am certain that I shall not live twelve days!' This was Lady Sanderson's cue. As if it were the most natural thing in the world, she produced a new will which was in Huntington's name although Huntington was the only one present who knew nothing about it. The exhausted pastor read through the will and shook his head. He would have nothing to do with it. The will has been preserved and it is obvious why Huntington refused to sign it. Hermes Hill was to remain as it was and not a screwdriver, chair or gardening hose was to be removed from it. It would all belong to Lady Sanderson. The cottage which Huntington had built for his daughter would become Lady Sanderson's property. A piece of ground which he had bought for his three poor elderly sisters was also to be transferred to Lady Sanderson's name after their death. Whatever money was available would go to his widow.

Huntington's children were now mentioned in the most loathsome terms, obviously reflecting Lady Sanderson's views, which were fully out of place in a last will and testament. Ebenezer was accused of being a ne'er-do-well and left £10! The black sheep of the family, Benjamin, was to receive £200 which was to be put in trust. Gad was to receive £300 and Huntington's daughters were to have what was left of his belongings after Lady Sanderson's death. This all turned out to be pure fiction as, after Huntington's death, Lady Sanderson was not willing to pay Huntington's children a penny.

The whole will is couched in Lady Sanderson's peculiar jargon. For instance, she had Huntington call her 'my invaluable wife'; the word 'invaluable' being one of her favourites and not her husband's way of referring to her at all. In Huntington's will of 1810, he had referred to his 'beloved wife' by name, as appropriate in a legal document saying who should receive what. In this will, Lady Sanderson's name was not mentioned at all, she being referred to merely as 'my invaluable wife'. This reflects Lady Sanderson's custom of never using her own name in conjunction with her husband. As was stated earlier, she never referred to herself as Mrs Huntington and always called her husband 'our invaluable friend' or 'the Prophet'.

Ebenezer was to have more of Lady Sanderson's wrath poured on him. The copyright of all her husband's writings was to be given to Thomas Bensley and W. Clark (Lois' husband) and Bensley was to have the sole printing rights, 'as I have no doubt my son Ebenezer is determined to live without work'. This was tantamount to thoroughly ruining Ebenezer and putting even more money into Bensley's pocket. It is obvious that Bensley was privy to Lady Sanderson's designs but the business deal did not go as he wished and he and Lady Sanderson quarrelled soon after Huntington's death.

The greatest surprise was what should happen to Providence Chapel itself. In this very questionable will, it was claimed that Huntington bequeathed the chapel to his wife as her own property and for her to manage as long as she lived. After Lady Sanderson's death four trustees (Bensley, Goulding, Holland and Aldridge) should pay Huntington's son William and his son-in-law Mr Blake £100 each in rent. The Rev. Joseph Chamberlain was to be installed as pastor with a salary of £200 per annum. This move on Lady Sanderson's part was just the opposite of anything Huntington would ever have done. His one big argument against the Huntingdon Connexion was that a woman had no calling from God to manage a Christian congregation and appoint ministers. He was also completely against lay people patronizing churches. Now his beloved Providence Chapel was to be run by another 'Lady'!

The will was a preposterous display of Lady Sanderson's own grasping hand and jealousy regarding Huntington's children. All of them, including the trustees, were as likely to die before Lady Sanderson as after and the whole will, though two baronets were appointed as its executors, was a farce. Though only to live another few days, the dying Huntington still knew what was right and what was very wrong. Unable to write himself, and unable to convince the foe in his own family and her allies that the will could never bear his signature, Huntington changed the subject whenever it was brought up. Lady Sanderson's legal advisers, however, were so cunning (one might equally say, criminal), that after Huntington's death they were able to 'prove' that the will was nuncupative and Huntington would have signed it, 'if he had been in his right mind'. One of the men appealed to in defending the will was the Lord Chancellor himself, who took one look at the document and said that Huntington's action in not signing it was correct. 'It was such a will as ought never to be signed', was his comment.

With her husband's family far away, Lady Sanderson allowed callers of her choice to see her husband. She kept up a regular correspondence with Bensley, Miss Falkland (a personal friend and close relation) and her own daughter by her first marriage. She did not communicate in any way with Huntington's children and they were not aware how serious their father's illness was. To one caller Huntington said, 'I have had nothing but law and physic ever since I have been at Tunbridge Wells, and my soul is sick of it'. As her husband was in great pain Lady Sanderson gradually dropped pretending to be his financial manager and got down to the business of being his loving wife. She told him that she realised he was suffering acutely but her husband merely replied, 'I had worse pains once with a burning ague, not a bed to lay on, and without an earthly comfort; but now I have every blessing in Providence to alleviate my sufferings'. He told her that his heart was overflowing with the goodness of God and said, 'All lies straight before me; there are no ifs nor buts; I am as sure of Heaven as if I were in it'.

Huntington's final illness had been brought on by diabetes and he worsened speedily; his blood pressure and eyesight were severely affected and he began to have difficulty in speaking. Lady Sanderson wrote to Bensley, Falkland and her daughter to tell them to come to see the end. Huntington's children were still not informed. Meanwhile Ebenezer, Naomi, Ruth and her husband met to discuss how they could find out what was happening to their father. It was decided that Mr and Mrs Blake and Naomi (now Mrs Burrell) should take the stage coach to Tunbridge Wells and insist on seeing their father. When they arrived in the afternoon of 30 June, the servant let them in. Huntington called them up to his bedroom at once and hugs were given and tears shed. Their father seemed to receive new strength though his voice was weak and his mouth parched with fever. He asked his children about how the family was progressing and what was happening at Providence Chapel. He told them he wished to have a meal with them as a family and wondered why they had not got in touch with him earlier. Taking his daughters' hands, he said to them, 'You are my dear children, and I am glad to see you'.

It was quite obvious that Huntington had no idea that his wife had been warding his children off so selfishly. He was especially surprised to find that the three had booked a hotel and asked innocently why they had not written so that private accommodation could have been arranged. When they were alone, Huntington told them that he had not been able to settle his affairs but was trusting that the Lord would show him a way soon. He added, 'A prudent man guideth his affairs with discretion'. This is proof enough that the will Lady Sanderson produced was not of his making. His son-in-law Mr Blake said, 'I hope Sir, your work is not done, as there are many brought to the birth, but not able to come forth'. Huntington shook his head and merely said, 'My constitution is broken'. At this Ruth could not contain herself and told her father that all she desired was to follow her father and soon be with the Lord. Huntington replied, 'Keep there, and you will not lose your hire'.

These facts from the pen of Ruth Blake are extremely important in accessing Huntington's final days. The 'official' report sponsored by Lady Sanderson and written by Miss Falkland leaves out completely any reference to a visit from his children and gives the quite false impression that he did not wish to be bothered by them and was not interested about what was happening at the chapel. She even wrote that it was Huntington's idea to visit Tunbridge Wells! The whole account by Miss Falkland shows that she knew little of what happened during Huntington's last days – she only arrived in Tunbridge Wells on the eve of his death – and her sole purpose was to paint Lady Sanderson in the best colours possible. She even had the audacity to write of her ladyship, 'To his family [meaning Huntington's children] she has been a most generous benefactress, and a real friend'. Such departures from the truth led Ebenezer Hooper to comment that 'Miss F's account was *not* entitled to be regarded as full and faithful, and that it *did* deserve some of the censures bestowed upon it'.[5] Such a comment may be described as a classical understatement!

Miss Falkland, Thomas Bensley and John Over arrived the same day as the Blakes and Mrs Burrell. When Bensley saw Huntington, he was shocked at the way he had deteriorated physically but said to him, 'I am glad sir, to see you look so comfortable'. His pastor replied, 'Why should I look otherwise? Death with me has lost its sting these forty years. I am no more afraid of death than I am of my nightcap.' The entire party ate a meal together around Huntington's bed during which

[5] Hooper, *Facts and Letters*, p. 117.

Huntington told them how the dead who die in the Lord are blessed and said that he was full of joy at the prospect.

Naomi and the Blakes had to catch the stage coach very early the next morning but they stayed with their father until 11 o'clock when they realised that he could not talk any longer and needed rest. Huntington gave them the impression that though he was seriously ill, there were chances of a recovery. After telling them they would not see him again in that room, he blessed them, kisses were exchanged and his children left him never to see him in this world again. Three hours later Huntington took a turn for the worst and, though it was only two o'clock in the morning Lady Sanderson sent for her lawyers. Both Mr Morgan and Mr Stone turned up. She also sent for two doctors, who were unable to relieve Huntington's sufferings though cupping was applied.

Throughout the day, Huntington could not say much but he was obviously constantly in prayer. He could not see and his throat was continually blocked with phlegm. Now and then he could be heard saying, 'My Father, come!' and, 'Bless God; praise Him!' When Mr Morgan wet his lips, Huntington replied, 'God bless you, Sir. I thank you and bless His holy name'. It must have been a great trial to the lawyer, who was intent on getting a signature from Huntington by stealth in his dying weakness, only to find himself being blessed by the saint! At times Huntington seemed to be in raptures; at other times he was heard saying, 'He tarries long. Why is his chariot so long in coming?' Just before he died, Huntington tried to raise himself and obviously wanted to speak, but as he could not, he laid himself down again. Those around him came closer and put their ears to his mouth. The old coalheaver was heard to say, 'Bless his precious name'. He then gave a deep sigh and died. Someone in the room said those typical and true Huntingtonian words, 'Mark the perfect man, and behold the upright, for the end of that man is peace'. Though Huntington had been separated from his friends and family and been whisked away to be cared for by strangers, with lawyers about him like vultures around a dying victim, he yet died in peace because Jesus, who can calm every storm, was with him until the end. Though he had talked of things he still had to do in this life the day before, when the Lord called him he was neither surprised nor unprepared.

The funeral services

When the news reached Huntington's congregation in London there was a general mourning and many tears were shed. Cornelius Tozer confessed that he sat and wept with his wife for hours. The news that Lady Sanderson was now to be head of their church shattered them and they felt like sheep without a shepherd. Both the congregation and Huntington's family were shocked at the will which Lady Sanderson insisted was legal and they were thus not surprised when her ladyship sent parties of men off to guard Hermes House and other possessions of her deceased 'invaluable friend' so that nothing of what she claimed as her property could be taken.

Huntington had long wished to be buried at the side of his great friend Jenkin Jenkins, the 'Welsh Ambassador' and the funeral was arranged to take place at Lewes on Thursday, 8 July. On that day the streets of London were as good as deserted as the Huntingtonians hired every coach and wagon they could lay their hands on to take them to Lewes. When they all lined up to begin the funeral procession, they stretched for well over a mile. First there was Huntington's hearse, drawn by six horses, followed by seven mourning coaches containing Huntington's children. Next came Lady Sanderson, her daughter and Miss Falkland in a coach of their own, followed by coaches belonging to, or hired by, friends and members of Providence Chapel. Well over a thousand people attended on foot. During the long march to the graveyard, against Huntington's wish, hymns were sung and all down the lanes leading to Lewes the neighbours came out to watch the largest procession they had ever seen. Huntington was laid in his vault without undue ceremony and his family and closest friends retired to Jenkins' old chapel where Joseph Chamberlain preached on Isaiah 57:2, 'He shall enter into peace: they shall rest in their beds, each one walking in his uprightness'. The chapel was not packed as the mourners were queuing in a seemingly never-ending stream to pay their last respects at their pastor's graveside. On that tombstone the words were engraved:

HERE LIES THE COALHEAVER: –
BELOVED OF HIS GOD; BUT ABHORRED OF MEN.
THE OMNISCIENT JUDGE AT THE GRAND ASSIZE
SHALL RATIFY AND CONFIRM THIS TO THE CONFUSION
OF MANY THOUSANDS;
FOR ENGLAND AND ITS METROPOLIS SHALL KNOW
'THAT THERE HATH BEEN A PROPHET AMONG THEM'.

On the following Sunday Chamberlain preached to over 2,000 hearers at Providence Chapel, all of them in deep mourning. His text was Psalm 92:13, 'Those that be planted in the house of the Lord shall flourish in the courts of our God'. Huntington had given strict orders that no funeral eulogies should be proclaimed from the pulpit and, like a good workman who need not be ashamed, Chamberlain expounded the words of resurrection hope to his receptive congregation. The funeral hymns the Huntingtonians sang were all from Hart's collection. Number 164 expresses exactly what the faithful were feeling on that day:

Sons of God by blest adoption,
View the dead with steady eyes.
What is sown thus in corruption,
Shall in incorruption rise;
What is sown in death's dishonour,
Shall revive to glory's light;
What is sown in this weak manner,
Shall be rais'd in matchless might.

Earthly cavern, to thy keeping
We commit our brother's dust;
Keep it safely, softly sleeping,
Till our Lord demand thy trust.
Sweetly sleep, dear saint in Jesus,
Thou, with us, shalt wake from death;
Hold he cannot, tho' he seize us:
We his power defy by faith.

Jesus, thy rich consolations
To thy mourning people send;
May we all, with faith and patience,
Wait for our approaching end.
Keep from courage vain or vaunted;
For our change our hearts prepare;
Give us confidence undaunted,
Cheerful hope and godly fear.

Appendix I

Fullerism Weighed And Found Wanting

Though the anonymous author of *The Voice of Years* attacked Huntington mercilessly, he nevertheless testified to his subject being a Christian and argued that Huntington's theology was highly Christocentric.[1] It was left to Maria De Fleury, John Ryland and Andrew Fuller to deny outright that Huntington was a Christian. Whereas De Fleury and John Ryland Senior removed Huntington's title S.S. (Sinner Saved) from his name and substituted for it MBA (Master of the Black Arts), Fuller declared that he could find absolutely nothing of a Christian nature in either Huntington's theology or his way of life.[2] De Fleury prophesied that when Huntington's writings had been banned to oblivion, Ryland's works would still be read far and wide. This has not come to pass and though Huntington's works are still in print, very little of Ryland's is either read or published these days.

Fuller is a different case completely. Indeed, he has more preeminence nowadays than he enjoyed in his lifetime and feats of theological strength are attributed to him which would have surprised his contemporaries. Fuller, it is claimed, rescued theology from the Hyper-Calvinism of his predecessors, thus making Calvinism

---

1 'Mr Huntington, in thus preaching Christ, was of more value to his hearers than thousands and tens of thousands, who are "qualified" for the office of the ministry, but are ignorant of the *"unsearchable riches of Christ"*.' *(The Voice of Years*, p. 14f. See the author's section entitled 'Evangelical', pp. 13-15).

2 Fuller, *Works*, vol. II, *The Voice of Years*, pp. 762-764.

'evangelical'. He also, it is alleged, worked out a system of theology which made the missionary movement possible.[3] No praise of Fuller is too great for Tom J. Nettles of the Mid-America Baptist Theological Seminary, who maintains there was no awakening in the eighteenth century amongst Baptists until Fuller came on the scene to fill the same role in England that Luther had filled in Germany.[4] Writing concerning political revolutions in his preface to the Sprinkle reprint of Fuller's *Works*, Nettles says:

> Though the history books focus almost entirely on those admittedly formative and pivotal events, another revolution of remarkable proportions, often ignored by the powers of the age, rippled through a significant sector of the Kingdom that will have no end. The shot heard around the world in this spiritual offensive was fired from the pen of Andrew Fuller (1754-1815), an English Particular Baptist.

The theory that Fuller was a theological revolutionary is in keeping with Fuller's own view of himself. He is quoted as saying, 'When I first published my treatise on the nature of faith, and the duty of all men who hear the gospel to believe it, the Christian profession had sunk into contempt amongst us; insomuch that had matters gone on but a few years longer, the Baptists would have become a perfect dunghill in society'.[5] Thus nowadays many believe with Fuller that he has rescued the Christian profession from being contemptible and saved the Baptists from being a dunghill in society. Be this as it may, in accomplishing his goal, it will be shown that Fuller relied far more on the old-fashioned rationalism of fallen men rather than the wisdom that comes from above.

---

[3] See, for instance, E. M. Clipsham's various articles under the general heading, 'Andrew Fuller and Fullerism: A Study in Evangelical Calvinism', Baptist Quarterly, 1963-1964, vol. 20, pp. 99-114; 146-154; 214-225; 268-276.See also Clipsham's 'Andrew Fuller and the Baptist Mission', Foundations (Am.), 1967. vol. 10, pp. 4-8.

[4] Tom J. Nettles, Preface, *Works*, vol. I, Sprinkle Publications reprint, 1988.

[5] *Memoirs of the Life and Writings of the Rev. Andrew Fuller*, John Webster Morris, 1816, p. 267. Fuller is talking about Baptist churches which had produced Gill, Brine and Booth and a Christian profession by men such as Hervey and Whitefield.

In his book *The Gospel Worthy of All Acceptation*, an argument for a universal atonement but with a particular application, Fuller informs the reader that he has rejected his former (Calvinistic?) beliefs. Jonathan Edwards' *Inquiry* and two short passages of Scripture were the means of persuading him to take this step, 'Kiss the Son, lest he be angry' (Psalm 2:12) and, 'Repent ye: for the kingdom of heaven is at hand' (Matthew 3:2).[6] This book and the Bible texts convinced Fuller that it is the known duty of all unconverted sinners to 'kiss the Son' and 'repent'. It is worthy of note that in claiming this, Fuller does not, and will not, distinguish between reprobate sinners and the unconverted elect. Nor does he distinguish between repentance relating to the broken law and faith relating to a gift of God. Nevertheless, by a roundabout way which will be outlined below, Fuller concludes on meditating on these verses that all unbelievers have the capacity to understand the good news immediately on hearing it. They also automatically realise that it is their solemn duty to believe and accept the gospel. As Huntington puts it succinctly, the Fullerites preach that, 'It is the duty of men, whom God hath concluded in unbelief, to believe the gospel'.[7]

Traditionally, Reformed commentators have viewed those who are commanded to kiss the Son as those who are given to Christ to be his people. The Bride of Christ may legitimately kiss Christ and, apart from the Father, none other. This would then be an argument in favour of a limited atonement rather than a universal one. The whole of Psalm 2 shows the sovereignty of God, and not the obliging nature of man to follow his inherently recognised duties to accept a fictive invitation. This is clearly emphasised by the psalmist, who uses the imagery of a potter making his pots to suit his own will.[8] It is also difficult to see, on face value, how the words of John the Baptist in Matthew 3 can be

---

[6] Fuller, *Works*, vol. II, p. 328ff., p. 343ff. In private correspondence Fuller maintains that reading the Arminian Abraham Taylor caused him to reject the Calvinism of his day. See Ryland's *Memoirs of Fuller*, p. 34, p. 36ff.

[7] *Excommunication* (Letter to Dr John Ryland concerning the excommunication of John Adams), p. 145.

[8] See Spurgeon's approach to this passage in his *Treasury of David*. In my edition (Stockholm, 1896), Spurgeon makes it clear that Christ's Bride, Christ's inheritance the church, alone may kiss their Lord.

understood as a general appeal to the supposed known duty of reprobates to believe in Jesus – but we shall see how Fuller argues his case.[9]

Fuller first tackles the problem from a negative angle. Let us suppose, he argues, that nobody wishes to kiss the Son or repent and nobody wishes to believe. What would this signify? It would mean that either the sinner was in want of the 'natural powers and advantages' necessary to believe, or he was in 'want of a heart to make a right use of them'. He concludes that it must be the heart of the sinner which is at fault because all the 'natural powers and advantages to read, hear, repent, pray' are awake in all unconverted sinners. In other words, the unconverted sinner is able to recognise the truths of the gospel by nature and if he rejects the gospel, it is because he does not want to believe it. Fuller argues in this way as he is fully convinced that God would not command all unconverted sinners to believe if they did not know that it was their inherent duty to do so. Where there is no knowledge of duty, he tells us, there can be no transgression. He then goes on to argue that God would not ask anyone to repent who could not. Those who repent can believe and those who believe can have faith and those who have faith can put their trust in Christ, so it is the duty of all men to repent, believe, have faith and trust in Christ.[10]

This is where the difference between Fuller and Huntington makes itself very evident. Huntington argued that you cannot expect a fallen man to have non-fallen insight. The sinner does not fall by refusing to accept the gospel when it is preached. He fell in Adam. He is dead in trespasses and sins and thus cannot understand spiritual things. He is a stranger to grace.[11] Fuller denies this completely. If man cannot believe, it would be detrimental to God's justice to condemn that man. There

---

[9] Anglicans especially will be surprised to see how Fuller equates the preaching of John with the full Christian gospel and the baptism of John with a full Christian baptism. This teaching was current amongst Baptists of the time and was one of the reasons why John Newton wrote his *Apology*. Newton pointed out that Christian baptism, as opposed to the baptism of John, is in the name of the Father, Son and Holy Ghost. (See also Fuller, *The Gospel Worthy of All Acceptation*, p. 357, p. 364ff.)

[10] Fuller, *Works*, vol. II, pp. 331, 332. See especially 'On the Inability of Sinners to Believe in Christ, and Do Things Spiritually Good', p. 376ff.

[11] See Huntington's *The Loss and Restoration of the Image of God in Man*, Collingridge, vol. III.

must be an ability to believe in fallen man, otherwise God would have no right to demand that he exercise that ability. Here Fuller loses all sight of the fact that God does not first condemn and punish a man when he decides to reject the gospel of salvation in Christ. He is already condemned and punished as man in Adam because he breaks God's laws by his very fallen nature. Often Fuller comes very near to speaking of man as if each individual were an untried Adam in the Garden of Eden. Man's fault is not that he is incapable of belief. It is that, when put to the test, man does not act positively on the insight God has given him. Fuller obviously does not see the Fall as a once-and-for-all action which has condemned man in Adam for all time. He sees the Fall as a recurring event every time a man with full insight into the gospel nevertheless rejects it.

Now Fuller attacks James Hervey, Walter Marshall and the 'Marrow Men' for teaching that the gospel brings with it the gift or grant of Christ.[12] Naturally, Hervey and his like-minded brethren did not believe that this gift would be given to all men, but only to the elect. Fuller misses this point as his theology does not allow him to believe that there is a saving distinction between the elect and reprobates before conversion. He argues that the 'gospel contains no gift or grant to mankind in general, beyond that of an offer or free invitation'. In preaching, he believes, all hearers must be given the same chance of receiving the gospel whether they eventually believe it or not. Thus a free invitation or offer must be given to all hearers and they must decide whether they wish to accept the offer or reject it. It is not clear at this stage what the contents of this 'invitation' or 'offer' are. Fuller is more interested here in arguing that fallen man should be invited to exercise his sense of duty rather than in describing the object of that duty.[13] It is, however, clear what Fuller is trying to protect himself against. He wishes to avoid placing salvation (the gift of Christ) before belief; a

---

[12] Fuller, *Works*, vol. II, p. 335ff.

[13] Later, on page 345, he is more explicit and says, 'Faith in Jesus Christ, even that which is accompanied with salvation, is there [in the New Testament] constantly held up as the duty of all to whom the gospel is preached'. This is the great paradox in Fuller's system. God expects of all men that they exercise saving faith but he only gives it to some to exercise.

mistake which he believes the 'old' Calvinists made. He argues that Christ becomes the believer's possession after the invitation to believe the gospel is accepted, and not before. It seems, then, that Fuller would not preach a gospel sermon on Acts 5:31, 'Him hath God exalted with his right hand to be a Prince and a Saviour, for *to give* repentance to Israel, and forgiveness of sins'. He prefers to argue that conversion does not occur on being given the gift of salvation; it occurs when salvation is accepted. The onus is on man, not on God.

Fuller goes on to argue that if Christ is the believer's antecedent to his believing, then it does not matter whether he believes or not. He is saved, however he may behave. This is his argument against Huntington, who taught that Christ died for his sheep – and for them alone – and that salvation is a gift of God and not a human response to a divine invitation. Fuller thus accused Huntington of living like a heathen. Huntington's position was that if Christ indwells a man and that man is led by the Spirit to be God's child for ever, how can he live like a heathen?

Huntington, of course, *did* argue that personal belief was most important. He emphasised, however, that natural man knows nothing of any duty, awareness or obligation to believe and that such an awareness belongs to the elect alone by God's special gift. Fuller could not accept this 'gift' theology, as he held that all men have the wherewithal to believe[14] – whether they eventually believed or not. A gift of such a 'wherewithal' is thus not necessary.

Fuller concludes the first part of his treatise on the scope of the atonement by criticising Particular Baptist pastor Abraham Booth for 'designedly' avoiding the question, 'Whether faith in Christ be the duty of the ungodly?' in his *Glad Tidings to Perishing Sinners*. This is the attitude Fuller took from the early 1780s on. He could not believe that his fellow-pastors did not really see eye to eye with him on his theory of non-Christian duty, so he accused them of duplicity if they did not preach it from the housetops. Fuller never seemed to understand that these men did not teach such a theory because they emphasised God's work in redemption and not man's. They did not emphasise man's work

[14] In the sense of a knowledge of their obligation to believe and an awareness of what the gospel entails.

in redemption because they believed man had nothing whatsoever to do with it.

Fuller opens Part II by referring back to his 'kiss the Son' theory which is proof, he argues, that 'Unconverted sinners are commanded to believe in Christ for salvation; therefore believing in Christ for salvation is their duty'. He now looks at passages in both Testaments to back up his view. The first evidence which he introduces is Isaiah 55:1-7, 'Ho, every one that thirsteth, come ye to the waters, and he that hath no money; come ye, buy and eat'. This is the language of a general invitation, Fuller argues, and is proof enough that an appeal is being made here to all the unconverted.

Now this very verse was often used by Fuller's critics, such as William Huntington and William Gadsby, as proof that only those who had been given a thirst for the gospel knew what Isaiah was talking about. Here, they felt, was evidence that the gospel is only for those who thirst, and not for every man. Fuller denies this outright and says this is an appeal that every man jack can understand. He argues thus because he believes that fallen man is capable of discerning spiritual things – to a certain extent – and this word of Isaiah's is addressed to 'the natural desire of happiness which God has implanted in every bosom'. Nevertheless Fuller argues, rather unconvincingly, after explaining what 'athirst' means, that 'The *duty*, to a compliance with which they are so pathetically urged, is a relinquishment of every false way, and a return to God in His name who was given for "a witness, a leader, and a commander to the people"; which is the same thing as "repentance towards God, and faith towards our Lord Jesus Christ".' Fuller adds, 'The whole passage is exceedingly explicit, as to the duty of the unconverted; neither is it possible to evade the force of it by any just or fair method of interpretation'.[15] None the less, Fuller is guilty here of 'evading the force' of his own argument. All he proves is that man is ready to selfishly promote his own happiness. For this, he gives God the blame. This is a long way from believing that man, in his fallen state, is aware of an inbred duty towards God in Christ in any way. If man were conscious of such a duty, then his fall was not total, as the

[15] Fuller, *Works*, vol. II, p. 344.

Scriptures imply in 1 Corinthians 2:14, 'But the natural man receiveth not the things of the Spirit of God: for they are foolishness unto him: *neither can he know them*, because they are spiritually discerned'.

On turning to the New Testament, Fuller argues, 'The New Testament is still more explicit than the Old. Faith in Jesus Christ, even that which is accompanied with salvation, is there constantly held up as the duty of all to whom the gospel is preached'. He goes on to quote John 6:29, 'This is the work of God, that ye believe on him whom he hath sent'.[16]

Now if ever a text explicitly says that faith is the work of God and any efforts through false ideas of duty wrought by man are in vain, this must be it! Fuller thinks differently. He argues that the statement, 'This is the work of God' ... is the same as saying, 'This is the first and greatest of all duties, and without it no other duty can be acceptable'.[17] Here Fuller is not only talking about a universal feeling of duty in all unconverted sinners but 'an acceptable duty'. He is again emphasizing what man ought to do in a text which explains what God does. Though his title tells us that the gospel is worthy, Fuller is now almost halfway through his book and has merely shown how worthy *fallen man* is in realising his duty to accept the gospel.

This teaching brought a great deal of unrest in the churches and many left churches that had previously been sound in biblical doctrine because of new Fullerite ideas. Those who refused to go or change their doctrines were excommunicated. The change in Fuller's theology created havoc amongst pastors, turning brother against brother. Huntington's words of defence of one who was excommunicated from Dr John Ryland's church for sticking to traditional Calvinism are worthy of being quoted in full. Huntington's main point was that in emphasizing giving a gospel invitation to all sinners, the Fullerites were ignoring the evangelistic duty to preach the law. Sin must be known as sin before grace can be understood as grace. Huntington thus says:

> 1. This doctrine can never be established by the practice or example of Jesus: for though he called all that laboured and were heavy laden to come to him, and those that were sick, that were

[16] *Ibid.*, p. 345.
[17] *Ibid.*, p. 345.

hungry, and thirsty, etc. yet it is clear that he always sent the curious, the pharisaical, and the wholehearted inquirer to the law. 'What is written in the law? How readest thou? This do, and thou shalt live'. 'If thou wilt enter in to life, keep the commandments'. And, if they asked 'Which?' he replied, 'Do not kill, do not steal, do not commit adultery; and Honour thy father and mother'. This sending them to the law to work, is a sufficient proof that Christ made not his gospel the rule of these men's duty. Mr Ryland and Mr Fuller act contrary to Christ, who is the best example; for it is clear that the Saviour went a different way from them, in making the two tables of the law, not the gospel, the rule of these men's obedience.

2. I think, with respect to the unconverted, sir, that you begin at the wrong end. You tell them, it is the duty of all men to believe; but, as faith is produced in the soul by the Spirit, and is brought forth into exercise by a spiritual birth, I think you should tell the unconverted, that it is their duty first to beget themselves; then to quicken their own souls; then to make a new heart and a new spirit; and then by perfect love, to cast out fear from their hearts; and then their faith would work by their love. A child cannot walk before it is born, nor can any man walk by faith till he is born again. Marvel not at this: before a man can believe, he must be born again.

3. This extorting evangelical obedience to the faith from infidels shut up in unbelief, is a doctrine that cannot meet with the approbation, nor be attended with the impression, of the Holy Ghost; for he is the Spirit of faith, and produces faith: but, by this doctrine the unconverted are set to perform what none but the Spirit of God can effect. A man receives grace for the obedience of faith; but that which is produced by the Spirit's energy, is here made the carnal man's duty. Man is made the agent, where the Spirit is the efficient; and, can it be expected that the Spirit will attend with his seal a doctrine that brings no honour to him? He will not give his glory to another, nor his praise to the unconverted. This doctrine will never add one soul to the household of faith.

> 4. If it is the duty of all men to believe, they must believe that Jesus died for all men; that he will pardon all men, and save all men. If they believe not this, their faith is vain, and they are yet in their sins; and if all men do believe this, they believe a lie, for the bible affords no such warrant for the universal faith of these unconverted legions. 'I will take you one of a city, and two of a family, and I will bring you to Zion'. Were I to go to the condemned criminals in the cells of Newgate, and tell them, it is their duty, one and all, to believe; that the king will pardon them at the gallows, and that he will save them from death: should I succeed with this doctrine, and bring them all to believe the report, I should think that I had acted as the false prophets did in the days of Jeremiah, make this people to trust in a lie; and, when the rope came to be put round their necks, they would have just cause to curse my false doctrine, and me also as an impostor and a deceiver. And if all men believe Mr Ryland's doctrine, they will go down to the grave with a lie in their hand; and he will appear but little better in their sight, when they lift up their eyes in hell, than I should in the eyes of the above criminals, when cast off at Tyburn.[18]

The weakness Fuller has shown up to now is in assuming that fallen man has enough spiritual discernment to recognise and understand the gospel – even though he might still reject it. Now Fuller explains his theory of natural theology which transforms anything Paul said in Romans 1:20. Paul taught that nature points to a Creator and stops there. Fuller builds on this, saying:

> And the same law that obliged them [Adam, Moses and Israel] to love him in these discoveries of himself obliges us to love him in other discoveries, by which he has since more gloriously appeared, as *saving sinners through the death of his Son.*[19] To suppose that we are obliged to love God as manifesting himself in the works of creation and providence, but not in the work of redemption, is to suppose that in the highest and most glorious

---

[18] *Excommunication*, pp. 147ff.

[19] Fuller's italics.

display he deserves no regard. The same perfections which appear in all his other works, and render him lovely, appear in this with a ten-fold lustre; to be obliged to love him on account of the one, and not the other, is not a little extraordinary.[20]

Fuller is speaking here of what the sinner has a duty to see 'notwithstanding the depravity of his nature'!

This account of natural revelation far transcends anything that the Scriptures teach. Though David says that the heavens declare God's glory (Psalm 19:1) and Paul says that God's eternal power is seen in creation, neither David nor Paul teach that through contemplating nature a fallen man is enabled, or even obliged, to love God in a saving way. Fuller teaches that love engendered through natural revelation produces spiritual discernment. Surely Paul's argument in Romans is that fallen man, faced with natural revelation, has changed its truths into lies and God has thus left man in his ignorance, an ignorance which can only be removed when Christ comes into his life? It is a maxim of Fuller, however, right through his book that what is discernible rationally is also discernible spiritually. 'He that loves God for any excellency, as manifested in one form, must of necessity love him for that excellency, let it be manifested in what form it may'.[21] Fuller seems to have now lost all sight of the fact that his idea of the 'natural operation of love to God' occurs nowhere in this world where God has not given his love. We love, says the Scriptures, because Christ first loved us. Since the Fall, there is no 'natural' love for God in this world apart from the love Christ shows to his Father and Christ's love to his church directed back to him in thanksgiving.

Fuller again thinks otherwise and argues that there are laws of natural religion which prompt a man to love God. He can thus argue, quoting 'an able writer', 'If a sinner, therefore, who hears the gospel have these suitable affections of love to God and hatred of sin, to which he is obliged by the laws of natural religion, these things cannot be separated from a real complacency in that redemption and grace which

[20] Fuller, *Works*, vol. II, p. 345.
[21] *Ibid.*, p. 351.

are proposed in revealed religion'.[22] Huntington summed up Fuller's faith by saying his 'points of thought' were his 'points of faith' in order to stress that Fuller's gospel was all in the mind and not in the Scriptures.

Now we are in a position to understand why Fuller emphasises so much that fallen man is conscious of a duty to love God on hearing the gospel. Though he is cursed by the Mosaic law, indeed, slain by it, and is thus dead in trespasses and sins, there is another law which is stronger than the Mosaic law, i.e., 'the law of natural religion', which opens a man's eyes to the love of God. This is highly romantic and speculative thinking and it may thrill many a heart to hear that man is not as fallen as supposed. It is also a theory that is becoming more and more prominent in the writings of so-called 'Christian authors' today. That king of fantasy J. R. R. Tolkien tells us in his poem *Mythopeia:*

> Man is not wholly lost nor wholly changed,
> Disgraced he may be, yet is not dethroned,
> And keeps the rags of lordship once he owned.

Tolkien believed in a fall but a fall which did not leave man fully reprobate. Appealing as Fullerism might be, like Tolkien's optimistic view of man, it is a false gospel and as far from the biblical account of the fall of man as hell is from heaven. The ideas which Fuller expresses here are the ideas of the so-called Enlightenment which can be found in the writings of Lessing, Locke and Paine but not in the Scriptures. It is thus no wonder that after the publication of *The Gospel Worthy of All Acceptation*, Christian leaders accused Fuller of denying the total depravity of man. Fuller took up this criticism by arguing that man was not 'totally unable to believe in Christ' in the sense of 'unable in every respect'.[23]

It is obvious that Fuller cannot accept the total depravity of man as he does not view what he calls man's 'moral inability' to believe as pervading his total nature. Apart from in the field of morals, fallen 'men have the same natural powers to love Christ', he tells us, 'as to hate him,

---

[22] *Ibid.*, p. 352.

[23] *Ibid.*, p. 438. 'Reply to Mr Button's eighth letter, on the causes to which the want of faith is ascribed'.

to believe as to disbelieve'.[24] He seems to be saying that just as fallen man is free to hate Christ, he is also free to believe in him. The only thing that is stopping him is not his completely fallen nature but his lack of moral principles. Man could believe if he would! This is reducing man's fall to one aspect of his nature only. The Bible teaches that not only man as man but the entire creation in all its aspects is groaning and travailing under sin. As Cowper the poet puts it, 'Sin marr'd all'. The very blood and bones, body, soul and spirit of man are fallen. There is nothing in him which is perfect. He is fully scarred by the wages of sin and even the elect must bear their physical and mental deficiencies, not merely moral inabilities, with them to the grave. Man has no natural, nor rational, powers to believe in Christ because sin permeates his very being. If what Fuller teaches were true, a man with changed morals would immediately become a perfect Adam as before the Fall. Saved man, however, must wait until this body of sin is changed in the resurrection before this happens.

The key to Fuller's faulty view of man's depravity is perhaps to be found in his unwillingness to use theological and biblical conceptions such as 'sin'.[25] The Bible gives this word a theological content and it must be dealt with theologically. Sin is a revolt of the whole man and needs divine atonement. One does not, however, read in the Bible of 'moral inabilities' being atoned for. Christ's redemptive atonement of his sheep, according to the Scriptures, destroys sin and makes fallen men new whole men – new creatures. But Fuller shies away from believing in redemption from sin. He does not like the language and in throwing overboard the language, he loses the conceptions.

Next Fuller looks closer at his critics' arguments that 'No man *can* come to Christ except the Father draw him', and 'The carnal mind is enmity against God; for it is not subject to the law of God, neither *can* be. So then they that are in the flesh *cannot* please God'.[26] These critics,

---

[24] Fuller, *Works*, vol. III, 'Moral Inability', p. 768.
[25] See Fuller's 'Conversation on Imputation, Conversation on Substitution, and Imputation', *Works*, vol. II, where he argues time and time again that biblical doctrines must not be taken literally or must be understood metaphorically.
[26] *Ibid.*, p. 356ff.

including Huntington and Gadsby, argued that such passages from Scripture show clearly that fallen man is both unable and unwilling in his natural state to come to Christ He has no natural ability and no moral ability to do so. Fuller argues that this interpretation is false because it would suggest that if natural aversion were removed, there would still be a natural inability to believe. He then states that the Scriptures teach no such inability. If fallen man is by nature unable to believe, he argues, then he is also unable to disbelieve because, 'It requires the same powers to reject as to embrace'.[27] Here Fuller is reasoning the wrong way. He does not see that there is an aversion against Christ in natural man because he is fallen and has no natural ability to understand the truths of the gospel. Thus the 'powers' that make him believe must come from outside of himself. Fuller's high view of natural revelation is, once again, getting in his way. He *cannot*, and *will not*, see that he must argue according to the chronological facts revealed in God's Word. Adam had communion with God in his natural state. He rebelled and lost contact with God – he hid himself from God. Since then man in Adam's fallen nature *will not* believe. It is only when the nature of the Second Adam is applied to the life of man that he *can* and *will* believe.

It is most likely Fuller's teaching on natural revelation that moved his followers to use the unscriptural term 'universal holiness', a holiness that encompassed man. It was John Adams' rejection of this pseudo-holiness that was in part the cause of Ryland's fierce antagonism against him. Huntington commented in his open letter to Ryland:

> As to your insisting too much upon universal holiness, Mr Adams might be at a loss to know what you mean by the term, as I now am; for the bible has no such expressions: and, as for true holiness, anybody that has read your sermon on the promises of God, might easily discern, if they had any eyes at all, that you had very little, if any, real knowledge of the Spirit of holiness. Holiness is no more universal than the gospel; but, 'tis right that your holiness should be as extensive as your rule of duty.[28]

---

[27] *Ibid.*, p. 357.

[28] *Excommunication*, p. 146.

Sadly, as shown in previous chapters, Fuller has no consistent doctrine of the Second Adam and the new man in Christ, as he never came to terms with the doctrine of the imputed righteousness of Christ which is so closely related to it. At times, it is as if Fuller sees no natural differences between a fallen reprobate and the saved elect. Writing against an Arminian who stated rightly that fallen man has 'no will nor power to believe in Christ, nor any concern in the matter', Fuller says he could never affirm such a thing, saying, 'On the contrary, I maintain that men have the same power, strictly speaking, before they are wrought upon by the Holy Spirit, as after; and before conversion as after; that the work of the Spirit endows us with no new rational powers, nor any powers that are necessary to moral agency'.[29] Here it seems that Fuller is even questioning a total moral fall.

Nor has Fuller any clear idea of God's use of the law in conversion. Fuller demands the repentance of the sinner without confronting him with the law he has broken. The sinner who accepts God does so because he accepts the gospel out of a feeling of duty. Fuller develops this theory to such a length that he persuades himself that the covenant of works[30] is entirely abolished on man's and God's side, as regards both the sinner and the believer. In its place he puts a legal system which is but a faint shadow of the 'fiery law' written by the finger of God in the midst of his glory and given to Moses on Mount Sinai; a law from which no jot or tittle could ever be erased.

In Part III of his treatise[31] Fuller answers objections to his system which he feels might arise. He conditions his (Calvinist?) readers to support his arguments by telling them that the greater part of the objections are Arminian in origin and unscriptural in nature. He then proceeds to set up a row of Aunt Sallies and to knock them down with the choicest of coconuts. His first argument may be given as an example of his technique. A Mr Johnson of Liverpool had argued that 1 Corinthians 15:47, 'The first man was of the earth, earthy', showed that Adam had only an earthly mind and not a spiritual one. Fuller (in

[29] *Works*, vol. II, pp. 546, 547.
[30] *Works*, vol. II, p. 375ff.
[31] *Ibid.*, p. 366ff.

complete harmony with Huntington here) shows that Adam was created a spiritual man. This is perhaps of importance to Fuller as he delighted in showing that the natural man can discern spiritual things. The argument, though true in relation to unfallen Adam, is irrelevant concerning reprobate minds who cannot, according to Scripture, understand spiritual things.

Next, although Fuller has quoted a number of critics from the seventeenth and eighteenth centuries, such as Owen, Gill, Hervey, Marshall, Booth, Brine and the Marrow Men, who would obviously disagree with him, he now tells his readers that no less than Augustine, Calvin, all the other Reformers, the divines of the Council of Dort and all the nonconformists of the seventeenth century are of his opinion. Later he claims that Perkins, Goodwin, Charnock, Bunyan and M'Laurin support him. He caps this by saying that his opponents are so extreme that they would believe that Calvin was an Arminian in comparison to them. This is a strange charge to make as Fuller seems now to imply that his opponents are Hyper-Calvinists although he has just stated that they are Arminians! To make the confusion greater Fuller goes on to say that he admits his views 'may be inconsistent with the doctrines of grace', but claims that the leading advocates of the doctrines of grace all agree with him!

It might be demonstrable that many of the host of believers of bygone days mentioned by Fuller had made claims at some time or other during their doctrinal development which were contradictory to the doctrines of grace. In the same way it is demonstrable that Fuller was a Calvinist before he became a Neonomian. To argue, however, that all these men agreed with him in principle cannot be maintained. Fuller gives no proof of his allegations and to deal with the theology of all the people Fuller claims to have on his side would fill volumes. It is sufficient here to say that, in Book II, Chapter XXII of his *Institutes*, Calvin, quoting Augustine, certainly teaches a different doctrine of election and reprobation from Fuller's. In the same chapter it is also obvious that Calvin argues for the discriminating love of God and that Christ died to secure salvation for his sheep alone. Anyone reading Book II of the *Institutes* must be impressed with the truth that the atonement was limited to Christ's elect,[32] Calvin urged that election and predestination should be preached, whereas Fuller said the doctrines of grace should be kept secret in preaching. It would be a clever commentator indeed who could bend the theology of the writers Fuller quotes to fit into his theory of a universal conditional atonement.[33]

Turning to John Owen, any person who reads his *The Death of Death in the Death of Christ* and thinks he is arguing for a universal conditional atonement must have a very strange pair of spectacles on indeed! Jim Packer sums up the matter succinctly in his preface to the Banner of Truth reprint, 'Christ did not win a hypothetical salvation for hypothetical believers, a mere possibility of salvation for any who might possibly believe, but a real salvation for His own chosen people'. Owen, however, is the one writer whom Fuller quotes the most, continually giving the impression that he is using him as his authority.

None of the commentators Fuller mentions would accept his idea of election. In Fuller's theology, election is not determined before the foundation of the world through the sovereign council of God. Election came merely via God's prescience. He looked ahead as the invitation went out to all sinners for whom he had sent his Son to die, but nobody bothered to accept it. It had all been done in vain. He thus was compelled to reorganise his strategy and influence some in a special way to follow their inborn duty and accept his invitation. This is nothing else but the most primitive Arminianism and is a terribly low view of God's sovereignty.

Fuller is very slippery in his presentation of his case and his proof for it. His is an argument from silence from start to finish. All the authorities who Fuller claims back him up do not demonstrably do so at all. It is not that they openly support him, but that they do not openly

32 See also Calvin's *The Eternal Predestination of God* and *The Secret Providence of God* for a detailed exposition of this doctrine.

33 Several such attempts have been made, such as in Paul van Buren's *Christ in Our Place: The Substitutionary Character of Calvin's Doctrine of Reconciliation.* See John Murray's refutation of Buren's views in *Collected Writings of John Murray*, Banner of Truth Trust, 1982, vol. iv, pp. 310-314. It is still common for letters to editors in Christian magazines to find over-eager correspondents claiming that Calvin was really an Amyraldian or even an Arminian at heart. But what saith the Scripture?

denounce him, which he finds of value. They do not deny his theory. Fuller then naively concludes that those who do not tell him that they are against him must be for him. This is his position throughout. The argument from silence is used in almost all Fuller's expositions to prove that sinful man still has natural abilities which enable him to spiritually discern what his Christian duty is. The texts, however, merely show that God commands the sinner to change his ways. Because God does this, Fuller presumes that man is able to sense that God is right. Fuller, however, is not consistent here. The Bible makes it plain that man cannot discern spiritual things. There is no silence about the matter at all! This does not worry Fuller who, in face of such evidence, resorts to theories of natural revelation to 'prove' his point and give him the last word. Fuller's high view of natural revelation and low view of the law and its curse led him and his close friends the Rylands and their spokeswoman De Fleury to drop the doctrine of the covenant of works completely, thus revealing their Neonomian position. The term 'the covenant of works' or 'the covenant of life' is used amongst Calvinists to express the fact that eternal life is given to man on condition that he obeys God's law perfectly and perpetually.[34] God's demand on man is that he should always live a life of perfect righteousness. The law not only says, 'Break this and die', but also 'Do this and live'. As man has broken the law, he has forfeited his eternal life. Huntington's position is that this covenant has never been annulled by God and remains his standard through all time. It is therefore the standard Christ set for himself and accomplished. Though man has broken the covenant of works, Christ has fulfilled the law, and thus the covenant, completely for his elect and has imputed his own righteousness to them. This righteousness Huntington describes as the wedding gown which will allow the saved sinner to partake in the Marriage Feast of the Lamb. Neonomians reject this view and say that God no longer keeps to his covenant and is satisfied when mankind shows love to him by striving to keep the moral law, robbed of its curse and bondage. He will not expect of the believer what he is unable to provide. It is worthy of note that usually Fuller is very generous with his references to Herman Witsius (1636-1708). In his *The Gospel Worthy of All Acceptation*, he refrains from quoting him. This is because Witsius' great work *The*

[34] See *Westminster Confession*, chapter VII, Sections I, II and chapter XIX, Section I.

Economy of the Covenants between God breaks all the bubbles in Fuller's rationalistic dreams of a universal atonement and an annulment of God's perfect standards for his people. Witsius makes it quite clear that the covenant of works is the covenant by which man will be judged whether in the old or new dispensations.[35] Fuller fails here because he cannot see how God made it possible, through Christ's indwelling the believer, to work out actual righteousness in man, thus holding up his own standards. Fuller's emphasis centres on man's responsibility over God's availability. When man accepts, God gives; when man refuses what God has for him, God withdraws his offer. The onus is always on man. Thus Fuller argues that because men have thwarted God's will, 'God is not in covenant with them, nor they with him'.[36] Here Fuller is rejecting the teaching of his Baptist predecessors and Witsius, who argued that one must distinguish between elect sinners and the reprobate. God is in covenant with his elect whom he has determined to save from the foundation of the world. Fuller says of the unregenerate, 'As unbelievers are not under the covenant of works, it is improper to say that whatever is required of them in the Scriptures is required by that covenant, and as a term of life. God requires nothing of fallen creatures as a term of life. He requires them to love him with all their hearts, the same as if they had never apostatised'.[37] This is strange and confused talk indeed for a person who is always underlining man's duties. Here lie the very roots of Antinomianism, yet it was Fuller who accused Huntington of Antinomianism though the 'Coalheaver' argued that God's standards never drop.

---

[35] Witsius argues that the perfect performance of duty is still demanded by God and eternal life can be obtained under no other condition. The covenant of works is 'on no account abolished, but insofar that it is become impossible for man to attain to life by his own personal works' (Herman Witsius, *The Economy of the Covenant*, vol. I, pp. 151, 161). Witsius makes it clear that there is a covenant between the Father and the Son concerning the elect *(Ibid.*, p. 165). Fuller does quote Witsius to back up his duty-faith teaching in 'A Reply to Philanthropos' *(Works*, vol. II, p. 489, footnote) but Witsius is merely speculating that Christ *could* have atoned for all had *it so pleased God.* Witsius makes it clear in the context that the atonement was sufficient for all who come to Christ.

[36] Fuller, *Works*, vol. I, p. 375.

[37] *Ibid.*, p. 375ff.

Fuller is guilty of faulty logic here. He is arguing that because man has broken the covenant of works, he no longer comes under its jurisdiction. Man is, however, under its jurisdiction as he has been condemned by it, for breaking it, and carries its sentence of death with him until rescued by a righteousness which is not his own.

Fuller argues in this way because he does not believe that the covenant of works was a covenant of life.[38] He finds that the law never orders the sinner to 'Do this and live'. This, too, is strange exegesis as Fuller obviously writes as though he believes that the broken law brings death with it. Surely if breaking the law means death, keeping the law must mean life? Fuller, who claims to be so rational, is not prepared to accept this logic. But logic is not our yardstick. Is this teaching of Fuller's scriptural? That breaking the law means death cannot be a secret as both Exodus and Deuteronomy show this repeatedly. The entire New Testament testifies to the fact that man fell because he sinned. But what did he fall from? He fell, according to the Old and New Testaments, from life which he would have had if he had not fallen, 'And the Lord commanded us to do all these statutes to fear the Lord our God, for our good always, that he might preserve us alive, as it is at this day. And it shall be our righteousness, if we observe to do all these commandments before the Lord our God, as he hath commanded us' (Deuteronomy 6:24, 25). The words of our Lord are clear enough here. In Luke 10:25-28 we read, 'He [Jesus] said unto him, What is written in the law? how readest thou? And he answering said, Thou shalt love the Lord thy God with all thy heart, and with all thy strength, and with all thy mind; and thy neighbour as thyself. And he said unto him, Thou hast answered right: this do, and thou shalt live'.

Huntington deals with Fuller's theory concerning God's eternal standards in his reply to De Fleury's and Ryland's barnstorming pamphlets against him. After claiming that Huntington is an Antinomian who finds lying as natural as breathing and that he has a 'familiar spirit' and is a conjuror void of any grace of God, his accusers go on to argue that the covenant of works has been done away with.[39]

---

[38] *Ibid.*, p. 375.

[39] *The Broken Cistern and the Springing Well*, p. 82. De Fleury is 'expounding' 1 John 2, 'A new commandment I write unto you'. (See also Huntington's comments on p. 37

Huntington replies:

> I read that the old veil of ignorance is done away in Christ; but I never read that the law was done away. Christ came to fulfil it; the apostles preached to establish it. Christ is a just God and a Saviour; and all Adam's race, saints and sinners, must and shall appear before the judgment-seat of Christ. And he will appear as a just God with the book of the law, and pronounce the curse from thence upon the bondservant, for it is a covenant of works to him. And he will appear with the book of life as a Saviour, and pronounce the blessing of life from that, as a covenant of grace. Thus the Pharisee and the believer will both be judged according to their works. He that is of the works of the law will be tried by the book of the law; and he that is of the works of faith will be tried by the law of faith, and be proclaimed a good and faithful servant … The law is not done away as a covenant of works; it will entangle a foolish Galatian still: and the weak believer, when deceived by these vain janglers, finds, to his sorrow, that the law is a covenant of works still; and genders to bondage still, for it binds him hand and foot, as sure as ever he goes to work by that rule, unless he performs a perfect task, which he never can; for, while he seeks to the law to be made perfect by the flesh, Christ profits him nothing; and without Christ he can do nothing.[40]

Huntington argued in this way as De Fleury and Ryland, following Fuller, believed that the gospel invitation of God's love in Christ should be given to the unrepentant sinner and then the law, without its curse, as a mere moral guide, should be given to the believer to teach him the way of righteousness. This to Huntington was not using the law as a schoolmaster to bring a sinner to Christ, but was using Christ as a

---

and his *An Answer to Fools and a Word to the Wise*, where he takes De Fleury and Ryland to task on similar teaching.)

[40] *Ibid.*, pp. 82, 83.

schoolmaster to bring the believer to a meaningless law robbed of its function.[41]

Taking up De Fleury's and Ryland's accusation that he was an Antinomian, Huntington replies:

> I will not say that the authors of this book are antinomians; but this I will say, that the book contains the worst antinomianism that I ever read; and is a vile and damnable harangue, both against the law, the gospel, and the grace of God. Against the law, because it declares, the law has ceased to exist, and is done away, as a covenant of works. Against the gospel, because it is no rule of right or wrong.[42] And against the grace of God, by declaring that the new man is taken captive by sin.[43]

Here we see the confused state of the Fullerites' theology. They believe that the law is robbed of its commanding and condemning power, yet the new man in Christ can be taken captive by sin.

Summing up Fuller's doctrine of the law, Huntington argues:

> They tell you that the law is the believer's only rule of life, walk and conduct; but only with the allowance of this grand and glorious truth, namely, that it has ceased to exist as a covenant of works; and therefore, has no power to command works to be done, nor any power to condemn the slothful, who does nothing. The law has ceased to exist with respect to works, that it may be substituted as the bond of the covenant of grace. This is destroying the law for ever, and establishing the gospel on the destruction of it.[44]

---

[41] *Ibid.*, p. 42.

[42] The Fullerites empty the gospel of its moral content and its teaching of the law written on the hearts of believers. The covenant of works is no longer seen as a gospel ideal fulfilled in Christ. Furthermore, they argue that the gospel without the law is for sinners and the pared-down law is for the saints. Sinners are thus put under grace and believers under the law.

[43] *Ibid.*, pp. 99, 100.

[44] *Ibid.*, p. 68.

Huntington could argue like this as he saw the law as being the very nature of Christ, who is 'the end of the law for righteousness' – the word 'end' here meaning 'goal', and not 'termination' as the Fullerites naively supposed. He argued that Christ is 'not only the fulfilling end, but the grand end of the law is answered in and by him. And the same end is answered and fulfilled by a work of grace in us. We are redeemed from under the law, and are under grace, and not under the law. But the law is still what it ever was – an everlasting, unalterable, unrepealable law; and a covenant of works in every sense; and to him that works under it the reward is still reckoned of debt'.[45] Christ came debtless through the fiery furnace of the law and he shares this victory with his church, and his church will not be sent to hell, not because the law has been annulled but because the eternal law has been established and fulfilled in the eternal Christ who indwells the believer.

In defence of De Fleury and Ryland it must be stated that Huntington was taking a rather unfair advantage of his opponents here. De Fleury and Ryland could not match Huntington's theological and spiritual acumen and they had no idea of what the new man in Christ was. Owing to their weak doctrine of imputed righteousness they merely believed that the old sinner in Christ had changed his ways and had a new goal in life though he still did not have the law inscribed on his heart. Christ's indwelling the believer and the latter's living under the influence of the Holy Spirit were not actual realities for them but metaphorical ways of explaining spiritual truths.[46] What the Fullerites really believed this 'metaphor' was is a conundrum. William Rushton, in his book *Particular Redemption*, tried hard to understand and analyse their teaching, but it is difficult to see order in chaos. De Fleury and Ryland acted as if they still had tablets of stone round their necks and were 'doing their best for Jesus'. In other words, they were acting as pious Jews who still had not encountered the Messiah. Jesus' death to them

---

[45] *Ibid.*, pp. 64, 65.

[46] See Fuller's *Works*, vol. II, pp. 681, 682, 688 and 690, where the author argues that imputation, Christ's being made sin for us, sin as a debt and Christ's redemption are not to be understood literally but metaphorically. See also Fuller's rationalistic arguments against the vicarious, penal, redemptive death of Christ in *The Gospel Worthy of All Acceptation.*

was not a substitutionary redemption but an example of a moral victory.[47]

Fuller realises that he is arguing foursquare against all the Calvinists who have gone before him, i.e., those who believed in a limited atonement. If Christ died to save his Bride and her alone, all Fuller's paradoxical difficulties concerning a universal atonement with a limited application would be avoided. Fuller cannot, however, accept that Christ gave his life for his sheep alone. His arguments to prove this are bizarre, to say the least, and he ties himself up in the most twisted of mathematical knots. Under the title 'On Particular Redemption' in his work, *The Gospel Worthy of All Acceptation*, he argues:

> Objections to the foregoing principles [Fuller's theory], from the doctrine of election, are generally united with those from particular redemption; and, indeed, they are so connected that the validity of the one stands or falls with that of the other.
>
> To ascertain the force of the objection, it is proper to inquire wherein the peculiarity of redemption consists. If the atonement of Christ were considered as the literal payment of a debt – if the measure of his sufferings were according to the number of those for whom he died, and to the degree of their guilt, in such a manner as that if more had been saved, or if those who are saved had been more guilty, his sorrows must have been proportionally increased – it might, for aught I know, be inconsistent with indefinite invitations. But it would be equally inconsistent with the free forgiveness of sin, and with sinners being directed to apply for mercy as supplicants, other than as claimants. I conclude, therefore, that an hypothesis which in so many important points is manifestly inconsistent with the Scriptures cannot be true.
>
> On the other hand, if the atonement of Christ proceed not on the principle of commercial, but of moral justice, or justice as it relates to crime – if its grand object were to express the Divine displeasure against sin, (Romans 8:3) and so render the exercise of mercy, in all the ways wherein sovereign wisdom should

[47] See Fuller, *The Gospel Worthy of All Acceptation*, 'On Particular Redemption', *Works*, vol. II, p. 373ff.

> determine to apply it, consistent with righteousness (Romans 3:25) – if it be in itself equal to the salvation of the whole world, were the whole world to embrace it – and if the peculiarity which attends it consists not in its insufficiency to save more than are saved, but in the sovereignty of its application – no such inconsistency can justly be ascribed to it ... [48]

The inconsistencies here are entirely of Fuller's making, showing, as always, his weak view of the atonement and imputed righteousness. The traditional 'commercial' interpretation of the atonement is in keeping with the commercial language which the Bible uses and is in no way reflected in Fuller's caricature of it The Bible does not teach that Christ's atonement was relative to the number of sins committed by fallen man. He bore the sins of his flock and those only. His atonement was particular. Nor was Christ's atonement relative to the degrees of guilt amongst his subjects. There is only one judgment for all degrees of sin – death. This judgment Christ took upon him. Nor did Christ's atonement work out a different ransom for the different stages in his subjects' holiness. They had no holiness. The same degree of righteousness – Christ's total righteousness – was imputed to all the elect. Thus the elect are clothed in Christ's righteousness and not their own. This is the teaching which rids the confused mind of 'inconsistencies', and not Fuller's teaching of 'moral justice', which is just another way of saying God may not have mercy on whom he will have mercy. Such a view is totally 'inconsistent' with God's sovereignty and Christ's love for his flock of whom he loses none. Though Fuller at times claims that he has the whole church in history behind him, he nevertheless had to append over 150 pages to his pamphlet to take up the many arguments which came thick and fast in a widespread and almost violent protest against his theories. Mostly, Fuller merely underlined what he had written before, laying more importance on natural revelation and arguing more from silence than ever. One new argument was that the relationship between children and parents proves his point regarding the duty of sinners, including

[48] *Ibid.*, pp. 53, 54.

reprobates, to believe. He tells us that nobody doubts that children have a duty to obey their parents and are aware of this duty. Therefore we must logically conclude that sinners realise that they must obey God.[49]

This argument was felt to be the trump card of all Fullerites and was used in all their campaigns against Huntington. He, of course, turned their gaze from false logic back to the Scriptures and showed them that they were confusing the state of a slave with that of a son. They were confusing the children of Hagar with those of Sarah. Bondservants have neither the duties nor the freedom of those who have received the adoption of sons and been *made free* from sin to become servants of righteousness.[50] The natural man is a slave to sin and dead to righteous works. He 'receiveth not the things of the Spirit of God: for they are foolishness unto him: neither can he know them, because they are spiritually discerned'. Only the child of God has the mind of Christ and can thus understand his spiritual commitments and duties (1 Corinthians 2:14-16). Verses 9 and 10 are even more explicit, 'Eye hath not seen, nor ear heard, neither have entered into the heart of man, the things which God hath prepared for them that love him. But God hath revealed them unto us by his Spirit'. Paul makes it very clear, here, that to 'know the things that are freely given to us of God' one must have been freed from the spirit of the world and have been given the Spirit which is of God.

Fuller's philosophical system fails sadly as a Christian demonstration of God's intended scope for the gospel. It is rationalistic to the core, depending on the *a priori* ideas of a limited fall and the notion that God's eternal standards are not higher than man's ability to reach them. Though Fuller always maintained that he was the most orthodox of Calvinists, he was not a Calvinist at all in the sense of one who holds the 'five points'. Fuller certainly rejects the total depravity of man and the atonement is not unconditional in his system. There is no particular redemption in Fullerism at all, as Christ's death atoned for the non-particular sins of the reprobate and elect alike – should they

---

[49] See, for instance, Fuller's *Works*, vol. II, p. 418, footnote *et passim*. This is the natural consequence of Fuller's teaching that both the unsaved and saved are put under the same modified law. See Huntington's commentary on this heresy in *The Broken Cistern*, pp. 56-67.

[50] See Romans 6 and Galatians 4.

believe. He denied even the basic meaning of the word 'redemption' and left it to speculate in the realms of metaphor and imagery. Likewise it cannot possibly be said that Fuller believed in irresistible grace, as he held that there are those in hell for whom Christ died. All that is left is the doctrine of the final perseverance of the saints. Fuller has not much to say about this but, judging by his criticism of Huntington for openly preaching such a doctrine,[51] he does not seem to have viewed it with favour. Fuller's gospel is thus in no respect good news to anyone, as it expects a man, too big for his boots, to accept the offer of a God cut down to size.

[51] Fuller, *Works*, vol. III, p. 830.

Appendix II

The Wording Of Huntington's Epitaph

It is widely believed that Huntington wrote his own epitaph. The author of The Banner of Truth article on *The Voice of Years* states this categorically and judging by his faulty reference to Romaine in conjunction with the epitaph, assumes that it was written before Romaine's death in 1795. Even the Gospel Standard Magazine, well familiar with William Huntington's story, states that Huntington was the author of his own memorial inscription.[1] This, of itself, would not have been unusual as it was the custom for both men and women to write their own epitaphs in previous centuries, as it still is, in certain cases, today. A well-known example of such a practice is John Newton's epitaph which was written on white marble and placed in St Mary's Woolnoth Church in 1807:

JOHN NEWTON
CLERK
ONCE AN INFIDEL AND LIBERTINE,
A SERVANT OF SLAVES IN AFRICA
WAS
BY THE RICH MERCY OF OUR LORD AND SAVIOUR
JESUS CHRIST
PRESERVED, RESTORED, PARDONED
AND APPOINTED TO PREACH THE FAITH
HE HAD LONG LABOURED TO DESTROY

[1] The Gospel Standard, January, 1993.

Huntington's enemies, however, have seized on his epitaph to 'prove' that he claimed to be a prophet who could look into the future and predict things to come. They thus regard him as a kind of self-proclaimed Nostradamus. This is obviously the stance of the Banner author who says of the words,

HERE LIES THE COALHEAVER:-
BELOVED OF HIS GOD; BUT ABHORRED OF MEN.
THE OMNISCIENT JUDGE AT THE GRAND ASSIZE
SHALL RATIFY AND CONFIRM THIS
TO THE CONFUSION OF MANY THOUSANDS;
FOR ENGLAND AND ITS METROPOLIS SHALL KNOW
'THAT THERE HATH BEEN A PROPHET AMONG THEM'.
W.H.S.S.

'As he vilified all indiscriminately, he could hardly expect all to speak well of him. In the event, many idolised him. People certainly learned that there had been a prophet among them – one whose prophecies did not always come to pass!' It is interesting to note here that the author is not aware of any inconsistencies in his words to the effect that Huntington vilified *all* yet *many* idolised him!

Huntington's traducers, in order to underscore their point, usually adopt a slight modification of the epitaph's wording. This is the case in the Banner article but the Gospel Standard, sympathetic to Huntington, has made no such modification. The words, 'That there hath been a prophet among them', are in inverted commas in the original, as also in the Gospel Standard reference but the quotation marks have been left out of the Banner citation. It is thus made to appear as if Huntington is directly calling himself a prophet according to the author's faulty interpretation of the word.

The true sources of the passage, as the critics must know, are Ezekiel 2:5 and 33:33. The internal evidence of these passages was obviously used as the interpreting factor by the author of the epitaph. The verses in question show how Ezekiel is commanded not to be afraid but to go to a 'rebellious nation' and preach to them the Word of God. These verses have been traditionally used by pastors entering the full-time ministry or by those conducting ordination services to emphasise that a minister of the Word should have a strong calling from God before attempting to shepherd a flock. Suddenly, however, in Huntington's case, this passage is misapplied to compare Huntington with Mother Shipton! Taken in its correct sense and context, the epitaph emphasises that Huntington was called to be a preacher, just as Newton felt himself called to 'preach the faith that he had long laboured to destroy'. This is made quite obvious by the final words of the epitaph (left out in all critics' quotes) engraved in the marble tablet at Providence Chapel:

> 'He that goeth forth and weepeth, bearing precious seed, shall doubtless come again with rejoicing, bringing his sheaves with him.'

When referring to unfair criticism concerning Huntington's epitaph, William Stevens, a member of Providence Chapel, says of his pastor that, 'Nothing was more condemned by him than predictions made by the fancies of men, without the authority of the word of God'.[2] True to Stevens' opinion of his pastor's teaching, there could hardly have been a popular preacher in the late eighteenth century who dealt so little in prophetic speculation as did Huntington. He wrote only one pamphlet on prophecy for publication and this pamphlet was really more an anti-prophetic pamphlet than an exposition of any prophecy or prophetic view.

This is all the more noteworthy as very many churches in Huntington's day were busily using the Scriptures as a kind of *Old Moore's Almanac* to find out what the future would bring instead of using them as a doctrinal guide for the present. Many expositors of the Scriptures were finding proof that England was the home of the supposed ten lost tribes of Israel and the New Jerusalem was to be set upon English soil.[3] Even the secular newspapers of Huntington's day were full of the subject of prophecy. The *Northampton Mercury*, which claimed to be England's most-read newspaper, loved to publish astonishing prophecies, such as Pastor Ziehen's account of Europe's

---

[2] *Recollections of William Huntington*, p. 40.

[3] This theme is dealt with in the poetry of William Cowper and William Blake.

destruction. Ziehen professed to have received the news direct from God that a great earthquake was to destroy 7,000 towns and villages on its way from the Alps to England and the Rhine, Zuider Sea and the British Channel would be entirely drained away. Richard Brothers was courting fame by proclaiming himself to be God's nephew and the Branch or Rod of Jesse which was to save the world. He proudly stated that God had chosen him to lead the saints out of doomed Britain and take them in safety to the promised land. Unlike the poet Blake, Brothers asserted that Britain, far from being a paradise, was really Babylon the great harlot and was to be destroyed by God's wrath. He, like Ziehen, proclaimed the exact date when these astounding things were to be accomplished. Ziehen said that his pan-European catastrophe would occur in 1786, but Brothers gave Britain more time and said that London would be destroyed in 1798. The self-proclaimed experts disagreed! Such 'prophecies' were not made in some backwater of society but were preached in the metropolis and believed by thousands. Ziehen, a learned Lutheran divine, was no less than the personal chaplain to the Hanoverian Court and Brothers, an ex-marine officer, had Pall Mall politician Nathanial Brassey Halhed as his spokesman in Parliament. Halhed wrote a book in support of Brothers, claiming that he had seen proof upon proof that Brothers' prophecies concerning the downfall of the great whore, Babylon, alias London, would come to pass.

It is quite plain to see that these 'prophetic schools' in Huntington's day sprang up like mushrooms because believers had rejected the old prophetic view of the Puritans concerning Rome. They had developed a low view of Scripture, especially in relation to God's covenants with man and his Son and they maintained a high view of man's rational abilities and his inbred awareness of God's purpose in nature.

Huntington combats Halhed's 'proofs' and those of other 'modern prophets' on five counts. First, he argues that what God has not revealed in the Scriptures cannot be seen in nature and the just are to live by faith and not by 'sight' and 'signs'. Next, he affirms that Scripture makes it plain that only God in Christ knows the times and seasons of the end. Huntington then argues that it is preposterous to identify London with the Babylon of prophecy as this would mean the capital would suddenly have to spread to seven hills which were in no wise geographically available at the time. Huntington pleads for the traditional identification of prophetic Babylon with Rome. All evidence, Huntington teaches, points to the fact that Babylon (i.e. the Roman Catholic institution) in London, is not being pulled down but rather built up with renewed strength. For this stance, Huntington, as indicated in the introduction to this book, was ridiculed because sceptics and evangelicals alike felt that Rome's power had been curbed for ever. Next, Huntington attacks the belief that the outcome of the events of the end of the world would be through the agency of a modern 'prophet'. Christ alone will usher in the end, he argues and makes short work of Brothers' theory that the Branch was to be a man of flesh and blood (i.e., Brothers himself) and not Christ who is God. It was to be expected that such a theory would develop as leading London pastors such as Garrett were proclaiming that flesh and blood cannot deliver sinners, so Christ must have shed divine blood. This theory was a direct denial of the incarnation. Huntington pointed out time and time again in his works that it was a faulty view of the incarnation which led to a faulty view of Christ and thus to faulty views of the atonement and of the church. This is nowhere seen more clearly than in Huntington's exposure of Fullerism, with its refusal to accept the God-man Jesus as the perfect human Lawkeeper who ransomed his church, not with silver and gold but with his own precious human blood.[4] Finally, Huntington maintains that all these heresies have come to pass because the biblical covenants of law and grace are not respected and mere men are seen as the executors of God's covenants, and not Christ.

Oddly enough, it was Huntington's teaching concerning Christ as the Executor of God's Testament for his people that caused widespread ridicule amongst many so-called evangelicals. Just as they had set up evening lectures at sixpence a head to defend rationalism and Thomas Paine against Huntington's biblical theology, now, realising what a box-office attraction Huntington's name was, his critics organised Assembly Hall debates entitled, 'Which is the greatest enthusiast, Mr Brothers, for styling himself God's Nephew, or William Huntington, for making Christ his Executor?' This time, however, Huntington's

[4] 1 Peter 1:18

enemies did not charge sixpence per head but the grand entrance fee of a shilling each. They had to finance the trip to Israel somehow!

Apart from Huntington's sceptical views concerning extra-biblical prophecy published against Halhed and Brothers, one must look hard to find any references to prophetic theories of his own. He does take up the topic two or three times in private letters to friends which he obviously never intended to publish. They were, however, published by Lady Sanderson immediately after his death. This was definitely against Huntington's will and happened under circumstances which reaped no praise for her ladyship.[5] These writings which were for private eyes only show that Huntington believed that Rome would gain great power in England through allying with the Arminians and filling Protestant churches with Catholic priests. True Christians[6] would go through a short time of persecution, Rome's power would wane before the onslaught of Islam and at last Rome would come to some agreement with the Moslems after which gospel truths would again come to their own, the time of the Gentiles would be fulfilled and the Jews would accept the gospel before the Second Coming of Christ.[7]

Having said this concerning Huntington on prophecy, it must be firmly stated that there is no evidence whatsoever to show that Huntington wrote his own epitaph years before his death, calling himself a prophet. There is, in fact. no evidence whatsoever that Huntington penned it himself at any time. There is certainly strong evidence that Huntington refused to be called a prophet even though he was often proclaimed as such by those of his flock who used the word in its correct, scriptural, new covenant context. He simply felt uncomfortable at being called a prophet as it was not the kind of name that a Christian would use of himself. He stressed that it would be the prerogative of Christ at the resurrection to proclaim who was a true

---

[5] The story of Lady Sanderson's unflattering attempt to cash in on Huntington's unpublished writings, in fear of competition from his children, in particular Ebenezer and Ruth can be read in Hooper's books *The Celebrated Coalheaver* and *Huntington: Facts and Letters*.

[6] Stevens interprets the three and a half years of persecution mentioned by Huntington as referring to Dissenters. Bills were, of course, being debated in Parliament at the time to curb Dissenting preachers.

[7] See *Posthumous Letters*, vol. I. Letter 77 to Bensley and Letter 163 to Joseph Morris.

prophet or not.[8] Furthermore, Thomas Bensley, in his rather confused account of Huntington's last days, which he allegedly obtained from Lady Sanderson, expressly says that even on his deathbed, Huntington testified that 'it was not for him to say' that he was a prophet.

As noted previously, Lady Sanderson never referred to her husband as such but insisted on calling him 'the apostle' or 'the prophet'. Huntington reproved her often for this practice, telling her, 'I will not suffer it. I am a saved sinner, and that is enough for me'.[9] Nevertheless when Lady Sanderson published Huntington's so-called *Posthumous Letters* she wrote, 'Some were written more than twenty years ago; by which it will be clearly seen that *our Prophet*[10] then held the same great truths of the gospel which he constantly and invariably maintained to the last'. Moreover, according to Thomas Bensley, Lady Sanderson confessed to writing the epitaph albeit at her husband's dictation, some time during his final hours. When Bensley visited Huntington the day before his death, he says there was no indication that his pastor was about to die and the 'Coalheaver' told his family that day that he had not settled his affairs and hoped to do so yet. The accounts of Huntington's last day would rule out any dictation on his part as he was too ill by far. Furthermore, Miss Falkland's account of Huntington's last few days is the only first-hand eyewitness account and though she says that Huntington wished to dictate certain matters, she also says, 'But this, to our great regret, never could be done – that night was his last!' No reference whatsoever is made by Eliza Falkland to an epitaph being dictated.

On studying the evidence carefully, it would appear that the story that Huntington actually wrote his own epitaph is quite untrue and the story that he dictated his epigraph cannot be confirmed. Lady Sanderson obviously wrote Huntington's will for him, in the conviction that she was acting on his behalf and the evidence suggests that she wrote his epitaph under the same conviction. In forcing the will on Huntington, she did her husband, his family and Providence Chapel a great

---

[8] See *Gleanings of the Vintage*, Letter 173.

[9] See *Posthumous Letters*, vol II. p. 227

[10] Author's italics.

disservice, but the epitaph she wrote is a true testimony to the opposition Huntington received and the triumph of the faith which he represented. Lady Sanderson indirectly admitted that she was the author behind Huntington's alleged last wishes as, when members of Providence Chapel complained about them, she defended herself by saying, 'I hope never to deviate from what *I believe to have been*[11] his will'.

[11] Author's italics. See *Posthumous Letters*, vol I. p. 4.

Bibliography

Huntington's works

I wish to thank Mr H. M. Pickles and Mr John Crowter of Coventry and the Evangelical Library, London for supplying me with books which were not available in local libraries or bookshops.

The Bensley and Collingridge Editions

Bensley (20 volumes 1811) and Collingridge (6 volumes 1856) editions with dates of first publication. Collingridge was reprinted in 1989 by J. R. Broome and distributed by Gospel Standard Trust Publications.

	Bensley	Collingridge	
1780	1	2	A Spiritual Sea Voyage. Verse
1783	2	4	The Arminian Skeleton
1783	2	1	The Naked Bow
1784	3	1	The Bank of Faith, Part 1
1784	1	1	The Kingdom of Heaven Taken by Prayer
1784	2	2	Spiritual Birth. Verse
1784	3	3	An Innocent Game for Babes in Grace
1784	2	1	The Poor Christian's Last Will and Testament
1785	5	6	Epistles of Faith, Part 1
1785	8	4	Letters on Ministerial Qualifications
1786	3	6	The Law Established by the Faith of Christ
1786	4		Tidings from Wallingford
1786	4		Zion's Alarm

1787	2	2	A Sermon on the Dimensions of Eternal Love
1787	4	2	The Justification of a Sinner and Satan's Lawsuit with him
1787	4		The Modern Plasterer Detected
1787	7	2	The Shunamite
1787	7	2	Music and Odours of the Saints
1788	7		Free Thoughts in Captivity
1788	7	6	The Servant of the Lord Described
1788	7	3	Spoils taken from the Tower
1788	8		Way and Fare of a Wayfaring Man
1789	8	6	A Rule and a Riddle, Part 1
1789	8	6	A Rule and a Riddle, Part 2
1789	8		The Bond Child Brought to the Test
1789	8	6	The Coalheaver's Confession
1789	8		A Lawyer's Complaint
1789	10		Letter to Rev. Caleb Evans
1790	9	1	The History of Little Faith
1790	9	1	The Cry of Little Faith
1791	11		The Broken Cistern and the Springing Well
1791	11		Excommunication
1792	10		The Barber: or, Timothy Priestley Shaved, Part 1
1792	10	5	The Funeral of Arminianism
1792	11		The Moral Law not injured by the Gospel
1792	11		An Answer to Fools and a Word to the Wise
1792	10		The Barber; or, Timothy Priestley Shaved, Part 2
1793	12		A Feeble Dispute with a Wise and Learned Man
1793	12		Forty Stripes Save None for Satan
1794	12		Letter to the Rev. Torial Joss
1794	12		Advocates for Devils Refuted
1794	12	2	The Mystery of Godliness
1794	13		Living Testimonies, Part 1
1794	15	5	Moses Unveiled in the Face of God
1794	17	4	The Child of Liberty in Legal Bondage
1795	17		A Lying Prophet Examined
1796	15	3	Light Shining in Darkness, Part 1

1796	16	6	Utility of the Books and Excellency of the Parchments
1797	14		Living Testimonies, Part 2
1797	18	5	The Breath of the Lord and the Sieve of Vanity
1797	6	6	Epistles of Faith, Part 2
1797	17	2	The Wise and Foolish Virgins
1798	17	4	Discoveries and Cautions from the Streets of Zion
1798	17		Watchword and Warning
1799	18	4	Correspondence between Noctua Aurita and Philomela
1800	18	4	A Portion to Seven and also to Eight
1800	19	3	The Loss and Restoration of the Image of God in Man
1801	19		Letter to Joseph Britton of Downham
1802	19	2	Contemplations on the God of Israel
1803	3	1	The Bank of Faith, Part 2
1804	20	2	The Destruction of Death by the Fountain of Life
1804	20	5	The Joy of Faith in the Shadow of Death
1804	20		'Onesimus' in the Balance
1804	20	3	Every Divine Law in the Heart of Christ
1806	16	3	Light Shining in Darkness, Part 2
1809		1	The Coalheaver's Scraps
1809		6	The Apartments, Equipage and Parade of Immanuel
1811		6	Zion's Gates and Pleasant Fruits
1811		6	The Colour of the Fields and their Fitness for the Sickle
1812		6	Naphtali, or Holy Wrestling
1814		5	Gleanings of the Vintage

Further works of Huntington

Popish Controversy: Letters to and from Miss Morton, C. Verral, 1787, reprinted under the confusing title of 'Epistles of Faith' (See works for 1785 and 1797 of that name), Focus Christian Ministries Trust, 1990
The Doctrine of Garrett Refuted, E. Huntington, 1808
Last Fragments of the Rev. J. Jenkins, E. Huntington, 1811, reprinted by John Crowter, Coventry, 1993
The Glory of the Second House, E. Huntington, 1811, reprinted by John Crowter, Coventry, 1993
The Lord Our Righteousness, S. Huntington, 1811, reprinted by John Crowter, Coventry, 1993
Farewell Sermon, T. Bensley, 1813, reprinted by John Crowter, 1993
Further Gleanings of the Vintage, Pickles, H. M. (Ed), Coventry, undated
Posthumous Letters, 4 vols, 592 letters, T. Bensley, 1814-1822

Secondary literature on Huntington

Anonymous, *The Voice of Years*, A. Maxwell, 1814, reprinted by John Crowter, Coventry
Hooper, Ebenezer, *The Celebrated Coalheaver*, Gadsby, 1871, reprinted by John Crowter, Coventry, 1993
Hooper, Ebenezer, *Huntington: Facts and Letters*, Collingridge, 1872, reprinted by John Crowter, Coventry, 1993
Sant, Henry and Ella, George M., *William Huntington: The Sinner Saved*, Focus Christian Ministries Trust, undated (Essays published courtesy of the Bible League Quarterly)
Stevens, William, *Recollections of the Late William Huntington*, Gadsby, 1868, reprinted by John Crowter, 1993
Wright, Thomas, *The Life of William Huntington*, Farncombe & Son, 1909

Works on Huntingtonians

Alexander, J. H., *More Than Notion*, Zoar Publications, 1976
Burrell, Joseph Francis, *The Triumph of Christ*, Gardiner, 1819, reprinted by John Crowter, 1993

Hazelrigg, Grey, (Ed.), *Footsteps of Mercy*, Coventry, 1993
Morton, Elizabeth, *The Daughter's Defence*, London, 1788
Philpot, J. C., *Reviews*, 2 vols, London, 1901 (Contains numerous essays about Huntingtonians and works of Huntingtonians)
Pickles, H. M. (Ed.), *James Abbott: A Witness of the Truth*, Coventry, undated
Pickles, H. M. (Ed.), *John Rusk: Sailmaker and Well-Instructed Scribe*, Coventry, undated
Pickles, H. M. (Ed.), *John Rusk: Collected Letters and Extracts*, Coventry, 1993

Magazine articles

Abbott, William, 'A Letter by the Late W. Abbott', The Gospel Standard, January, 1861, pp. 23, 24
Abbott, William, 'A Letter by the Late William Abbott', The Gospel Standard, April, 1860, pp. 111, 112
Abbott, William, 'A Letter by the Late William Abbott', The Gospel Standard, February, 1856, pp. 55-57
Abbott, William, 'A Letter from the Late W. Abbott', The Gospel Standard, March, 1859, pp. 80-82
Anonymous, 'Thus Says a Writer Concerning Mr Brook', The Gospel Standard, January, 1856, p. 34
Beeman, Isaac, 'A Letter from Mr Beeman to Mr Keyt', The Gospel Standard, September, 1850, pp. 302-304
Brick, John, 'The Funeral of William Huntington S.S'., Chapel Society Newsletter, No. 2, December, 1989 (Letter written 12 July 1813)
Brook, W. J., 'A Letter by the Late Mr. W. J. Brook', The Gospel Standard, 1850, pp. 69-71, 379-381, 202, 203
Brook, W. J., 'A Letter to a Friend', The Gospel Standard, 1875, pp. 259-261
Brook, W. J., 'Unpublished Letters by the Late Mr Brook', The Gospel Standard, April, July 1861, pp. 112-114, 203, 204
Editor, 'Unpublished Anecdotes of Mr. Huntington', The Gospel Standard, May, 1861, pp. 144, 145

Ella, George M., 'Sequel to 'To a Sinner Saved'', Bible League Quarterly, January-March, 1990, pp. 305-312
Fradgley, Mrs, 'A Letter by the Late Mrs Fradgley, of America', The Gospel Standard, August, 1860, pp. 238, 239
Huntington, W., 'Extracts from Mr. Huntington's Letters', The Gospel Magazine, August, 1870, pp. 444, 445
Huntington, William, 'A Correspondence between Mr H. and a Friend', The Gospel Standard, 1850, pp. 166-172
Huntington, William, 'A Letter by Mr Huntington', The Gospel Standard, pp. 17-19
Huntington, William, 'A Short Discourse on Sanctification', The Gospel Standard, 1850, pp. 228-232
Huntington, William, 'An Unpublished letter of W. H. to John Rusk', The Gospel Standard, April, 1861, p. 114
Huntington, William, 'Extracts from Mr Huntington's Letters', The Gospel Magazine, September, 1870, p. 462
Huntington, William, 'Mr Huntington's Dying Testimony to the Power', The Gospel Standard, March, 1860, pp. 77, 78
Huntington, William, 'Short Discourses by Mr Huntington', The Gospel Standard, 1850, pp. 369-373
Huntington, William, 'The Wedding Garment' (Sermon), The Gospel Standard, March, 1861, pp. 77-81
Huntington, William, 'Unpublished Letter from Mr H. to Mr Brook', The Gospel Standard, January, 1860, pp. 21,22
Huntington, William, 'Unpublished Letters by Mr Huntington', The Gospel Standard, November, 1861, p. 337
Jenkins, J., 'A Letter by J. Jenkins the Welsh Ambassador', The Gospel Standard, March, September, 1859, pp. 87, 270, 271
Jenkins, J., 'A Letter by the Late J. Jenkins', The Gospel Standard, October, 1861, pp. 302, 303
Keyt, John, 'A Letter from the Late John Keyt', The Gospel Standard, 1850, pp. 319-322
Keyt, John, 'A Letter by the Late John Keyt', The Gospel Standard, September, 1856, pp. 276-278
Keyt, John, 'A Letter by the Late J. Keyt', The Gospel Standard, March, 1859, pp. 84, 85
Keyt, John, 'A Letter by the Late J. Keyt to W. Moore', The Gospel Standard, April, 1860, pp. 109, 110

Keyt, John, 'A Letter by the Late John Keyt', The Gospel Standard, June, 1860
Keyt, John, 'A Letter upon Important Business by a Shopman', The Gospel Standard, September, 1860, pp. 269-272
Keyt, T., 'A Short Account of the Last Days of Mr W. Taylor', The Gospel Standard, January, 1860, pp. 20, 21
Rusk, John, 'Marks and Evidences of a Real Citizen of Mount Zion', The Gospel Standard, 1875, pp. 245-251
Rusk, John, 'Mr Huntington on Ps. 69:32', The Gospel Standard, May, 1859, p. 154
Rusk, John, 'Perilous Times', The Gospel Standard, October, November, December, pp. 295-301, 327-334, 359-366
Rusk, John, 'Poverty and Princedom', The Gospel Standard, 1861, pp. 14, 37, 69, 101, 133
Rusk, John, 'Sorrow and Comfort', The Gospel Standard, 1850, pp. 45, 93, 130, 149, 189
Rusk, Mary Anne, 'Experiences of the Late Mary Anne Rusk', The Gospel Standard, June, July, August, 1861, pp. 181-187, 205-212, 231-236
Sant, Henry, 'The Sinner Saved', Bible League Quarterly, January-1989, p. 205f.
'The Old Pilgrim, Personal Recollections of Mr W. Huntington', The Gospel Magazine, October, 1870, pp. 533-538
W. S., 'An Anecdote of Mr. Lock, the Assistant of WH', The Gospel Standard, November, 1859, pp. 338-340
Young, Henry, 'Experience of the Late Henry Young', The Gospel Standard, October, November, December, 1860, pp. 293-302, 325-333, 357-362

Reviews

Anonymous, *The Voice of Years*, The Banner of Truth, July 1988, pp. 8-11
Anonymous, 'The Celebrated Coalheaver', The Gospel Advocate, 1872, Ebenezer Hooper, pp. 25, 49, 95, 128

Broome, J. R., 'William Huntington: Sinner Saved', The Gospel Standard, March, 1991, Henry Sant and George Ella, pp. 76-78

Editor's Review, 'Life and Letters of James Bourne', The Gospel Standard, August, October, 1861, pp. 251-260, 312-322

Philpot, J. C., 'Isaac Beeman, The Remains of Isaac Beeman'. The Gospel Standard, February, 1859, A J. Baxter

Philpot, J. C., 'Recollections of the Late William Huntington'. The Gospel Standard, February, 1869, William Stevens

Philpot, J. C., 'God the Guardian of the Poor and the Bank of Faith', The Gospel Standard, William Huntington

Philpot, J. C., 'William Huntington, Epistles of Faith', The Gospel Standard, September, 1853, pp. 285, 318

Philpot, J. C., William Huntington, 'The Posthumous Letters of the Late William Huntington', The Gospel Standard, August, 1856, pp. 250-260

Miscellaneous

Abbey, Charles and Overton, John, *The English Church in the Eighteenth Century*, Longman's Green, 1887

Balleine, G. R., *A History of the Evangelical Party*, Longman's Green, 1911

Berkhof, Louis, *Systematic Theology*, Banner of Truth Trust, 1959

Berkhof, Louis, *The History of Christian Doctrines*, Banner of Truth Trust, 1969

Calvin, John, *Institutes of the Christian Religion*, Eerdmans, 1979

Clarke, John, *The Life and Times of George III*, Weidenfeld and Nicolson, 1972

Coxon, Francis, *Christian Worthies*, Zoar Publications, 1981

Fuller, Andrew, *The Complete Works of the Rev. Andrew Fuller*, Holdsworth and Ball, 1832, also 3 volumed Belcher edition reprinted 1988 by Sprinkle Publications. Quotes are from the Sprinkle edition

Furneaux, Robin, *William Wilberforce*, Hamish Hamilton, 1974

Haldane, Alexander, *The Lives of Robert & James Haldane*, Banner of Truth Trust reprint, 1990

Hart, Tindal, A., *The Curate's Lot*, John Baker, 1970

Jay, William. *The Autobiography of William Jay*, Banner of Truth Trust, 1974 (includes biographies of Newton, Ryland Sr., Wilberforce,

More, Rowland Hill, Cecil, Pearce, Robert Hall, Hughes, Foster, Haweis and a number of other eighteenth-century evangelical leaders)
Lecky, W. E. H., *The History of England in the 18th Century*, Longman's Green, 1899
Middleton, Erasmus, *Biographia Evangelica*, 1784-86
Overton, John and Relton, Frederic, *The English Church*, 1906
Pibworth, Nigel R., *The Gospel Pedlar*, Evangelical Press. 1987
Pollock, John, *Wilberforce*, Lion, 1977
Quinlan, Maurice James, *Victorian Prelude, A History of English Manners 1700-1830*, Columbia University Press, 1941
Romaine, William, *Select Letters*, James Taylor, 1876
Romaine, William, *The Life, Walk and Triumph of Faith*, Routledge, Warne & Routledge, 1860
Ryle, J. C., *Christian Leaders of the 18th Century*, The Banner of Truth Trust, 1978
Sidney, Edwin, *The Life of the Rev. Rowland Hill A.M.*, Seeley, Burnside and Seeley, 1844
Stephen, Leslie, *English Literature and Society in the Eighteenth Century*, Duckworth, 1940
Traill, Robert, *The Works of the Late Reverend Robert Traill, A.M.*, William Brownlie, 1795
Venn, John, *The Life and A Selection from the Letters of the Late Rev. Henry Venn, M.A.*, John Hatchard and Son, 1835
Witsius, Herman, *The Economy of the Covenants Between God and Man*, Presbyterian and Reformed Publishing Company, 1990 reprint.
Wood, A. Skevington, *The Inextinguishable Blaze*, Paternoster Press, 1960

Index Of Names And Topics

Note: This index does not include names of biblical characters

Index Of Places

Note: This index does not include biblical place-names

Index Of Biblical Characters And Places

Index Of Scripture References

Old Testament

New Testament

Index Of Works Quoted

Periodicals and newspapers

Articles

Books

Huntington's works

www.ingramcontent.com/pod-product-compliance
Lightning Source LLC
Chambersburg PA
CBHW060315100426
42812CB00003B/788